DESIGN THEORY AND COMPUTER SCIENCE

Cambridge Tracts in Theoretical Computer Science

Managing Editor Professor C.J. van Rijsbergen, Department of Computing Science, University of Glasgow

Titles in the series

DESIGN THEORY AND COMPUTER SCIENCE

Processes and Methodology of Computer Systems Design

SUBRATA DASGUPTA

Computer Science Trust Fund Eminent Scholar & Director
Institute of Cognitive Science
University of Louisiana at Lafayette

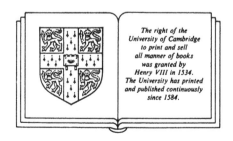

The right of the
University of Cambridge
to print and sell
all manner of books
was granted by
Henry VIII in 1534.
The University has printed
and published continuously
since 1584.

CAMBRIDGE UNIVERSITY PRESS

Cambridge

New York   Port Chester   Melbourne   Sydney

CAMBRIDGE
UNIVERSITY PRESS

University Printing House, Cambridge CB2 8BS, United Kingdom

Cambridge University Press is part of the University of Cambridge.

It furthers the University's mission by disseminating knowledge in the pursuit of
education, learning and research at the highest international levels of excellence.

www.cambridge.org
Information on this title: www.cambridge.org/9780521390217

© Cambridge University Press 1991

First published 1991

A catalogue record for this publication is available from the British Library

ISBN 978-0-521-39021-7 Hardback
ISBN 978-0-521-11815-6 Paperback

To my mother

Protima Dasgupta

When we mean to build,
We first survey the plot, then draw the model;
And when we see the figure of the house,
Then we must rate the cost of the erection;
Which if we find outweighs ability,
What do we then but draw anew the model
In fewer offices or at last desist
To build at all?

Henry IV, Part 2, I, iii

Though this be madness, yet there is method in 't

Hamlet, II, ii

Contents

Contents

Contents

Preface

In this book I intend to examine the logic and methodology of design from the perspective of computer science. Computers provide the context in two ways. Firstly, I shall be discussing the structure of design processes whereby computer systems are, or can be, designed. Secondly, there is the question of the role that computers can play in the design of artifacts in general – including other computer systems.

The aim of any systematic enquiry into a phenomenon is to uncover some intelligible structure or pattern underlying the phenomenon. It is precisely such patterns that we call *theories*. A theory that claims to explain must exhibit two vital properties. It must be *simpler* – in some well defined sense – than the phenomenon it purports to explain; and it must be *consistent* with whatever else we know or believe to be true about the universe in which the phenomenon is observed.

The phenomenon of interest in this book is such that it cannot be adequately described by a single sentence. That itself is an indicator of its inherent complexity – and therefore of its intrinsic interest. It is, perhaps, best described in terms of the following entities:

(a) *Computer systems.* I include in this term all nontrivial discrete computational devices (e.g., algorithms, logic circuits, computer architectures, operating systems, user-interfaces, formal languages and computer programs). Computer systems are characterized by the fact that they are artifacts; that they may be physical or abstract in form; and that, in general, they are complex entities.

(b) *Design processes.* These are characterized by the fact that they are cognitive and intellectual in nature. Design as an activity is, thus, psycho-biological in origin. It is a human activity.

(c) *Computer-aided design (CAD) systems.* These are also computer systems to which are assigned some of the tasks encountered during design. CAD systems are, thus, artifacts that either augment the cognitive/intellectual processes in design or, more ambitiously, attempt to mimic these same processes.

The central topic of this book – the phenomenon of interest – is the relationship among these entities. More specifically the question addressed here is the following:

Can we construct a theory of the design process – an explanatory model – that (a) can serve to clarify and enhance our understanding of how computer systems are, or can be, designed; and (b) consequently, provides a theoretical basis for building methods and computer-aided tools for the design of such systems?

Let us label this question 'Q'. There are at least two important issues that pertain to Q.

Firstly, it has been observed by many that the cognitive/intellectual activity we call design has a significant component that is domain-independent. Whether we are designing buildings, organizations, chemical plants or computers there are some principles or 'laws' that are common to all. Thus, quite independent of the specific design domain, it makes sense to talk of *general* theories of design – that is general, domain-independent explanatory models of the design process. The theoretical and intellectual value of any theory that we may propose in response to Q will, to a great extent, be determined by its generality – its domain-independence. A theory of design that is applicable to computer architecture, software and VLSI circuits is clearly preferable to one that is only applicable to VLSI circuits. A theory that is applicable to both computer systems and buildings is clearly more valuable than one that is only valid for buildings.

At the same time a theory of design is of heuristic value only when it provides advice on how to design specific systems within a specific domain. A grand theory of design is pointless if it is so general that no one knows how to relate it to specific problems. Thus, our search for a design theory must attend to both the theoretical need for generality and the practical quest for domain-specificity.

The second major issue relevant to Q is the debate on whether a theory of design is to be descriptive or prescriptive. A *descriptive* theory is an explanation of a given phenomenon as we observe it. All theories in the natural sciences are, of course, descriptive. When we enter the realm of artifacts – the realm of what Herbert Simon memorably termed the 'Sciences of the Artificial' – the issue becomes somewhat more problematic. For, given that design is a cognitive/intellectual process, it is clear that no design theory can afford to ignore or bypass the constraints imposed by human nature and intellect. To this extent, a theory of design must in part be descriptive. It must explain how design is conventionally carried out by humans.

In contrast, a *prescriptive* (or *normative*) theory is one that prescribes how something should be. Design is concerned with the making of artifacts – that is, entities that are in some well defined sense not natural; design is concerned with the purposive effecting of change. Thus, it is clear that a theory of design must have the capability of specifying how such change is best effected.

We can conclude that anyone embarking on constructing a theory of the design process must navigate cautiously between the Scylla of description and the Charybdis of prescription.

The urge to construct theories of design – to construct a logic of design – is neither new nor specific to the computer system domain. In particular, architectural design theory has a lineage that can at least be traced back to the Roman writer Vitruvius. One of the most celebrated treatises on the principles of architecture was by the 15th century Renaissance writer Leoni Alberti. In our own times, many architectural theorists and practitioners, including such pioneers such as Christopher Alexander and Christopher Jones, have pondered and written on the methodology and logic of their discipline, and I shall have occasion to refer to some of their ideas in this book.

In computer science[1] one of the earliest discussions of what we now call program correctness (an important aspect of computer systems design) is a relatively little known paper by Alan Turing published in 1949. Soon after, Maurice Wilkes's invention (circa 1951) of microprogramming must surely count as an important event in the methodology of computer design. In hardware logic design (or what is also called 'gate level' design) one of the debates of the late 1950s (as has been traced by Glen Langdon (1974) in his historical study of the discipline) was on a methodological issue. The so called 'Eastern School' favored the use of block diagrams in designing logic circuits while the 'Western School' advocated the use of boolean algebra. This is, in fact, a classic instance of the ever recurring debate between what might be called the 'naturalistic' and 'formalistic' schools of design methodology.

In computer science, design methodology really came of age in the mid 1960s when the problems of constructing and managing large scale software began to be openly and widely discussed. Perhaps the most influential figure from these times is Edsgar Dijkstra who in an important series of publications between 1965 and 1969 brought to our attention the intrinsic complexities attending programming and who prescribed

---

[1] In this book, I shall use the term 'computer science' to encompass all disciplines pertaining to computers and computing – including algorithms, languages, computer architecture, software, artificial intelligence, computer-aided design, VLSI design, etc. Similarly the term 'computer scientist' will refer to practitioners of any of these disciplines. I shall thereby avoid the tiresome distinction sometimes made between 'computer science' and 'computer engineering'.

techniques that were to crystallize into the, now well established, principles of structured programming. In this same period Robert Floyd and Tony Hoare published papers as a result of which the idea of programs as formally provable theorems in an axiomatized system was born. Contemporaneously, Herbert Simons's highly influential book *The Sciences of the Artificial* appeared in which the author presented the outline of what he termed a 'science of design'.

Since that very fruitful period the design process has become a subject of interest in all those areas of computer science where one has to come to terms with the problems of large scale complexity. These areas range from such relatively 'soft' areas as computer architecture and the design of human–computer interfaces to the relatively 'hard' domains such as microprogramming and VLSI circuit design. Finally, interest in design theory amongst computer scientists and amongst engineers and architects has been further sharpened by two computer related advances: computer-aided design and applied artificial intelligence.

If one examines the literature on design theory – both inside computer science and outside it – one encounters a small number of recurrent and closely intertwined themes. Is design art or science? Can we construct a genuine logic of design? Should we try to formalize the design process? What is the relationship between design and mathematics? What is the connection between design and science? Are designs computable? What is the nature of design knowledge?

These themes form, so to speak, the very stuff of this book. By addressing these and other questions I hope to draw the reader's attention to the enormously complicated phenomena surrounding the design act and their implications for design methodology and design automation. At the same time by attempting to respond to these issues within the framework of a systematic and coherent set of ideas I hope to shed some further light on the structure of design processes. This, as previously noted, is the primary aim of any theory of design.

This book consists of three parts. In Part I the fundamental characteristics of the design process are identified, discussed and analyzed. In the context of the description/prescription duality, Part I is descriptive in spirit and intent. I shall examine design as an activity that is 'out there' in the 'real' world – an activity that can be empirically studied and analyzed just as one studies any other empirical phenomenon. In the course of this discussion examples and illustrations will be drawn from various types of computer systems, notably computer architectures, operating systems, logic and VLSI circuits and user-interfaces. However, since many of the ideas discussed in Part I also apply to other 'Sciences of the Artificial' – specially engineering and architecture – I shall also have occasion to refer to the work of design theorists in these other disciplines.

Part II is wholly prescriptive in spirit and intent. It is concerned with *design paradigms* – that is, specific philosophies of, or approaches to, design (with or without the assistance of computers). Obviously, any prescription that one may make about what the design process *should be* – that is, any design paradigm that one may invent – is severely constrained by *what is possible*. Thus, the characteristics discussed in Part I establish the framework within which the various paradigms appearing in Part II are analyzed, criticized or recommended.

To this writer, the most interesting question in design theory is the relationship between design and those two great intellectual enterprises, mathematics and science. A substantial portion of Part II is devoted to design paradigms that are explicitly or implicitly modeled on the relationship between design, mathematics and science. However, if there is a single thesis that this book may claim to advocate, it is that from the perspective of methodology, one may actually conduct design in a manner that makes it indistinguishable from the activity we call science. Part III is concerned entirely with arguments and evidence in support of this thesis and its consequences, especially in the realm of computer-aided design.

Acknowledgements

Quite apart from the hundreds of authors cited in the text, I owe a massive debt of gratitude to many individuals and organizations who, in one way or another, have influenced the final shape of this work. In particular, I thank the following:

- Tony Hoare (Oxford University), Werner Damm (University of Oldenberg, Germany) and B. Chandrasekaran (Ohio State University) for their various and very individualistic insights into the design process.
- Bimal Matilal (Oxford University) and James Fetzer (University of Minnesota) – two philosophers – for discussions or correspondences regarding matters philosophical.
- Karl Klingsheim (University of Trondheim and Elektroniklaboratoriet ved NTH, Norway) – engineer turned design philosopher – who suffered my theorizing with patience and good humour.
- Sukesh Patel, Ulises Aguero, Alan Hooton and Philip Wilsey – wonderful collaborators and former students.
- N.A. Ramakrishna – my research assistant without whose heroic help the manuscript would never have been finished.

The book was conceived during a summer spent at the University of Oldenberg, Germany in 1988. I am deeply grateful to the German Science Foundation for supporting me with a Guest Professorship and to Werner Damm and members of his 'group' for their intellectual, social and logistical support.

I thank the US National Science Foundation for their award of a grant for the period 1988–9 and the University of Southwestern Louisiana (USL) for a Summer faculty award in 1989. As ever, I am grateful to USL and, in particular, the Center for Advanced Computer Studies for the unusual, flexible and collegial atmosphere that is so conducive to projects such as this.

I thank Keith van Rijsbergen (Glasgow University) – the editor of the series in which this book is being published – and David Tranah (Cambridge University Press) for their initial, warm support of this project. And, of course, my editor at Cambridge University Press, Alan Harvey, for his continuing, friendly and patient help throughout the production process.

I thank the following for granting me permission to use material from their publications:

- Harvard University Press, for the quote from C. Alexander, *Notes on the Synthesis of Form* (1964), p. 1, appearing on page 3.
- John Wiley and Sons, for the excerpts from J.C. Jones, *Design Methods: Seeds of Human Future* (1980), p. 64 appearing on page 145, and from Y.E. Kalay (Ed), *Computability of Design* (1987), p. xi, appearing on page 2.
- Springer-Verlag, for adaptation of material from S. Alagic and M.A. Arbib, *The Design of Well-Structured and Correct Programs*, pp. 124–7, appearing on pages 83–91.
- The Institute of Electrical and Electronic Engineers, for material from the papers: (a) 'Domain Specific Automatic Programming' by D.R. Barstow, *IEEE Transactions on Software Engineering*, Vol. SE-11, #11, Nov. 1985, pp. 1321–36. (b) 'Understanding and Automating Algorithm Design' by E. Kant, *IEEE Transactions on Software Engineering*, Vol. SE-11, #11, Nov. 1985, pp. 1361–74. (c) 'Automatic Data Path Synthesis', by D.E. Thomas *et al.*, *Computer*, Vol. 16, #12, Dec. 1983, pp. 59–70.
- Lissa Pollacia and Lisa Levy for excerpts from their project report 'PDI Constraints' (USL Center for Advanced Computer Studies, April 1988).

Finally, my thanks to my wife Sarmistha and sons Jaideep and Monish. As always, they suffered the domestic consequences of this enterprise with phlegmatic forbearance.

Part I

The Architectonics
of Design

Chapter 1

The Inadequacy of Definitions

The natural point to begin any discussion of design is its definition – that is, to state succinctly in a single sentence what it is that one does when one designs and what the end product is. Such an enterprise has been attempted in a variety of contexts including architecture, engineering, computer science, and the hybrid discipline of computer-aided design. As might be expected these definitions range from the very prosaic to the very abstract and each reflects quite clearly the specific perspective, tradition, and bias of its author. Invariably, such attempts to capture an entire human (or more recently, human–computer) enterprise within the bounds of a single sentence are unsatisfactory at the very least and fail abysmally at the worst.

One reason why definitions fail is the ubiquity of design as a human activity. As Simon (1981) has pointed out, anyone who devises courses of action to change an existing state of affairs to a preferred one is involved in the act of design. We have all been involved in devising such courses of action; hence from the very experience of living – or at least from the very experience of purposively controlling our lives – we have an intuitive idea of what design is. Thus, any single all embracing definition leaves us dissatisfied as much by what it excludes as by what it contains. For every definition one can point to instances of what is intuitively or experientially felt to be design but which have been excluded from the definition.

Consider for example, the following characterization by Alexander (1964):

> The process of inventing physical things which display new physical order, organization, form in response to function.

Our intuition and experience as naive designers tell us that the derivation of 'organization' or 'form' in response to 'function' is rightly an essence of design. So is the property of newness demanded of the form. But we may protest at the idea of design being the *process of inventing physical things*. At the very least this seems misleading. For, experience and intuition inform us that a design is a pattern, a template or a plan *based on which* a physical thing – an artifact – may be devised. Thus, a design itself is an *abstract* entity – an abstract representation of an artifact. It is one level removed from the artifact itself.

Even after this clarification we may still object to Alexander's characterization wherein the artifact (of which the design is a representation) is a *physical* entity. Computer programs and company organizations are both artifacts that are not physical. They are abstract entities. And, experience and intuition tell us, programs and organizations are designed exactly in the same sense that one designs chemical plants, bridges, and computers. Thus, the artifacts that one designs need not necessarily be physical; they may well be abstract artifacts.

Consider as a second example the following statement due to Kalay (1987).

> Design is an ill-understood process that relies on creativity and intuition as well as judicious application of scientific principles, technical information, and experience, for the purpose of developing an artifact or an environment that will behave in a prescribed manner.

Intuition (and knowledge) tell us that many of the ingredients of design have indeed been incorporated into this definition. Yet if we examine the statement carefully we realize that design here is stipulated to be a *process* for the purpose of developing an artifact (or environment) yet it fails to say what the output of the process *is*. It misses, once more, the fact that designs are abstractions.

In his text on engineering design, Dieter (1983) adopted, as a 'formal' definition, a characterization due to Blumrich (1970) in which design is equated solely with problem solving. Thus, the proof of a new mathematical theorem, or a new proof of an old theorem, or the elucidation of the hitherto unknown structure of a particular protein molecule would all count as design processes according to this characterization. Intuitively, this rings false.

Clearly, an over-simplified or single-sentence definition of design will not do. A more fruitful approach is, first, to rely on our common intuitive (and probably superficial) grasp of what design is. We can then attempt to identify some of the fundamental characteristics exhibited by design – that is, the process and its product – across the sciences of the artificial, and use these characteristics as a means for *understanding* design at a deeper and less intuitive level. These characteristics and the consequent understanding will, then, constitute the 'architectonics' of design. I shall discuss these characteristics in the ensuing chapters under four headings:

  (i) Design as the initiation of change.
 (ii) The nature of design problems.
(iii) The form of design solutions.
(iv) The evolutionary nature of design processes.

Chapter 2

Design as the Initiation of Change

Most design theorists including Simon (1981) and Jones (1980) among the more influential agree that, in an ultimate sense, the goal of design is to initiate *change* in some aspect of the world. We perceive an imperfection in the state of affairs in some specific domain and we conceive or design an artifact which when implemented will, we believe, correct or improve this state of affairs.

There are a number of consequences of this seemingly obvious observation.

2.1 DEMARCATING ENGINEERING FROM SCIENCE

I shall use the term *engineering* here (and throughout the book) as a synonym for the more cumbersome 'sciences of the artificial'. That is, the term encompasses the activities involved in the production of *all useful artifacts* – both material, such as buildings, computers and machine tools, and symbolic or abstract such as organizations and computer programs. Clearly, except in the simplest of situations, *engineering entails design.*[1]

The notion of design as an agent of change appears to establish a firm criterion for demarcating engineering from the natural sciences (such as physics, chemistry, biology or geology). According to conventional wisdom, the latter disciplines are concerned with understanding the natural universe; the engineering disciplines are concerned with its purposeful, artificial alteration or extension.

The tendency to distinguish between the natural sciences (or simply, 'science') and engineering has, over the years, assumed almost mythical proportions. This difference has been articulated in a variety of ways, for example:

(a) That science is concerned with 'analysis' and engineering with 'synthesis'.
(b) That science is 'theory-oriented' while engineering is 'result-oriented'.

---

[1] In chapter 4 I shall discuss such engineering situations that have historically not necessitated nor have cognitively demanded an explicit and separate act of design.

(c) That engineering is 'creative, spontaneous and intuitive' while science is 'rational'.

Thus for example, Lawson (1980, pp. 30–33) describes a simple experiment in which two groups of students, one architectural the other scientific, were required to solve a simple design problem involving the arranging of a set of colored wooden blocks of varying shapes so as to satisfy a particular set of constraints. The scientists in this case carried out a series of experiments involving the blocks in order to discover a rule governing the allowable combination of blocks; if such a rule could be identified this could then be used to produce an optimum design (arrangement) that satisfies the constraints. The architects, in contrast, were found to be more concerned with finding a solution by systematically combining the blocks, examining if the arrangement was acceptable, selecting another combination if not, and so on. Lawson's conclusion was that the scientists adopted what he called a 'problem-focused' strategy and the architects, a 'solution-focused' strategy; that is, his conclusion was essentially along the line of (b) above.

As another example, Schön (1983) in his analysis of 'professional' disciplines – which includes such design disciplines as process engineering, architecture, and civil engineering – makes a distinction between two kinds of epistemologies: technical rationality and reflection-in-action. *Technical rationality* is the fruit of the rationalism that resulted from the developments in science from the 17th century onwards. It is based on the notion that scientific knowledge is the only type of genuine knowledge we can acquire about the world.[2] Technical rationality is concerned with the application of scientific theory and techniques to problem solving. It takes as axiomatic that the professions – medicine, architecture, engineering – are concerned with the application of the *basic* (i.e., the natural) sciences to the relevant domain of the practitioner.

Schön contrasts technical rationality with what he calls *reflection-in-action* in which knowledge and thinking about that knowledge are not independent of the practitioner's action. Knowing and thinking are contained in, and are a part of, the action itself.

Schön's main thesis is that the professional disciplines *as they are actually practised* rest more on reflection-in-action than on technical rationality. Thus, in the specific context of the design disciplines the epistemology of design rests not on technical rationality but on a kind of knowledge and cognitive capability that are inextricably

---

[2] This is the philosophy of *Positivism* advocated in the 19th century by such thinkers as Auguste Comte.

intertwined with the act of design itself. This line of argument is along the direction of (c) above.

Arguments very similar to those of Schön's have been made recently by Winograd and Flores (1987). They use the term *rationalist tradition* for Schön's technical rationality and have critically examined and indicted much of the work in cognitive science and artificial intelligence (AI) for the fact that the practitioners of these fields take for granted that the rationalist tradition is the only appropriate basis for these disciplines. Winograd and Flores have no single term that corresponds to reflection-in-action; rather they describe a whole complex of concepts that collectively represent the same notion. Perhaps their terms that are closest in naming this complex are *thrownness* – a word due to Heidegger (1962) – and *readiness-to-hand*. The point they make in their densely argued book is similar to Schön's thesis: that there are compelling reasons for basing the design of systems (specially computer systems) on the foundations of thrownness and readiness-to-hand rather than the rationalist tradition.

It is important to note that the distinction of engineering from science is argued from two different directions:

(i) That the *aims* of science and engineering differ.
(ii) That the *methodology* of science and engineering differ.

That there are indeed differences in aims will not be questioned.[3] I will also agree with Schön (1983) and Winograd and Flores (1987) that the design disciplines are indeed founded on an epistemology akin to reflection-in-action rather than technical rationality. What is questionable is the assumption that the natural sciences themselves conform to the model of technical rationality. This matter will be discussed at length in Part III but in anticipation the following can be said: recent researches in the history and philosophy of science belie the technical rationality of the natural sciences; the epistemologies of the natural sciences and engineering are much closer to one another than would appear from the writings of Schön (1983) or Lawson (1980); and that, more specifically, under certain conditions the logic and methodology of design (and, thus, of engineering) are indistinguishable from the logic and methodol-

---

[3] Although even here it is possible, in some cases, to cast doubts on this proposition. Consider, for instance, the design of a special purpose computer to be used as part of a radio-telescope system for studying the properties of galaxies; or a computer integrated into a high-energy particle accelerator. Generalizing these examples one could legitimately argue that the aim of any artifact designed for, and as an instrument in, scientific experiments is as much for the understanding of nature as for changing the world.

ogy of the natural sciences. Consequently, the demarcation between engineering and science is far from obvious or may even be viewed as fictitious.

2.2 THE MATTER OF VALUES

If design is indeed concerned with change it is obviously concerned with how things *ought* to be. In other words the very act of design implies the influence of a particular set of *values* on the designer.[4]

The question of values becomes explicit in at least two different ways.

Firstly, the *recognition* of a design problem – the realization that the 'current' state of affairs in a particular domain demands change – is intimately a function of the designer's 'value system'. A state of affairs that appears unsatisfactory to one person may not be so to another; the former 'sees' a design problem where the latter does not or at least is unwilling to admit.

Example 2.1

In the early to mid 1970s, a small group of computer scientists – almost all in universities – began to investigate the design and implementation of *high level microprogramming languages* (HLMLs).[5] At that time microprogramming as a technique for implementing a computer's control unit, though two decades old, was in a primitive state. The very best tools then available for developing microprograms were assemblers, debugging aids and software simulators.

Note that this was a time when such programming languages as Algol 60 and PL/1 were widely deployed and a language of the sophistication of Algol 68 was in the process of being implemented. The state of microprogramming contrasted rather strikingly with the state of programming.

---

[4] Design, may, of course, be initiated by a non-designer. Such a person identifies a particular problem and then commissions a designer or an organization to solve that problem. The person thus becomes a *client* on behalf of whom the designer works. In this book, I shall make a distinction between 'client' and 'designer' only when it is necessary to do so. Otherwise, that is when the distinction is not made, it will be assumed that the word 'designer' subsumes 'client' – that is, the designer's actions are in full agreement with the client's desires and that their values coincide. Obviously, it is only when a conflict arises between the two parties that the distinction needs to be made.

[5] See, e.g., Kleir and Ramamoorthy (1971), Eckhouse (1971), Jackson and Dasgupta (1974), Yau *et al.* (1974), Ramamoorthy and Tsuchiya (1974), Tsuchiya and Gonzalez (1976), Patterson (1976) and Dasgupta and Tartar (1976). For later reviews and surveys of this topic, see Landskov *et al.* (1980), Dasgupta (1980b), Sint (1980), Davidson *et al.* (1981), Dasgupta and Shriver (1985), Davidson (1986), Davidson (1988).

The early investigators of HLMLs and HLML compilers *perceived* a problem here. The perceived problem was the unsatisfactoriness of microprogramming methods and the desired change was to elevate the microprogramming effort to a more abstract and, therefore, more manageable level. These designers of the early HLMLs and HLML compilers believed that higher level tools were *intrinsically more desirable* than what were then available.

Yet it was not till a decade later that the validity of this design problem came to be conceded in the industrial sector. The result is that HLMLs are now being commercially designed and implemented.
End Example

Example 2.2
The search for *simplicity* or *clarity* has often served as a powerful valuational motive in determining design problems. Thus, Dijkstra (1968) suggested that the *goto* statement be eliminated from high level programming languages because of its proneness to exacerbate the incomprehensibility and complexity of programs. This latter characteristic and the fact that it was already known through the work of Bohm and Jacopini (1966) that one could compose arbitrary programs without using the *goto* led on the one hand to a new style of programming and, on the other, to a new class of programming languages that did not contain the *goto*. One of the earliest of these languages was BLISS (Wulf, Russell and Haberman 1971) and one of the most recent in this line is Occam (Inmos 1984).

The extent to which the elimination of *goto* was a matter of subjective values rather than objective technical judgement is revealed by the controversy that Dijkstra's article raised. The prehistory and the subsequent developments of program and language design without the *goto* statement have been traced in detail by Knuth (1974).
End Example

A second way in which the question of values becomes explicit in design is that while a particular community of practitioners may indeed agree on a common design *problem* there may be wide disagreements as to the nature of the *solution*. The latter may also be a function of the individual designer's value system.

For example, one school of thought may adopt such principles as 'simplicity' or 'understandability' as their ruling design philosophy; others facing the same problem may well be guided by the principle of providing complete 'functionality'; a third school may espouse as their philosophy the goal of achieving the best performance/cost ratio. Clearly, while all these are likely to be important objectives in designing systems the adoption of any one approach, style, or design philosophy as the ruling principle is a matter of the designer's values.

Example 2.3

A striking example of how values may determine solution approaches in the domain of *structural engineering* is described by Billington (1979) in his detailed study of the bridge designs of the Swiss engineer Robert Maillart. Using as examples a class of bridges called 'deck stiffened arch bridges' – of which Maillart designed over a dozen between 1923 and 1934 – Billington shows that Maillart's fundamental *modus operandi* was to first select a structural form (a) from which the analysis and computation of the internal forces in the structure followed and (b) for which the analysis could be kept relatively simple. In Maillart's design philosophy the mathematical analysis of structural forces was subordinated to, or a handmaiden for, the development of structural form. Or as Billington put it, 'force follows form'.

Maillart's approach contrasted sharply with the views of other contemporaries – both in Europe and the U.S.A. – according to which sophisticated analysis of the structural forces has priority over, and determines, structural form (Billington 1979).
End Example

Example 2.4

As another example from the domain of structures, the Italian engineer–architect Pier Luigi Nervi has frequently stated that the fundamental principle that has served as his philosophy of design is the maxim that a *necessary* condition for architectural (i.e., aesthetic) excellence in a building is the excellence of its structural (i.e., engineering) characteristics. That is, good architecture implies good structure (Nervi 1957, 1966).
End Example

Finally, it may be observed that if values determine valid design problems and solution approaches they may also determine valid *research* topics in engineering – or at least in those areas of engineering concerned with design issues. This, of course, has important consequences for the role of values in the *funding* of research in the design disciplines. We may see these consequences in two different ways.

Firstly consider an investigator who puts forth a grant application for a project in which a new design problem or a new solution to a known design problem is to be investigated. The validity of this research topic – and thus, whether it is worth investigating – may often hinge on whether the grant application reviewer agrees with the investigator that the problem is *indeed* a problem – that is, on whether the reviewer 'sees' the same problem and in the same way as the investigator.

Quite obviously, the reviewer's *not* seeing the same problem as the investigator may well be a cognitive or intellectual matter – and, therefore, not a question of values at all. For instance, an investigator may propose to study the structure of a new hardware description language (HDL) intended to span several levels of hardware description, and the proposal is based on a detailed analysis of the failure of previous HDLs to model 'time' adequately across these different levels. The reviewer in this case may simply not cognitively *appreciate* the subtlety of the problem that the investigator has identified.

I am not concerned here with such types of perceptual distances between investigator and grant reviewer. Consider instead an *ideological* difference between investigator and reviewer. This may simply blind the latter to the intellectual or technical merits of the proposed project and cause the proposal to be rejected.

Example 2.5
A grant proposal is concerned with the investigation of a new technique for the optimization of the width of microprogram control memories. However, the reviewer believes that such problems are no longer 'important' because the developments in reduced instruction set computers (RISCs) suggest (to the reviewer) that microprogramming is rapidly becoming obsolete at least in the domain of microcomputers. The reviewer rejects the proposal on this ground alone.
End Example

A second consequence of the impact of values on research is by virtue of the fact that a funding agency may institutionally decide that a particular research topic is 'important' for one or several reasons – for example, because of its relevance to a wide variety of applications, its economic consequences or its military implications. A particular grant proposal may then be rejected simply because it falls outside the scope of the research topic – regardless of the proposal's intrinsic merits. More alarmingly the sanctioning, by a funding agency, of a research topic that it may wish to support may serve to *define* which problems are important and which are not. One may, thus, see the insidious influence of the agency's particular biases on what the relevant research community *believes* to be important. Researchers begin to 'see' valid research problems only insofar as they fall within the agenda of the funding agencies.

Chapter 3

The Nature of Design Problems

In practical terms, the notion of design as the initiation of change – that causes some aspect of the world to change from a less preferred state to one that is more preferred – translates to the fact that the designer begins with a *problem*. The act of design, thus, starts with a description of the problem stated in terms of a set of *requirements*. The designer's brief is to develop a *form* – what we conventionally call 'the design' – such that if an artifact is built according to this form (that is, if we were to *implement the design*) it will *meet* the requirements. In that case we may as a convenient abbreviation say that the design meets the requirements. The design problem will, then, have been solved. This scenario, depicted in fig. 3.1, can be taken as our initial 'model' of the design process.

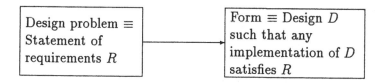

Design problem ≡
Statement of
requirements R

Form ≡ Design D
such that any
implementation of D
satisfies R

Fig. 3.1 M_d: Initial model of the design process.

Clearly, design problems are not all of the same type or complexity. It is evident to us intuitively – though we may at first be hard pressed to justify our intuition – that the problem of designing an arithmetic/logic unit (ALU) to be placed on a 'state-of-the-art' 32-bit processor chip differs *in kind* from the problem that motivated the conception and development of the first reduced instruction set computers (RISCs) – though they are both aspects of 'hardware' design. Intuitively, it also seems correct to assume that the problem of designing a parser that would serve as a front end to a compiler differs in kind from that of designing the optimizing code generator that would serve as the back end of the same compiler; or that the problem of designing a parallel program that simulates the behavior of a computer architecture differs (quite distinctly) from the problem of designing the architecture itself.

On the other hand, our intuition may also tell us that there is *a kind of* resemblance facing the designers of user-interfaces and the exo-architecture of computer systems.[1]

Clearly, it is of great interest to examine and try to understand the *nature* of design problems in such a way that we can definitely state in what manner two given problems differ or are similar.

3.1 EMPIRICAL REQUIREMENTS

The commonest and most basic type of problems that a designer is called upon to deal with are characterized by what I shall call *empirical requirements*. These are requirements that specify *externally observable* or *empirically determinable* qualities desired of the target artifact. That is, empirical requirements are such that whether or not a design meets these requirements can be determined by solely observing (possibly through controlled experiments) the external behavior and functioning of any implementation of the design.[2] The general nature of empirical requirements can be best understood through examples.

Example 3.1

A computer manufacturer produces a vector processor (call it VP_1) that provides a maximum throughput of 600 megaflops and a sustained (or average) throughput of 300 megaflops (relative to a particular set of benchmarks).[3] The main design group in this organization is given the task of exploiting improved logic and memory technologies to design a successor to VP_1 that is functionally identical to (or compatible with) VP_1 but has twice the maximum and average throughputs.

Here, the primary stated requirements are a given functionality (i.e., the new processor must have the same exo-architecture as VP_1) and a particular level of performance. Once this new computer has been designed and a real or simulated implementation

---

[1] By *exo-architecture* (or outer architecture) is meant the structure and behavior of a computer as seen by the lowest level users of that system, viz., the assembly language programmer or compiler writer (Dasgupta 1984, 1989a).

[2] As will be further discussed in chapter 4, a design's implementation may well be an *abstract* entity. For example, a program expressed in an executable programming language may be the implementation of a software design specified in a more abstract program design language.

[3] 1 megaflop = 10^6 floating point operations per second. This is the primary unit of performance for computers intended for scientific–numeric computations.

has been constructed one may determine whether these requirements are met by observing its functional behavior and measuring its performance.
End Example

Example 3.2
Up to the late 1970s, the most important and widely known concurrent programming languages were based on the *shared memory* model. These included Concurrent Pascal (Brinch Hansen 1977) and Modula (Wirth 1977, 1985a). In such languages interprocess communication and synchronization are achieved by access to shared memory and the use of suitable shared-memory-based synchronization primitives. Thus, these languages could not be directly used to implement programs that followed the *message passing* paradigm. For example, if a module M_1 wishes to communicate data directly to another concurrently active module M_2 it can only do so in these languages by depositing the data in a buffer B that can be accessed by both M_1 and M_2, and by using synchronization constructs to guarantee that (a) access to B is mutually exclusive and (b) data sent by M_1 to B is actually consumed by M_2 in the same order.

Various language designers began to work in the late 1970s on the development of programming languages where a fundamental (if not the only) requirement was the direct and explicit support of the message passing model of concurrent programming. Two of the most important of such languages are Ada[TM] (U.S. Department of Defense 1981)[4] and Occam[TM] (Inmos 1984).[5]

The problem common to these language design efforts was one of realizing a certain type of functionality – the ability of modules or processes to directly communicate data via messages. Whether or not the designers of a particular language are able to solve this problem and how adequate the solution is can be empirically determined by using the resulting language to develop a defined set of message-passing-based concurrent programs and assessing the quality of the latter.
End Example

Example 3.3
In the early 1970s, the development of high level microprogramming languages and their compilers began to be seriously investigated (Dasgupta and Shriver 1985). A crucial component of *horizontal microcode compilers* is the 'back end' which would parallelize the sequential code (i.e., a sequence of micro-operations) produced as intermediate output by an earlier phase of the compilation process, and generate a

---

[4] Ada[TM] is a trademark of the U.S. Department of Defense.

[5] Occam[TM] is a trademark of the Inmos group of Companies.

sequence of horizontal microinstructions – where each microinstruction consists of a collection of concurrently executable micro-operations.

For the first developers of such *microcode compactors*, the primary requirement was functional: to design a compactor (for a particular model of micro-architectures)[6] that would input a sequential microprogram and produce a horizontal microprogram. This is obviously an empirical problem since one can easily observe whether a compactor designed in response to this problem does indeed parallelize and compact sequential microcode.
End Example

Example 3.4
A microcode compactor has been designed and implemented. However, it is found that (a) its asymptotic time complexity is $O(n^2)$ where n is the length of the input microcode and (b) the quality of its output is rather poor – e.g., it is observed that when the compactor is executed on benchmarks the resulting output sequences of microinstructions are significantly suboptimal. The compiler builder is required to design a new compactor that is as efficient as the 'current' one but which significantly improves the quality of the output, for the same benchmarks. The design problem here is to maintain functionality and performance of the predecessor system and improve the degree of compaction. Whether the new system meets these requirements can be empirically determined.
End Example

The above examples provide instances of requirements that in one way or another relate to function or performance. These are, of course, not the only types of empirical requirements and, while it is not possible to specify all the varieties of such requirements, the most important ones can certainly be identified as belonging to the following broad classes:

- Functionality
- Performance
- Reliability
- Fault-tolerance
- User-friendliness
- Modifiability

---

[6] *Micro-architecture* refers to the structure and behavior of a computer as seen by the microprogrammer (Dasgupta 1989a). Thus the code produced by a microcode compiler would be executed by a computer at the micro-architectural level.

Functionality

In its most elemental sense functionality refers to the capability of the designed (or yet to be designed) artifact to *do* certain desirable things – that is, to provide certain desirable functions. This requirement perhaps characterizes the most fundamental type of problem in design. It is, further, empirical in nature in that whether or not a design provides certain desired functions is determinable by observing the behavior of any implementation of that design or by the direct analysis of the design itself.

It is important to emphasize that functionality is an externally observable characteristic demanded of the target artifact *as a whole* rather than of any of its internal components.

Example 3.5

Suppose the problem is to design a processor data path that satisfies a particular range of requirements R. Assume that the outcome of this exercise is a data path the structure of which conforms to the block diagram shown in fig. 3.2. Amongst the requirements in R will (one hopes) be a functional requirement F such that given the data path design D we can, either by simulating the behavior or operation of D or by physically implementing it, determine whether D provides the functions F. F may, for instance, be a description of the operations (instructions) that the data path is to execute. Correspondingly, whether D satisfies F can be determined by observing the outer behavior of D and seeing whether D does indeed perform the operations specified in F. Note that while the functionalities of the internal components of the data path (e.g., that of the ALU/Shifter complex) will obviously contribute to F they are not part of the empirical problem as far as the data path *as a whole* is concerned. The functionalities of the internal components become empirical problems only in the context of the design of the components themselves.

End Example

In spite of its apparent innocuousness the quest for functionality is often fraught with difficulties. Firstly, we may not always be able to distinguish between functionality and other types of requirements – that is, whether a requirement belongs to the functional category, or to some other category may not be clear. For instance, it is not always evident when discussing functionality whether we should make a distinction between the artifact *merely* doing something and it doing something *well.* Secondly, a functional requirement when identified may not always be *empirical.* Thirdly, what it is that we desire an artifact to do – that is, what its functionality is to be – may not always be objectively definable or characterizable to the satisfaction of all concerned.

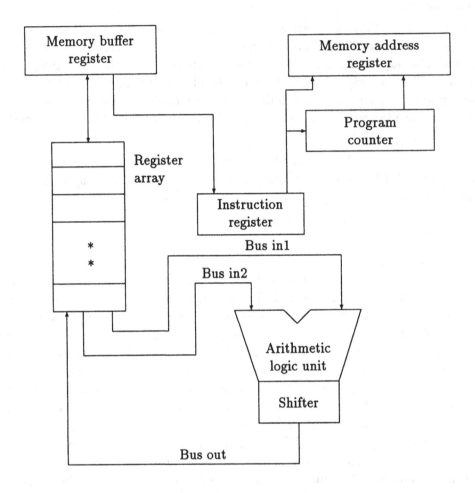

Fig. 3.2 Structure of a data path.

Example 3.6

Consider the design of a user-interface for a workstation-based operating system. During the initial phase of this project, it was decided that one of the requirements for the interface would be:

*R*1: The interface must be adaptable to the skill level of the user.

Is this a functional or some other kind of requirement? It may be argued, for instance, that the *functionality* of a user interface is defined solely in terms of the command language at the user's disposal and that adaptability is itself a different kind of requirement that enhances the interface's performance. We may counter this by arguing that the *raison d'être* for a user interface is to provide a means of human–computer communication that greatly facilitates the human user's tasks; that adapting to a user's skill level is, therefore, indeed something that the interface may be required to do and, consequently, that adaptability constitutes an intrinsic functional requirement rather than a performance or some other requirement.

Suppose it is agreed that $R1$ is indeed part of the interface's functionality. Is it an *empirical* requirement though? For it to be so, we must know how to assess the adaptability of the user interface by observing the latter's behavior (once it has been designed and implemented). That is, the intuitive notion that we possess about what it is to be adaptable must be translated into an empirically testable requirement. Further consideration of this may lead the designer to propose the following. Define

$R2$: The user-interface supports a number of different task domains. Let TD = set of task domains.

$R3$: The user-interface recognizes a number of distinct and discrete user skill levels. Let SL = set of skill levels.

$R4$: A user's skill level is defined (by the user) as an ordered pair $\langle s, t \rangle$ where $s \in$ SL, $t \in$ TD.

$R5$: The screen displays items appropriate to each ordered pair $\langle s, t \rangle$.

$R6$: Feedback is appropriate to each ordered pair $\langle s, t \rangle$.

Then $R1$ is said to be satisfied if $R2$, $R3$, $R4$, $R5$ and $R6$ are all satisfied.

Notice that $R5$ and $R6$ mentions 'items' and 'feedback' that are 'appropriate' to the user's skill level. Thus, although we have gone some way in clarifying what 'adaptability to skill level' is, the original requirement $R1$ has still not been fully transformed into an empirical form since it is not yet known how 'appropriate items' and 'appropriate feedback' can be empirically characterized. Thus, further refinement of $R5$ and $R6$ must be done.

Finally, even after $R1$ has been translated into a wholly empirical problem there may be disagreement on the part of potential users – the clients – as to whether the concept of adaptability has been adequately characterized by $R2$–$R6$. For instance, it might be argued that adaptability implies an additional property:

$R7$: Ease of navigation is appropriate to the skill level of the user.
End Example

Performance

Performance refers to the capability of the target artifact to achieve its functionality *well*. And, while in some cases it is possible and necessary to make the distinction between functionality and performance, in other cases the separation is either less clear or undesirable.

Example 3.7

An instance of the former is the design of a *family of computers* where each member of the family has the same exo-architecture (that is, identical functionality) but distinct performance characteristics. Here, the necessity of distinguishing between functionality and performance is quite obvious. In contrast, consider the design of a 'reactive' computer system that is intended to respond appropriately, 'in real time', to signals received as inputs from the environment. Here, the responses – that is, its functional characteristics – must not only be the *correct* ones, they must also be effected within tight time constraints otherwise the whole purpose of the system is lost. In this case, any distinction between functionality and performance is artificial, even undesirable.

End Example

Performance as an *empirical* requirement – as I shall show in section 3.2, it need not necessarily be empirical – usually refers to *economy* in the use of some observable set of *resources*. The architect of a very high performance vector processor establishes as a goal an 8 nanosecond cycle time – that is, in performing each of its defined operations, each functional unit in the processor (e.g., floating point adder, multiplier, etc.) can accept operands every 8 nanoseconds and can produce an output every 8 nanoseconds. The 'resource' of concern here is, of course, processing time. In designing a microcode compiler (see examples 3.3, 3.4) the requirement is to develop a program that produces, for a given set of benchmark microprograms, horizontal microcode that is within 20% of the optimal. The resource here is the number of microinstructions produced – an abstract resource which translates more concretely into the amount of control memory space required to hold the compiler output. In designing a new circuit simulation program one of the requirements is that the simulator should require no more than 60% of the time required by an extant simulator for a particular set of test circuits. The resource is, once more, that of processing time.

Quite a different type of resource may be engendered in the design of human–computer interfaces – including programming languages and other forms of formal notations. An oft-cited requirement in such design problems is ease of use (or alternatively, ease of learning). This is a performance requirement insofar that the resource of concern here is the time required by humans to learn how to use the interface. Unfortunately, it is not a type of requirement that lends itself easily to quantification though it is clearly empirical in nature.

Reliability

Consider a system S designed to satisfy a particular set of functional requirements F. F may be viewed as a specification of how S is expected to behave when it is in operation. A *failure* is said to occur when the actual behavior of S deviates from its expected behavior. The *reliability* of S, denoted by the symbol $R(t)$, is formally defined as the probability that S will conform to its expected behavior (as defined by F) throughout a period of time t (Anderson and Lee 1981).[7]

Various reliability models that allow $R(t)$ to be predicted have been constructed for different types or classes of systems. For instance, assuming a *constant failure rate* λ for the artifact in question it can be shown that (Kraft and Toy 1981)[8]

$$R(t) = e^{-\lambda t}$$

As another example, assuming a time-varying failure rate, $\lambda(t)$, Musa (1980, 1984) proposed a reliability model for software of the form

$$R(t) = e^{-\int_0^\infty \lambda(t)\ dt}$$

In the context of design problems several alternative ways of expressing reliability requirements have been proposed. The most well known is the *mean time between failures* (MTBF) – also called *mean time to failure* (MTTF) – which specifies the average time for which an artifact may be expected to function between failures. In the event of a constant failure rate, λ, this measure is simply

$$MTBF = \frac{1}{\lambda}$$

For example, assume that a system is being developed for which the failure rate is 10^{-3} failures/hour. The system will then fail, on the average, once every 1000 hours – this is its MTBF.

The failure rate may itself also serve directly as a design requirement. For instance, in designing the 'Software Implemented Fault Tolerant' (SIFT) system (Wensley *et al.* 1978) – a computer system intended for on-board aircraft control – the reliability requirement was a failure rate of 10^{-9} per hour for a ten-hour flight period.

---

[7] Other ways of characterizing reliability have also been proposed. Thus, according to Siewiorek and Swarz (1982), the reliability $R(t)$ is the conditional probability that a system has survived the interval $[0, t]$ given that it was operational at time $t = 0$.

[8] The instantaneous *rate* at which an artifact may fail is generally a function of time and would be denoted by $\lambda(t)$. In the above equation $\lambda(t)$ is taken to be a constant.

Fault tolerance

An important empirical requirement intimately related to reliability is fault tolerance. As discussed above, reliability is a measure of how long a system may conform to specified behavior. Any deviation from specified behavior is termed a failure.

Failure is caused by some sort of *fault* in the system. Given reliability as an empirical requirement the designer may attempt to achieve this objective by techniques or design features that *prevent* faults from occurring. However, there are clearly limits to the extent to which such *fault prevention* may be achieved.

An alternative approach is to recognize that faults may be present or will appear in a system or that all possible faults are not anticipatable at design time; and, consequently, to design the system so that it continues to meet its other critical requirements (e.g., functionality or performance) in spite of the occurrence of faults. Systems exhibiting this characteristic are said to be *fault tolerant*. In other words, a fault tolerant system is one in which the presence of a fault (or the failure of a component) does not lead to a failure of the system as a whole, in the course of its operation.

While fault tolerance may be viewed as denoting a collection of techniques or an approach by means of which the reliability requirement is achieved, it can and does serve as an empirical requirement in its own right. To put this in slightly different terms, fault tolerance can constitute a rather specific *kind* of reliability requirement.

Example 3.8

The design and implementation of the C.vmp multiprocessor system was undertaken as an investigation of fault tolerant architectures for real time industrial environments [Siewiorek *et al.* 1978]. Its specific fault tolerance requirement was that the system should have the capability to continue correct operations in the presence of

(i) A transient fault in a component or subsystem; or

(ii) A permanent failure of a component or a subsystem.

End Example

Example 3.9

Amongst the requirements for Tandem 16 Nonstop[9] system [Katzman 1977] were the following:

---

[9] Nonstop is a trademark of Tandem Computers.

(i) The operating system was to remain operational in the presence of a detected failure of any single module or bus.

(ii) The operating system should permit any such failed module to be repaired on-line and thereby be reabsorbed into the system.

End Example

Example 3.10
The Pluribus was a multiprocessor computer developed by Bolt, Beranek and Newman, to serve as interface message processors in the ARPANET computer network [Katsuki *et al.* 1978]. In formulating the requirements for this system its designers recognized that, rather than reliability in the sense of failure-free operation, what was required was that the computer should have the ability to recover 'gracefully' from failures. That is, while faults such as occasional loss of message packets or brief periods of down time were acceptable, the system should not be unavailable for more than a few minutes.

End Example

User-friendliness
In discussing functionality I pointed out, using an example, that the separation between functionality and other types of requirements cannot always be clearly understood or legislated. In general, functional requirements – that is, what the artifact is supposed to do – are often determined by, or are consequences of, other requirements. It is, then, possible to imagine a hierarchy of requirements in which there is a *causal structure* between members of the hierarchy; requirements higher in the hierarchy generate or imply those lower in the hierarchy (fig. 3.3).

An important type of requirement that may appear rather high in a requirement hierarchy is *user-friendliness*. This has emerged as a rather fundamental class of requirements in the case of artifacts that interact with, stimulate, or react to the stimulus provided by, the human user. In the domain of computing systems user-friendliness is particularly relevant to the design of programming or other machine-executable languages, user-interfaces and interactive software.

User-friendliness need not necessarily be empirical. For example, amongst the many characteristics that have been identified for constructing user-friendly computing systems are the following:

(UF$_1$) A system intended for some task domain D should appear (to the user) to be *like a more familiar environment* pertinent to D so that the user may employ existing or previously acquired knowledge (pertinent to that environment) in both understanding and responding to the system.

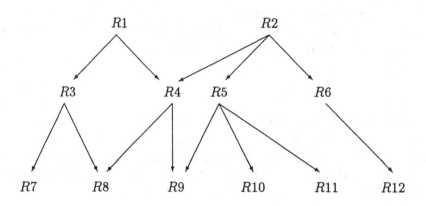

Fig. 3.3 A hierarchy of requirements: requirement Rj is (partially) caused by (is the partial effect of) Ri if there is a directed edge from Ri to Rj.

(UF$_2$) An interactive system *should not be reclusive or taciturn*; that is, it should respond in some positive manner to user commands (Norman 1981).

(UF$_3$) A system intended for some task domain should allow the user to interact with it in terms of the user's *mental model* of the task domain (Norman 1986).[10]

(UF$_4$) The system should exhibit what Winograd and Flores (1987) termed as *readiness-to-hand*. That is, the system (or tools, or environments) must so appear to the user that any involvement of the latter with the system should be unselfconscious or unreflective.[11]

Note that with the possible exception of (UF$_2$) these characteristics, *as stated*, are

---

[10] In cognitive science, the term *mental model* refers to the construction, on the part of an agent (human or robotic) of appropriate internal symbolic structures that represent more or less directly those aspects of the external world or task domain that the agent is engaged with at any particular time. To use an example from Johnson-Laird (1988) on hearing an assertion 'the dishwasher is on the right of the cupboard' the agent constructs an internal model in which symbols representing the entities 'dishwasher' and 'cupboard' are placed in a representation of a spatial array so that the overall situation matches the assertion. This model, then, has the same structure as the actual scene in the external world that prompted the assertion to be uttered.

[11] See also chapter 2, section 2.1 above. As an example of readiness-to-hand, Winograd and Flores cite the act of driving a nail during which, under normal conditions, it is the notion of *hammering* that determines the action rather than the structure or representation of the *hammer*. It is only when there is a *breakdown* of some sort – e.g., when the hammer slips from one's hand, cannot be found, or breaks – that one becomes conscious of the hammer itself (Winograd and Flores 1987, section 3.4). Another example cited by the authors is that in driving a car one does not think in terms of *exercising a control device* (viz., the steering wheel); one is simply driving along a road. Again, it is only when a breakdown occurs – the sudden need to avoid a pothole, for example – that the steering wheel becomes a consciously perceived control device.

not empirical in nature. We would be hard pressed to imagine or devise an experiment that could be conducted to determine whether a system does indeed appear as a 'more familiar' environment (UF$_1$) unless we characterized that 'familiar environment' more exactly. Likewise, for any particular user-interface it would be necessary to determine the nature of the mental model associated with that interface before one can determine empirically that an interface design satisfies the mental model requirement (UF$_3$). A similar remark can be made about readiness-to-hand (UF$_4$).

Thus, the above stated instances of user-friendliness are not empirical at all. They are examples of a wholly different type of requirement which I shall call *conceptual* requirements. These will be further discussed in section 3.2. But what is important to note is that given such requirements as (UF$_1$), (UF$_3$) or (UF$_4$), we may be able to *refine* them into empirically significant criteria of user-friendliness.

Example 3.11
Consider the design of an architecture description language (ADL) and its execution environment. ADLs constitute a special subclass of the class of hardware description languages that are intended to describe computers at the architectural levels rather than at the chip layout, circuit or logic levels (Dasgupta 1989b). The associated execution environment allows descriptions of architectures to be translated and then executed so as to simulate architecture-level behaviors. The simulation can be interactively controlled by the architect/user through a user interface (fig. 3.4)

Suppose that a major explicit goal in such a language/execution-environment design effort is that the system as a whole be user-friendly in the sense of the criterion (UF$_3$). This may be stated as the requirement

(UF$_3'$): The ADL and the user interface must both directly support what is, in some sense, the designer's characteristic mental model of the architectural domain.

As stated (UF$_3'$) provides no criterion for determining how we may test whether any design does or does not satisfy the mental model requirement. The notion of a mental model must, therefore, be further explicated.

The universe of architectural discourse broadly consists of two levels of concepts: the *exo-architecture* (Dasgupta 1984, 1989a) – or outer architecture – which specifies the most primitive view of a computer as seen by its users – i.e., the view as seen by the operating system designer and the compiler writer; and the *endo-architecture* – or inner architecture – which is concerned with the abstract structure and behavior of the constituent components of the computer (Dasgupta 1984, 1989a).

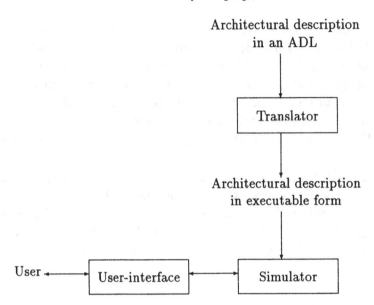

Fig. 3.4 An architectural description language and its execution environment.

At the exo-architectural level, the relevant concepts are addressing modes, data types, stores (register arrays, main memory, stacks, queues), instructions and their meanings, instruction formats, exception conditions, word lengths and processor cycles. At the endo-architectural level the relevant concepts are structures such as data paths and interconnection networks; stores such as register arrays, main memory and cache; and processes that fetch instructions, translate virtual to real addresses, execute instructions, update cache memory, and control the parallel or serial activation of such processes.

Thus, a conceptual user-friendliness requirement of the type (UF'_3) may be refined into a collection of empirical requirements of the following types:

(UF'_{31}): When designing exo-architectures or simulating the behavior of exo-architectures it should be possible for the language or interface user to directly describe, reference, and manipulate stores such as register arrays, main memory, stacks and queues without referring to implementations of these entities.

(UF'_{32}): In designing or describing endo-architectures, the user should be able to directly describe, refer to, manipulate, and control entities such as data paths, instruction fetch/execute processes, or address translation mechanisms without having to define these in terms of more primitive concepts.[12]

---

[12] It is interesting to note that (as far as is known to this author) at the time of writing no ADL

Two interesting aspects of these requirements may be noted. Firstly, the term 'mental model' does not appear in either of them. This is because the non-empirical concept of mental model is defined in terms of the empirically determinable concepts (UF'_{31}) and (UF'_{32}) (and others not stated here). Alternatively one may say that requirements (UF'_{31}) and (UF'_{32}) are *justified* because they *contribute* to the more abstract requirement of user-friendliness.

Secondly, (UF'_{31}) or (UF'_{32}) seem as much to be part of the functional requirements for the ADL/execution-environment system as they are of the user friendliness requirements. In general, many components of functionality are consequences of other, non-functional requirements.
End Example

Modifiability
This term, in general, refers to the ease with which changes may be incorporated into an artifact or in the design of an artifact. A special case of modifiability is *enhanceability* – that is, the ease with which new functional capabilities can be added to a system.

In an important sense, modifiability is as fundamental a design requirement as functionality. For, as I shall further relate in chapter 5, design is inherently an *evolutionary process*. Just why this is so will be discussed in that chapter but for our present purposes it suffices to note that this is a primary characteristic of design processes. What it signifies is that *there is a propensity for designs to be modified*. Modifiability is, then, the requirement that relates to the ease with which such modifications can be effected. If evolution is a fact of design then modification is, so to speak, inevitable. Modifiability requirements when stated explicitly focus the designer's attention on where such changes are most likely to take place.

Example 3.12
In the domain of software, modifiability requirements may take the following forms (Parnas 1972, 1979):

(a) The ability to correct a program component without needing to know the internal architecture of other components.
(b) The ability to recompile or reassemble a program component without recompilation or reassembly of the entire program.
(c) The ability to release an early version of a software system with a subset of the total set of intended capabilities without the need to design the whole system.

has yet been designed that meets the requirements (UF'_{31}) or (UF'_{32}). (Dasgupta 1982, 1989b).

(d) The ability to add functional capabilities to an extant program without the necessity of modifying more than a small fraction of the current program.

(e) The ability to eliminate unneeded functional capabilities or other features (so as to enhance performance, for instance) with minimal change or rewriting of the existing system.

End Example

Example 3.13

In the context of their assessment of the Digital Equipment Corporation PDP-11, Bell and Strecker (1976; see also Bell 1977) identified as a critical requirement in computer design, the ability of the architecture to absorb future increase in the size of the main memory address space without the architecture having to be redesigned.

A second important modifiability criterion in computer architecture is the capability provided for adding new instructions to the instruction set

(a) without having to redesign the exo-architecture as a whole or even significantly;

(b) without having to redesign the implementation of the exo-architecture – that is, the processor data path or the control unit;

(c) without causing a significant lowering in the performance of the current processor.

End Example

3.2 CONCEPTUAL REQUIREMENTS

A design problem may be defined or characterized by requirements that are not necessarily empirical in nature. Rather, these requirements reflect certain doctrines or values related to style, aesthetics or design philosophies. I shall call these *conceptual* requirements and they play an important role in the *recognition* or *generation* of design problems.

Examples of such requirements were presented in chapter 2 where I discussed the role of values in design (see, in particular, examples 2.1 and 2.2). Consider in addition, the following example.

Example 3.14

In example 3.3 I discussed briefly the design and implementation of horizontal microcode compilers and, in particular, the development of microcode compactors as components of such compilers. The primary requirements for these compactors (when they were initially being developed) were empirical in nature, notably, the need to meet certain obvious functional and performance goals. Suppose one such compaction

algorithm has been designed and it meets the stated functionality requirement, produces output of acceptable quality and has a satisfactory asymptotic time complexity. However, the algorithm is difficult to understand and difficult to implement. The developer of the compiler is reluctant to use this algorithm without further investigation of an alternative compactor that is more transparent and/or easy to implement. A new design problem is generated as a result of this requirement. It is a requirement that is not empirical in nature; rather it reflects a certain (subjective) desire on the part of the compiler developer to produce a system that is aesthetically or cognitively more appealing. The requirement is, in these senses, conceptual in nature.
End Example

A design problem produced fundamentally as a consequence of a set of conceptual requirements will be referred to as a *conceptual design problem*. Such requirements and problems exhibit the following interesting features.

(a) Because conceptual requirements reflect issues related to values, e.g., stylistic or aesthetic issues, such requirements when sufficiently at odds with the prevailing wisdom may often generate controversy. Conceptual requirements and problems represent perceptions in the minds of some (e.g., that 'such and such is an unsatisfactory state of affairs') that are not readily perceived by others. Solutions to such problems may therefore – at least at first – generate scepticism, disbelief or dismay. Dijkstra's (1968) perception of the problems attending the *goto* statement, his suggestion of *goto*-less programming, and the controversy that ensued is a classic instance of this situation. Another example is the set of arguments first advanced by Patterson and Dietzel (1980) which eventually led to the design of the first reduced instruction set computers (RISCs). These early proponents of RISCs perceived a conceptual design problem based essentially on issues related to architectural complexity; this led not only to considerable controversy as to the nature of the problem itself but to disagreements concerning the validity of solutions to the problem.[13]

Of course, most conceptual requirements or problems are not likely to be so radical as to produce controversies of the above sort. However, by their very nature conceptual arguments are highly likely to lead to *original* (and *interesting*) design problems and, consequently, to *new classes* of artifacts and designs. Conceptual requirements are thus likely to produce new lines of thought for designing systems in a particular domain.[14]

---

[13] The literature on RISCs is considerable. The key documents are Patterson and Dietzel (1980), Strecker and Clark (1980), Patterson and Sequin (1982), Hennessy and Gross (1983), Hennessy (1984), Patterson (1985) and Colwell *et al.* (1985). A review of the RISC problem is presented in Dasgupta (1989a).

[14] In Part III of this book, the role of the conceptual design problems in advancing a design

(b) Conceptual problems must eventually be translated into empirical requirements. Otherwise whether or not a design satisfies the requirements (see fig. 3.1) can never be objectively confirmed or refuted. For instance, we have previously noted (see section 3.1 above) that the requirement

    (UF_3): A system intended for some task domain should allow the user to interact with it in terms of the user's mental model of the task domain.

may be viewed as a conceptual requirement as it is based essentially on a belief that such a system is desirable from a human point of view. However, whether a design actually meets (UF_3) can only be determined when the concept of 'mental model' has been refined into empirically determinable characteristics. Such an exercise was described in example 3.11.

In other words, conceptual requirements (or a conceptual design problem) will often *determine* empirical requirements; alternatively, empirical requirements may often be *justified* on the grounds that they capture, in an empirical way, conceptual requirements.

3.3 THE IMPRECISENESS OF DESIGN PROBLEMS

According to section 3.1, a requirement is empirical when it specifies externally observable or empirically determinable qualities for an artifact. In many situations a requirement can be naturally stated in a sufficiently precise manner to immediately satisfy this definition. In other words, some requirements are 'naturally' empirical in that one knows exactly and precisely what procedures to construct or use in order to determine whether or not a given design meets such requirements. Design problems that are *entirely characterized* by such requirements fall within the category of what Simon (1973) termed *well-structured* problems.

Example 3.15

Many algorithm design problems fall in this category. Consider, for instance, the design of an algorithm that computes the greatest common divisor (GCD) of two positive integers, a, b. One formulation of the requirements would be (Hoare 1987)

    Let $Z = GCD(a, b)$. Then Z is such that (i) Z divides a exactly; (ii) Z divides b exactly; (iii) Z is the largest of the set of integers satisfying (i) and (ii).

Notice that although the requirements are stated in prose they are precise in that such properties as 'divides exactly' and 'largest of the set of integers' can be defined

---

discipline and its role in establishing a connection between design and science are discussed.

precisely according to the laws of arithmetic and set theory. Given a proposed algorithm A we can devise a procedure that can test conclusively whether or not A satisfies these requirements.
End Example

Example 3.16
The preciseness of the requirements of a well-structured problem provides the added advantage of permitting the problem to be *formally* characterized. As an example, consider the problem of designing a symbol table. The requirements may be stated quite formally as follows.[15]

(a) Initially, the symbol table ST is empty. Notationally

$$ST = \{\ \}$$

(b) The symbol table ST consists of a set of ordered pairs

$$\langle S, V \rangle$$

where $S \in$ SYM, $V \in$ VAL, and SYM, VAL are sets of entities of predefined types. SYM is the set of symbols, VAL is the set of values.
(c) The set of symbols in ST is denoted as **dom** (ST)
(d) For a given symbol $S \in$ **dom** (ST), let ST(S) denote the value V such that $\langle S, V \rangle \in$ ST.
(e) The operation UPDATE(S,V) is defined by

$$\textbf{if } \langle S, V \rangle \notin \text{ST } \textbf{then}$$
$$\textbf{return } \text{ST} \cup \{\langle S, V \rangle\}$$

(f) The operation LOOKUP(S) is defined by:

$$\textbf{if } S \in \textbf{dom } (\text{ST}) \textbf{ then}$$
$$\textbf{return } \text{ST}(S)$$
$$\textbf{else return } \text{errormessage}$$

(g) The operation DELETE(S) is defined by

$$\textbf{if } S \in \textbf{dom } (\text{ST}) \textbf{ then}$$
$$\textbf{return } \text{ST} - \{S, \text{ST}(S)\}$$
$$\textbf{else return } \text{errormessage}$$

End Example

---

[15] This problem and its characterization are largely inspired by Hayes (1985).

Unfortunately, many design problems are not characterized by requirements that can be so precisely defined. A requirement may at first blush *appear* empirical but on further consideration is found to be too imprecise to really *be* an empirical requirement. Furthermore, as we have seen, conceptual requirements by their very nature are inherently imprecise. Design problems characterized by *at least one requirement* that is not empirical – largely because of its impreciseness – are instances of what Simon (1973) termed *ill-structured* problems.

Example 3.17
Suppose that a major requirement in a computer design project is that the instruction set must support frequent time consuming operations in a significant sample of high level language programs. Clearly this is *intended* to be a functional and, therefore, an empirical requirement. However, such attributes as 'efficient support' or 'significant sample' are inherently imprecise. It is only when they have been translated into requirements for which we can devise objective criteria to determine whether an instruction set satisfies the requirements that we will have a set of functional requirements that are also empirical. Until then the design problem remains ill-structured.
End Example

3.4 BOUNDED RATIONALITY AND THE INCOMPLETENESS OF DESIGN PROBLEMS
Yet another important characteristic of many design problems is that they may be *incomplete* – in the sense that at the time a design problem is posed the requirements characterizing the problem are only partially identified.

At first this may seem perplexing. A design problem P is defined in terms of its set of requirements R. Even if R consists of a single requirement this should suffice to define P; it may seem unclear as to how or why P can be construed as incomplete.

The problem is twofold. First, given a requirement set R an arbitrary pair of elements r_i, r_j in R may *influence* or *interact with* one another. For instance an artifact designed to satisfy r_i *cannot* also satisfy r_j (and vice versa); or a decision to satisfy r_i may result in a design *that can only partially satisfy r_j*.

Second, a design problem frequently acquires a 'life of its own' not in any obscure sense but in the sense that in order for a design to satisfy a given set of requirements R, it may also be required to satisfy other requirements not explicitly contained in R or even conceived of, at the time the design problem is first posed. The design problem is elaborated or further refined in the course of design as new, previously unidentified requirements surface.

We have already seen ways in which requirements may spawn other requirements (sections 3.2, 3.3). If a given requirement is conceptual in form or it is an insufficiently precise (quasi-) empirical requirement, then it must be made precise. This is done by redefining the hitherto imprecise requirements and, in the process of doing so, generating new requirements. But here we are concerned with attempting to understand in more general terms the underlying causes of the incompleteness of design problem.

A 'first order' reason for this is that design problems are often *poorly understood* at the time design begins. The deeper reason – or indeed the reason *why* design problems are so often poorly understood – is, at least to a large measure, the fact that designers and their clients, as all human beings, are limited in their capabilities to make fully rational decisions.[16] Designers and clients act and behave under conditions of *bounded rationality* (Simon 1976, 1981, 1982).

The concept of bounded rationality (which will play an important and ubiquitous role throughout this book) was developed by Simon in the mid 1940s in the context of administrative decision making (Simon 1976). It has been subsequently elaborated into a general theory of rationality as much applicable to game playing and design as it is to organizational and economic behavior (Simon 1981, 1982).

The crux of the concept is that in a decision making situation there are two components: the decision making *agent*, and the *environment* in which decisions are to be made.

In 'classical' models of rationality, all the constraints or conditions attending the decision making situation are assumed to be contained in the environment. The agent is assumed to have perfect or complete knowledge of these constraints and be able to perform all the computations necessary to arrive at a decision.

In contrast, the model of bounded rationality takes for granted that there are constraints on the cognitive and information processing capabilities of the decision making agent. These may arise in several ways: even assuming that the conditions associated with the decision making situation are all precisely defined or known, the agent may be unable to perform the computations necessary to produce the most optimum decision because the cost of computation is prohibitive; or the complexities

---

[16] I am discounting the possibility of design problems being posed, formulated or recognized by non-human agents – specifically, by computers. At this time of writing such a possibility seems sufficiently remote as to merit exclusion from this discussion. The role of computers in *solving* design problems will of course, be discussed at length in later chapters.

of the constraints or conditions and their interaction are so great as to prevent the agent from deciding on the best course of action; finally, the agent may have only incomplete or imperfect knowledge of all the alternative courses of action.

Example 3.18
The contrast between classical and bounded rationality models can be illustrated with the example of a scheduling algorithm of the type required to assign processes to processors in multiprocessor systems (Coffman and Denning 1973) or for compacting horizontal microprograms (Dasgupta 1989b). Consider a list of tasks (or processes) each of which requires a specific amount of time for execution; a partial ordering of these tasks according to their data precedence relation;[17] and a finite set of identical processors. The objective is to design a scheduling algorithm that will produce a schedule (i.e., an assignment of tasks to processors) so as to minimize the execution of the task set.

From the perspective of the classical model of rationality it would be assumed that the execution times for the tasks are all *known* beforehand or that some assumption can be made about their respective expected execution times. The scheduler is designed according to whichever of these assumptions is used. Furthermore, according to the classical model of rationality, the scheduler would explore all alternative choices of schedules and produce the one that leads to the least total execution time.

From the perspective of bounded rationality, it would be recognized that in general, the task execution times would *not* be known *a priori*; and furthermore, even if they were known or some reasonable assumption could be made about them, the cost of computing the optimal solution would be far too prohibitive.
End Example

Bounded rationality is, then, a characteristic of the decision making agent. In the context of design it plays as significant a role in the stage of requirements identification and problem formulation as it does (as we shall see later) in the course of design development. Its obvious consequence for characterizing design problems is, as I have discussed above, the fact that requirements are likely to be grossly incomplete in the beginning or the early stages of the design process.

The incompleteness of design problems in turn has its own consequences:

---

[17] Informally, given a pair of tasks T_i, T_j in a task stream such that T_i precedes T_j in the task stream, T_i is said to *data precede* T_j if (i) a variable written into by T_i is read by T_j; or (ii) a variable read by T_i is written into by T_j; or (iii) both T_i, T_j writes into the same variable. If T_i data precedes T_j, then T_i *must* be executed before T_j begins execution. (For more, see Dasgupta 1989b, chapter 5, section 5.4.)

(a) It blurs the distinction between 'requirements' and 'design'. That is, whether a particular requirement belongs in the design problem or is a part of the solution to the problem is a moot point.

(b) Regardless of how we view such requirements it is clear that in a design problem of any reasonable complexity, an inherent component of the design process is, in fact, the development or expansion of the set of requirements.

3.5 SUMMARY

We may conclude our examination of the nature of the design problems by summarizing their salient features.

(i) A design problem is characterized in terms of a set of requirements such that if an artifact or system implemented according to the proposed design satisfies the requirements, the design problem will have been solved.

(ii) The most basic type of requirement is *empirical* in nature. Empirical requirements are such that whether or not a design meets them can be determined empirically by observing the behavior or functioning of a (possibly abstract) implementation of the design. A design problem that is characterized entirely in terms of empirical requirements is said to be *well-structured*.

(iii) A design problem may also be generated as a result of requirements that are not empirical. Such requirements are termed *conceptual* and any reasonably complex, interesting, or original design problem will contain one or more conceptual requirements. A design problem characterized by at least one conceptual requirement is an instance of an *ill-structured* problem.

(iv) Because of the fact of bounded rationality, design problems are often incomplete.

(v) In order that a design can be shown to satisfy a set of requirements, all requirements – including those that are conceptual or imprecisely stated – must eventually be transformed into a set of requirements that are entirely empirical. In other words, an ill-structured design problem must, in order to be demonstrably solvable, be transformed into one or more equivalent well-structured problems. The elaboration, expansion, or refinement of the requirements is thus an integral part of the development of a design.

(vi) As a consequence of the above, the distinction between requirements (i.e., the design problem) and design (i.e., the solution to the problem) is quite often blurred.

Chapter 4

The Form of Design Solutions

As stated at the beginning of chapter 3 the designer's brief is to develop a *form* such that an artifact constructed according to this form would satisfy the requirements. The form *is* the design. The ultimate output of a design process must, then, be an explicit description or representation of the form in some abstract or symbolic language. I shall use the term *design description* to refer to such symbolic representations of forms. When 'design' is used as a noun it becomes essentially a synonym for 'form'.

The concept of form is elusive, abstract, and complex. It may refer to the visible shape of an entity – as when naturalists and biologists talk of biological forms.[1] It may refer to the essential or ultimate nature of a thing – as when philosophers talk of Platonic forms. It may denote the way in which certain parts are arranged and related to one another in an entity – as when one talks of the form of an essay, an argument, a solution, or a musical composition. Finally, architects talk of forms or 'built' forms (March 1976, Alexander 1964) in which term they embrace in a complex, diffuse fashion, the totality of shape, structure and relationships of parts as manifested in buildings.

These examples clearly reveal that form as a general concept is multifaceted. Thus, when we undertake to design an artifact the end product of our activity – the form of the artifact itself and how it is to be described – is critically dependent on how or for what purpose the design is to be used.

4.1 DESIGNS AS BLUEPRINTS
The most basic purpose of design is for it to serve as a plan, a coded set of instructions or, in general, a *blueprint* for implementing an artifact. In designing, then, a clear and deliberate distinction is made between *conceptualizing* an artifact and its

---

[1] A celebrated treatise on biological forms *qua* forms is Sir D'Arcy Wentworth Thompson's (1917) *On Growth and Form*.

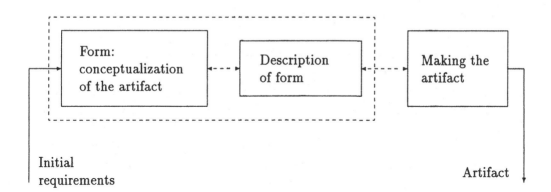

Fig. 4.1 Separation of conceptualization and making.

making. This distinction is enforced by *externalizing* the conceived form by explicitly describing the form in some artificial language (fig. 4.1).

Such a separation of conceptualization and making has not always been necessary. Jones (1980) has pointed out that the earliest initiators of change – the skilled craftsmen of old – did not distinguish between the two. Rather, conceptualization and making were inextricably intertwined; the former was *in* the latter, the latter *in* the former.[2] Using as an example a classic account by Sturt (1923) of how 19th century wagon wheels were formed or developed by wheelwrights, Jones termed this mode of artifact development *craft evolution* and characterized it as follows:

1. Craftsmen do not (usually) externalize their works in terms of symbolic descriptions; nor do they give reasons for many of the decisions they make.
2. The form of an artifact evolves over many years, decades, or even centuries by a process of trial and error and involves many failures and successes of the evolving artifact.
3. The form of an artifact is changed only to correct errors or in order to meet new requirements.
4. The accumulated knowledge concerning the evolution of form is stored in the artifact itself and in the minds of the craftsmen. Such knowledge is transmitted by craftsmen and learnt by their successors through a process of doing and watching during apprenticeship.

---

[2] Refer also to chapter 2, section 2.1 above, in which Schön's (1983) concept of reflection-in-action and Winograd's and Flores' (1987) notions of thrownness and readiness-to-hand are discussed.

In a very similar vein, Alexander (1964) in the context of buildings writes of the *unselfconscious process* whereby buildings in highly traditional cultures have been or continue to be created. The main characteristics of this process are the following:

1. The form maker is also the form user. That is, the builder of a dwelling is also its owner and occupant.
2. There is little *explicit* thought about what rules to apply. The notion of what to do when creating or modifying a dwelling is directly embodied in the doing itself.
3. Failure of a building and its repair are closely intertwined. Indeed, building and repair are integral to everyday life. [3] Furthermore, while there may be general 'remedies' for particular types of failures, there are no general principles of design.
4. There are no external or written means for communicating ideas.
5. Decisions are essentially made according to tradition or custom rather than the builder's new ideas.
6. There is practically no division of labor and, thus, specialization is rare.

The transition from craft evolution to what Jones (1980) termed *design-by-drawing* – that is, to a mode in which there came about a separation of conceptualization from making, of thinking from doing – is attributed by Jones to at least two important reasons.

First, design-by-drawing became necessary when the size and complexity of the artifact exceeded the cognitive capacity of a single craftsman. [4] In order for many craftsmen to be able to cooperate a representation of the artifact – a dimensioned scale drawing – was required to be first created before implementation could begin. The drawing served as the craftsmen's blueprint and to establish or define the interfaces between the different craftsmen's tasks.

---

[3] For instance, the Eskimo reacts constantly to small changes in temperature inside the igloo by opening holes or closing them with snow. The Eskimo also builds a new igloo every night during winter hunts. Alexander (1964) cites several other fascinating examples of this intimate connection between the activities of building, repair and daily life.

[4] Based on introspection alone this seems a plausible enough explanation. But there is of course objective, empirical evidence obtained by cognitive psychologists in support of this suggestion. Conceptualization is a conscious cognitive process. According to current ideas in cognitive science in order for such a process to be performed properly the knowledge required must be contained in the agent's short term or working memory (Atkinson and Shiffrin 1968). And, according to a celebrated paper by Miller (1956) the number of meaningful units of information – or *chunks* – that can be held in working memory is roughly seven (plus or minus two). (Lachman, Lachman and Butterfield 1979, Anderson 1980, Johnson-Laird 1988).

Secondly, there is the fact that by dividing the work of building the artifact amongst several craftsmen, the building process can be greatly *expedited*. This again necessitated the availability of an explicit, shareable representation of the artifact.

When a design is intended to serve *only* as a blueprint for implementation it will usually suffice for the design or form to consist of the *invariant arrangement of the components* of the artifact together with a specification of the *invariant properties* of the components. The design will, then, be a *structural form*; and the description will be a description of this structural form.

Example 4.1
Consider the design of a 16-bit computer data path down to the micro-architectural level of abstraction – that is, at the abstraction level as seen by the microprogrammer or control unit designer (Dasgupta 1989a, chapters 1,5). The intended output of the design process is a data path *form* that will be the basis for implementing the data path chip.

What should be the form of this design? To answer this, we note that the implementer (who will *also* be a designer – the chip level designer) must know *what* the components of the data path are and how they are arranged with respect to each other; he or she must also know the *functional characteristics* of the components as well as the *constraints* (such as timing properties) that they must satisfy. These are all invariant characteristics of the data path. From the implementer's viewpoint – that is, viewing designs as blueprints – the data path design must necessarily be a structural form.

Figs. 4.2 and 4.3 are (partial) *descriptions* of such a data path design. Fig. 4.2 shows, pictorially, the *arrangement* of the principal components in terms of their patterns of interconnections. Fig. 4.3 is a textual description, expressed in the architecture description language S*M (Dasgupta, Wilsey and Heinanen 1986, Dasgupta 1989b, chapter 4). It first specifies the stores with their dimensions; it then describes a 3-phase clock with a cycle time of 100 nanoseconds and phase durations of 25, 50 and 25 nanoseconds respectively; finally, it specifies the functional and timing characteristics of the operational components in the data path, viz., the arithmetic logic unit (ALU) and the various buses. In the case of the ALU module, for instance, the description indicates the input and output ports to this module and tells us that the module is invoked for the duration of the second phase of the clock. Depending on the value of CTL, the module performs one of a set of operations. Each operation is specified in terms of what the 'new' value of the output is, as a function of the 'old' values of the inputs – where 'old' refers to the values at the start of the module's activation and 'new' refers to the value at the termination of activation.
End Example

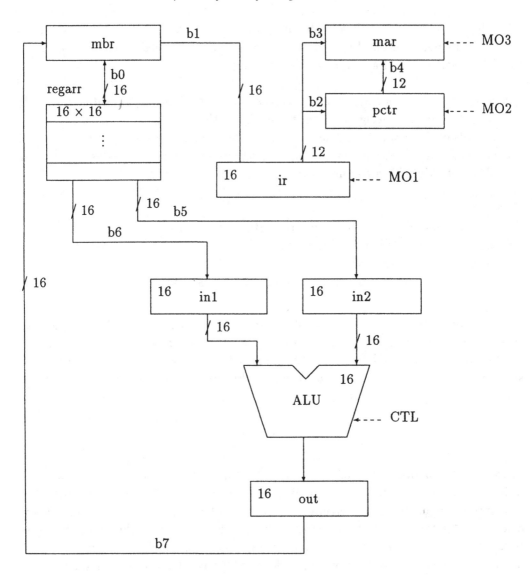

Fig. 4.2 A data path fragment: the arrangement of components.

Example 4.2

Consider the design of an algorithm expressed in pseudocode.[5] As a specific instance we may take the algorithm shown in fig. 4.4 for performing a breadth-first search of a graph G starting at some vertex v (see also Horowitz and Sahni 1978).

---

[5] Pseudocode (or 'program design language') refers to any language that combines natural language sentences with notations and concepts from mathematics and programming languages for the purpose of describing software and algorithms.

```
store mbr, ir, in1, in2, out: seq[15..0] of bit ;
store mar, pctr : seq[11..0] of bit ;
store regarr : array[0..15] of seq[15..0] of bit ;
store CTL : seq[3..0] of bit ;
store MO1, MO2, MO3, ... : bit

clock clk dur 100nS
   subclock   ph1 : dur 25ns
              ph2 : dur 50ns
              ph3 : dur 25ns
endclock

module ALU
   inport in1, in2, CTL outport out
   guard {clk.ph2}
   effect
      case CTL is
         when 2#0010# ==> new out = in1 and in2
         when 2#0011# ==> new out = in1 or in2
         ...
         ...
      endcase
endmodule

module b1
   inport mbr outport ir
   guard {clk.ph1}
   effect
      if MO1 = 1 then new ir = mbr endif
endmodule
   ...
   ...
```

Fig. 4.3 Data path fragment: specification of components.

In this case, the algorithm is a design – a form – that satisfies the requirements that the vertices of a graph are searched in a 'breadth-first' manner. An implementation of this algorithm will produce a program (expressed in a compilable programming language) that would also satisfy the requirement. The algorithm is, thus, a structured set of commands or a plan that tells the implementer what to do in order to build a program for performing the breadth-first search of a graph. It is, in other words, a blueprint.

Algorithm BREADTHFIRST SEARCH (G, v) ;
— The array Visited is such that Visited[i] = 1 if Vertex i has
— been visited ; initially Visited[i] = 0 for all vertices i in G.
— The variable ToExplore is a queue of vertices from G that have
— yet to be explored.
— The variable Temp holds the 'currently visited' vertex
Visited$(v) \leftarrow 1$;
Temp $\leftarrow v$;
while true **do**
    for all vertices u adjacent to v **do**
        if Visited$(u) = 0$ **then**
            Visited$(u) \leftarrow 1$;
            add u to ToExplore
        endif
    endfor ;
    if ToExplore is empty **then return** ;
    Temp $\leftarrow$ first vertex in ToExplore
endwhile

Fig. 4.4 Algorithm for performing breadth-first search.

The form itself is explicitly structural in the following way. The control structure specifies the arrangements of the components. In fact this arrangement is *hierarchical* and *nested* as shown in fig. 4.5.[6] The invariant properties of the components are behavioral or functional properties and they are specified in terms of the *semantics* of the components. For instance, the properties of the complex components A, B, C and D are defined in terms of the semantics of the control structures **while ... do**, **for ... do** and **if ... then** along with the properties of their constituent components; and the invariant properties of the primitive components $1, 2, \ldots, 10$ are given by the meanings of these expressions and statements.
End Example

In the realm of software, the distinction between a 'design' and an 'implementation' of that design is less sharp than in other cases because of the inherently abstract nature of software. Broadly speaking, one can distinguish between software design and software implementation in one of two ways.

(A) The software is said to have been designed when it is developed entirely in a prespecified *design language* (based on a set of textual and graphic notations).

---

[6] Note, in contrast, that the structural form of figs. 4.2 and 4.3 was *not* hierarchical.

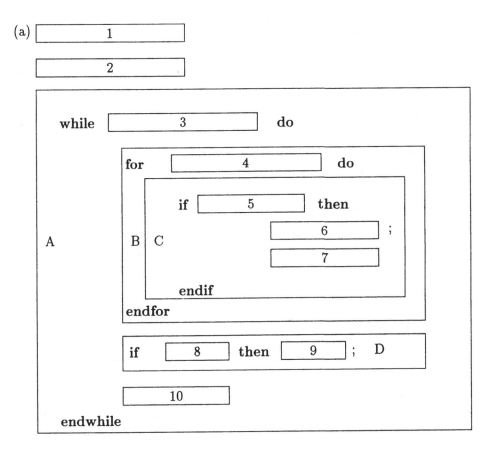

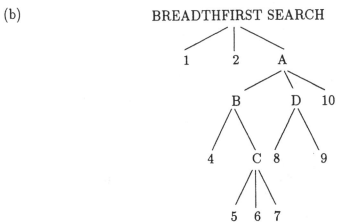

Fig. 4.5 The nested and hierarchical arrangement of parts in BreadthFirst Search.

Implementation is the process of *translating* this design into a program expressed in the target programming language and subsequently making the program *operational* in a particular programming environment.

(B) The software design process terminates at the point at which it is described entirely in the target programming language. That is, the program expressed in that language *is* the design. Implementation is what happens when that piece of software becomes operational in a particular computing environment.

The first of these two views appears to be the most widely accepted viewpoint. It is embedded in the so called 'waterfall-model' of the software life-cycle (Boehm 1984) and appears in the discussions of software development by Zelkowitz, Shaw and Gannon (1979), Sommerville (1985), and Freeman (1980a, 1980b, 1987). Freeman (1987) in particular, provides a detailed and illuminating discussion of (amongst many other things) the role of software design as a blueprint for implementation where 'design' is interpreted in the sense of (A) above.

The second view of what constitutes software 'design' is held at least implicitly by the proponents and practitioners of the techniques of *formal design* (e.g., Dijkstra 1976, Hoare 1986, 1987, Gries 1981). As I shall discuss in detail in chapter 8, the formalists view programs as mathematical objects and the design process as an exercise in applied mathematics. A program designed according to this viewpoint should be provably correct according to strict and rigorous mathematical reasoning. And the basis for such proofs of correctness is the formal *proof theory* for the programming language in which the program is described. [7] Thus, by implication, the design of software must proceed down to the level of detail at which it may be expressed in a programming notation for which a proof theory exists.

In short the form of the designed software will at least in part depend on which of these two views one takes of the boundary between design and implementation. But in either case, the design forms the blueprint for implementation; in either case the design form is a structural form.

Example 4.3
Consider the design of a user-interface for a workstation-based operating system (see also example 3.6), and assume that the design is to be expressed according to (A) above – that is, in a design language such that it may be subsequently translated into executable software.

---

[7] The nature of such proof theories is discussed in chapter 5.

Suppose that one particular very high level requirement that the user interface is to satisfy is the following (Levy and Pollacia 1988):

R_1: For each user skill level in each of the task domains recognized by the user-interface, the user-interface provides an online help facility.

Further refinement of R_1 leads to (amongst others) the following requirements:

R_{11}: For each skill level in each task domain there exists an online help facility that provides information for all interface features, commands and parameters.

Further decomposition of R_{11} produces (amongst others) the following requirement:

R_{112}: There exists an online help utility that accesses the help files to display information for each item requested.

In response to R_{112} a 'help routine module' is designed and expressed in Ada-like psuedocode. Omitting details, the form of this module is shown in fig. 4.6. Note, once more, that the form is structural and that the structure is hierarchical. The package HELP_ROUTINE is at the highest level of the hierarchy; its immediate *components* are the procedure DISPLAY_HELP, the function CHECK_FOR_VALID and any other procedures contained inside the package. The invariant *arrangement* of these components is defined in terms of the calling protocol – specifically, DISPLAY_HELP invokes CHECK_FOR_VALID and the other procedures in HELP_ROUTINE (fig. 4.7). The components themselves have an inner invariant form determined by their internal control structure. Finally, the *primitive components* are the individual natural language or quasi-formal statements.
End Example

Consider the design of a *formal computer language* – as, for example, a programming, a specification, a microprogramming or a hardware description language. In these cases, 'implementation' refers *primarily* to the development and implementation of a compiler for the language for some given target machine or a class of target machines.[8] Thus if one views the language design *as a blueprint for the compiler writer* it is necessary that the design should take the form that is most relevant to the compiler writer's purpose. This involves a definition of the *syntax* of the language – using which the compiler writer may develop the routines to check whether or not a given program in that language is grammatically correct or not; and a definition

---

[8] See later in this discussion for other aspects of a language's implementation.

```
package HELP_ROUTINE ;
   DISPLAY_HELP (item : in string) ;
   function CHECK_FOR_VALID (item : in string) return boolean ;
end HELP_ROUTINE

   package body  HELP_ROUTINE is

     procedure DISPLAY_HELP (item : in string) ;
        type skill_level_type is (novice, experienced, expert) ;
        type task_domain_type is (core, programming, textprocessing,
        system_admin, system_programming);
        . . .
     begin
        determine the user's skill level and current task domain by
        examining the system maintained pair ⟨s1, td⟩ ;
        next_item := first_item from item ; − select first entry in item
        item := item without first_item ;    − delete first entry from item
        while next_item is nonblank loop
           valid := CHECK_VALID(next_item) ;
           if not valid then print 'No help available for ', next_item
           else    begin
                    − display information for next_item for
                    − the user's ⟨s1, td⟩ pair

                    . . .
                   end
        endloop
     end DISPLAY_HELP
     function CHECK_FOR_VALID (item : in string) return boolean ;
        list_of_items : array of string ;
        begin
           if item is in list_items then return (true)
           elseif item is a valid abbreviation
              then return (true)
              else return (false)
           endif
        end CHECK_FOR_VALID
     − other procedures invoked from inside DISPLAY_HELP
     . . .
   end package HELP_ROUTINE
```

Fig. 4.6 The design of HELP_ROUTINE.

of the language's *semantics* – whereby the compiler writer can write the executable code generation routines for the constructs in the language.

The actual *form* of the language – its design, that is – is, once more, structural and hierarchical. The components of the design are the various syntactic categories corresponding to the language constructs; the hierarchical relationships between the syntactic categories constitute the invariant arrangement of the components; and the semantics of the syntactic categories constitute the invariant properties associated with the components.

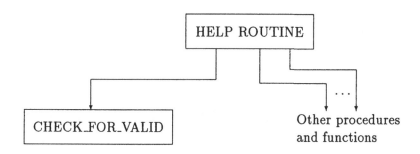

Fig. 4.7 Hierarchical arrangement of HELP_ROUTINE's components.

Example 4.4
As a specific instance, the following grammar gives a partial description of the syntax of a Pascal-like language expressed in Backus Naur form (BNF):

⟨program⟩ ::= **program** ⟨identifier⟩ ; ⟨block⟩
⟨block⟩ ::= ⟨var decl part⟩ ⟨proc decl part⟩ ⟨stmt part⟩
⟨stmt part⟩ ::= **begin** ⟨stmt⟩ {; ⟨stmt⟩ } **end**
⟨stmt⟩ ::= ⟨simple stmt⟩ | ⟨structured stmt⟩
⟨simple stmt⟩ ::= ⟨assign stmt⟩ | ⟨input_output stmt⟩ | ⟨proc stmt⟩
⟨structured stmt⟩ ::= ⟨if stmt⟩ | ⟨while stmt⟩
⟨assign stmt⟩ ::= ⟨variable⟩ := ⟨expression⟩
⟨if stmt⟩ ::= **if** ⟨expression⟩ **then** ⟨stmt⟩ |
       if ⟨expression⟩ **then** ⟨stmt⟩ **else** ⟨stmt⟩
⟨while stmt⟩ ::= **while** ⟨expression⟩ **do** ⟨stmt⟩

The components are the syntactic categories ⟨program⟩, ⟨block⟩, etc. Their relationship with one another can be described by a hierarchical structure of the form shown in fig. 4.8.

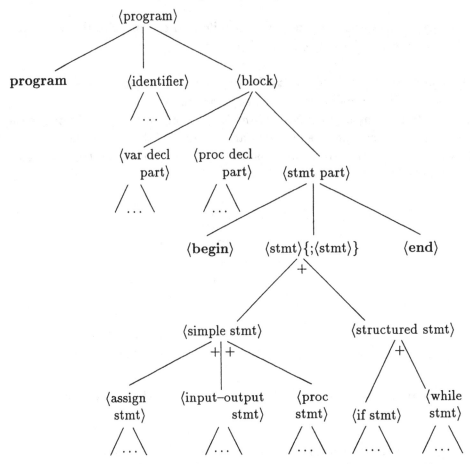

Fig. 4.8 Hierarchical arrangement of components in a language design.

The functional properties of each of the components can be specified by means of a description of what each construct does. For instance, the functional property of ⟨assign stmt⟩ could be given by the informal *operational* description of its semantics:

'The current value of ⟨variable⟩ is replaced by the value of ⟨expression⟩. The ⟨variable⟩ and ⟨expression⟩ must be of identical type.'

Similarly, the functional property of ⟨while stmt⟩ can be defined by means of the following operational semantics:

'The type of ⟨expression⟩ is boolean. ⟨stmt⟩ is executed as long as the evaluation of ⟨expression⟩ yields TRUE. ⟨while stmt⟩ terminates when ⟨expression⟩ evaluates to FALSE'

End Example

I noted above that the primary meaning of 'implementation' for a language design is the building of a compiler for that language. A language's implementation may also entail other aspects. For instance it may be required to construct a program that will *mechanically verify* the correctness of a program (or microprogram or hardware description) written in that language. If one of the principal requirements that a language design was supposed to satisfy was that programs written in the language should be amenable to formal mechanical verification then an implementation of the language must entail a verifier for that language. Alternatively, it may be required, as part of the implementation, to construct a program that will mechanically effect *correctness preserving transformations* of a (relatively less efficient) program to one that is more efficient.

In either of these cases, it is not enough for the design to consist only of the syntax and semantics as given in example 4.4.

Example 4.5
Consider, in particular, an implementation that involves the development of a correctness preserving transformation program for programs written in the language that is to be designed. In this case, the language design must, in addition to its various syntactic components and their hierarchic relationships, also include *transformation rules* for its various constructs. Examples of such rules are:

$(R1)$ X_1, X_2 := e_1, e_2 ≡ X_2, X_1 := e_2, e_1
$(R2)$ X := e ≡ X, y := e, y
$(R3)$ **if** b **then** S_1; S_3 **else** S_2; S_3 **endif**
      ≡ **if** b **then** S_1 **else** S_2 **endif** ; S_3
$(R4)$ **if** b_1 **then** S_1 **elseif** b_2 **then** S_1 **else** S_2 **endif**
      ≡ **if** b_1 ∨ b_2 **then** S_1 **else** S_2 **endif**

$(R1)$ and $(R2)$ are rules affecting simple and multiple assignment statements while $(R3)$ and $(R4)$ involve transformations of conditional statements. Note that these rules define invariant functional properties of (combinations of) syntactic categories other than those defined by their conventional semantics alone.
End Example

4.2 DESIGNS AS USER GUIDES
In the preceding section I discussed the question of what form a design should take assuming that the sole purpose of a design is for it to serve as a blueprint for implementation. However, the latter is *not* the only purpose that a design is intended to serve.

To begin with, recall from chapter 3 that some of the most significant requirements that characterize a design problem are *functional* requirements. An artifact is meant to *do* something. Functional properties define what it is that the intended artifact is supposed to do. Thus, any thinking that goes into the development of the artifact must pay as much attention to how these functional properties *are to be made available* to the environment in which the artifact will be placed as to how these same properties are to be actually realized. The designer has to recognize the fact that every design is Janus-faced: from one side it reflects the usability of the artifact, from the other side it reflects its implementability.

Thus it is simply not enough for designs to be blueprints for implementation – fundamental though this role is. A design should also be a specification of how the intended artifact is to be used in some anticipated environment. Designs should, in addition to being blueprints, serve as *user guides* for the designed artifact.

It was stated at the start of this chapter that the ultimate output of a design process is an explicit representation of form. Later, it was pointed out that if one views designs only as blueprints for implementation then it is sufficient for the form to be structural in nature. But now we add the caveat that designs may also need to serve as user guides. And, the question then is, how does this caveat affect the form that designs should take?

As always, given the empirical nature of our enquiry into the design process, we may best address this question by way of examples.

Example 4.6
Consider the language design problem of example 4.4. Its syntax and semantics characterize the structure of the language. Consider, in particular, one of the components, the **while** statement. Its syntax

$$\textbf{while } \langle\text{expression}\rangle \textbf{ do } \langle\text{stmt}\rangle$$

characterizes the internal structure of the statement. Its semantics is given informally and operationally as:

'The type of ⟨expression⟩ is boolean. ⟨stmt⟩ is executed as long as the evaluation of ⟨expression⟩ yields TRUE. ⟨while stmt⟩ terminates when ⟨expression⟩ evaluates to FALSE'.[9]

---

[9] This is not, of course, the only way in which the semantics of the *while* statement can be stated. It can also be defined *denotationally* (Stoy 1977, Gordon 1979, de Bakker 1980) or *axiomatically* (Hoare and Wirth 1973, de Bakker 1980).

Notice, though, that neither syntax nor semantics tells us where or when the **while** statement can be used. Indeed, unless we are already familiar with the types of language constructs from prior experience with, or knowledge of, programming languages, we would be at a loss to make much sense of such constructs. The syntax and semantics tell us the structure and properties of the **while** statement but not how one should use it. Additional information is thus required. It usually takes the form of a statement of the following form:

'The **while** statement is used whenever a particular computation is required to be performed repeatedly as long as some condition holds. The repetitive computation is specified by ⟨stmt⟩. The condition that controls the repetitive performance of the computation is specified by ⟨expression⟩.'

This statement, thus, establishes the *context* in which the **while** statement is relevant. Borrowing a term from philosophy, this statement defines the *pragmatics* of the **while** statement.
End Example

Example 4.7
The architects of the IBM System/360 (Blaauw and Brooks 1964) and later, the IBM System/370 (IBM 1981) provided an instruction called the TEST-AND-SET as part of the exo-architecture of these systems. The TEST-AND-SET, thus, constitutes a component of the architectural designs for these machines.

From the viewpoint of implementation it is sufficient to characterize this instruction in terms of its syntax (its internal structure) and semantics. The syntax may be stated as

TS Addr

where 'TS' is the opcode and 'Addr' is a main memory byte address. Its semantics may be given informally (and operationally) by a statement such as

'The leftmost bit of the addressed byte is used to set the condition code (0 if leftmost bit was 0, otherwise 1) and the addressed byte is set to all ones'

A more formal, nonoperational specification of the semantics may be

$$\textbf{new } \text{cond\_code} = \text{main\_mem[Addr].high\_order}$$
$$\& \textbf{ new } \text{main\_mem[Addr]} = 2\#11111111$$

(where the prefix **new** indicates the 'new' value of an entity – upon termination of the instruction – and the absence of **new** signifies a value at the start of the instruction's execution).

This design for the TEST-AND-SET instruction while perfectly adequate for the purpose of implementation gives us no clues as to the context in which the instruction is to be used – nor, more fundamentally, why this instruction was concocted at all! We, thus, need an additional component in the design that *explains* where or when the TEST-AND-SET may be required:

'The TEST-AND-SET may be used to implement a higher level synchronizing operation such as a LOCK operation as follows:

$$\text{LOCK}(k) : \textbf{repeat } \text{TS k } \textbf{until } \text{cond\_code} = 0\text{'}$$

End Example

In both the above examples the place of the 'user' in the scheme of things was quite obvious. In the case of a programming language, the user is the programmer; in the case of the exo-architecture, the user is the operating systems designer or the compiler writer. It behooves us, however, to consider a design context in which the notion of a user (and, therefore, of a user guide) is less obvious.

Example 4.8
Consider the design of a pipelined computer – more specifically, the processing unit which fetches, decodes and executes instructions in pipelined mode (Kogge 1981, Hwang and Briggs 1984, Dasgupta 1989b). Let us in particular, assume a 4-stage pipeline as shown in fig. 4.9. Here, the IFETCH stage fetches an instruction from memory and places it in an instruction register, IDECODE decodes the instruction, EADDR computes the effective address, and IEXEC fetches the operands and executes the instruction. Furthermore, while each instruction in the input instruction stream goes through all the four stages, at any given time the four stages are operating in parallel on different instructions: while IEXEC is executing instruction i, EADDR is processing instruction $i + 1$, IDECODE is decoding instruction $i + 2$, and IFETCH is fetching instruction $i + 3$.

A pipeline of this sort is not normally visible at the exo-architectural level; it is essentially a feature of the computer's internal logic, structure and behavior – that is, a part of the computer's *endo-architecture* (Dasgupta 1989b). Thus, it would appear that the notion of design as a user guide does not apply in this case. One might assume that the sole role of a pipeline design is as a blueprint for implementation

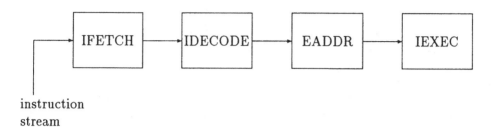

instruction
stream

Fig. 4.9 A 4-stage instruction pipeline.

and, therefore, it suffices for the description of the pipeline design to be that of a structural form. The design would then consist of:

(i) A specification of the functional properties of each of the stages.
(ii) A specification of the amount of time required by each of the stages and the overall timing characteristics.[10]
(iii) A specification of the channels of communication between the stages.

One would assume that there is no need for the design to serve as a user guide as there are no obvious 'users' for this design other than the implementer.

This may indeed be true in general. But there are specific situations in which the pipeline design *does* have a 'user'. I refer here to the compiler writer who may want to exploit the structure of the pipeline in order to rearrange the generated object code so as to increase the inter-instruction parallelism and, thus, the overall throughput (Hennessy and Gross 1983). Thus, even in this case, the output of the design process – the design itself – may be required to serve not only as a blueprint for implementation but as a user guide for the compiler writer. The design must, accordingly, be in a form that is appropriate for both.

To understand this further, consider a specific sequence of instructions:

$$\text{IS} \;\equiv\; I_1 \;:\; R_2 \;\leftarrow\; \text{Mem}[R6]$$
$$I_2 \;:\; R_4 \;\leftarrow\; R_2 + R_4$$
$$I_3 \;:\; R_3 \;\leftarrow\; R_3 + 1$$
$$I_4 \;:\; \text{Mem}[R6] \;\leftarrow\; R_3$$

produced as the object code by a compiler for our four-stage pipeline processor. Suppose further that the compiler writer was cognizant of the following facts:

---

[10] For example, whether instructions are moved from one stage to the next simultaneously under the control of a single clock or whether the stages operate asynchronously.

(i) For a pair of instructions I_j, I_k in the instruction stream, where I_j precedes I_k, and I_j is already in the pipeline, if I_j data precedes I_k (see footnote 17, chapter 3) then I_k will be held up in IDECODE and not allowed to proceed to EADDR until I_j has completed execution.

(ii) For each instruction in the instruction set, there exists one or more possible functional units within the processor that can be used to execute the instruction. In the case of I_3 above, for example, it may be that the 'add' operation can be performed either by a general purpose ALU or an incrementer.

(iii) All the stages in the pipeline take the same amount of time to perform their respective tasks. This time is referred to as the 'time unit'. Under these circumstances, the processing of IS by the pipeline would take 9 time units as shown by the Gantt chart of fig. 4.10. [11] However, if the compiler has been developed to take into account the aforementioned characteristics, it may recognize the facts that I_1 data precedes I_2, I_3 data precedes I_4 and I_2, I_3 are mutually independent; it may accordingly *reorder* IS to the sequence

$$IS' \equiv I_1 : R_2 \leftarrow \text{Mem}[R6]$$
$$I_3 : R_3 \leftarrow R_3 + 1$$
$$I_2 : R_4 \leftarrow R_2 + R_4$$
$$I_4 : \text{Mem}[R6] \leftarrow R_3$$

IFETCH	$I1$	$I2$	$I3$	$I3$	$I4$				
IDECODE		$I1$	$I2$	$I2$	$I3$	$I4$	$I4$		
EADDR			$I1$	–	$I2$	$I3$	–	$I4$	
IEXEC				$I1$	–	$I2$	$I3$	–	$I4$
	1	2	3	4	5	6	7	8	9 →

time units

Fig. 4.10 Gantt chart for IS.

Providing that the execution of I_3 involves the incrementer and that of I_2 the general purpose ALU, IS' can be processed in 7 time units (fig. 4.11). Furthermore, all stages of the pipeline are effectively utilized for this particular code sequence.

---

[11] A Gantt chart is a two dimensional diagram with time as the horizontal axis. It contains as many rows as there are stages in the pipeline and as many columns as there are distinct intervals of time required to be depicted. Entries in the row corresponding to a stage show tasks that are processed by the stage over successive time intervals.

IFETCH	I1	I3	I2	I4			
IDECODE		I1	I3	I2	I4		
EADDR			I1	I3	I2	I4	
IEXEC				I1	I3	I2	I4

| 1 | 2 | 3 | 4 | 5 | 6 | 7 $\rightarrow$ |

time units

Fig. 4.11 Gantt chart for IS'.

Now, it may well be that a design (and its description) intended as a blueprint for implementation *could* serve as a source for the information required by the compiler writer. However, it may as well be the case that at least some of the information relevant to the compiler writer is not easily or directly extractable from such a design description. Thus the pipeline design should be in such a form that both the implementer's and the compiler writer's tasks are equally facilitated.
End Example

4.3 DESIGNS AS MEDIA FOR CRITICISM AND CHANGE
Based on the foregoing analysis our current picture of what a design process must produce – the form itself – may be depicted as in fig. 4.12. The form must be such that the implementer can extract the information necessary to implement the artifact; it must also contain a specification of how the artifact is to relate to its operational environment – that is, how it is to be used.

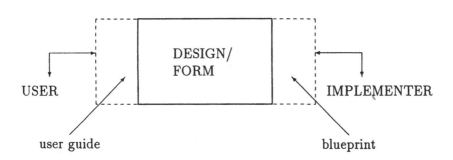

Fig. 4.12 Relationship between the design/form, user, and implementer.

Let us suppose that we have produced such a form and it is described in a particular design language. I shall now consider several scenarios concerning the fate of this design.

In the first, the designer is satisfied that the form is the correct response to requirements; the design is passed on to the implementer and the artifact is implemented. The artifact is then tested to determine whether it satisfies the requirements as the designer expects it to, or has claimed that it will. Unfortunately, the artifact *fails* the test in one or more ways. The requirements that the artifact fails to meet are so critical that the latter *must* be modified so that it does satisfy the requirements.

In the second scenario, the implemented artifact does meet the requirements satisfactorily. It is then made operational in its target environment. However, in the course of time the environment for which the artifact had been designed in the first place *changes* in one way or another. The artifact no longer operates satisfactorily in the changed environment. The original requirements no longer all hold; the changed environment generates new or a modified set of requirements. However, the environment shift is not so stark as to cause the artifact to become entirely obsolete – rather, it is expected that relatively small changes to the original design will accommodate the new requirements.

In the third scenario, the design never reaches the implementer. Rather, it becomes the focus of critical assessment by the client or the designer's colleagues. They ask questions such as *why* a particular decision – producing a particular feature – was at all necessary, or *what if* a solution approach Y had been adopted rather than the approach X that actually was.

All three scenarios lead to the condition of *redesign*. In the case of the first two scenarios redesign is necessitated simply because the artifact does not meet the (original or changed) requirements. In the third case redesign is the basis for experimenting with alternative choices – not only to address 'what if' questions but also in response to 'why' questions. What is common to all three scenarios is their respective starting points – the original design/form itself. For it is *this* design that must be modified; and the precise *nature* of this change is to be determined by *critically examining* the current design. The design itself becomes the medium for criticism, change and experimentation.

This, then, becomes a third fundamental role for the form that is produced by a design process (fig. 4.13). Its implications for the form that should be produced and manner in which such a design should be described are profound. For it is clear that whenever the issue of change or experimentation comes up, a design cannot be viewed as a static entity in the sense that a blueprint and a user guide are static. In these latter cases it is imperative that the implementation be given, not merely a structural form in which the components have specific invariant properties and the

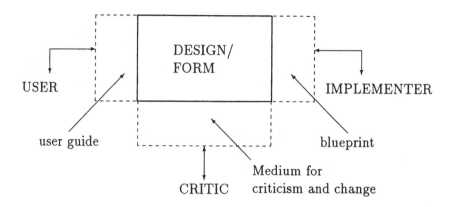

Fig. 4.13 The three functions of a design/form.

arrangement of the components is invariant, but exactly *one* such structural form. Many alternative pathways may have been explored in the course of the design process but what the implementer receives is the final structural form. [12] In the context of change, in contrast, a design becomes a shifting, dynamic entity in more ways than one:

(a) Before a feature or component is modified it must be known *why* decisions were made in favor of that feature in the first place. Thus, the *evolutionary history* of the design decisions that led to the emergence of the feature or component must be available in order to address such a question.

(b) When a feature or a component is modified the ramifications of such a change on other features or components must also be understood. Such ramifications are double edged: on the one hand a change in design component *A* may necessitate changes in components *B*, *C*, ..., with which *A* interfaces or interacts; on the other, a change to *A* may render other design decisions invalid – in which case such decisions may have to be re-evaluated. In order to determine and evaluate these sorts of ramifications, a network depicting the *causal structure* or *dependencies* amongst design decisions *must* be available as part of the design description itself. In other words, the evolutionary history of the 'final' form must, once more, be a part of the design description. Furthermore, with every change in the design, the form must not only change, but also the network of causal dependencies amongst the design decisions.

---

[12] It is not for nothing that we refer to a design as being 'frozen' when it is passed on to the implementer.

Example 4.9
The 'final' form of a particular user-interface called PDI (Levy and Pollacia 1988) is
specified in an Ada-like pseudocode. One module of this design is the HELP_ROUT-
INE package shown previously, in fig. 4.6. To understand *why* or *how* this module
became a part of the 'final' design – an understanding that is essential for any critique or evaluation of the design – necessitates a documentation of the evolutionary
pathway of which the HELP_ROUTINE is an end product. Fig. 4.14 displays a path
through the network (strictly speaking, directed acyclic graph) of decisions culminating in HELP_ROUTINE. Each node in this diagram signifies a requirement that was
generated in the course of design. [13] An edge from node i to node j signifies that
a necessary condition for requirement i to be satisfied is that requirement j is also
satisfied (alternatively, requirement j is part of the refinement of requirement i).
End Example

Example 4.10
In designing a special purpose multiprocessor to support the efficient simulation
of computer architectures (Hooton 1987, Hooton, Aguero and Dasgupta 1988) the
processor–memory interconnection network finally decided upon was a *multiple bus*
scheme (fig. 4.15). In assessing this design the critic may legitimately enquire why a
multiple bus scheme rather than a *crossbar* or a *multistage* network was used.[14] This
information, or the implication of substituting one network scheme for another on
this particular architecture, is not available in a design description that shows only
the final structural form – as represented, for instance, by a diagram such as fig. 4.15
(or a more detailed version thereof), or a formal specification of the network in an
architecture description language. What is required in addition is the causal history
of this design decision or feature – that is, a specification of how the design evolved
such that the multiple bus scheme emerged as its end product.
End Example

4.4 SUMMARY
The solution to a design problem – the output of a design process – is a form. It
is this form that constitutes 'the design'. I have suggested in this chapter that the
nature of a design/form will (or should) be influenced by three distinct roles that the
design/form plays in the development of an artifact.

First, it serves as a blueprint to guide the artifact's implementation. For this purpose

---

[13] This is an example of a situation where requirements generation formed a substantial part of
the design process (see chapter 3, section 3.3).

[14] For discussions of such interconnection schemes see, for example, Hwang and Briggs (1984),
Hayes (1988) or Dasgupta (1989b).

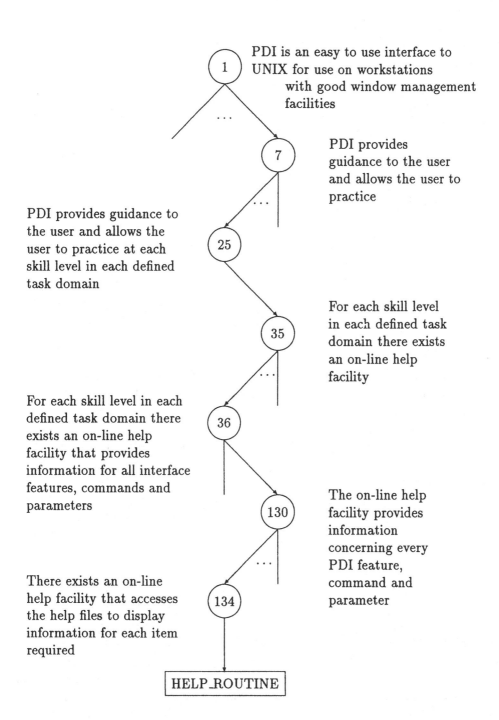

PDI is an easy to use interface to UNIX for use on workstations with good window management facilities

PDI provides guidance to the user and allows the user to practice

PDI provides guidance to the user and allows the user to practice at each skill level in each defined task domain

For each skill level in each defined task domain there exists an on-line help facility

For each skill level in each defined task domain there exists an on-line help facility that provides information for all interface features, commands and parameters

The on-line help facility provides information concerning every PDI feature, command and parameter

There exists an on-line help facility that accesses the help files to display information for each item required

HELP_ROUTINE

Fig. 4.14 Evolutionary history of HELP_ROUTINE.

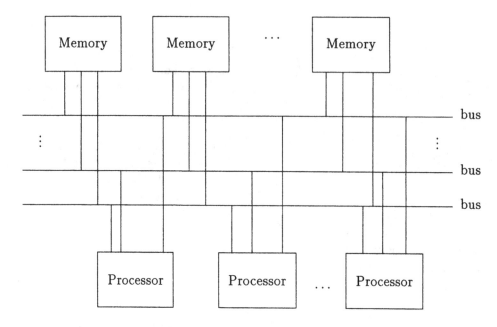

Fig. 4.15 Multiple bus interconnection scheme.

it is required that the design be a *structural* form. By this is meant that the form should contain a description of the functional properties of the components of the form, and the relationship or arrangement of the components.

The language in which designs *qua* blueprints are expressed must, then, be capable of specifying structures. In the case of computer systems such design descriptions range from specifications in formal languages (such as programming, hardware description or microprogramming languages) through descriptions in quasi-formal notation (that combine, for instance, mathematical, formal language and natural language statements) to very informal and visual descriptions (such as block diagrams, charts or flow diagrams).

Second, a design/form serves as a user-guide in the sense that it characterizes the artifact's pragmatics – that is, the context in which the artifact 'makes sense'. In general, this context should have been taken into account in the formulation of the requirements so that the design/form will implicitly reflect it. By recognizing the user-guide role of a design/form this context is, however, rendered explicit. The design description must, then, not only be a description of structural form; it must also serve as a document that describes how the target artifact is to be harnessed by the potential user.[15]

---

[15] An 'artifact' in this context may of course be a component that participates in the formulation

In the case of computational artifacts such as programming languages, operating systems, user interfaces, application software or exo-architectures the *user manual* serves as such a document. However, user manuals are not normally viewed as part of the design description. And, in many cases, such user manuals are restricted to describing the structure of the artifact rather than its pragmatics.

Third, a design or form is a medium for criticism, experimentation and change. In contrast to designs *qua* blueprints where the form of relevance is structural in nature, and designs *qua* user guides where the information of relevance is the context of the artifact's deployment, designs viewed as media for criticism and change must express the justification of design decisions and the causal relationship amongst design decisions so that 'why' questions and 'what if' questions can be addressed by referring to the design itself.

It is striking that though this role of design is so fundamental – since it is this that allows us to 'play' with our ideas, explore alternatives, and recover from mistakes of judgement or of decisions prior to the building of the artifact – it is an aspect that is grossly neglected in most discussions of design descriptions or languages. For what it signifies is that the output of the design process must not only consist of the 'final' structural form, but also the evolutionary history that led to the emergence of the structural form. It is only by virtue of this history that the design can serve as a medium of criticism and change. In later chapters we shall explore the practical implications of these observations in more detail.

---

of the 'total' artifact.

Chapter 5

The Evolutionary Structure of Design Processes

5.1 THE SATISFICING NATURE OF DESIGN DECISIONS

In chapter 3 (section 3.4) I introduced the concept of bounded rationality. As noted there, bounded rationality is a model of rationality proposed by Simon (1976, 1982) that recognizes the severe limits on the cognitive and information processing capabilities of the decision making agent. Such limitations may arise in a variety of ways: the various factors or parameters affecting a decision may be so complex or they may interact in such complicated ways the agent may be unable to decide the best course of action; or the agent may simply not know all the alternative courses of action; or even when all the factors or alternatives are known fully, the cost of computing the best possible choice may be far too prohibitive.

Bounded rationality explains why design problems are so very often formulated in an incomplete manner (see section 3.4, chapter 3). But it has an even more profound consequence for the design process itself, and for the nature of design solutions.

Example 5.1
To understand this, consider a computer architect who has been given a particular set of initial requirements and is required to design a *micro-architecture* that meets these requirements. A computer's micro-architecture, it will be recalled (see footnote 6, chapter 3) refers to the internal architecture of the computer as seen by the microprogrammer (see also Dasgupta 1989a, chapter 1).

We shall further assume that the initial requirements, though sparse, are quite precise and complete. For instance, the requirements may state that the micro-architecture (and the associated microcode) should (a) implement a specific well defined exo-architecture; and (b) be realizable on a single chip using a specific feature size and technology.[1]

---

[1] Typically, this kind of a design problem arises when a commercially successful exo-architecture (such as IBM System/370 or the VAX-11) previously implemented in an older, medium scale integrated circuit (MSI) technology is required to be reimplemented in a newer, large scale or very large

The principal components of any micro-architecture are the following:

(a) The types and organization of stores that are visible or accessible at the micro-architectural level. Typically, these include memory buffer and address registers, the instruction register, the program counter, one or more arrays of general registers, arithmetic registers and latches, the microinstruction register, the control store, and the control store address register (Dasgupta 1989a, chapter 5).[2]

(b) The organization of the data path connecting stores to one another or to functional units. For example, the data path may be organized in a distributed fashion or around one or more centralized buses.

(c) A set of functional units (e.g., ALUs, counters, shifters, etc).

(d) The modes of parallelism to be deployed. Modes include pipelining of the instruction fetch/decode/execute process, horizontal microcoding, and overlapping of microinstruction fetch/execute.

(e) The temporal structure of the micro-architecture. Choices include, for example, a polyphase clock cycle and the choice of the number of phases in the cycle.

(f) The set of microoperations and their semantics.

(g) The formats or organization of microinstructions.

(h) The sequencing logic for microprogram execution.

(i) The distribution of control information between the microcode and the registers.

It is not only that the space of possible choices for each of these components *considered independently* is (in a practical sense) unbounded! It is also the case that these components *interact* with one another in the sense that a set of decisions concerning one component will influence the design of, or design choices for, one or more of the other components. For example:

(i) The mode(s) of parallelism chosen will determine microinstruction organization (and vice versa).

(ii) The choice of the temporal structure will influence the effective degree (and hence, modes) of parallelism as well as the microinstruction formats.

(iii) The data path organization and the set of functional units will determine the repertoire of micro-operations and, consequently, the organization of the microinstructions.

(iv) The microprogram sequencing logic influences both temporal structure and microinstruction organization.

---

scale integrated circuit (LSI/VLSI) technology.

[2] Note that all the programmable stores visible at the (higher) exo-architectural level (main memory, floating point registers, the program status word) are also visible at this level.

(v) Decisions regarding the distribution of control information will determine the composition of the storage organization, the microinstruction organization and the nature and complexity of the microcode.

Furthermore, practically none of these relationships can be captured by a mathematical expression such that one can quantitatively predict the effect of varying one component on another. The computer architect can hardly make *any* optimum decisions regarding the design of the micro-architecture.
End Example

This example is quite typical of the more complex kinds of design problems encountered by system designers, planners and architects. In the light of my earlier discussion of the nature of design problems (chapter 3), the *initial* requirements in this case are quite precise and complete. They are, furthermore, empirical requirements. The complexity of this problem stems from the nature, variety and mutual interdependence of the choices available to the computer architect in the course of the design process. The space of possible designs or design choices is, in a practical sense, unbounded. This, in Simon's (1973) terminology, is another characteristic of ill-structured problems.[3]

It is bounded rationality, then, that limits our ability to deal with problems involving many alternative and mutually interacting choices in an optimal manner. This led Simon (1981) to suggest that for most non-trivial design problems one must be content with 'good' rather than the 'best' solutions. The designer sets some criterion of satisfactoriness and if the design meets the criterion the design problem is considered to have been 'solved'. Such a strategy can be adopted not only for the design problem as a whole but also for the smaller subproblems encountered during the design process. In Simon's terms decisions made during the process of design are, in general, *satisficing procedures* in that they aim to produce 'acceptable' or 'good' rather than optimal solutions. Designs then, are in general, *satisficing solutions*.

Example 5.2
In the case of the micro-architecture design problem of example 5.1 many satisficing decisions will have to be taken. The large space of possible choices may initially be reduced by a decision to adopt a particular *architectural style* or a particular *combination of styles*.[4] For instance, the architect may decide, with suitable justification,

---

[3] Recall the earlier discussion of ill-structuredness in chapter 3, section 3.3.

[4] A style is a set of characteristics or attributes that allows us to distinguish one group of artifacts from another – artifacts that may otherwise be functionally similar or serve some common purpose. Thus, a style signifies certain *acts of choice* on the part of the designer the result of

to adopt a bus-organized style for the data path design, a pipeline style for the overall control unit operation, and a horizontal style for microinstruction organizations. Justification for these early decisions may be based on a small number of goals that serve as *criteria of satisfactoriness* for the computer architect – though these may not be requirements that the *client* is necessarily concerned with. The goals may be:

(i) The need for a *regular data path structure* – as necessitated by VLSI technology. This goal serves as a pointer to a bus organized data path style.

(ii) The need to achieve a *high level of parallelism* in the operation of the processor. This goal suggests the selection of the pipelined style for the control unit operation as a whole, coupled with the style of horizontal microinstruction organization.

Note the satisficing nature of these decisions. The argument is essentially of the following form:

$G1$: A regular data path structure is desired
$C1$: The bus organized style is conducive to regular data path structures

Therefore

$D1$: Select the bus organized style.

$C1$ stipulates the choice that is expected to lead towards the satisfaction of goal $G1$. Hence the decision $D1$. Similarly:

$G2$: A high level of parallelism in the operation of the processor is desired.
$C21$: Pipelining the microinstruction fetch/decode/execute phases is one means to achieve this.
$C22$: Executing micro-operations in parallel through a horizontal microinstruction organization is one means to achieve this goal.

---

which is the presence of one particular set of characteristics in the artifact rather than another. The role of style in computer architecture *design* is discussed at length in Dasgupta (1984) and as a basis for *classifying* computer architectures, in Dasgupta (1989b). The general place of style in design is discussed perceptively by Simon (1975). Style, of course, occupies a major and highly visible position in the domain of building architecture – as, for example, when we talk of gothic, romanesque or baroque styles of buildings (Pevsner 1963) – and in painting – as when artists and art historians talk about impressionism, pointillism or cubism (Gombrich 1969, Jansen 1969). The notion of style will often be encountered in this book and is discussed at greater length in chapter 10, section 10.7.

Therefore

D2: Select pipelining and horizontal microinstruction organization.

In this case, $C21$ and $C22$ are choices that, individually, are expected to contribute towards the goal $G2$. Hence the decision $D2$.

Other satisficing decisions will appear later in the decision process. For instance, given an initial decision to adopt a horizontal organization for microinstructions, there remains the problem of what the *precise format* will be – i.e., how to distribute the micro-operations to different fields of the microinstruction. Many different possibilities exist (Dasgupta 1979, 1989a, Mueller and Varghese 1988). To make this decision the following criterion may be established:

'If the micro-operations control disjoint resources of the data path (viz., registers, buses, functional units) then they should be assigned to distinct fields of the microinstructions (so as to exploit the potential parallelism in the data path).'

A microinstruction format meeting this criterion would constitute a satisficing solution. A very different satisficing solution may emerge if the criterion was that

'The microinstruction width should not exceed 64 bits.'

The important point to note is that given the many possibilities posed even in the relatively low level design of the microinstruction format, the architect may still be forced to satisfice; he or she may be forced to establish a criterion (or criteria) of satisfactoriness such that a design that meets the criterion (or criteria) is *accepted* as the solution to the problem. The architect will, on most occasions, not be able to do any better than this – either because he or she does not know how an optimal decision may be derived or, even if this *is* known, the time required to derive an optimum solution is simply too much.
End Example

5.2 THE INTRACTABILITY OF DESIGN OPTIMIZATION PROBLEMS

In the preceding section it was noted that designers may have to (and most often do) rest content with satisficing solutions. This is due to several closely connected reasons: (a) the various design decisions may interact such that the precise effect of the interactions may not be predictable; (b) the space of possible choices or decisions is, for all intents and purposes, unbounded; and (c) the designer may not even know all the possible courses of action.

It was also noted that even in the case that all possible alternatives *are* known in advance (in the sense that we know how to *generate* the alternatives) the *cost* of deriving an optimum or 'best possible' design may be so high as to be simply prohibitive. In spite of knowing that there does indeed exist an optimal solution to a design problem – in spite of knowing the procedure that would yield the optimized design – the designer may still be forced to satisfice.

Since optimization is a recognized topic in many engineering disciplines, is part of the curriculum of engineering design courses, and is discussed at length in texts on engineering design theory (Siddall 1982, Dieter 1983) it is important for us to understand the scope and limits of design optimization – particularly in the context of computer systems – and to appreciate why designers are so often forced to satisfice even when it is known that a problem is optimally solvable. Towards this objective let us first identify a number of design optimization problems.

Example 5.3
The typical structure of a compiler is shown in fig. 5.1. As indicated, the 'back end' of a compiler is concerned with the generation and optimization of object code for the target machine. The input to the code generation/optimization phase is a description of the original program in some convenient target-machine-independent ('intermediate language') representation.

It should be recognized that the compiler in general, and the code generator in particular, are instances of *automated* or *computer-aided* design tools. They are representative and embodiments of the *algorithmic design paradigm* that I shall discuss in chapter 11. The code generator/optimizer, then, is a *design problem solver*[5] charged with the task of producing or synthesizing a program in the language of the target computer from an equivalent program in machine-independent form.

For a given target machine the optimization problem posed to the code generator/optimizer is to produce an 'optimal' object program. The optimality criterion (or, in the language of mathematical optimization theory, the 'objective function') may be the *smallest* object program (measured in bytes of main memory or in the number of instructions) that is functionally equivalent to the input program, or the

---

[5] We may balk against actually using the anthropocentric term 'designer' to refer to the code generator/optimizer!

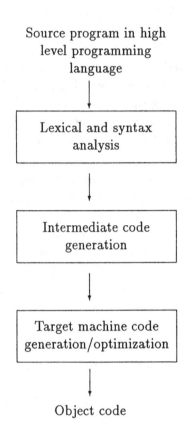

Fig. 5.1 Structure of a compiler.

fastest object program (measured in the number of processor cycles, say) that is equivalent to the input.[6]

As a specific instance, given the assignment statement

$$Z := (a + b) * (b - d)$$

Figs. 5.2(a) and (b) show the object codes for a target *register machine* (Dasgupta

---

[6] There is, of course, a second order design activity involved here – that of the *compiler writer* who is responsible for designing the whole compiler. His or her brief is to develop a compiler that will produce correct and the 'best possible' object code for the given target machine in the 'least possible' time. This is, of course, a fundamentally ill-structured design problem when viewed holistically. It is a good example of an ill-structured problem which may have constituent subproblems that are well-structured.

1989a, chapter 4) with two general registers that are, respectively, optimal and non-optimal in terms of the number of instructions.
End Example

LOAD b, Reg0	LOAD b, Reg0
ADD a, Reg0, Reg1	ADD a, Reg0, Reg0
SUB d, Reg0, Reg0	LOAD b, Reg1
MPY Reg0, Reg1, Reg1	SUB d, Reg1, Reg1
STORE Reg1, Z	MPY Reg0, Reg1, Reg1
	STORE Reg1, Z

(a)   (b)

Fig. 5.2 (a) Optimal and (b) nonoptimal object code for $Z := (a + b) * (b - d)$.

Example 5.4
One of the most fundamental problems in microprogrammed computer design is that of automatically generating horizontal microcode for a target micro-architecture from a high level abstract description of the microprogram (Landskov *et al.* 1980, Dasgupta 1989b, Dasgupta and Shriver 1985, Mueller *et al.* 1988, Linn 1988). The basic problem here is that given a sequence of micro-operations (*vertical* microcode)

$$S = m_1\, m_2\, \cdots\, m_n$$

produced as the intermediate output of a microcode compiler such that each m_i in S is a micro-operation of the target micro-architecture T, to generate a sequence of *horizontal microinstructions*

$$H = I_1\, I_2\, \cdots\, I_m$$

where each I_j in H encodes or represents a concurrently executable subset of the micro-operations in S such that:

(a) Each I_j is a legitimate microinstruction for T;
(b) Each m_i in S appears in exactly one I_j in H;
(c) The data dependencies between the micro-operations in S are preserved in H;[7]
(d) There are no conflicts in the usage of the functional units between the micro-operations within each I_j;[8] and
(e) The number of microinstructions in H is minimal.

---

[7] Let m_i, m_j in S be such that m_i precedes m_j. Then possible data dependencies between m_i and m_j are: (i) m_i writes into a register/store which is read by m_j; (ii) m_i reads a register/store which is written into by m_j; (iii) m_i, m_j both write into a common register/store.

[8] That is, no two concurrently executable micro-operations in I_j should use the same functional unit.

This problem is usually referred to as the *horizontal microcode compaction* problem. Fig. 5.3 shows the overall structure of a horizontal microcode compiler. Fig. 5.4(a) displays a small *straight line microprogram* segment for which fig. 5.4 (b) depicts an optimal horizontal microinstruction sequence that may typically be generated by the compaction phase.

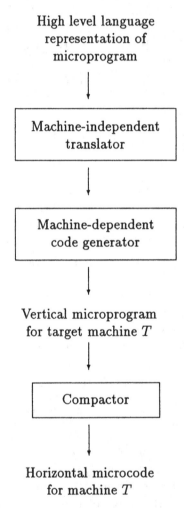

Fig. 5.3 Structure of a microcode compiler.

Like the code generation/optimization problem of example 5.3 this is a well-structured automated design problem that exemplifies the algorithmic design paradigm. *End Example*

$$
\begin{array}{l}
m_1 : \text{AIL} := \text{REG3} \\
m_2 : \text{MBR} := \text{MEM}[\text{MAR}] \qquad I_1 = \{m_1, m_2\} \\
m_3 : \text{AIR} := \text{MBR} \qquad\qquad\quad I_2 = \{m_3, m_7, m_8\} \\
m_4 : \text{AOUT} := \text{AIL} + \text{AIR} \quad\ I_3 = \{m_4\} \\
m_5 : \text{MBR} := \text{AOUT} \qquad\qquad I_4 = \{m_5\} \\
m_6 : \text{MEM}[\text{MAR}] := \text{MBR} \quad\ I_5 = \{m_6\} \\
m_7 : \text{REG3} := \text{`10'} \\
m_8 : \text{PCTR} := \text{PCTR} + 1
\end{array}
$$

(a) (b)

Fig. 5.4 (a) Straight line microprogram; (b) corresponding minimal horizontal microcode.

Example 5.5
Another example from the domain of microprogrammed computer design is the problem of designing an optimal *minimally encoded microinstruction organization* (Dasgupta 1979, Banerji and Raymond 1982, Hayes 1988, Mueller and Varghese 1988). This can be specified precisely as follows:

(i) Let $M = \{m_1, m_2, \ldots, m_r\}$ be the set of micro-operations for the computer that is being designed.
(ii) Let C_i denote a subset of M such that any pair of micro-operations in C_i cannot be executed in parallel from the same microinstruction (because of conflicts in their resource usage, say). Call C_i a *compatible set*.
(iii) Let $C = \{C_1, C_2, \ldots, C_k\}$ be a set of such compatible sets such that each $m_j \in M$ appears in exactly one such $C_i \in C$. (In general there may be more than one set of such compatible sets).
(iv) Let $|C_i|$ denote the number of micro-operations in C_i.

Each C_i can, then, be encoded in a single *field* F_i of the microinstructions using

$$
B_i = \lceil \log_2(|C_i|) + 1 \rceil
$$

bits. This takes into account the necessity of being able to encode uniquely each of the micro-operations on C_i and also the encoding of the 'no-operation' (i.e., none of the micro-operations in C_i). The total length of the microinstruction would be

$$
B = \sum_{i=1}^{k} B_i
$$

bits. The problem is, to determine a set $C_{\min}$ of compatible sets such that the corresponding length, B, is the minimum.

As a specific instance, let $M = \{m_1, m_2, \ldots, m_8\}$ be such that the following pairs of *potentially parallel* micro-operations can be identified – that is, each of these pairs of micro-operations could be executed concurrently without any conflict in their resource usage:

$$\langle m_1, m_3 \rangle, \langle m_1, m_4 \rangle, \langle m_1, m_5 \rangle, \langle m_1, m_6 \rangle, \langle m_1, m_7 \rangle, \langle m_1, m_8 \rangle,$$
$$\langle m_2, m_4 \rangle, \langle m_2, m_5 \rangle, \langle m_2, m_8 \rangle, \langle m_3, m_5 \rangle, \langle m_3, m_8 \rangle, \langle m_4, m_6 \rangle,$$
$$\langle m_5, m_6 \rangle, \langle m_5, m_7 \rangle, \langle m_6, m_8 \rangle$$

Two possible sets of compatible sets (among others) satisfying the above potential parallelism are:

(a) $\langle m_1, m_2 \rangle$; $\langle m_3, m_6, m_7 \rangle$; $\langle m_4, m_5, m_8 \rangle$; $B = 6$ bits

(b) $\langle m_2, m_6 \rangle$; $\langle m_4, m_5, m_8 \rangle$; $\langle m_3, m_7 \rangle$; $\langle m_1 \rangle$; $B = 7$ bits

The smallest number of bits for this problem happens to be 6 bits. Thus (a) is one possible microinstruction organization (with 3 fields) that constitutes an optimal design.
End Example

Example 5.6
Two critical tasks in the design of large or very large scale integrated (LSI/VLSI) circuit chips or printed circuit boards (PCBs) composed of such chips, are placement and routing (Muroga 1982, Rubin 1987, Gajski 1988).

Broadly stated, *placement* is concerned with the positioning of modules in a larger entity so that the interconnections of the modules satisfy certain constraints and the entity as a whole meets certain area and time constraints. In the case of chip design – where placement is also called *floor planning* – the entity is the chip itself and the modules are low complexity circuits or cells. In the case of PCBs, the entity is the board and the modules are the chips.

Generally speaking, *routing* is the process of actually connecting modules that have been placed in specified positions so as to satisfy certain connectivity constraints. For example, an important constraint is that the wires must not cross one another. Another is the minimization of the total area required for interconnections.

Clearly, the placement and routing tasks are closely related and a satisfactory layout of a chip or board may involve several cycles of placement and routing. The natures of the problems are, however quite different.

Many of the placement, routing, and other VLSI design problems can be formally defined in the form of well-structured optimization problems, and have been systematically studied as such by Sahni and Bhatt (1980). A small selection of these problems are given below.

(a) *The module placement problem*

Let

$$m = \text{the number of modules}$$
$$p = \text{the number of available locations or positions}$$
$$S = \text{the number of signals}$$
$$d_{ij} = \text{the distance between locations } i \text{ and } j$$
$$N = \{N_1, N_2, \ldots, N_s\} \text{ be the set of signal nets where}$$

$$N_i \subseteq \{1, \ldots, m\}$$

$$W_i = \text{the weight of net } N_i, 1 \leq i \leq s$$

Then

Produce an *assignment* $X = [x_{ij}]$ where $x_{ij} \in \{0, 1\}$, and $x_{ij} = 1$ iff module i is assigned to location j such that

(i) $\sum_{j=1}^{p} x_{ij} = 1$ (that is, module i is assigned to exactly one location j)
(ii) $\sum_{i=1}^{m} x_{ij} \leq 1$ (that is, location j has been assigned to no more than one module, or to none at all).
(iii) $\sum_{i=1}^{s} W_i f(i, x)$ is minimized, where $f(i, x) = \text{cost of net } N_i$ in assignment X

(b) *Euclidean wire layering problem*

Given

A set of wires $W = \{(u_i, v_i), (x_i, y_i) \mid 1 \leq i \leq n\}$ where $(u_i, v_i), (x_i, y_i)$ are the coordinates of the end points of wire i; and the end points of wires are connected by straight lines.

Then

Obtain a partitioning $W_1, W_2, \cdots, W_k$ of W such that

      (i) $W_i \cap W_j = \emptyset$ for all $1 \leq i, j \leq k$

      (ii) $\bigcup W_i = W$ for $i = 1, \ldots, k$

      (iii) No two wires in any W_i intersect

      (iv) k is a minimum.[9]

(c) *Wire routing problem*

Given

    (i) A set of wires $W = \{(u_i, v_i), (x_i, y_i) \mid 1 \leq i \leq n\}$ where $(u_i, v_i), (x_i, y_i)$ are the coordinates of the end points of wire i

    (ii) A rectangular $m \times n$ grid such that the end points of each wire correspond to grid points

    (iii) Each pair of end points $(u_i, v_i), (x_i, y_i)$ in W can be connected by a wire that can make only right angle bends.

To obtain

    A routing of each wire such that total wire length is minimized and no two wires intersect.

End Example

Examples 5.3–5.6 above, along with many other optimization problems share a common characteristic: they are *intractable* in the sense that their solutions require algorithms of *exponential time complexity*. That is, in the worst case, the time required to produce a solution is $O(k^n)$ where k is a constant and n, a parameter characterizing the 'size' of the problem.[10,11] The very high computational cost of arriving at

---

[9] The Euclidean layering problem is an instance of the *layering* problem which is concerned with the identification of a minimal number of layers (i.e., planes) along which connecting paths may be established such that an assignment of each wire to one of the layers can be made without the wires intersecting (Sahni and Bhatt 1980)

[10] For the microcode compaction problem (example 5.4), for instance, n is the length of the input vertical microcode sequence S; for the minimally encoded microinstruction organization problem (example 5.5) it is the number of micro-operations in M; for the wire layering and routing problems (example 5.6), n is the number of wires in W.

[11] More exactly, according to the theory of computational complexity, such problems are said to be *NP-hard* or *NP-Complete* (Horowitz and Sahni 1978, Garey and Johnson 1979, Sedgewick 1983). According to complexity theory, algorithms are 'efficient' or 'inefficient' in a very precise sense: A *polynomial time algorithm* – i.e., an algorithm whose time complexity is a polynomial function of n, the size of the problem (i.e., is $O(p(n))$ where $p(n)$ is a polynomial in n) – is 'efficient'. An *exponential time algorithm* – i.e., an algorithm whose time complexity is $O(k^n)$ – is 'inefficient'. A problem is *intractable* when no polynomial time algorithm can be found to solve it. Intractable problems are precisely those problems that are said to be NP-hard or NP-Complete.

an optimal solution (specially for large values of n) would suffice to discourage the designer (even using automated tools) to seek solutions that are guaranteed to be optimal.

Table 5.1. Summary of microcode compaction algorithm performances (based on Davidson *et al.* (1981))

SLM	MOs	BAB		RBL		Pick1		FCFS-VS	
No		Time	MIs	Time	MIs	Time	MIs	Time	MIs
6	32	6.9	6	6.9	6	2.4	6	1.8	6
28	52	15.6	10	4.8	10	4.5	10	3.8	10
10	62	26.3	12	10.6	12	5.5	12	4.5	12
42	96	10.0	19	6.4	19	6.3	19	4.1	19
44	99	12.6	21	6.3	21	6.0	21	4.1	21
2	149	3839.1	30	43.4	30	19.4	30	15.2	30
24	163	180.9	34	24.6	34	14.6	34	12.4	34
26	208	2302.0	47	118.9	47	15.6	47	13.3	47
5	231	2639.3	50	99.9	50	17.8	50	14.0	50
30	375	> 35000[*]	–	741.3	74	73.4	74	40.7	74

Notes:

 Time: Seconds of CPU time required on a Honeywell 68/80 processor running the Multics operating system. This includes operating system overheads.

 MOs: No. of micro-operations in input SLM

 MIs: No. of microinstructions produced

 (*) BAB failed to terminate as the time exceeded the maximum time allowed by Multics.

Example 5.7

The practical impact of executing polynomial and exponential time algorithms is exemplified by the experiments of Davidson *et al.* on the comparative performance of several horizontal microcode compaction algorithms for straight line microprograms (SLMs) (see also example 5.4). Davidson and his colleagues studied and compared the performance of an exponential time *branch and bound* (BAB) algorithm that is guaranteed to produce the smallest number of microinstructions (and is, therefore, optimal) with three polynomial time algorithms that are not guaranteed to perform optimally. Table 5.1 summarizes their measurements for a representative sample of 10 SLMs. Here, the 'efficient' polynomial algorithms are shown as RBL, Pick 1 and FCFS-VB. It turns out that in the case of these particular SLMs, the three polynomial algorithms produced optimal output but in far less time than BAB. In

one case, BAB even failed to terminate! Thus, RBL, Pick 1 and FCFS-VS represent satisficing procedures for this particular problem.
End Example

Two important qualifications must be made to the above conclusion. Firstly, the fact that an optimal solution can be determined in time $O(k^n)$ applies to a 'worst case' scenario. That is, at least one problem instance of size n requires that much time. Many other problem instances may, in practice, require less time – hence optimal solutions may be obtained in reasonable time for many instances of the problem. For instance, Garey and Johnson (1979) have pointed out that though the simplex algorithm for linear programming (Hadley 1962) is of exponential time complexity, the algorithm runs in reasonable time in practice. [12] Such cases are, however, the exceptions rather than the rule.

Secondly, while a particular problem in its most general form may be known to be intractable, special cases of the problem may be solved through efficient (i.e., polynomial time) algorithms.

Example 5.8
The optimal code generation problem was described in example 5.3. Several versions of this problem as well as other related problems of code generation are known to be intractable (Horowitz and Sahni 1978, Garey and Johnson 1979). These include:

---

[12] The general form of the *linear programming* is as follows. Given a set of linear *constraints* of the form

$$a_{11}x_1 + a_{12}x_2 + \cdots + a_{1n}x_n = b_1$$
$$a_{21}x_1 + a_{22}x_2 + \cdots + a_{2n}x_n = b_2$$
$$\cdots\cdots\cdots\cdots$$
$$a_{m1}x_1 + a_{m2}x_2 + \cdots + a_{mn}x_n = b_m$$

where the a_{ij}'s $(1 \leq i \leq m, 1 \leq j \leq n)$ and the b_k's $(1 \leq k \leq m)$ are constants and x_p's $(1 \leq p \leq n)$ are variables such that

$$x_p \geq 0 , 1 \leq p \leq n$$

to determine values for the x_p's such that the *objective function*

$$U \equiv c_1x_1 + c_2x_2 + \cdots + c_nx_n$$

(where c_p $(1 \leq p \leq n)$ is a cost associated with the corresponding x_p) is *minimized*. The *simplex algorithm*, originally developed by Dantzig (1963), is an important and widely used method for solving this problem. Whether or not the LP problem was NP-hard remained open till 1979 when Kachian (1979) published a polynomial algorithm for solving the problem. Thus, the LP problem is tractable.

(i) Optimal code generation for expression with common subexpression (e.g., $(a + b - d) * (a + b + c)$) on a 1-register machine.

(ii) Determining the smallest number of registers needed to evaluate an expression containing common subexpressions without having to store intermediate values in main memory.

However, if the expressions have no common subexpressions (e.g., $(a + b) * (c - d)$, say) then both these problems can be solved in polynomial time (Horowitz and Sahni 1978).
End Example

5.3 DESIGN AS AN EVOLUTIONARY PROCESS

The contents of sections 5.1 and 5.2 may be summarized as follows:

(i) Because of bounded rationality the ramifications of a design decision or of a chain of such (possibly interacting) decisions cannot always be comprehended at the time the decisions are made. Bounded rationality also limits the designer's ability to explore the space of design choices which, for ill-structured problems, is virtually unbounded. Under such circumstances the designer is forced to adopt solution procedures that produce satisficing rather than optimal designs.

(ii) While there *are* well-structured design problems that can be formulated as optimization problems, their optimal solutions may turn out to be intractable in the sense that the computation time required to produce an optimal design is, in the worst case, an exponential function of the problem size. Computationally speaking, most design optimization problems are NP-hard. Thus, *in practice*, designers are forced to resort to satisficing procedures even for such problems.

Under these conditions it is fruitful to view the act of design as an *evolutionary process* and the design itself at *any* stage of its development as a *tentative solution* to the problem originally posed. The design is not only tentative at intermediate stages of its development but also at the stage at which the designer sees fit to 'terminate' or 'freeze' the design.

In other words, according to this evolutionary model, a design at any stage of its development (including the 'final' stage) is

(a) an evolutionary offspring of an earlier design form; and
(b) likely to evolve further in the future.

The use of the word 'evolution' in the context of artifacts is prone to raise the ire of many thinkers (particularly biologists) as they (often rightly) feel that the concept of biological evolution is misinterpreted or corrupted when adopted in non-biological contexts; that the analogy between the evolution of organic forms and the development of artifacts or ideas is basically false.

For example, Steadman (1979), an architect, presents a highly critical study of the entire history of the analogy between biological and artificial (or technical) evolution and forcefully rejects the validity of the analogy. Medawar (1975), a biologist, has also pointed out the distinction between evolution and the development of artifacts. Recently, Thagard (1988), a cognitive scientist, and Ruse (1986), a philosopher, have both taken issue against the argument propounded by some philosophers and scientists – most notably the psychologist Campbell (1974) and the philosophers of science Toulmin (1972) and Popper (1972) – that the development of scientific knowledge follows essentially an evolutionary process.[13]

Given this background it is necessary for me to *establish exactly in what sense* the design process may be said to be evolutionary.

In biology, 'evolution' refers to the unfolding and changing of organisms across generations through natural means. At the obvious risk of oversimplification, the hallmarks of *Darwinian evolution* can be summarized as follows (Ruse 1986, Maynard Smith 1975, Bendall 1983):

(a) Within any population of organisms of a given species, there is considerable *variation* among individuals largely brought about by genetic factors (i.e., by randomly generated genetic mutations).

(b) In a given environment the likelihood of an individual surviving to adulthood and reproducing successfully will be influenced by the particular genetic characteristics or *traits* of that individual.

 If it does survive so as to reproduce then the offsprings will inherit the traits and increase the frequency of occurrence of these traits in the population. On the other hand if the traits are such that the individual organism is unable to reach maturity and reproduce, then the traits will be less likely to perpetuate in the population. This process is termed *natural selection*.

(c) By this process, organisms are constantly *tested* against the environment and those that are genetically endowed to survive and reproduce successfully may be

---

[13] This theory is often referred to as *evolutionary epistemology*. For a judicious examination of this topic see Ruse (1986).

said to be 'fit' relative to that environment.[14] If the environment changes then some forms of the organism within the population may become fit relative to the new environment while other forms may die out and even become extinct. Thus, organisms appear to constantly *adapt* to its surroundings.

Returning to the subject of design I am *not* claiming that the principles of variation and natural selection in the specific Darwinian sense apply to the design process. What *are* highly relevant, however, are the concepts of *testing* and *adaptation* in the following precise sense:

(i) Because of bounded rationality a design at any stage of development is, in general, a *conjectural* or *tentative solution* to the design problem. The adequacy (or satisfactoriness) of the design is determined solely according to whether it meets the requirements prevailing at that stage of the design process. Hence the design must be *critically tested* against the available requirements.

(ii) If the design is found to meet the requirements we may say that there is a *fit* between design and requirements and that the former is *adapted* to the latter.

(iii) In the course of the critical test, there may be found a *misfit* between the design and the requirements. The causes of the misfit may be many: (a) The design is *incorrect* with respect to the requirements; that is, the test shows conclusively that the design does not satisfy the requirements. (b) The design is *incompletely* or *imprecisely described* so that it cannot be shown whether or not the design satisfies the requirements. (c) The *requirements* are stated in such a form that it cannot be shown whether or not the design satisfies the requirements.

(iv) Depending on the sources of the misfit, the design (or the requirements) must be *modified* so as to eliminate or reduce the misfit, thus, producing a new ⟨design, requirements⟩ pair.

(v) The design process may be halted when the design is found to be adapted to the requirements (or, stated otherwise, the design and the requirements have reached a state of mutual adaptation). However, the design process never *formally* ends since (a) given that designs are, in general, satisficing solutions,

---

[14] This, as many writers have previously pointed out, makes the phrase 'survival of the fittest' a tautology. For, according to the above, those who survive are, *by definition*, the fittest! It must, of course, be also pointed out that the phrase was not coined by a biologist at all but by Herbert Spencer, prolific Victorian social thinker and 'systems builder'. For a critical view of Spencer's ideas on evolution, see Medawar (1963). In the 5th and 6th editions of his *'Origin of Species* (1859, first edition) – the 6th and final edition appearing in 1872 – Darwin adopted 'survival of the fittest' to mean the same as 'natural selection'. See Appleman (1970).

for fixed requirements one can always *improve* a design so as to achieve a more satisfactory fit; or (b) the *requirements may change* in which case the prior state of adaptation is disturbed and a misfit between the design and the (new) requirements is re-generated.[15]

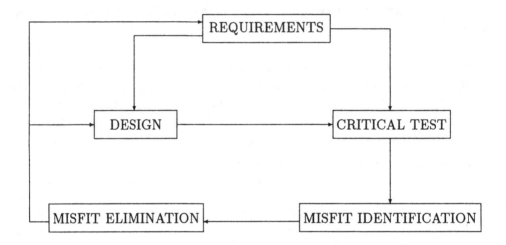

Fig. 5.5 Design as an evolutionary process.

This view of the design process may be depicted according to fig. 5.5. As shown here, design is a continuous process in which each cycle begins with a ⟨design, requirements⟩ pair (where the design component may, in fact, be the 'null' design) and ends with a ⟨design, requirements⟩ pair. The cycles are characterized by the facts that:

(i) The ⟨design, requirements⟩ pair changes from one cycle to the next.

(ii) The nature of the misfit may differ from one cycle to the next.

(iii) Consequently, the nature of the misfit elimination may differ from one cycle to the next.

---

[15] When a design is *optimal* in the sense that for fixed requirements no improvement in the design can be made, the design process *could* formally end provided of course the requirements were guaranteed not to change. However, as I have attempted to make clear in sections 5.1 and 5.2 optimal design is a limiting – and very limited – case of satisficing design. Satisficing is the norm; optimizing is the special case. Furthermore, an optimal design becomes suboptimal as soon as requirements change. In the case of a problem couched in terms of the LP problem, for example (see footnote 14), the costs C_p, $(1 \leq p \leq n)$ appearing in the objective function may change thereby necessitating a redesign using the new cost terms.

The process may come to a temporary halt when adaptation has been achieved. It will resume when some condition in the adapted situation – specifically related to the requirements – is disturbed, thereby generating a new misfit.

Two quite obvious questions may arise in the reader's mind at this stage:

(a) Is a claim being made here that evolution (in the sense described above) is a *universal* characteristic of design processes? That is, is it, in some sense, a *law* of the artificial sciences?
(b) Regardless of the answer to (a), does the evolutionary model serve any useful *purpose* in explicitly carrying out the act of design? That is, regardless of whether or not the evolutionary model is a universal feature of design processes, does it have a *heuristic value*?

Clearly, the first question addresses whether evolution is a description of reality while the second is a prescriptive issue. I shall address the former in this chapter below and the latter in chapter 9.

5.4 EMPIRICAL EVIDENCE OF EVOLUTION IN DESIGN

The evolutionary model described in section 5.3 was arrived at by a process of reasoning that follows what the 19th century philosopher C. S. Pierce termed *abduction* (or *retroduction*). Abduction allows inferences to be made according to the following schema or rule:

1. A phenomenon or property Q is observed or known to be the case
2. If property (or law or proposition) P is true then Q is also true.

It is believed that P is true.

Abductive reasoning is, then, a form of plausible inference. It allows for an *explanation* to be offered as to *why* Q is observed or known to be the case. However, the resulting inference or explanation – that P is true or is the case – is only a plausible *hypothesis* that may subsequently be falsified.[16]

---

[16] Abduction will play an important role in this book in later discussions of design paradigms (Part II) and – in particular – in the discussion of the relationship of design and science (Part III). For an introduction to abductive reasoning from the perspective of computer science, see Charniak and McDermott (1985, chapters 1,8). The place of abduction in design is (as far as is known to this author) first discussed by March (1976). Its role in the formation of scientific theories is explicitly discussed by Hanson (1972) and, more recently, by Thagard (1988).

The evolutionary model of design described in section 5.3 above, is a hypothesis inferred abductively. The basic schema followed was:

(i) Observations of actual design processes P_1, P_2, ..., P_n

(ii) Each P_i ($1 \leq i \leq n$) can be shown to be a special case or instance of the general evolutionary model of design.

It is hypothesized that the evolutionary model is a true general model of design processes.

Thus, the answer to the first question posed at the end of section 5.3 is that the evolutionary model is an abductively determined *empirical hypothesis* which – like all such hypotheses – can and must be subjected to critical tests. Furthermore, following Popper (1965, 1968), in order to qualify as a *scientific* proposition, the hypothesis must be *falsifiable*. That is, we should be able to construct tests for the evolutionary model hypothesis that attempt to falsify or refute the hypothesis.

Clearly, there is no such thing as *conclusive* evidence for a general empirical hypothesis – although there may be conclusive evidence *against* it! All we can try to do is to critically test the hypothesis in attempts to falsify it. If the falsification attempts fail the tests may be said to provide *corroborative* evidence for the hypothesis. The hypothesis, thus, becomes that much more plausible. Towards this end, I shall provide below, a set of such corroborative evidence for the evolutionary model of design.[17]

My approach will be to describe some specific design methods that have been developed over the years. Some of these methods (and I will identify them) *may* have been influenced by the idea of evolution but never explicitly and certainly not in the very precise sense proposed in section 5.3. To the extent that they appear to have an evolutionary flavor these methods may be construed as (relatively) *weak* corroborative evidence. They constitute evidence nonetheless. The other methods as conceived have no explicit links with the evolution model at all and, indeed, appear so far removed from the evolutionary model as to constitute genuinely *critical* tests that have the potential to falsify the evolutionary model hypothesis. Their failure to falsify would then make these methods *strong* corroborative evidence.

---

[17] The reader familiar with modern philosophy of science will recognize a strong Popperian flavor to this whole discussion on the nature of scientific propositions (Popper 1965, 1968). However, as I shall discuss at length in Part III, the view of the scientific method that I shall espouse is not 'purely' Popperian. Rather it combines the ideas of several writers that include, in addition to Popper, Kuhn (1962), Lakatos (1976), Hanson (1972) and Laudan (1977).

I will demonstrate how each of these methods can be naturally mapped onto the evolutionary model. Thereby, I will hope to show these examples collectively provide compelling corroborative evidence for the evolutionary model hypothesis.

Example 5.9

One of the most influential principles of program design is that of *stepwise refinement* first proposed as an explicit doctrine in the early 1970s by Dijkstra (1972) and Wirth (1971). This principle can be stated concisely as follows:

(i) If the problem is so simple that its solution can be obviously expressed in a few lines of a programming language then the problem is solved.

(ii) Otherwise decompose the problem into well-specified subproblems such that it can be shown that if each subproblem is solved correctly, and these are composed together in a specified manner, then the original problem will be solved correctly.

(iii) For each subproblem, return to step (i).

A more formal version of stepwise refinement combines this principle with the mathematical theory of program correctness originally due to Floyd (1967) and Hoare (1969). This version is based on the idea of developing a proof of correctness and the program together, and allowing the proof of correctness to *guide* stepwise refinement and program development. This version of program development – which we may call the *design-while-verify* (DWV) method – has been widely studied by Mills (1975), Dijkstra (1976), Alagic and Arbib (1978), Jones (1980), Gries (1981), Hoare (1987) and many others. The DWV approach also has been applied to firmware development (Dasgupta 1984, Damm *et al.* 1986, Damm 1988), the specification of computer architectures (Dasgupta 1984, Damm and Doehmen 1987) and hardware circuits (Gopalakrishnan *et al.* 1985, 1987).[18]

The reader may detect a vague whiff of the evolutionary principle in the above statement of stepwise refinement. Thus, to provide as critical and stringent a test as possible, I have selected a programming example that was developed using DWV and published a decade ago by Alagic and Arbib (1978) and which provides absolutely no indication whatsoever that the authors had design evolution in mind (in the precise sense of the evolutionary model of section 5.3) when they developed this program. I shall first present the program development effort as Alagic and Arbib (1978) presented it. I shall then demonstrate how this approach maps onto the evolutionary model.

---

[18] As will be seen in chapter 8, the DWV method is an important instance of the *formal design paradigm*.

The problem is to develop a Pascal program that will permute the scalar elements of an array A with indices ranging from 1 to N so that $A[1] \leq A[2] \leq \cdots \leq A[N]$. The program development – as presented by Alagic and Arbib (1978) but with some paraphrasing for the sake of conciseness and added clarity – will be outlined in terms of a number of steps.

Step 1 The basic algorithm that will be developed rests on viewing A as consisting of a sorted partition $A[1 .. i - 1]$ and an unsorted partition $A[i .. N]$. Initially (for $i = 1$) $A[1 .. 0]$, the sorted partition is empty and the unsorted partition is $A[1 .. N]$. Furthermore, each element in $A[i .. N]$ is greater than or equal to every element in $A[1 .. i - 1]$. This state of affairs can be depicted as follows:

$$
\begin{array}{|l|r|}
\hline
\overset{\displaystyle 1}{A[1 .. i - 1]} & \overset{\displaystyle i-1}{A[i .. N]} \\
\hline
\end{array}
\tag{A}
$$

$$
\qquad\qquad i \qquad\qquad\qquad N
$$

$$
\text{sorted} \qquad\qquad \text{unsorted; each } A[j] \in A[i .. N]
$$
$$
\geq \text{ every } A[k] \in A[1 .. i - 1]
$$

In each step of the algorithm, the sorted partition is extended by one element and the unsorted partition decreased by an element. This is depicted as follows:

$$
\begin{array}{|l|l|r|}
\hline
\overset{\displaystyle 1}{A[1 .. i - 1]} & \overset{\displaystyle i-1}{A[i]} & A[i + 1 .. N] \\
\hline
\end{array}
\tag{B}
$$

$$
\qquad\qquad\qquad i+1 \qquad\qquad N
$$

$$
\underbrace{\qquad\qquad\qquad}_{\text{sorted}} \qquad \text{unsorted}
$$

Step 2 The only permissible operation on A is the *permutation of its elements*. Thus to achieve the transition from (A) to (B), the elements of $A[i .. N]$ can be permuted so as to place its smallest element in $A[i]$.

Step 3 This suggests the following program outline

```
for i := 1 to N − 1 do
    PERMUTE VALUES IN A[i .. N]                           (5.1)
    TO PLACE SMALLEST VALUE IN A[i]
```

When the **for** statement terminates, $A[1 .. N]$ will be sorted. That is, the following assertion will hold:

$$\forall\, p, q: \; (1 \leq p < q \leq N) \;\supset\; (A[p] \leq A[q]) \qquad (5.2a)$$

At this stage, some notation requires to be introduced. The symbol $[1 .. i)$ signifies that the range of any index variable is $1 .. i - 1$. More generally:

$$
\begin{aligned}
[a \ldots b] &= \text{the set of } i \text{ such that } a \leq i \leq b \\
[a \ldots b) &= \text{the set of } i \text{ such that } a \leq i \; < \; b \\
(a \ldots b] &= \text{the set of } i \text{ such that } a \; < \; i \leq b \\
[a \ldots a) &= (b \ldots b] = [\;] = \text{the empty set}
\end{aligned}
$$

Furthermore, $P(W)$ will signify an assertion P about the interval W.

Based on this notation, assertion (5.2a) can be restated as

$$\text{SORTED}([1 .. N]) \;\equiv\; \forall\, p, q: \; (1 \leq p < q \leq N) \;\supset\; (A[p] \leq A[q]) \qquad (5.2)$$

Step 4 Given the **for** statement (5.1), the fact that on termination the assertion (5.2) will hold, and that in the i-th iteration the objective is to transform array state (A) into array state (B), we can capture the state of the computation at the start of the i-th iteration by the following assertions:

(i) The block $A[1 .. i - 1]$ is sorted. That is,

$$\text{SORTED}([1 .. i)) \;\equiv\; \forall\, p, q: \; (1 \leq p < q \leq i) \;\supset\; (A[p] \leq A[q]) \qquad (5.3)$$

(ii) Each element in $A[i .. N]$ is greater than or equal to every element in $A[1 .. i-1]$. That is,

$$
\begin{aligned}
\text{GREATER\_THAN}&([1 .. i)) \;\equiv\; \\
&\forall\, p, q: \; (1 \leq p < i \leq q < N) \supset (A[p] \leq A[q]) \qquad (5.4)
\end{aligned}
$$

Step 5 Referring to the **for** loop (5.1) consider its body:

'PERMUTE VALUES OF $A[i .. N]$ TO PUT
SMALLEST VALUE IN $A[i]$'

If this is done by manipulating $A[i .. N]$ *only* – that is, without manipulating $A[1 .. i - 1]$ – then neither $\text{SORTED}([1 .. i))$ nor $\text{GREATER\_THAN}([1 .. i))$ will be affected. Furthermore, the assertion

$$\text{I\_SMALLEST}([i .. N]) \;\equiv\; \forall\, q: \; (1 \leq q \leq N) \;\supset\; (A[i] \leq A[q]) \qquad (5.5)$$

will also hold. This merely says that $A[i]$ is the smallest element in $A[i .. N]$.

Step 6 Observe that since $[1 .. i + 1) = [1 .. i]$, from (5.3) and (5.4) the following definitions obtain:

$$\text{SORTED}([1 .. i]) \equiv \forall p, q : (1 \leq p < q \leq i) \supset (A[p] \leq A[q]) \quad (5.6)$$
$$\text{GREATER\_THAN}([1 .. i]) \equiv$$
$$\forall p, q : (1 \leq p \leq i < q \leq N) \supset (A[p] \leq A[q]) \quad (5.7)$$

We now see that

$$\text{SORTED}([1 .. i)) \wedge \text{I\_SMALLEST}([i .. N]) \supset \text{SORTED}([1 .. i]) \quad (5.8)$$
$$\text{GREATER\_THAN}([1 .. i)) \wedge \text{I\_SMALLEST}([i .. N]) \supset$$
$$\text{GREATER\_THAN}([1 .. i]) \quad (5.9)$$

Step 7 Thus, since $\text{SORTED}([1 .. i))$ and $\text{GREATER\_THAN}([1 .. i))$ hold at the beginning of the i-th iteration of the **for** loop, $\text{SORTED}([1 .. i])$ and $\text{GREATER\_THAN}([1 .. i])$ will hold at the end of the i-th iteration (see diagram (B)).

Step 8 Before the next execution (if at all) of

'PERMUTE VALUES OF $A[i .. N]$ TO PUT
SMALLEST VALUE IN $A[i]$'

i will have been incremented by 1. Thus the state of the array A will again be as shown in diagram (A). In other words $\text{SORTED}([1 .. i))$ and $\text{GREATER\_THAN}([1 .. i))$ will hold every time the loop body begins execution. Let

$$\text{INV}([1 .. i)) \equiv \text{SORTED}([1 .. i)) \wedge \text{GREATER\_THAN}([1 .. i)) \quad (5.10)$$

$\text{INV}([1 .. i))$ is, thus, the *invariant* for the **for** loop.

Step 9 The statement

'PERMUTE VALUES OF $A[i .. N]$ TO PUT
SMALLEST VALUE IN $A[i]$'

must now be refined such that the following Hoare formula holds:[19]

$$\{(1 \le i \le N) \wedge \text{INV}([1..i))\}$$
$$\text{'PERMUTE VALUES OF } A[i..N] \text{ TO PUT} \qquad (5.11)$$
$$\text{SMALLEST VALUE IN } A[i]\text{'}$$
$$\{\text{INV}([1..i])\}$$

Step 10 The proof rule for the **for** statement is (Alagic and Arbib 1978):[20]

$$\frac{\{(a \le x \le b) \wedge P([a..x))\} \; S \; \{P([a..x])\}}{\{P([\,])\} \text{ for } x := a \text{ to } b \text{ do } S\{P([a..b])\}}$$

where $P([\,]) = P([a..a)) = P((b..b])$

In that case, if the Hoare formula (5.11) can be proved true, and if $\text{INV}([\,])$ is true on entering the **for** loop, then by this proof rule

$$\text{INV}([1..n])$$

will hold when the loop terminates. That is, the assertions

$$\text{SORTED}([1..N]) \equiv \forall\, p, q \;:\; (1 \le p < q \le N) \supset (A[p] \le A[q])$$
$$\text{GREATER\_THAN}([1..N]) \equiv \forall\, p, q :\; (1 \le p \le N < q \le N) \supset (A[p] \le A[q])$$

---

[19] Let P and Q be assertions (such as the logical formulas (5.2)–(5.6) above) and let S be a program (or part thereof). The notation

$$\{P\} \; S \; \{Q\}$$

is called a *Hoare formula* and is read as follows: if P is true at the beginning of S's execution then when (and provided that) S terminates the assertion Q will be true. Hoare formulas are, of course, at the very heart of proving the correctness of program and system designs using the so-called *axiomatic approach* (Dijkstra 1976, Alagic and Arbib 1978, de Bakker 1980, Gries 1981). For an extended discussion of this topic see chapter 8.

[20] A *proof rule* (or *rule of inference*) is a rule of the form

$$\frac{H_1, \; H_2, \; \ldots, \; H_n}{H}$$

where $H_1, \ldots, H_n$ are logical formulas and which is to be read as: if it can be shown $H_1, \ldots, H_n$ are individually true, then H is also true. $H_1, \ldots, H_n$ are called the *antecedents* (or *premises*) of the proof rule and H the *consequence* (or *conclusion*). In applying the axiomatic approach to proving correctness each composite programming (or system description) language construct (e.g., the sequential statement, **if**, **while** or **for** statement etc.) has associated with it – as in the case of the **for** statement above – a proof rule. For discussions of such proof rules see de Bakker (1980), Gries (1981) or Alagic and Arbib (1978). The topic is discussed in chapter 8 also, in the general context of the formal design paradigm.

will hold. These correspond to the state of the array

$$1 \qquad\qquad\qquad\qquad\qquad\qquad\qquad\qquad N$$

$$A[1 .. N]$$

(C)

sorted

Step 11 INV([ ]) $\equiv INV([1 .. 1))$ is true since SORTED([1 .. 1)), $1 \leq p < q < 1$ is always false and in GREATER_THAN([1 .. 1)), $1 \leq p < 1$ is always false. INV([ ]) denotes the *initial* state of the array:

$$i = 1 \qquad\qquad\qquad\qquad\qquad\qquad\qquad N$$

$$A[i .. N]$$

unsorted

Step 12 Consider now, the refinement of 'PERMUTE VALUES OF $A[i .. N]$ TO PUT SMALLEST VALUE IN $A[i]$' such that (5.11) holds. Suppose we use

```
m := i
for j := i + 1 to N do
    if A[j] < A[m] then m := j
EXCHANGE A[i] AND A[m]
```
(5.12)

Clearly, (5.12) does not affect the partition $A[1 .. i - 1]$, hence SORTED([1 .. i)) remains unchanged. Furthermore since (5.12) only permutes elements in $A[i .. N]$, GREATER_THAN([1 .. i)) is also unaffected. Hence (5.12) leaves

$$\text{INV}([1 .. i)) \equiv \text{SORTED}([1 .. i)) \wedge \text{GREATER\_THAN}([1 .. i))$$

true. It now remains to prove that LSMALLEST([i .. N]) holds in which case the Hoare formula (5.11) will also hold.

Step 13 Consider now, the program fragment (5.12). Informally, the effect of the **for** statement body is to make $A[m]$ the smallest value in the range $A[i .. j - 1]$. Furthermore, when **for** terminates, $A[m]$ will be the smallest value in the range $A[i .. N]$. Define:

$$\text{M\_LOWEST}([i .. j)) \equiv \forall q : (i \leq q < j) \supset (A[m] \leq A[q]) \qquad (5.13)$$

The purpose of this assertion is that we want to show that

$\{\text{M\_LOWEST}([\,])\}$
for $j := i + 1$ **to** N **do**
   if $A[j] < A[m]$ **then** $m := j$
$\{\text{M\_LOWEST}([i \mathbin{..} N])\}$ (5.14)
EXCHANGE $A[i]$ AND $A[m]$
$\{\text{I\_SMALLEST}([i \mathbin{..} N])\}$

Step 14 To prove

$\{\text{M\_LOWEST}([\,])\}$
for $j := i + 1$ **to** N **do**
   if $A[j] < A[m]$ **then** $m := j$ (5.15)
$\{\text{M\_LOWEST}([i \mathbin{..} N])\}$

according to the proof rule for the **for** statement, it is required to prove that

$\{\text{M\_LOWEST}([i \mathbin{..} j))\}$
   if $A[j] < A[m]$ **then** $m := j$ (5.16)
$\{\text{M\_LOWEST}([i \mathbin{..} j])\}$

The proof rule for the **if** statement in Pascal is (Alagic and Arbib 1978, Hoare and Wirth 1973):

$$\frac{\{P \wedge B\}\, S\, \{Q\}, \quad P \wedge \neg B \supset Q}{\{P\}\ \textbf{if}\ B\ \textbf{then}\ S\ \{Q\}}$$

Using this proof rule and observing that

$\{\text{M\_LOWEST}([i \mathbin{..} j)) \wedge (A[j] < A[m])\}$
   $m := j$ (5.17)
$\{\text{M\_LOWEST}([i \mathbin{..} j])\}$

and

$$\text{M\_LOWEST}([i \mathbin{..} j)) \wedge \neg (A[j] < A[m]) \supset \text{M\_LOWEST}([i \mathbin{..} j])$$

we may infer that (5.16) is true.[21]

---

[21] The proof of (5.17) relies on using the *axiom of assignment* for the general form of the assignment statement, viz., $X := E$. The axiom is the Hoare formula $\{P[X/E]\}\ X := E\ \{P\}$, where $P[X/E]$ is the assertion P with all free occurrences of X in P replaced by E (Alagic & Arbib 1978, Hoare and Wirth 1973, de Bakker 1980).

Step 15 Finally, we have to *refine* 'EXCHANGE $A[i]$ AND $A[m]$' such that

$$\{\text{M\_LOWEST}([i..N])\}$$
$$\quad \text{EXCHANGE } A[i] \text{ AND } A[m] \qquad\qquad (5.18)$$
$$\{\text{I\_SMALLEST}([i..N])\}$$

is true. Suppose the refinement is

$$t := A[i];$$
$$A[i] := A[m]; \qquad\qquad (5.19)$$
$$A[m] := t$$

By applying the axiom of assignment backward thrice and the proof rule for sequential composition

$$\frac{\{P_1\}\ S_1\ \{P_2\},\ \{P_2\}\ S_2\ \{P_3\},\ \dots\ ,\ \{P_n\}\ S_n\ \{P_{n+1}\}}{\{P_1\}\ S_1;\ S_2;\ \dots\ S_n;\ \{P_{n+1}\}}$$

It can be shown that (5.18) is true.

Step 16 The complete program with appropriate annotations is shown in fig. 5.6.

$$
\begin{array}{l}
\{\text{true}\} \\
\textbf{for } i := 1 \textbf{ to } N-1 \textbf{ do} \\
\quad \{\text{INV}([1..i))\} \\
\quad m := i\ ; \\
\quad \textbf{for } j := i+1 \textbf{ to } N \textbf{ do} \\
\quad\quad \textbf{if } A[j] < A[m] \textbf{ then } m := j \\
\quad \{\text{M\_LOWEST}([i..N])\} \\
\quad t := A[i]\ ; \\
\quad A[i] := A[m]\ ; \\
\quad A[m] := t \\
\quad \{\text{I\_SMALLEST}([i..N])\} \\
\quad \{\text{INV}([1..i))\} \\
\{\text{SORTED}([1..N])\}
\end{array}
$$

Fig. 5.6 The annotated sort program.

I shall now explain the evolutionary structure underlying the DWV method followed in designing the sorting problem.

(E1) The problem is to design a Pascal program that will permute the elements of A such that $A[1] \leq \cdots \leq A[N]$. There are, thus, two requirements:

R_f: The program must permute the elements of A so as to satisfy the constraint $A[1] \leq \cdots \leq A[N]$.

R_i: The program must be implemented in Pascal.

Here R_f is a *functional* requirement and R_i, an *implementation* requirement. Let

$R_o = \langle R_f, R_i \rangle$ signify this initial set of requirements.

(E2) The initial solution suggested is the algorithm outlined in steps 1–2. Thus, the first design version D_1, is given by the **for** statement (5.1).[22]

(E3) In DWV the *only* mode for testing whether a design D satisfies a functional requirement R – which, following Hoare (1986), I shall denote by the symbol $D \subseteq R$ – is by *formally proving* that $D \subseteq R$. Thus an attempt to test D_1 against R_o immediately results in the following *misfit* $M_1 = \langle M_{10}, M_{11} \rangle$ being defined where

M_{10}: D_1 is not written in Pascal – thus violating R_i

M_{11}: Even had D_1 been written in Pascal, R_f is not in a form that allows one to prove (or disprove) that $D_1 \subseteq R_f$.

(E4) The misfit M_{11} is eliminated (in step 3) by formalizing the requirement R_f in the form of the assertion SORTED$[1 .. N]$ (equation (5.2)). Let this formal version of R_f be denoted by R_{ff}. The first cycle of design evolution is, thus, completed. At this stage, the design, requirements pair is $\langle D_1, R_1 \rangle$ where $R_1 = \langle R_{ff}, R_i \rangle$. The evolutionary cycle may be depicted as follows:

---

[22] It is important to note that nothing is said about *how* the designers arrived at this design. D_1 may have been suggested through the designers' prior knowledge of sorting algorithms; or prior experience with problems pertaining to array data structures; or through a *gestalt*-like insight; or in some other way. How a designer may actually discover a design is *not* a matter of concern in the evolutionary model of design. The evolutionary model is concerned with what happens *after* a design is tentatively suggested – i.e., with how designs are justified and what kinds of factors and reasonings cause a transition from one design solution to the next in order to converge to a design that satisfies the requirements. See Part III for a more extensive discussion of this distinction between the 'context of discovery' and the 'context of justification'.

$$R_{\mathrm{o}} = \langle R_{\mathrm{f}}, R_{\mathrm{i}} \rangle \quad\longrightarrow\quad M_1 = \langle M_{10}, M_{11} \rangle \quad\longrightarrow\quad \text{Eliminate } M_{11}$$

$$D_1 \quad\longrightarrow\quad R_1 = \langle R_{\mathrm{ff}}, R_{\mathrm{i}} \rangle \quad\longleftarrow$$

$$D_1 \quad\longleftarrow$$

(E5) The 'current' state of the design process is given by the pair $\langle D_1, R_1 \rangle$. The first part of step 4 represents the beginning of the the next evolutionary cycle. D_1 is tested against R_1 and this produces the misfit

$$M_2 : D_1 \text{ is not written in Pascal – thus violating } R_{\mathrm{i}}$$

M_2 is, of course, identical to M_{10}, one of the misfits identified in the previous cycle (see (E3)). Recall that in the course of that cycle, only M_{11} had been eliminated but not M_{10}.

Obviously D_1 must be modified in order to eliminate M_2. However, the 'gap' between D_1 and R_1 is too wide for modification to D_1 to be done in a single step. The task of eliminating M_2 is thus effected by a sequence of the evolutionary cycle each of which only *partially* eliminates (or reduces) the misfit. This sequence of partial eliminations is described below.

(E6) As the first step of the misfit elimination process a set of new requirements are generated in steps 4–8. These requirements are 'intermediate' or 'internal' in the sense that they would have to be satisfied by a *single* iteration of the **for** loop (5.1) – in contrast to R_{ff}, for example which would have to be satisfied by the program when it finally terminates. These internal requirements are specified by (a) the assertions SORTED($[1..i)$) and GREATER_THAN($[1..i)$) (equations (5.3) and (5.4) respectively) which would be required to be satisfied at the start of the i-th iteration of the **for** loop (5.1); and (b) the assertions I_SMALLEST($[i..N]$), SORTED($[1..i)$) and GREATER_THAN($[1..i)$) which would have to be satisfied at the end of the i-th iteration of the **for** loop (equations (5.5), (5.3) and (5.4) respectively; see also equations (5.6), (5.7), (5.8) and (5.9)).

Denoting these two sets of internal requirements as R_int1 and R_int2 respectively, the second cycle of design evolution can be represented by the following schema:

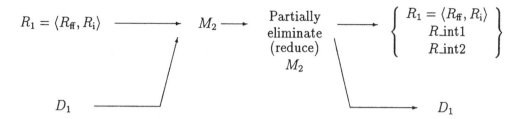

In passing, it should be noted the assertions (5.3), (5.4), (5.5), (5.8) and (5.9) were identified because it is *expected* that if the body of the **for** loop is developed so as to satisfy these assertions then upon termination of the **for** statement the desired requirement R_{ff} will be satisfied. The arguments in support of this expectation are presented in steps 5–8. But these arguments are informal and are not admissible as justifications in the DMV method. They represent, rather, the kinds of cogitating mentioned in footnote 22.

(E7) As a result of identifying the internal requirements R_int1 and R_int2 – thereby completing the previous cycle – the 'current' state of the design process is given by the design, requirements pair $\langle D_1, \{R_1, R\_int1, R\_int2\}\rangle$. Let D_1_body denote the body of the **for** loop. Step 9 represents the beginning of the next evolutionary cycle. The statement of the Hoare formula (5.11) represents the test of whether $D_1\_body \subseteq \{R\_int1, R\_int2\}$. More specifically, (5.11) states exactly how D_1_body must satisfy these two requirements: R_int1 must always hold at the beginning of D_1_body's execution; R_int2 must always hold at the end of D_1_body's execution.

(E8) The resulting misfit is obvious! We cannot even determine whether or not $D_1\_body \subseteq \{R\_int1, R\_int2\}$ because of the misfit

$$M_3 \ : \ D_1\_body \text{ is not expressed in Pascal}$$

(E9) M_3 is (partially) eliminated in step 12 by replacing the previous version of D_1_body: 'PERMUTE VALUES OF $A[i..N]$ TO PUT THE SMALLEST VALUE IN $A[i]$' by the code shown in (5.12).[23] Call the latter, D_2_body, and call the modified version of D_1, D_2. This completes the third evolutionary cycle which is depicted by the schema

---

[23] Steps 10 and 11 simply reiterate the expectation that if $D_1\_body \subseteq \{R\_int1, R\_int2\}$ according to the Hoare formula (5.11) then by the proof rule for the **for** statement, $D_1 \subseteq R_{ff}$.

$$\left\{\begin{array}{c} R_1 = \langle R_{f\!f}, R_i \rangle \\ R\_int1 \\ R\_int2 \end{array}\right\} \longrightarrow M_3 \longrightarrow \begin{array}{c} \text{Partially} \\ \text{eliminate} \\ M_3 \end{array} \longrightarrow \left\{\begin{array}{c} R_1 = \langle R_{f\!f}, R_i \rangle \\ R\_int1 \\ R\_int2 \end{array}\right\}$$

$$D_1 \qquad\qquad\qquad\qquad\qquad\qquad\qquad\qquad D_2$$

where D_2 is

> for $i := 1$ to $N - 1$ do
>
> $\quad D_2$_body

(E10) The later part of step 12 and the whole of step 13 are concerned with testing D_2_body against $\{R\_int1,\ R\_int2\}$. In accordance with the DWV method (or formal design in general) the mode of testing is formal, using the proof theory for Pascal. However, the test cannot be carried to completion. The misfit is

> $M_4\ :\ $ 'EXCHANGE $A[i]$ AND $A[m]$' is not a Pascal statement

(E11) Towards the elimination of this misfit a new set of 'internal' requirements is generated in steps 13–14. This consists of the assertions M_LOWEST ($[i .. j)$) and M_LOWEST($[i .. j]$) and their special cases M_LOWEST($[\ ]$) and M_LOWEST($[i .. N]$). These requirements are such that the Pascal part of the D_2_body

> for $j := i + 1$ to N do
> if $A[j] < A[m]$ then $m := j$

must satisfy them according to the Hoare formulas (5.15) and (5.16) and D_2_body must satisfy them according to (5.14).

Denote this new set of requirements by R_int3. The fourth evolutionary cycle is thus completed and can be depicted as

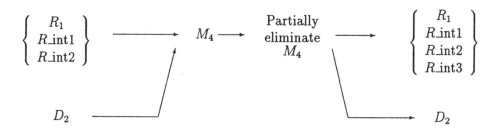

(E12) The state of the design process at this stage is defined by the pair $\langle D_2, \{R_1, R\_int1, R\_int2, R\_int3\}\rangle$. In step 14 the Pascal part of D_2_body is tested to see whether it satisfies the relevant requirements in R_int3 according to the Hoare formula (5.15). The test takes the form of a proof of correctness for the formula (5.16) and then, using the proof rule for the **for** statement, to show that (5.15) is correct. As a result no further misfit is produced in this cycle and the $\langle$design, requirements$\rangle$ pair at the end of this (the fifth) cycle remains as it was at the beginning:

$$
\left\{\begin{array}{c} R_1 \\ R\_int1 \\ R\_int2 \\ R\_int3 \end{array}\right\} \longrightarrow
\begin{array}{c} \text{No misfit between} \\ \text{the Pascal part of} \\ D_2\text{\_body and} \\ R\_int3 \end{array} \longrightarrow
\begin{array}{c} \text{Null} \\ \text{elimination} \end{array} \longrightarrow
\left\{\begin{array}{c} R_1 \\ R\_int1 \\ R\_int2 \\ R\_int3 \end{array}\right\}
$$

$$ D_2 \qquad\qquad\qquad\qquad\qquad\qquad\qquad\qquad\qquad\qquad D_2 $$

(E13) In the next cycle, the test that could not be completed in (E10) is resumed. The design D_2 is tested against the set of requirements $\{R_1, R\_int1, R\_int2, R\_int3\}$; specifically, the 'EXCHANGE $A[i]$ AND $A[m]$' part of D_2_body is tested for satisfaction of the assertion M_LOWEST($[i .. N]$) (in R_int3) and I_SMALLEST($[i .. N]$) (in R_int2) according to the Hoare formula (5.18). The misfit

$$ M_5 : \text{'EXCHANGE } A[i] \text{ AND } A[m]\text{' is not a Pascal statement} $$

is generated – this, of course, being identical to M_4 (see E10) which had not been eliminated previously. M_5 is eliminated by replacing 'EXCHANGE $A[i]$ AND $A[m]$' in D_2_body by the code segment (5.19) this producing, in step 15, a new design D_3. The completed (sixth) cycle is

$$\left\{\begin{array}{l} R_1 \\ R\text{\_int1} \\ R\text{\_int2} \\ R\text{\_int3} \end{array}\right\} \longrightarrow \quad M_5 \quad \longrightarrow \quad \text{Eliminate } M_5 \quad \longrightarrow \quad \left\{\begin{array}{l} R_1 \\ R\text{\_int1} \\ R\text{\_int2} \\ R\text{\_int3} \end{array}\right\}$$

D_2 ⟋ D_3

where D_3 is the complete Pascal program shown in fig. 5.6.

(E14) The current state of the design process is the pair $\langle D_3,\ \{R_1,\ R\text{\_int1},\ R\text{\_int2},\ R\text{\_int3}\}\rangle$. The test now performed (in step 15) is to formally prove that the formula

$$\{\text{M\_LOWEST}([i \mathbin{..} N])\}$$
$$t := A[i];$$
$$A[i] := A[m];$$
$$A[m] := t$$
$$\{\text{I\_SMALLEST}([i \mathbin{..} N])\}$$

is correct. It is shown that this is indeed the case. This is the final link in showing that $D_3 \subseteq R_{ff}$. The entire program is in Pascal, hence the R_i requirement is also satisfied. D_3 satisfies R_1. The design, thus, terminates at the end of this – the seventh – evolutionary cycle:

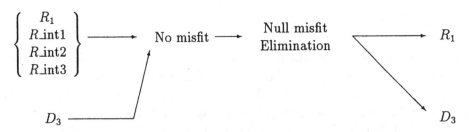

$$\left\{\begin{array}{l} R_1 \\ R\text{\_int1} \\ R\text{\_int2} \\ R\text{\_int3} \end{array}\right\} \longrightarrow \quad \text{No misfit} \quad \longrightarrow \quad \begin{array}{c}\text{Null misfit} \\ \text{Elimination}\end{array} \quad \longrightarrow \quad R_1$$

D_3 D_3

This completes our evolutionary explanation of the DWV-based development of the sorting program presented by Alagic and Arbib (1978). The complete series of evolutionary cycles is recapitulated by the sequence of (design, requirement) pairs shown in fig. 5.7.

End Example

As noted above, the DWV method develops a program and its proof of correctness together. I showed how the method can be explained in terms of the evolutionary

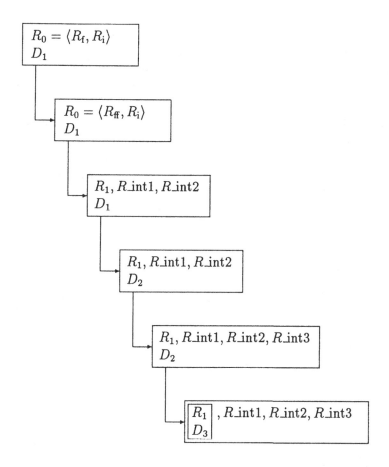

Fig. 5.7 Evolving sequence of the ⟨design, requirements⟩ pairs for the sorting program.

model. The design method discussed below appears on the surface quite different from the DWV approach. It is, in fact, an instance of the Artificial Intelligence (AI) paradigm (whereas the DWV method is an instance of the Formal Design paradigm) which is discussed in detail in chapter 10.

My pattern of explanation will differ slightly from that used in example 5.9. I shall describe the design method as it was originally described (again, subject to some paraphrasing for the sake of clarity and conciseness) but will stop at logical points; at each such point, an evolutionary explanation will be given for the immediately preceding design steps. Thus the description of the original design method will be *interleaved* with the evolutionary explanation.

Example 5.10

This particular problem and its solution were presented and discussed by Barstow (1985) and are related to *oil well logging*. Oil well logs are created by lowering measuring 'tools' into boreholes and recording measurements ('logs') of various properties of the rocks surrounding the borehole. These logs are then used to compute other properties which cannot be otherwise directly determined by measurement.

The issue of interest is to *automatically design* (using certain AI techniques) programs that calculate the values of the desired parameters from the available data. Barstow's (1985) concern is to demonstrate the *hypothetical synthesis* of such programs (i.e., the development of programs *as they might be carried* out by a hypothetical automatic program 'designer'). He does this by establishing a sequence of reasoning steps that an automatic 'designer' might follow in synthesizing the programs. In this example, we shall consider one such program.[24]

The overall approach towards synthesis is based on two basic stages:

(F) A *formalization* step – which given an imprecise and incomplete specification, produces a formal specification; that is, a specification that describes a mathematical relationship between the desired ('output') parameter and the known ('input') parameters that must be satisfied in the sense that the output parameter values can be uniquely determined from a set of input parameter values. Barstow (1985) calls these mathematical relationships *postconditions*.

(I) An *implementation* step: given the formal specification this produces the actual executable code.

In the discussion below, we shall be concerned only with the formalization stage. The initial problem as stated is: given logs of sonic transit time and resistivity, and assuming that the solid part of the rock formation consists of sandstone and the fluid part of water and hydrocarbon, to compute the fractional volume of hydrocarbon in the rock formation.

This can be stated succinctly as an 'informal specification' in the following format:

(IS1) *Inputs*   Sonic: real; Resistivity: real
       Outputs   VolHydrocarbon: real
       Assumptions   Solid is sandstone; fluid is water and hydrocarbon

---

[24] Barstow's ultimate intention in this exercise is to identify the types of knowledge that would be required by a knowledge-based automatic design system. In the current discussion, these knowledge items are stated or explicitly identified as either *heuristics* or *facts*. When attempting to explain the design process within the evolutionary framework the precise significance of the knowledge items in the evolutionary context will become clear.

Step 1 The general approach in a quantitative problem of this kind is to identify a quantitative relationship between the inputs and the outputs. In the case of (IS1) there are, according to Barstow (1985), a large number of such possible relationships. Thus, the problem is simplified by invoking the following domain-specific heuristic:[25]

(Heu1) In a volumetric analysis problem, separate the solid and the fluid analysis parts.

Applying (Heu1) to (IS1) causes the latter to be refined to the following informal specifications:

(IS1.1) *Inputs*   Sonic, Resistivity: real
          Outputs   VolFluid: real
          Assumptions   Solid is sandstone; Fluid is water and hydrocarbon

(IS1.2) *Inputs*   Sonic, Resistivity, VolFluid: real
          Outputs   VolHydrocarbon: real
          Assumptions   Solid is sandstone; Fluid is water and hydrocarbon

Step 2 In the case of (IS1.1) there is, in fact, a single equation relating the inputs and the outputs:

(Fact1) Sonic = VolFluid * SonicFluid + (1 − VolFluid) * SonicSolid

Given this, the domain-independent heuristic

(Heu2) Given a relationship involving the inputs and the outputs, if the relationship is consistent with the assumptions, add the relationship as a postcondition to the specification. If the relationship includes additional terms add them as inputs.

is applied to (IS1.1) resulting in

(IS1.1a) *Inputs*   Sonic, Resistivity, SonicFluid, SonicSolid: real
           Outputs   VolFluid: real
           Assumptions   Solid is sandstone; Fluid is water and hydrocarbon

---

[25] As will be further discussed in chapter 10, the use of heuristics to guide the problem solving activity is a fundamental characteristic of the AI paradigm. Heuristics that are specific to the particular design or problem domain are called *domain-specific*; those that are applicable across a range of domains are referred to as *domain-independent*.

$$Postconditions \quad Sonic = VolFluid * SonicFluid +$$
$$(1 - VolFluid) * SonicSolid$$

Step 3 Given the facts

(Fact2) Sonic transit time in water or hydrocarbon is 189 $\mu s/ft$

(Fact3) Sonic transit time in sandstone is 55 $\mu s/ft$

the application of the heuristic

(Heu3) If an input term has a constant value consider the term to be a local and add its value to the postcondition

to (IS1.1a) yields

(IS1.1b)	*Inputs*	Sonic, Resistivity: real
	Outputs	VolFluid: real
	Locals	SonicFluid, SonicSolid: real
	Assumptions	Solid is sandstone; Fluid is water and hydrocarbon
	Postconditions	Sonic = VolFluid * Sonic Fluid
		$+ (1 - VolFluid) * SonicSolid$
		SonicFluid = 189
		SonicSolid = 55

Step 4 (IS1.1b) is simplified by applying the following domain-dependent heuristic:

(Heu4) If the output terms are uniquely determined by the postconditions and a proper subset of the input terms delete the redundant input terms.

This yields the following formal specification.

(IS1.1c) ≡	*Inputs*	Sonic: real
(FS1.1)	*Outputs*	VolFluid: real
	Locals	SonicFluid, SonicSolid: real
	Assumptions	Solid is sandstone; Fluid is water and hydrocarbon
	Postconditions	Sonic = VolFluid * SonicFluid
		$+ (1 - VolFluid) * SonicSolid$
		SonicFluid = 189
		SonicSolid = 55

This is a convenient and logical point to pause and explain the preceding steps in evolutionary terms.

(E1) It was initially determined as overall strategy that the first of the two main stages of the design process would produce a formal specification. Thus the aim of this stage is to *design a specification* that meets the criterion of 'formalhood' as defined in (F) above. The initial state of the design process is the design–requirements pair $\langle D_o, R_o \rangle$ where

> R_o = A formal specification relating volume of hydrocarbon to sonic and/ or resistivity assuming that the solid part is sandstone and the fluid part is water and hydrocarbon.

$D_o = (\text{IS1})$

That is, the initial design is the formatted, but informal specification IS1.

(E2) The obvious misfit between D_0 and R_0 is

> M_0: The specification IS1 is not formal

As a first step towards eliminating M_0, the heuristic (Heu1) is invoked and as a result, the requirement R_0 is decomposed into two requirements

> R_{11}: A formal specification relating volume of the fluid to sonic and resistivity assuming that the solid part is sandstone and the fluid part is water and hydrocarbon.
>
> R_{12}: A formal specification relating volume of the hydrocarbon part of the fluid to sonic, resistivity and the volume of fluid, assuming that the solid part is sandstone and the fluid part is water and hydrocarbon.

The resulting requirement is $R_1 = \langle R_{11}, R_{12} \rangle$. This completes the first evolutionary cycle which can be depicted as follows.

$$\langle R_0 \rangle \longrightarrow M_0 \longrightarrow \begin{array}{c} \text{Reduce } M_0 \\ \text{(using Heu1)} \end{array} \longrightarrow R_1 = \langle R_{11}, R_{12} \rangle$$

$$D_0 = \langle \text{IS1} \rangle \qquad\qquad\qquad\qquad\qquad D_0$$

(E3) The current state of the (specification) design process is $\langle D_0, R_1 \rangle$. Testing D_0 against R_1 generates the misfit

> M_1: The input-output relationship in IS1 differs from the relationships required in R_{01} and R_{02}

M_1 is eliminated by refining (in step 1), IS1 into two simpler specifications, (IS1.1) and (IS1.2). The resulting design is $D_1 = \langle IS1.1, IS1.2 \rangle$. This completes the second evolutionary cycle which can be depicted as follows:

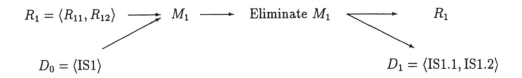

$$R_1 = \langle R_{11}, R_{12} \rangle \longrightarrow M_1 \longrightarrow \text{Eliminate } M_1 \qquad R_1$$

$$D_0 = \langle IS1 \rangle \qquad\qquad\qquad\qquad D_1 = \langle IS1.1, IS1.2 \rangle$$

It should be reiterated that the evolutionary model does *not* stipulate *how* or *by what rule* the misfit is to be eliminated or reduced. In this example however, as will become evident, the decision of how the elimination/reduction of a misfit is to be attempted is prompted mainly by the use of domain-specific and domain-independent heuristics and facts.

(E4) The current state of the design process is $\langle D_1, R_1 \rangle$. Testing D_1 against R_1 generates the misfit[26]

> M_2: The specification IS1.1 is not formal.

Towards the elimination of M_2, (Fact1) and (Heu2) are invoked (in step 2) producing as a result, a modification of IS1.1, viz., (IS1.1a). The new design is, thus, $D_2 = \langle IS1.1a, IS1.2 \rangle$ and the complete (third) evolutionary cycle is as follows:

---

[26] Of course, the alternate misfit M_2': 'IS1.2 is not formal' could also have been generated rather than M_2; or if the testing phase was concerned with the generation of *all* misfits then both M_2 and M_2' would have been concurrently generated. It merely turns out that tracing through Barstow's design strategy *in this particular problem* it was M_2 rather than M_2' (or both M_2 and M_2') that was first revealed.

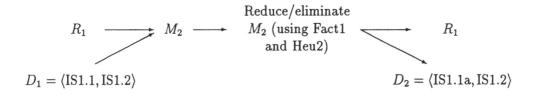

$$D_1 = \langle IS1.1, IS1.2 \rangle \qquad\qquad D_2 = \langle IS1.1a, IS1.2 \rangle$$

(E5) The current state of the design process is $\langle D_2,\ R_1 \rangle$. Testing D_2 against R_1 reveals the following misfit:

> M_3: New input variables (SonicFluid, SonicSolid) have been introduced with no values. Thus, VolFluid can still not be computed. Hence IS1.1a is not yet formal.

M_3 is eliminated by invoking (in step 3) (Fact2), (Fact3), and (Heu3); (IS1.1a) is modified to the form (IS1.1b). The resulting design $D_3 = \langle IS1.1b,\ IS1.2 \rangle$ and the fourth evolutionary cycle thus completed is as follows:

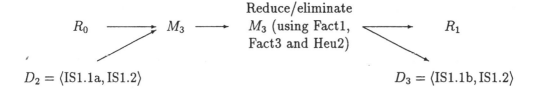

$$D_2 = \langle IS1.1a, IS1.2 \rangle \qquad\qquad D_3 = \langle IS1.1b, IS1.2 \rangle$$

(E6) The current state of the design is $\langle D_3,\ R_1 \rangle$. Testing D_3 against R_1 – specifically, testing IS1.1b against R_{11} – produces a *fit* since now IS1.1b is, in fact, a formal specification. Thus, in this – the fifth evolutionary cycle – no misfit is generated and none eliminated.

(E7) Strictly speaking the design of the formal specification corresponding to IS1.1b could have been terminated here; however, a new requirement is now explicitly introduced (in step 4). This is

> R_2: The formal specification should have no redundant terms. (That is, the specification should be 'minimal')

The new requirements set is now $R = \langle R_1, R_2 \rangle$. Testing D_3 against R produces the misfit

M_4: IS1.1b is not minimal

M_4 is eliminated by using (Heu4) and altering (IS1.1b) to yield the specification (IS1.1c) $\equiv$ (FS1.1). This is the final form for one part of the specification. The resulting design $D_4 = \langle FS1.1, IS1.2 \rangle$. The sixth evolutionary cycle can be represented as follows:

$$R = \langle R_1, R_2 \rangle \longrightarrow M_4 \longrightarrow \begin{array}{c} \text{Eliminate } M_4 \\ \text{(using Heu4)} \end{array} \longrightarrow R = \langle R_1, R_2 \rangle$$

$$D_3 = \langle IS1.1b, IS1.2 \rangle \qquad\qquad\qquad D_4 = \langle IS1.1c \equiv FS1.1, IS1.2 \rangle$$

Let us now return to Barstow's (1985) hypothetical program synthesis process as it was originally described.

Step 5 Attention is now transferred to the informal specification (IS1.2). There is no single relationship involving the inputs and the outputs of (IS1.2); however, by applying the domain-specific heuristic

(Heu5) In a fluid analysis problem, a useful intermediate step is to compute water ⟍ saturation.

(IS1.2) is refined to the following specifications:

(IS1.2.1) *Inputs*   Sonic, Resistivity, VolFluid: real
           Outputs   SaturationWater: real
           Assumptions Solid is sandstone; Fluid is water and hydrocarbon

(IS1.2.2) *Inputs*   Sonic, Resistivity, VolFluid, SaturationWater: real
           Outputs   VolHydrocarbon: real
           Assumptions Solid is sandstone; Fluid is water and hydrocarbon

Step 6 In the case of (IS1.2.1) the following relationship is relevant:

(Fact4) $\text{SaturationWater}^2 = \dfrac{A * \text{ResistivityWater}}{\text{VolFluid}^2 * \text{Resistivity}}$

where A's value depends on the nature of the solid part of the formation and ResistivityWater depends on local geological conditions.

Using (Fact4) in conjunction with (Heu2), (IS1.2.1) is refined to

(IS1.2.1a)   *Inputs*   Sonic, Resistivity, VolFluid, A,
                                 ResistivityWater: real
            Outputs   SaturationWater: real
            Assumptions   Solid is sandstone; Fluid is water and hydrocarbon
            Postconditions   SaturationWater^2 $= \frac{A \, * \, \text{ResistivityWater}}{\text{VolFluid}^2 \, * \, \text{Resistivity}}$

Step 7 Given the assumptions it is known that for sandstone

(Fact5): A = 0.81

This in conjunction with (Heu3) yields

(IS1.2.1b)   *Inputs*   Sonic, Resistivity, VolFluid, ResistivityWater: real
            Outputs   SaturationWater: real
            Locals A: real
            Assumptions   Solid is sandstone; Fluid is water and hydrocarbon
            Postconditions   SaturationWater^2 $= \frac{A \, * \, \text{ResistivityWater}}{\text{VolFluid}^2 \, * \, \text{Resistivity}}$
                                    $A = 0.81$

Step 8 Applying (Heu4) the redundant inputs are removed, yielding

(IS1.2.1c)   *Inputs*   Resistivity, VolFluid, ResistivityWater: real
            Outputs   SaturationWater: real
            Assumptions   Solid is sandstone; Fluid is water and hydrocarbon
            Postconditions   SaturationWater^2 $= \frac{A \, * \, \text{ResistivityWater}}{\text{VolFluid}^2 \, * \, \text{Resistivity}}$
                                    $A = 0.81$

Step 9 (IS1.2.2) is now considered. Once more, there is no single relationship relating inputs and outputs. There are, however, two other relationships that can be used:

(Fact6) SaturationWater $= \frac{\text{VolWater}}{\text{VolFluid}}$
(Fact7) VolWater + VolHydrocarbon = VolFluid

Applying (Fact7) and (Heu8) to IS1.2.2 produces:

(IS1.2.2a) *Inputs*   Sonic, Resistivity, VolFluid, SaturationWater,
                             VolWater: real
            Outputs   VolHydrocarbon: real
            Assumptions   Solid is sandstone; Fluid is water and hydrocarbon
            Postconditions VolWater + VolHydrocarbon = VolFluid

Step 10 Now, using (Fact6), since VolWater = SaturationWater * VolFluid, and
SaturationWater and VolFluid are both inputs, VolWater can be computed locally.
Thus, using a heuristic similar to (Heu3), viz.,

> (Heu6) If an input term can be computed from other input terms consider the for-
> mer term to be a local and add the relationship to the postcon-
> ditions.[27]

(IS1.2.2a) is transformed into

(IS1.2.2b) *Inputs*   Sonic, Resistivity, VolFluid, SaturationWater: real
            Outputs   VolHydrocarbon: real
            Locals   VolWater: real
            Assumptions   Solid is sandstone; Fluid is water and hydrocarbon
            Postconditions VolWater + VolHydrocarbon = VolFluid
                             $\text{SaturationWater} = \frac{\text{VolWater}}{\text{VolFluid}}$

Step 11 (Heu4) is now used to eliminate extra inputs, thus producing

(IS1.2.2c) *Inputs*   VolFluid, SaturationWater: real
            Outputs   VolHydrocarbon: real
            Locals   VolWater: real
            Assumptions   Solid is sandstone; Fluid is water and hydrocarbon
            Postconditions VolWater + VolHydrocarbon = VolFluid
                             $\text{SaturationWater} = \frac{\text{VolWater}}{\text{VolFluid}}$

(IS1.2.1c) and (IS1.2.2c) are, thus, the final formal specifications corresponding to the
informal specifications (IS1.2). (IS1.2.1c) and (IS1.2.2c) can, thus, also be renamed
(FS1.2.1) and (FS1.2.2).

Let us now resume the evolutionary explanation which was temporarily suspended
after the sixth evolutionary cycle (E7). At the end of this cycle the state of the design

---

[27] This heuristic is not explicitly stated by Barstow(1985). However it is necessary in order for
the transformation from (IS1.2.2a) to (IS1.2.2b) to take place.

process is represented by the pair $\langle D_4,\ R \rangle$ where $R = \langle R_1,\ R_2 \rangle$, $D_4 = \langle \text{IS1.1c} \equiv \text{FS1.1}, \text{IS1.2} \rangle$. It will also be recalled that the specification FS1.1 satisfies R_{11} as well as R_2.

(E8) Testing D_4 against R reveals the misfit

M_5: The specification IS1.2 is not formal

In order to eliminate or reduce M_5, (Heu5) is invoked, thus prompting (in step5) the refinement of IS1.2 into the two specifications (IS1.2.1) and (IS1.2.2). The new design is, now, $D_5 = \langle \text{FS1.1}, \text{IS1.2.1}, \text{IS1.2.2} \rangle$. The seventh evolutionary cycle can be schematized as

$$R = \langle R_1, R_2 \rangle \quad \longrightarrow \quad M_5 \quad \longrightarrow \quad \begin{matrix} \text{Reduce } M_5 \\ \text{(using Heu5)} \end{matrix} \quad \diagdown \quad R = \langle R_1, R_2 \rangle$$

$$D_4 = \langle \text{FS1.1}, \text{IS1.2} \rangle \qquad\qquad D_5 = \langle \text{FS1.1}, \text{IS1.2.1}, \text{IS1.2.2} \rangle$$

(E9) The current state of the design process is $\langle D_5,\ R \rangle$. Testing D_5 against R reveals the misfit

M_6: The specification IS1.2.1 is not formal

M_6 is eliminated in step 6 by using (Fact2) and (Heu2) to transform (IS1.2.1) into (IS1.2.1a). The resulting design is $D_6 = \langle \text{FS1.1}, \text{IS1.2.1a}, \text{IS1.2.2} \rangle$ and the (eighth) completed cycle is as follows.

$$R \quad \longrightarrow \quad M_6 \quad \longrightarrow \quad \begin{matrix} \text{Eliminate } M_6 \\ \text{(using Fact2} \\ \text{and Heu2)} \end{matrix} \quad \diagdown \quad R_1 = \langle R_1, R_2 \rangle$$

$$D_5 = \langle \text{FS1.1}, \text{IS1.2.1}, \text{IS1.2.2} \rangle \qquad\qquad D_6 = \langle \text{FS1.1}, \text{IS1.2.1a}, \text{IS1.2.2} \rangle$$

(E10) Testing D_6 against R reveals that

M_7: The specification IS1.2.1a is not formal

This misfit is eliminated (in step 7) by using (Fact5) and (Heu3) to transform (IS1.2.1a) into (IS1.2.1b). The resulting evolutionary cycle (the ninth) is as follows:

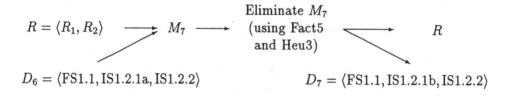

$$R = \langle R_1, R_2 \rangle \qquad\qquad M_7 \qquad \begin{array}{c}\text{Eliminate } M_7\\ \text{(using Fact5}\\ \text{and Heu3)}\end{array} \qquad R$$

$$D_6 = \langle \text{FS1.1}, \text{IS1.2.1a}, \text{IS1.2.2} \rangle \qquad\qquad D_7 = \langle \text{FS1.1}, \text{IS1.2.1b}, \text{IS1.2.2} \rangle$$

(E11) The state of the design process is now $\langle D_7, R \rangle$. Matching D_7 against R reveals the misfit

M_8: (IS1.2.1b) is not minimal

In other words, (IS1.2.1b) does not satisfy R_2. M_8 is eliminated (in step 8) by applying (Heu4) and, thus, transforming (IS1.2.1b) into (IS1.2.1c). The resulting design is $D_8 = \langle \text{IS1.1}, \text{IS1.2.1c}, \text{IS1.2.2} \rangle$. This (tenth) evolutionary cycle can be depicted as follows:

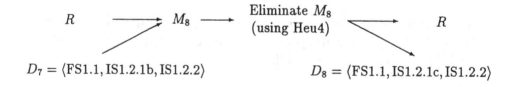

$$R \qquad\qquad M_8 \qquad \begin{array}{c}\text{Eliminate } M_8\\ \text{(using Heu4)}\end{array} \qquad R$$

$$D_7 = \langle \text{FS1.1}, \text{IS1.2.1b}, \text{IS1.2.2} \rangle \qquad\qquad D_8 = \langle \text{FS1.1}, \text{IS1.2.1c}, \text{IS1.2.2} \rangle$$

(E12) Testing D_8 against R reveals the following misfit:

M_9: (IS1.2.2) is not a formal specification

M_9 is reduced in step 9 by taking advantage of (Fact7) and (Heu2) and transforming (IS1.2.2) into (IS1.2.2a). This modification results in $D_9 = \langle \text{FS1.1}, \text{IS1.2.1c}, \text{IS1.2.2a} \rangle$. The (eleventh) evolutionary cycle is

$$R \longrightarrow M_9 \longrightarrow \begin{array}{c} \text{Reduce } M_9 \\ \text{(using Fact7} \\ \text{and Heu2)} \end{array} \longleftrightarrow R$$

$$D_8 = \langle \text{FS1.1}, \text{IS1.2.1c}, \text{IS1.2.2} \rangle \qquad\qquad D_9 = \langle \text{FS1.1}, \text{IS1.2.1c}, \text{IS1.2.2a} \rangle$$

(E13) Testing D_9 against R generates the misfit

M_{10}: (IS1.2.2a) is not a formal specification[28]

M_{10} is eliminated (in step 10) by invoking (Fact 6) and (Heu 6) and thereby transforming (IS1.2.2a) into (IS1.2.2b). The completed (twelfth) cycle is representable as

$$R \longrightarrow M_{10} \longrightarrow \begin{array}{c} \text{Eliminate } M_{10} \\ \text{(using Fact6} \\ \text{and Heu6)} \end{array} \longleftrightarrow R$$

$$D_9 = \langle \text{FS1.1}, \text{IS1.2.1c}, \text{IS1.2.2a} \rangle \qquad\qquad D_{10} = \langle \text{FS1.1}, \text{IS1.2.1c}, \text{IS1.2.2b} \rangle$$

(E14) A test of D_{10} against R produces the misfit

M_{11}: (IS1.2.2b) is not minimal

The misfit is eliminated (in step 11) by using (Heu 4) and transforming (IS1.2.2b) into (IS1.2.2c). The resulting design is, then

$$D_{11} = \langle \text{FS1.1}, \text{IS1.2.1c}, \text{IS1.2.2c} \rangle.$$

The (thirteenth) evolutionary cycle has the form

---

[28] The reader will note that though the misfits M_9 and M_{10} are of the same *type* – i.e., the fact that neither of the respective specifications are formal – the *specifics* of the misfits are different. (IS1.2.2) is not formal because there is no postcondition *at all* in the specification. (IS1.2.2a) is not formal because even though a postcondition exists the output cannot be computed since one of the inputs, 'VolWater' is still unknown.

$$R \quad\longrightarrow\quad M_{11} \quad\longrightarrow\quad \begin{array}{c}\text{Eliminate } M_{11}\\ \text{(using Heu4)}\end{array} \quad\searrow\quad R$$

$$D_{10} = \langle \text{FS1.1}, \text{IS1.2.1c}, \text{IS1.2.2b}\rangle \qquad\qquad D_{11} = \langle \text{FS1.1}, \text{IS1.2.1c}, \text{IS1.2.2c}\rangle$$

(E15) The current state of the design process is $\langle D_{11},\ R\rangle$. Testing D_{11} against R, it is now seen that the *sequential composition* of (IS1.2.1c) and (IS1.2.2c) satisfies the R_{12} part of R_1. Furthermore, the R_2 part is also satisfied by both IS1.2.1c and IS1.2.2c. Thus, (IS1.2.1c) and (IS1.2.2c) are indeed formal specifications and can be renamed (FS1.2.1) and (FS1.2.2) respectively. No further misfits are produced in this (the fourteenth) evolutionary cycle. The design process terminates (for the present, at least) in the state $\langle D_{11},\ R\rangle$ where $D_{11} = \langle \text{FS1.1, FS1.2.1, FS1.2.2}\rangle$ and $R = \langle R_1,\ R_2\rangle$.

The complete sequence of evolutionary steps – showing the successive 'generations' of $\langle$requirements, design$\rangle$ pairs – is schematically shown in fig. 5.8.
End Example

$$\langle R_0, D_0 = \langle \text{IS1}\rangle\rangle \quad\longrightarrow\quad \langle R_1 = \langle R_{11}, R_{12}\rangle, D_0\rangle \quad\longrightarrow\quad \langle R_1, D_1 = \langle \text{IS1.1}, \text{IS1.2}\rangle\rangle$$
$$\downarrow$$
$$\langle R = \langle R_1, R_2\rangle, D_3\rangle \quad\leftarrow\quad \langle R_1, D_3 = \langle \text{IS1.1b}, \text{IS1.2}\rangle\rangle \quad\leftarrow\quad \langle R_1, D_2 = \langle \text{IS1.1a}, \text{IS1.2}\rangle\rangle$$
$$\downarrow$$
$$\langle R, D_4 = \langle \text{IS1.1C} \equiv \text{FS1.1}, \text{IS1.2}\rangle\rangle \quad\longrightarrow\quad \langle R, D_5 = \langle \text{FS1.1}, \text{IS1.2.1}, \text{IS1.2.2}\rangle\rangle$$
$$\downarrow$$
$$\langle R, D_7 = \langle \text{FS1.1}, \text{IS1.2.1b}, \text{IS1.2.2}\rangle \quad\longleftarrow\quad \langle R, D_6 = \langle \text{FS1.1}, \text{IS1.2.1a}, \text{IS1.2.2}\rangle\rangle$$
$$\downarrow$$
$$\langle R, D_8 = \langle \text{FS1.1}, \text{IS1.2.1c}, \text{IS1.2.2}\rangle\rangle \quad\longrightarrow\quad \langle R, D_9 = \langle \text{FS1.1}, \text{IS1.2.1c}, \text{IS1.2.1a}\rangle\rangle$$
$$\downarrow$$
$$\langle R, D_{11} = \langle \text{FS1.1}, \text{IS1.2.1c}, \text{IS1.2.1c}\rangle\rangle \quad\longleftarrow\quad \langle R, D_{10} = \langle \text{FS1.1}, \text{IS1.2.1c}, \text{IS1.2.2b}\rangle\rangle$$

Fig. 5.8 Evolution of the oil well program specification design.

As I shall further discuss in Part II, the two foregoing examples belong respectively to the formal design and AI paradigms. Thus, from a paradigmatic perspective they are quite distinct. Yet, as we have just seen both processes are explainable by the evolutionary model.

The next example differs from the previous two in a very different way: while examples 5.9 and 5.10 embody the application of methods or approaches, example 5.11 below discusses the development of a design where the designer does not begin with a particular method. The design process is, thus, in a sense *unselfconscious* as far as the designer is concerned.[29]

Example 5.11
This example is based on the empirical studies by Kant and Newell (1984) – see also Kant (1985) – of how technically qualified people design *algorithms*. The experimental technique used for this purpose is to give subjects problems which are to be solved algorithmically and to have them talk aloud while they are developing the algorithm. This vocalization of their thinking is called a *protocol* which is recorded and subsequently analyzed.[30]

Here, I shall describe one particular study conducted by Kant and Newell. This involved the design of an algorithm to find the convex hull for any given set of points. The *convex hull* is the smallest subset of the points that when connected in a convex polygon contains all the other points (fig. 5.9). The subject assigned this task – referred to as S2 by Kant and Newell (1984) and as D1 by Kant (1985) – had a Ph.D. in computer science, was quite knowledgeable in algorithm design but knew little about convex hulls. The protocol produced by S2 was tape recorded.

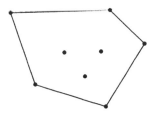

Fig. 5.9 The convex hull of a given set of points.

S2 developed two different algorithms for the convex hull problem. Here, we shall consider the first of these, termed by Kant and Newell (1984) Algorithm GT. The

---

[29] See section 4.1 for a discussion of Alexander's (1964) characterization of the unselfconscious design process in the context of buildings.

[30] Protocol analysis as a technique to study problem solving behavior is discussed and used extensively in (Newell and Simon 1972).

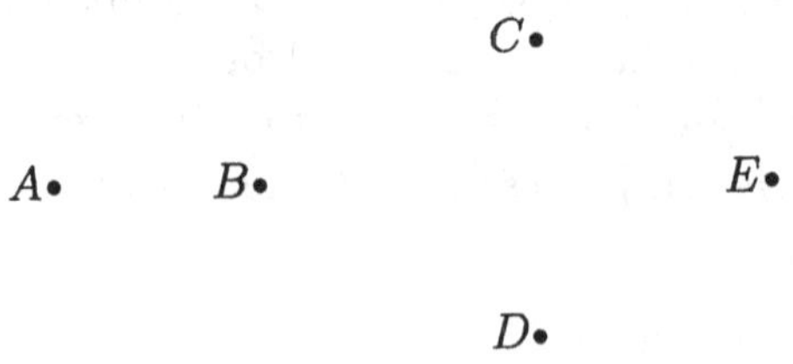

$$C \bullet$$

$$A \bullet \qquad B \bullet \qquad\qquad\qquad E \bullet$$

$$D \bullet$$

Fig. 5.10 Example used by S2 while developing Algorithm GT (Kant 1985). Reproduced with permission of IEEE. ©1985 IEEE.

particular set of points used as an example by S2 and mentioned in the protocol is shown in fig. 5.10.

An evolutionary explanation of the protocol as recorded in Kant and Newell (1984) is given below.

Phase 1: During this phase, the designer is given the problem in terms of the following requirement:

> R: Given a set of points, to identify the subset of these points that encloses all the other points.

Phase 2: An initial version of the algorithm is produced. Call this D_1 where

> D_1: Select a point and test whether it is on the convex hull or not.[31]

Phase 3: A misfit between D_1 and R is identified, viz.:

> M_1: It is not known *how* to determine whether the point selected is on the convex hull or not.

Phase 4: This phase is concerned with eliminating M_1. It identifies the test criterion for determining whether a selected line is on the convex hull or not. In S2's words:

---

[31] Kant and Newell (1984) note that this initial design is really the identification of a *schema* for generating the points on the set and testing whether or not they are on the convex hull. In other words, D_1 is an instance of the *generate and test* schema – one of the well known domain-independent problem solving heuristics developed within the AI paradigm (Newell and Simon 1972, 1976; Barr and Feigenbaum 1981).

'If it is the case that I can choose two points such that I can go on either side of the given line then this can't be on the convex hull.'

Let us call this test ON_CONVEX_HULL. This is used to eliminate M_1 producing a modification of D_1:

> D_2: Select a point and draw a line to that point from the previously selected point and apply the test ON_CONVEX_HULL

Phase 5: Testing the current design D_2 against R using an example with five points (fig. 5.10) reveals a new *misfit*:

> M_2: The algorithm will not succeed by selecting *any* arbitrary point as the starting point.

Phase 6: Precisely how to eliminate M_2 *in a general way* is not attempted yet. Instead M_2 is eliminated by *assuming* that the algorithm will start with a 'good' point (specifically, point A in fig. 5.10). This leads to a new design.

> D_3: [Assuming a good starting point] draw a line from the point most recently added to the 'convex_hull_so_far' to a new point such that all the given points in the set are on one side of the line.

Phase 7: D_3 tested against R reveals the misfit

> M_3: There is no guarantee that the algorithm will start with a good point.

M_3 is eliminated by exhaustively searching for a good starting point. Once a good starting point is selected (provided such a point exists), the rest of D_3 still holds. The resulting overall algorithm which is D_4 is sketched out in fig. 5.11.
End Example

5.5 ONTOGENIC AND PHYLOGENIC DESIGN EVOLUTION

It will be noted that examples 5.9–5.11 all refer to design processes that share the following characteristic: the observed evolutionary phenomenon occurs between the time when a problem is assigned to the designer and the time the design is passed on to the manufacturer or implementer. During this period the design, as it were, *unfolds* from the initial form to the acceptable form (see, e.g., figs. 5.7 and 5.8). Borrowing

---

Algorithm GT

Input X, the set of points

[1] Select a good starting point $X_0 \in X$ and place in Hull_so_far;
    delete X_0 from X

[2] **while** X is not empty **do**

[3]   Select a new point $X_i \in X$

[4]   Draw a line L_i from the most recently added points in
        Hull_so_far to X_i (That is, add X_i to Hull_so_far);

[5]   **if** Hull_so_far is not a convex hull
            then delete L_i (That is, remove X_i from
                Hull_so_far)

[6]   **else** delete X_i from X
    endwhile

Fig. 5.11 Algorithm GT $\equiv$ Design D_4.

yet another term from biology I have elsewhere referred to this as *ontogenic design evolution* (Dasgupta 1989a, 1989c).[32]

Note that the design processes described in examples 5.9–5.11 all happen to incur a relatively small amount of *time*. For example, Kant and Newell (1984) recorded that Algorithm GT was produced in 15 minutes while a second and more efficient algorithm was developed by the same subject, S_2, in about one hour. While I have no supporting data, it is also reasonable to surmise that a person with the same sort of background as S_2 would be able to design the sorting program using the DWV method in a matter of a few hours.

An artifact may, however, be so complex that its design necessitates the cooperation of several designers and demand time ranging from several months to several years. Many engineering projects as well as large computer systems design problems are obvious examples. However, in spite of the disparity in complexity and time requirements between these types of problems and those considered in examples 5.9–5.11, *evolutionarily speaking they are similar*: the design processes are ontogenic in nature. Thus, even in the case of a design activity spanning months or even a few years the process involves the unfolding and development of a form from some initial state that is at odds with the requirements to some state that fits the requirements.

I will contrast this with another type of process that may also consume large amounts

---

[32] Ontogeny: 'the life history of an individual, both embryonic and postnatal' (Gould 1977, p. 483).

of time (perhaps several years or even decades) and resources. However, here, the actual act of design involves *successive changes or improvements to previously implemented designs*. Evolution here operates upon 'completed' designs and usually reflects changes in one or more of the various parameters that had dictated the original design – e.g., change in technology, emergence of new modes of manufacture, changes in the operating environment of the system in question or the discovery (on the part of the user) of other purposes for the artifact than those previously assumed. Such parameter changes produce new problems – that is, new requirements. Again, borrowing a biological term I refer to this type of evolution as *phylogenic design evolution* (Dasgupta 1989a, 1989c).[33, 34]

The interesting point is that even the phylogenic design process appears to follow the same evolutionary model (fig. 5.5) that explains ontogenic design. In section 5.6, I shall describe in some detail evidence in support of this claim.

5.6 EMPIRICAL EVIDENCE OF EVOLUTION IN PHYLOGENIC DESIGN

It is not unusual in discussions of computer architecture to encounter the concept of *architectural families* where members of the family are related to one another through an ancestor/descendant relationship (Bell and Newell 1971, Siewiorek, Bell and Newell 1982). The classic examples are the Burroughs B5500, B5700, B6700, B7700 series (Doran 1979), the PDP-11 series (Bell and Mudge 1978), and the IBM System/360, System/370, 3030, 4300 series (Siewiorek, Bell and Newell 1982). Of more recent vintage are the various families of microprocessors such as the Motorola 68000 family – which include as members the MC68000, MC68010, MC68012, MC68020 and MC68030 processors (Wakerly 1989) – and the Intel 80×86 family –

[33,] Phylogeny: 'the evolutionary history of a lineage conventionally ... depicted as a sequence of successive adult stages' (Gould 1977, p. 483). The biologically informed reader may protest at the use of this word in the context of a few years or even a few decades since in evolutionary biology phylogeny is associated with entire geological time spans. The significance of the prodigious time spans involved in natural evolution has been recently articulated (for example) by Ruse (1986), and Dawkins (1986). However, even significant biological evolution may operate within much smaller time periods – say of the order of a few human generations. One of the most dramatic examples is the phenomenon of *industrial melanism* in which a profound change in the coloration of certain species of moths (the 'peppered moth') took place in Britain within the confines of a century. This change was in response to the change in the coloration of tree barks and rocks on which these moths rested during daytime. Originally, the predominantly light colored peppered moth was protected against predators by the light coloration of the lichen-covered tree barks and rocks. With the advent of industrialization the deposition of industrial smoke particles caused a darkening of the trees and the rocks. As a result, the dark (minority) mutants of the peppered moth survived more successfully to the extent that moths of this species in the industrial regions of Britain are now predominantly dark in color (Kettlewell 1959).

[34] Engineers refer to this kind of activity as *redesign* (IEEE 1987, Jones 1984, Ch. 3).

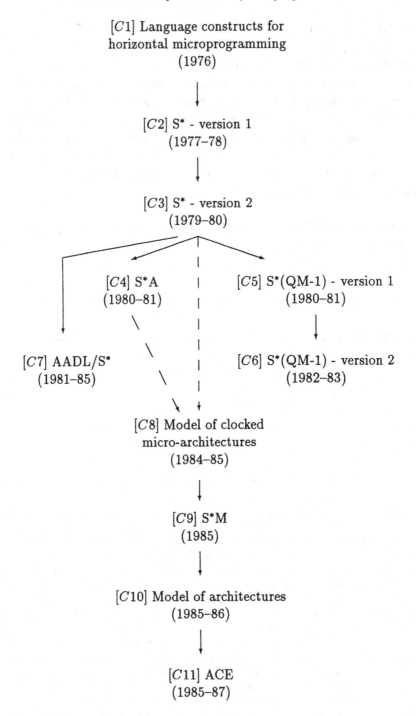

Fig. 5.12 Chronology of the S* family of languages.

which include as members, the 8086, 80186, 80286, and 80386 processors. (Liu and Gibson 1986, Morse, Isaacson and Albert 1987).

Similarly, one may encounter the notion of *language families* – as exemplified by the Euler/Algol–W/PL–360/Pascal/Modula series of programming languages designed and implemented by Wirth and his coworkers (Wirth 1985b).

Discussion of such families inevitably includes the notion of evolution. However, the word is very often used in an informal manner and there is rarely (if at all) any detailed description of the evolutionary mechanism or a description of the design decisions sufficiently detailed as to allow one to reconstruct the precise relationship between family members.[35]

In the absence of detailed documentation of the design decisions for those families for which evolutionary claims have been made it is virtually impossible to try and explain these phylogenic design processes in evolutionary terms. Instead, I shall present here a far more modest and specialized group of experimental languages designed between 1975 and 1985 and for which there is a sufficiently available record of the design processes for me to attempt to explain the phylogenic design processes in evolutionary terms.

Example 5.12
This particular group of languages was designed by the author and his collaborators and constitutes what I have elsewhere called the S* *family of languages* (Dasgupta 1984). The 'family' consists of the partially machine-independent microprogramming language scheme S*; a machine-specific instantiation of S* with respect to Nanodata QM-1, called S*(QM-1); and the three architecture description languages S*A, S*M and ACE. In addition, Damm and his colleagues developed a comprehensive micro-programming language and verification system based on the so called AADL/S*M system (Damm *et al.* 1986, Damm 1988). The actual chronology for this entire effort is shown in fig. 5.12. As can be seen, the language design efforts were interspersed with phases in which language features or concepts (rather than entire languages) and models were developed. These phases were essential components in the development of the entire family.[36]

---

[35] In a few rare cases, the original designers have provided insight in a very general way into the genealogy of particular families. See, for example, Wirth (1985b) for his account of the history of the 'Wirth family' of languages, or Bell and Mudge (1978) and Bell *et al.* (1978) for accounts of the evolution of the PDP-11 and PDP-10 families respectively. Perhaps the best such discussion has come from Brinch Hansen's (1982) description of the language Edison developed from predecessors, in particular, Pascal and Concurrent Pascal.

[36] The main references for the various components of the chronology shown in fig. 5.12 are:

There are in fact, two main phylogenic processes represented in fig. 5.12. The first of these consists of [C1]–[C3], followed by branches to [C4], [C5] and [C7] respectively. The other is composed of the sequence [C8]–[C11]. The link between these two distinct processes is commonality in some of the language constructs.

Let us consider for the present the first of these processes, viz., [C1]–[C3]. More specifically, I will show how the development of the set of parallel statements constitutes an interesting phylogenic process of its own, and that it can be mapped onto the evolutionary model as plausibly as were the examples of ontogenic designs in section 5.4.

Phase 1: The earliest ideas concerning the development of high level microprogramming tools had led to the design of sequential microprogramming languages. However, since the majority of microarchitectures executed horizontal microprograms it becomes necessary to transform automatically, such high level sequential microprograms into executable horizontal microcode. Between 1974 and 1976, several microcode compaction algorithms were developed for this purpose (Landskov *et al.* 1980; see also examples 5.4 and 5.7 above).

Largely as a result of these developments it was realized that the automatic generation of horizontal microcode may not always yield optimal code (for reasons discussed in section 5.2). Thus, it seemed desirable that the microprogramming language should at least provide constructs for specifying horizontal microprograms explicitly. This would allow the microprogrammer to exercise this option in the case of critical or heavily used microcode segments that have to be as efficient as possible.

In response to this requirement several parallel constructs were proposed (component [C1]). These were, specifically, the following:

(i) The statement

$$\textbf{cobegin } M_1; M_2; \ldots; M_n \textbf{ coend}$$

where the M_i's denote micro-operations. This construct was adopted from Dijkstra (1968) and is used to specify that the micro-operations are to execute concurrently within one microcycle.[37]

[C1]: Dasgupta (1977); [C2] Dasgupta (1978); [C3] Dasgupta (1980a, 1980b, 1984); [C4] Dasgupta (1983, 1984); [C5] Klassen and Dasgupta (1981); [C6] Dasgupta and Wagner (1984), Wagner and Dasgupta (1982); [C7] Damm *et al.* (1986), Damm (1988); [C8] Dasgupta (1985); [C9] Dasgupta and Heinanen (1985), Dasgupta, Wilsey and Heinanen (1986); Dasgupta (1989b); [C10] Wilsey and Dasgupta (1988, 1989a); [C11] Wilsey and Dasgupta (1989b).

[37] In the terminology of computer microarchitecture and microprogramming, a microcycle is

(ii) The statement

$$\text{shseq } S_1; S_2 \text{ end}$$

where S_1 is a single micro-operation or a **cobegin** statement, and S_2 is a single micro-operation, a **cobegin** statement or another **shseq** statement. This construct specifies that S_1 begins and completes execution before S_2 begins to execute; and that both S_1 and S_2 are completed within one microcycle.

(iii) The statement

$$\text{dur } S_1 \text{ do } S_2 \text{ end}$$

where S_1 is a micro-operation, and S_2 is another **dur** statement or a sequence

$$S_{21}; \ S_{22}; \ \ldots \ ; \ S_{2k}$$

in which S_{2i} is a micro-operation, a **shseq**, a **cobegin** or the 'empty' microstatement (which does nothing but consumes a micro-cycle; it corresponds to the 'no-op' microinstruction) such that the execution of S_{2i} is completed in a microcycle preceding the microcycle in which $S_{2,i+1}$ is initiated (for $1 \le i \le k-1$). The **dur** statement specifies that S_1 and S_2 will be executed concurrently. However, the duration of this statement may exceed a single microcycle which is not the case for the **cobegin** statement.

(iv) The statement

$$\text{lseq } S_1 \ ; \ S_2 \ ; \ \ldots \ ; \ S_n \text{ end}$$

where each S_i is a micro-operation or one of the statements defined above. This specifies, simply, that S_i completes execution in a microcycle preceding that in which S_{i+1} begins execution.

The **lseq** statement is, thus, the multicycle analog of the **shseq** statement while the **dur** statement is the multicycle analog of the **cobegin** statement.

The component $[C1]$ was concerned with the design of parallel statements only. It was assumed that other constructs existed for the representation of indivisible micro-operations.

Phase 2: The design problem in the case of component $[C2]$ was to develop the essential structure of a tool for abstraction that would facilitate the description, understanding and verification of microprograms and would be machine-independent in the following sense. It would provide:

---

the minimum possible time between the execution of two consecutive microinstructions. Thus a microcycle is taken as the 'typical' duration for the execution of a microinstruction (Dasgupta 1989a).

(a) A capability for constructing control structures for designating clearly and without ambiguity, both sequential and parallel flow of control.
(b) A capability for describing and arbitrarily naming microprogrammable data objects.
(c) A capability for constructing microprograms whose structure and correctness could be discerned and understood without reference to any control store organizations.

The result was the microprogramming language schema S* (component [*C*2]). Of special interest here are the following constructs in S*.

(i) The class of simple statements which can only correspond to machine-specific micro-operations. S* defines only the form (or schema) for these statements. The actual legal simple statements and their semantics are defined when S* is instantiated with respect to a specific microprogrammable machine.[38] The class of simple statements recognized in S* includes the assignment, a multiway **if** statement and the **goto**.
(ii) A set of parallel statements that allow various forms of micro-parallelism to be expressed. These are described more fully below.

There are essentially three constructs for expressing micro-parallelism. The first of these is the

$$\textbf{cobegin } S_1 ; S_2 ; \ldots ; S_n \textbf{ coend}$$

statement, where $S_1 , \ldots , S_n$ represent simple statements that are all executed concurrently within one microcycle.

However, as is well known, parallelism in microprograms is not simply limited to concurrently executable statements. In actual micro-architectures, two or more micro-operations may be executed in disjoint phases of a microcycle so that micro-operations may actually execute sequentially within the microcycle although if the latter is taken as the basic time unit, the micro-operations *appear* to execute in parallel during the microcycle. To allow such situations to be specified, S* provides the

$$\textbf{cocycle } S_1 ; S_2 ; \ldots ; S_n \textbf{ coend}$$

statement where (i) each S_i is either a simple or a concurrent statement; (ii) the execution of S_i must terminate before the execution of S_{i+1} begins (for $1 \leq i \leq n - 1$); and (iii) all statements are executed in the same microcycle.

---

[38] Thus, the schema S* cannot itself be used to write microprograms. It must be instantiated with respect to a particular machine before it can be used. S* (QM-1) ([*C*5] in fig. 5.12) is one such instantiation. For other instantiations see Damm *et al.* (1986).

The **cobegin** and **cocycle** statements correspond to single microcycle parallelism. Multi-microcycle parallelism is expressible in S* by means of the

$$\textbf{dur } S_1 \textbf{ do } S_2 \textbf{ end}$$

statement in which S_1 is a simple statement, S_2 is another (nested) **dur** statement, or a sequence

$$S_{21} \; ; \; S_{22} \; ; \; \dots \; ; \; S_{2k}$$

such that (i) S_{2i} $(1 \leq i \leq k)$ is a simple, **cobegin**, **cocycle** or empty statement; (ii) for $1 \leq j \leq k - 1$, the execution of S_{2j} is completed in a microcycle immediately preceding the microcycle in which $S_{2,j+1}$ begins; and (iii) S_1 and S_2 will execute concurrently.

Finally, S* includes the

$$\textbf{region } S_1 \; ; \; S_2 \; ; \; \dots \; ; \; S_n \textbf{ end}$$

construct, where S_i is any other S* statement, which carries with it, the meaning that each S_{i+1} can only begin execution in a microcycle following the one in which S_i terminates $1 \leq i \leq n - 1$.

Clearly, the progenitors of the parallel statements of S* are the constructs of component $[C1]$. The respective constructs are

	$[C1]$		$[C2]$
	cobegin		cobegin
	shseq	$\longrightarrow$	cocycle
	dur		dur
	lseq		region

However, there have been two modifications in adopting the constructs in $[C1]$ for $[C2]$: the **shseq** is replaced by the **cocycle** and the **lseq** has been replaced by the **region** statement. The question is: are these modifications explainable according to the evolutionary model?

For this to be the case, it will be required to be shown that the parallel statements of $[C1]$ produced a misfit as far as the requirements for S* were concerned and that the parallel statements in $[C2]$ were the new constructs produced in order to eliminate the misfit.

The arguments are as follows:

(a) One of the basic requirements in designing S* was that it must have the capacity to represent (machine-specific) micro-operations and concurrently executing sets of such micro-operations. Micro-operations are represented in S* by the class of simple statements. [C1] had provided the capacity to express concurrently executing micro-operations that completed within a single microcycle by virtue of the **cobegin** statement. There is a slight misfit between the **cobegin** in [C1] and the requirements of S* since in the latter, micro-operations are symbolized by simple statements. This discrepancy is corrected by a slight change in the syntax of the **cobegin** for S*. Thus, the **cobegin** in [C1] has been adopted in [C2] with the slightest of changes to eliminate a minor misfit.

(b) Another capability demanded of S* is the need to be able to express sets of micro-operations that all begin and complete execution in the same microcycle but, possibly, in different phases of the microcycle.

The **shseq** in [C1] provide this capability. However, suppose that the micro-architecture of concern (i.e., the architecture on which the microprogram is to run) has a 4-phase cycle; and if it is required to specify the execution of four micro-operations M_1, M_2, M_3 and M_4 where M_i executes in phases i ($1 \leq i \leq 4$).[39] Using the **shseq** statement of [C1] this situation is expressible as

        shseq M_1
            shseq M_2 ;
                shseq
                    M_3 ;
                    M_4
                end
            end
        end

Clearly this satisfies the basic functional requirement but is unduly cumbersome in structure. It would be much more convenient to be able to write

$$\textbf{shseq } M_1 \text{ ; } M_2 \text{ ; } M_3 \text{ ; } M_4 \textbf{ end}$$

which we cannot, given the defined syntax of the **shseq** statement in [C1].

---

[39] This is not a 'pathological' situation. Micro-architectures and polyphase microcycles are often designed so that it is possible to complete a particular sequence of micro-operations within a microcycle (Dasgupta 1989a).

Thus, there is a misfit between the **shseq** statement of [$C1$] and an *aesthetic* requirement on one hand – the requirement that stipulates simplicity and elegance – and a
pragmatic requirement on the other – that stipulates convenience of use.

There is a second misfit between **shseq** and another pragmatic requirement for S*;
and that is, the keywords prefixing the statements should reflect very closely the kind
of control structures the statements represent. The 'shseq' keyword does not clearly
express the fact that the constituents are to execute within a microcycle.

The result of eliminating these misfits is the **cocycle** statement in [$C2$].

(c) The capacity to express micro-parallelism that spans two or more cycles was also
a requirement for S*. The **dur** statement in [$C1$] appears to satisfy this requirement
almost completely (except that the term 'micro-operation' in [$C1$]'s **dur** statement
is to be replaced by 'simple statement' in [$C2$]).

(d) As pointed out, a major requirement that drove the design of S* was that the
microprogrammer must be afforded the choice of either leaving parallelism detection
and compaction to the compiler or specifying parallelism explicitly and thereby 'optimizing' the code at the S* level itself. In the latter case, the microprogrammer must
not only be able to describe exactly which operations should be done in parallel, and
how the parallel statements should be sequenced; he or she must also be allowed to
issue a compiler directive indicating that such program components should *not* be
analyzed for automatic parallelism detection and compaction; that, in other words,
such program components are 'optimized' *regions* in the above sense.

The **lseq** statement in [$C1$] essentially provided these capabilities. The only source
of dissatisfaction is, once more, a pragmatic one – the fact that the keyword 'lseq'
did not capture the sense of the construct. This misfit is eliminated by replacing in
[$C2$], the keyword 'lseq' by '**region**'. Hence the **region** statement in [$C2$].

Phase 3 A revised version of S* was developed in the year following its first publication and is shown as [$C3$] in fig. 5.12. The parallel statements in [$C3$] are as
follows.

Let the notation '$S_1 \theta S_2$' signify either '$S_1 \square S_2$' or '$S_1 ; S_2$', where '$S_1 \square S_2$' denotes
the parallel composition of S_1 and S_2 and '$S_1 ; S_2$' denotes the usual sequential
composition. Using this notation the following parallel statements were proposed:

    (P1) **cocycle** $S_1 \theta S_2$ **coend**
    (P2) **stcycle** $S_1 \theta S_2$ **stend**

where in (P1), S_1 and S_2 are simple or composites of simple statements, and in (P2) S_1, S_2 are simple, composites of simple, **cocycle** or **stcycle** statements.[40]

The **cocycle** statement signifies that the composite event $S_1 \; \theta \; S_2$ begins and ends in the same microcycle. Where 'θ' is the '$\square$' operator, S_1 and S_2 will execute concurrently; where it is the ';' operator, S_1 and S_2 will execute sequentially in the same microcycle.

The **stcycle** signifies that the composite event $S_1 \; \theta \; S_2$ begins in a new microcycle. Its termination is not defined by the construct itself. Rather, it is determined by the requirements of its constituent statements. Thus, the basic distinction between the two constructs lies in the specified duration of their actions – the duration of a **cocycle** is exactly one microcycle while that of the **stcycle** is at least one but possibly several microcycles.

The **region** statement in [C3] remains identical to its form in [C2].

We thus see the following differences in the parallel statements of [C2] and [C3].

[C2]		[C3]
cobegin		cocycle
cocycle	$\longrightarrow$	stcycle
dur		region
region		

The sequence of events that caused this modification in the parallel statements was as follows.

On completing the first version of S* [C2], two distinct sets of tests were conducted to assess its adequacy. On one hand, an instantiation of S* was performed with respect to the microprogrammable minicomputer Varian 75 (Varian 1975) to determine empirically whether S* was usable for this rather complex micro-architecture. The resulting instantiated language was called S*(V75) (Dasgupta 1980b).

On the other hand, *thought experiments* were conducted in which various 'scenarios' of microparallelism were contrived to see whether the constructs of [C2] could describe these scenarios.[41]

---

[40] A *composite* of simple statements $S_1, \ldots, S_n$ is the statement $S_1 \; \theta \; S_2 \ldots \theta S_n$ possibly with the addition of parenthetic delimiters **do** ... **od** or the delimiters **cocycle** ... **coend**, **stcycle** ... **stend**. In the absence of delimiters a left-to-right priority of the operator θ holds.

[41] As the term suggests, a thought experiment is an imaginary experiment often used to replace a real experiment. Thought experiments are essentially situations in which certain plausible conditions are imagined to hold from which certain consequences are derived through logical or empirically

In the course of the thought experiment stage, the 'problem of micro-parallelism' was re-analyzed into two orthogonal subproblems (Dasgupta 1980a):

(1) The necessity to be able to distinguish between: (a) Two or more micro-operations whose executions begin and end in a *single* microcycle; and (b) two or more micro-operations the execution of at least one of which spans *two or more* microcycles.

(2) The necessity to be able to distinguish between: (a) Two or more micro-operations executing concurrently in the same phase or in overlapping phases; and (b) two or more micro-operations executing in *disjoint* phases of the same microcycle.

Subproblem (1) is a problem of detecting single or multiple microcycle events. Subproblem (2) is one of distinguishing 'true' concurrency from 'apparent' concurrency.

These two subproblems, then, represented a *new* set of requirements which the parallel statements in [C2] were required to satisfy. And, though the parallel statements in [C2] were *functionally* adequate for this purpose, they were *aesthetically* inadequate in that the constructs in [C2] did not preserve a clean separation between the orthogonal subproblems (1) and (2).[42] The misfit was, thus, aesthetic in origin rather than functional. In the terminology of chapter 3, it was a conceptual requirement rather than an empirical one that caused the parallel statements in [C3] to replace those developed earlier in [C2].

To summarize, the development of S* between 1976 and 1980 comprised of three successive mature designs: first, a set of language features for expressing microparallelism, [C1]; next, the first version of S*, [C2]; finally, the second version of S*, [C3]. The path through these stages denotes a phylogenic design process which (as indicated by fig. 5.12) in fact subsequently branched along a number of different directions. Having supplied the details of the transitions between [C1] and [C2], and between [C2] and [C3], I have suggested that in this particular case there is sufficient evidence that it follows the evolutionary model described in section 5.3.

---

justified arguments. Thought experiments have played a specially important role in the history of physics (see, e.g., Holton 1952). As the above discussion indicates, it can also play a significant role in testing the satisfactoriness of designs.

[42] To appreciate this point note that the **cobegin** statement in [C2] encapsulates the issues of both 'real' concurrency and (single microcycle) timing. The **cocycle** in [C2] encapsulates the issues of both 'apparent' concurrency and (single microcycle) timing. Thus the concurrency subproblem is distributed between the two statements, and both statements embed the common concept of single microcycle timing. Likewise, the **dur** statement in [C2] embeds the 'real' concurrency issue so that real concurrency is expressible by both the **cobegin** and **dur** statements.

There are two additional points to note in this regard. Firstly, the designs in the phylogenic case are mature designs that either have been implemented or are operational and for which the time lapse for the entire design process may be significant, possibly measurable in terms of years rather than days, weeks, or months as in the ontogenic case.

Secondly, a single cycle of phylogenic design evolution will, in general, itself constitute one or (usually) more cycles of ontogenic evolution (fig. 5.13)

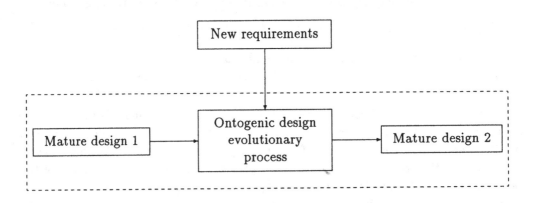

One cycle of phylogenic design evolution

Fig. 5.13 Nesting of ontogenic design in phylogenic design.

As I have already remarked, the S* family of fig. 5.12 includes one other major phylogenic pathway, consisting of [C8]–[C11]. It can be shown that [C8]–[C11] also constitute a phylogenic process in which the successive mature designs are either abstract models of micro-architectures or architecture description languages (ADLs) for specifying micro-architectures and that the transition between the successive designs can be mapped onto the evolutionary model.
End Example

Thus far in all the examples, I have followed the same method for presenting the evidence in support of the evolutionary model. A particular design process *as it was originally presented* in the literature was described in some detail. It was then shown how this process could be explained in terms of the evolutionary model of fig. 5.5. In the next example the nature of the evidence and the method of its presentation will be somewhat different. For this example is based not upon a single design process as has been the case so far but upon a range of *projects* which were studied and from which general conclusions were drawn, by other authors.

The main purpose of this example is to provide further – and rather massive – instances of phylogenic design processes for which, while it is not possible to *directly* explain the processes in terms of the evolutionary model of section 5.3, it appears *highly plausible* that the evolutionary model is empirically valid.

Example 5.13

The work considered here is the pioneering set of studies conducted for over a decade by Lehman and Belady on what they called *program evolution dynamics* (Lehman 1980a, 1980b, 1984, Lehman and Belady 1985, Belady and Lehman 1976, 1979).

As the empirical basis of their work, Lehman and Belady studied the changes in certain characteristics of several large programs across a succession of *versions* or *releases*. Specific examples of such programs were (Belady and Lehman 1979):

(i) The IBM OS/360 operating system consisting (at its final release) of approximately 3.5 million assembly language statements and over 6000 modules, involving 21 releases over 6 years.

(ii) The IBM DOS/360 operating system consisting of approximately 900,000 assembly language statements and over 2000 modules, involving 27 releases over 6 years.

(iii) A banking system consisting of about 45,000 Algol statements and involving 10 releases over 3 years.

(iv) Two electronic switching systems, the first consisting of approximately 178,000 assembly language statements involving some 28 releases over 4 years, the second consisting of approximately 212,000 assembly language statements and involving 18 releases over 3 years.

The specific characteristics that were studied and measured across the span of the programs' lives were:

(a) The actual number of statements in each program.
(b) The number of modules comprising the program.
(c) The average number of instructions per module.
(d) The number of modules that required change between successive releases.

The main results of these quantitative studies are summarized by Lehman and Belady in the form of their qualitative *laws of program evolution* (Lehman 1974, Belady and Lehman 1976, Lehman 1980):

Law I: The Law of Continuing Change. A system that is used undergoes continuous change until it becomes more economical to replace it by a new or restructured system.

Law II: The Law of Increasing Entropy (Unstructuredness). The entropy of a system increases with time unless specific work is executed to maintain or reduce it.

Law III: The Law of Statistically Smooth Growth. Growth trend measures of global system attributes may appear stochastic locally in time or space but are self-regulating and statistically smooth.

Law IV: The Law of Invariant Work Rate. During the active life of a program the global activity rate in the associated programming project is statistically invariant.

Law V: The Law of Perceived Complexity. During the active life of a program, the release content (changes, additions, deletions) of the successive releases is statistically invariant.

From the viewpoint of our evolutionary model the only relevant law here is the Law of Continuing Change. The causal basis for this law as suggested in (Belady and Lehman 1979, Lehman 1984) is as follows.

Large programs of the sort studied by Lehman and Belady are instances of what they call *Type E* systems. A Type E program is one that is embedded in its operational environment and implements an application in that environment. Type E programs model real world problems that cannot be precisely or completely specified (i.e., they model ill-structured problems – see chapter 3). Thus, such programs cannot be said to *satisfy* specifications in the ordinary sense of the latter term. The satisfactoriness or acceptability of a Type E program is meaningfully determined only by *user satisfaction* after the system becomes operational. And, once the system becomes operational its use will itself suggest functions, applications and purposes other than those originally envisioned. The operational environment itself changes and the program, if it is to continue to provide satisfaction to the user, will also be forced to change (or rather, be changed) accordingly. Hence the Law of Continuing Change.

The Lehman–Belady laws have been seriously criticized by Lawrence (1982) who conducted statistical tests to corroborate (or refute) the laws. In contrast to his largely negative conclusions concerning Laws II–V his tests did tend to confirm Law I. The basis for his confirmation of this law was the following argument.

If a program *does not* undergo continual change, the average number of modules handled per release should be zero. His findings were otherwise – to the extent that Lawrence proposed a stronger version of this law:

Systems *grow* in size over their useful life.

That is, not only do type E programs change continually; they increase in size until they are replaced.

It is quite clear that what Lehman and Belady studied were phylogenic processes. For a given system (the OS/360, the banking system, etc.), each release constituted a mature design. Thus the succession of releases or versions represented a phylogenic profile of the system.

Furthermore, the causal basis for the Law of Continuing Change (or its stronger version due to Lawrence (1982)) as described above appears to correspond to the cycle of events in the evolutionary model (fig. 5.5). At the start of any one such cycle an implemented design – the current release or version – is tested in the (then current) operational environment for user satisfaction (with respect to functionality, performance or any other requirement significant to the user). If a new requirement has been introduced – reflecting a change in the operational environment – then it is likely that the current system will not meet the requirement. The (implemented) design and the current requirement set are mutually maladapted. The misfit is eliminated by changing the system's design thereby releasing a new version. The (phylogenic) evolutionary cycle is thus completed.

End Example

Part II

Design Paradigms

Chapter 6

The Concept of a Design Paradigm

6.1 INTRODUCTION

This chapter initiates and serves as a preamble to a systematic discussion of several *design paradigms*. The concept of a paradigm is central, not only to this (the second) part of the book but also to the discussion of the relationship between design and science in Part III. It is, thus, of some importance to specify as exactly as possible what I mean when I use the terms 'paradigm' and 'design paradigm' in this work. The necessity for such clarification becomes specially urgent given the fact that in certain intellectual circles the word 'paradigm' has assumed the unfortunate status of a cult-word.

The present chapter also serves a second, less obvious, function. And that is, to demarcate the fundamentally *descriptive* spirit of the preceding chapters from the pronounced *prescriptive* character of the chapters to follow.

The discipline of design is necessarily Janus-faced. On the one hand the act of design is a cognitive and an intellectual process. Hence any theory of design must, at least in part, view design processes as *natural* processes that harness the capabilities inherent in, and are in turn harnessed to the limitations imposed by, human nature and intellect. A theory of design must at least in part be a cognitive theory and, therefore, descriptive in nature. Much of Part I was precisely that; in particular, the notion that design is an evolutionary phenomenon is a descriptive, empirical proposition – a consequence of the inherent bounds of our ability to make rational decisions.

On the other hand, design is also concerned with *constructing* artifacts and the deliberate effecting of change. A merely descriptive theory of design would be hopelessly inadequate in this regard. A theory of design that demands acceptance must also, necessarily, be a theory of action. It must prescribe, in general ways, *what to do* in order to effectively construct the artifacts we require and the changes we wish to make. This, then, is the *prescriptive* face of the discipline of design. Part II is fundamentally concerned with such prescriptive rules.

6.2 KUHNIAN PARADIGMS

In its ordinary or dictionary sense, a *paradigm* is an example, a pattern or a model as when we refer to the stored program computer conceived and described in the 1940s by Burks, Goldstine and von Neumann (1946) as a paradigm for all subsequent computer designs. Another instance of this dictionary sense is when we say that the Algol 60 report by Naur (1963) is a paradigm for the description and definition of a programming language.

This ordinary notion of a paradigm was greatly enlarged and enriched in the early 1960s by Thomas Kuhn's seminal treatise on the nature of the scientific process (Kuhn 1962). In this monograph Kuhn adopted this word in a very special way to advance a radically original account of the genesis and development of scientific disciplines. This work has exercised enormous influence, not only on the philosophy of science, but also on the social and behavioral sciences. Above all, it has profoundly affected how the more reflective working scientist views his or her craft.

Henceforth in this book, I shall use the term *Kuhnian paradigm* (or more briefly, *K-Paradigm*) whenever it is necessary to distinguish Kuhn's concept of a paradigm from either the dictionary sense or the sense that I shall shortly introduce in the context of design. Let me first, however, elucidate the concept of a Kuhnian paradigm.

It is now well known that in his original (1962) monograph, Kuhn employed the paradigm concept in a somewhat diffuse way to mean a number of different though loosely related things. In a paper that has become almost as celebrated as Kuhn's monograph itself, Masterman (1970) listed no less than twenty-one different ways in which 'paradigm' appears in Kuhn (1962). Largely in response to this and other criticisms of his work, in a series of later publications, Kuhn (1970a, 1970b, 1977) attempted to clarify and distill his notion of a paradigm. The discussion below is based on his later publications.[1]

A Kuhnian paradigm in its essence comprises two related concepts:

(a) A disciplinary matrix
(b) Exemplars

---

[1] Kuhn's (1962) work has been the subject of considerable discussion, analysis and criticism. Confining attention to its analysis from within Kuhn's discipline itself, viz., the philosophy and history of science, the reader is referred to Lakatos and Musgrave (1970) for several related discussions, Shapere (1964, 1966), Suppe (1977a) and the subsequent discussion in Suppe (1977b), and Laudan (1977, 1984).

The first of these is really a sociological entity. By a *disciplinary matrix* is meant a network of beliefs, values, techniques, theories, etc., that are shared by, or are common to, a given (scientific) community. More specifically, Kuhn (1970a, 1977) identifies the following sorts of components of a disciplinary matrix.

(A) Symbolic Generalizations: General, formal (or formalizable) assertions that are taken for granted and employed without question by members of the community. Typical examples are Newton's laws of motion in the domain of classical mechanics, Kepler's laws in planetary physics, Ohm's law and Kirchhoff's theorem in electricity, the definition of a formal grammar G as the 4-tuple $\langle V_N, V_T, P, S \rangle$ in the domain of computer languages or the characterization of Moore and Mealy machines in logic design.[2]

(B) Beliefs in metaphysical and heuristic models: That is, a commitment to, or a belief in, one or more abstract or physical *models* to which the relevant domain or discipline is assumed to conform. Historical examples of such beliefs in the natural sciences include: that molecules of a gas behave like small elastic billiard balls in random motion (Kuhn 1970a); that the orbital motions of planets obey the principle of uniform circular motion (Holton 1952); that species are immutable and are generated spontaneously (Mayr 1982); that when bodies are burnt (calcined) an entity called phlogiston escapes which must then be returned in order for the original body to be restored (Partington 1960); that the structure of an atom resembles a tiny planetary system (Holton 1952); and that two different kinds of blood flow in the arteries and veins respectively (Butterfield 1968).[3]

From the more recent domain of computer and related sciences examples of such commitments include: that computers are mathematical machines and, therefore, their behavior can be defined with mathematical precision and every detail deduced from the definition by the laws of logic (Hoare 1986); that any system (natural or artificial) capable of reasoning intelligently about a domain must, internally, contain

---

[2] Kuhn, as is the case with virtually all philosophers of science, concerns himself only with the natural sciences. His examples are thus entirely taken from the natural sciences and, in particular, from physics. The examples I shall give here span both the natural and the artificial sciences and, in particular, computer science.

[3] It is important to note – and this is in fact a central point in Kuhn's theory of paradigms – that many of these beliefs that are held by the practitioners of a discipline at particular points of time *may subsequently be shed* by these same practitioners or their successors. Thus, most of the above examples given above are, now, no longer part of *any* scientist's belief system. But they certainly were so in the past and, as further described below, they not only helped to determine the agenda of research in their relevant domains but also what were to be deemed as acceptable solutions.

representations of knowledge about that domain (Smith 1982); that at the micro-architectural level, a microprogrammed control unit functions as a computer within a computer (Dasgupta 1989a); and that functions are the primary building blocks for computer programs (Henderson 1980).

Note that some of these beliefs and commitments are virtually metaphysical or onto-logical in nature – that is, they are beliefs in some fundamental or essential character of the relevant domain. Uniform circular motion of the planets, the immutability of species and the mathematical nature of computers are examples of such *metaphysical models*. Others are more heuristic in nature – that is, they are not necessarily believed to be *really* true but are accepted *as if* they are true because it is useful to make such commitments. The billiard ball model of gas molecules, the notion of a control unit as an inner computer, functions as the primary building blocks for programs are examples of such *heuristic models*.

However, it does not really matter whether these models are construed as metaphysi-cal or heuristic. What is important is that each such model serves as a starting point for the solution of problems in the relevant domain or serves as a constraint which must be satisfied by solutions to problems in the domain.

Example 6.1
The assumption of the elastic billiard ball model led, very fruitfully to the develop-ment of the kinetic theory of gases (Holton 1952).
End Example

Example 6.2
The planetary model of the atom was first invented by Rutherford as a consequence of the celebrated experiments that he and his coworkers carried out in his laboratory. It then became the foundation for subsequent developments by Bohr and others of the quantum theoretical model of atomic structure (Holton 1952).
End Example

Example 6.3
The phlogiston theory was proposed in the latter half of the 17th century by the German chemists J.-J. Becher and G.E. Stahl. It was so firmly held to be true by chemists for well over a century, that many chemists were reluctant to accept Lavoisier's results on the role of oxygen in combustion when these were published a century later as his theory did not necessitate the presence of phlogiston (Partington 1960, Berry 1954).
End Example

Example 6.4

The strictly mathematical nature of computers was the starting point and the foundation for the development of the formal or mathematical theories of programming and programming languages as pioneered by Floyd (1967), Hoare (1969) and Scott (1970) and later developed by others (Dijkstra 1976, Stoy 1977, Gries 1981, de Bakker 1980).

End Example

Example 6.5

The notion of functions as the building blocks for computer programs formed the basis for the development of a distinct style of programming called functional programming (Backus 1978, Henderson 1980).

End Example

Example 6.6

Commitment to the view of a microprogrammed control unit as a computer-within-a-computer served as a basis, in the 1970s for the development of a class of computers called 'universal host machines' in which microprogramming was taken to be the fundamental mode of programming (Dasgupta 1989a, Neuhauser and Flynn 1988). This same commitment served as the foundation for the development of high level microprogramming languages (Dasgupta 1989b, Davidson 1988).

End Example

Example 6.7

The model of intelligent systems as containing their own representation of knowledge about the world has been the lynch pin in the development of much of the field of artificial intelligence (AI) in the past decade and a half and, in particular, in the technological development of knowledge-based systems (Brachman and Levesque 1985, Charniak and McDermott 1985).

End Example

(C) Values: This is the third type of component in the disciplinary matrix of a Kuhnian paradigm. One of Kuhn's examples is the constellation of values held by members of a scientific community regarding prediction: that they should preferably be quantitative rather than qualitative, that they should be accurate, and so on. Another instance is the desire for simplicity of a theory or a solution as embodied for example in the principle known as Occam's Razor. This principle, due to the medieval English philosopher William of Occam states that the hypothesis or explanation involving the fewest assumptions is the best. Like simplicity, the search for beauty is another powerful aesthetic imperative that may serve as a basic component of a

scientist's value system (Chandrasekhar 1987). Perhaps the most celebrated instance of values driving scientific investigation is Einstein's reluctance to accept quantum mechanics as an ultimate explanation of the physical world. This reluctance lay in his innermost conviction that the principles of causality and determinism were the fundamental governors of nature and, therefore, that the indeterminism implied by quantum mechanics was merely a consequence of our state of ignorance about the ultimate nature of physical reality.[4]

I have discussed at some length the central role of values in design and the effects they have on the selection and investigation of research problems in the design disciplines (chapter 2, section 2.2; see in particular, examples 2.1, 2.2 and 2.5). Values such as elegance, ease of use, simplicity and beauty are, thus, as commonly situated in the disciplinary matrix of the 'scientist of the artificial' or applied scientist as in that of the natural scientist.[5]

(D) Exemplars or Shared Examples: This is the fourth sort of component of what Kuhn calls a disciplinary matrix. Recall from above that 'disciplinary matrix' is, in turn, one of Kuhn's meanings of the word 'paradigm'. However, Kuhn (1962) also used the latter word to refer specifically to exemplars – which, of course, is more akin to the dictionary meaning. Thus, the concept of a set of shared examples or exemplars plays a very special role in the notion of a Kuhnian paradigm whether as a constituent of a larger disciplinary matrix or by itself. In his later publications, Kuhn (1970a, 1977) limited the use of 'paradigm' to the concept of a disciplinary matrix of which exemplars constitute an element.

Exemplars are the actual problem–solution complexes that the students of a scientific discipline encounter in the course of their education, training and research apprenticeship – through laboratory work, examinations and the solving of textbook exercises – and by scientific practitioners during their research careers. Exemplars become shared within a particular community in the sense that all members of that community will have encountered, studied, debated and solved these problems in the course of their apprenticeship and post-apprenticeship careers.

---

[4] One of Einstein's most memorable dicta on this matter was his remark 'Subtle is the Lord but malicious He is not' by which according to Pais (1982) he meant that 'Nature hides her secrets because of her essential loftiness but not by means of ruse'. It may be noted that holding causality as a fundamental tenet can be construed as much a metaphysical belief as a value. The borderline is quite fuzzy. For an extensive discussion of Einstein's values and beliefs, and their impact on both his own researches and his views on the development of quantum physics, see Pais (1982) and many of the papers in Holton and Elkana (1982) – in particular, Jammer (1982).

[5] 'When we recognize the battle against chaos, mess and unmastered complexity as one of computing science's major callings we must admit that "Beauty is our Business" ' (Dijkstra 1980).

Viewed conventionally, such problem–solution complexes are construed as applications of the theoretical principles – the symbolic generalizations referred to in (A) above – learned by the student or practitioner. Their intent is to sharpen the student's abilities to solve problems in the relevant discipline. Kuhn (1970a, 1977), however, insists that exemplars play a far more fundamental role in scientific education and research and, consequently, have a far deeper position in a scientific paradigm than mere application of theory. He suggests that in the course of dealing with exemplars relevant to a particular theoretical topic the student may be required to traverse amongst several symbolic generalizations. Kuhn's own example of this is taken from Newton's second law of motion which is denoted in standard form by the formula

$$F = ma$$

However, this law has many alternate guises that are pertinent to specific types of problems. For example, in the case of free fall the relevant symbolic generalization is

$$mg = m \frac{d^2 s}{dt^2}$$

and in the case of simple pendulum, it is

$$mg \sin \theta = -ml \frac{d^2 \theta}{dt^2}$$

and so on. In solving problems in classical mechanics the student learns to recognize which symbolic generalizations are relevant in given situations; see patterns; draw analogies between past problems and present ones and, as a consequence (using Kuhn's (1970) elegant phrase), to 'interrelate symbols and attach them to nature' in ways that had proved fruitful before.

Exemplars are, thus, means of acquiring *ways of seeing* and *intimately knowing* a discipline.

Example 6.8
In chapter 5, example 5.5, the problem of designing optimal minimally encoded microinstruction word organizations was described. To repeat, this problem can be specified as follows:

(i) Let $M = \{m_1, m_2, \ldots, m_r\}$ be the set of micro-operations for the computer that is being designed.
(ii) Let C_i denote a subset of M such that any pair of micro-operations in C_i cannot be executed from the same microinstruction (because of conflicts in their resource usage, say). Call C_i a *compatible class* (CC).

(iii) Let $C = \{C_1, C_2, \ldots, C_k\}$ be a set of such CCs such that each $m_j \in M$ appears in exactly one such $C_i \in C$. (In general there may be more than one set of such CCs).

(iv) Let $|C_i|$ denote the number of micro-operations in C_i.

Each C_i can, then, be encoded in a single field F_i of the microinstructions using

$$B_i = \lceil \log_2(|C_i|) + 1 \rceil$$

bits. The total length of the microinstruction would be

$$B = \sum_{i=1}^{k} B_i$$

where $|C| = k$. The problem is, to determine a set of $C_{\min}$ of CCs such that the corresponding length, B, is the minimum.

This problem, the way it is posed above, and its subsequent series of solutions constitute a classic example of the role of Kuhnian exemplars in the domain of computer science. For, almost all the early solutions were based on seeing similarities between this problem and a class of problems in finite automata and switching theory.

More specifically, Grasselli and Montanari (1970) were the first to couch the problem in the form of a *prime implicant covering problem* such that well known methods in switching theory for solving such cover table problems (Kohavi 1970, McCluskey 1986) could be applied. In their approach, they defined a *prime* compatibility class as follows.

A *maximal compatibility class* (MCC) is a CC to which no micro-operation can be added without violating the pairwise compatibility relation. A CC C_i is a *prime* CC if:

(a) C_i is nonmaximal and $|C_i| = 2^p - 1, p = 1, 2, \ldots$; or
(b) C_i is maximal and $|C_i| \neq 2^q, q = 1, 2, \ldots$

Grasselli and Montanari then show that a minimal solution can be obtained from the set of prime CCs by constructing a cover table that lists all the prime CCs and the micro-operations each of these covers. Any of the techniques to solve a cover table (Kohavi 1970, McCluskey 1986) can then be applied to obtain an optimal solution.

A more efficient method was subsequently devised by Das, Banerji and Chattopadhyay (1973). In their case, the set of all MCCs were first computed and a cover table based on these MCCs (rather than on the much larger number of prime CCs) was constructed. Once more the word length minimization problem is formulated as a cover table problem which is then solved using or by modifying techniques well known in switching theory.[6]

In summary, the prime implicant cover table problem is precisely an instance of the exemplars that Kuhn writes of: a standard problem with several well known solution techniques that are widely studied by, and familiar to, students of logic design and switching and finite automata theory. Grasselli and Montanari, Das and his coworkers all *saw* the word length minimization problem in terms of this exemplar and were, then, able to fruitfully develop methods for its solution by drawing upon the similarity.
End Example

6.3 DEFINING THE DESIGN PARADIGM CONCEPT

One of the major themes of this book is that the concept of the Kuhnian paradigm plays a role in the design disciplines that is very similar to – indeed is indistinguishable from – its role in the natural sciences (as elucidated by Kuhn (1962, 1970a, 1970b, 1977) and Laudan (1977)). Exactly how and why this is the case is the subject of Part III. Furthermore, while in section 6.2 above I have described what a Kuhnian paradigm is, the exact role that Kuhnian paradigms play in the development of a scientific discipline was left unexplained. This too will be discussed in Part III.

Our concern in this chapter (and this section in particular) is the elucidation of the concept of a *design paradigm* in the light of what has been said about Kuhnian paradigms.

A design paradigm is to design what a set of heuristic and/or metaphysical models (within a Kuhnian paradigm) is to science. Thus, the concept of a design paradigm is not (even approximately) equivalent to the concept of a Kuhnian paradigm; it is much less than that in the very same sense that beliefs in models is less than (being a part of) a Kuhnian paradigm. The scientist assumes, believes in, or is committed to, one or more abstract or physical models such that these models serve as a framework or starting point for the identification and solution of problems in that scientist's domain. Similarly, a design paradigm serves as a framework or starting point for the solution of design problems.

---

[6] For further discussions on this problem and its history see, in particular, Das, Banerji and Chattopadhyay (1973), Agerwala (1976), Dasgupta (1979), Banerji and Raymond (1982) and Mueller and Varghese (1988).

More precisely, a design paradigm

(a) Is an abstract prescriptive model of the design process that
(b) serves as a useful schema for constructing practical design methods, procedures, and tools for conducting design.

Some additional comments are required to qualify the above 'working' definition.

First, a design paradigm is fundamentally a *prescriptive* model of the design process. That is, a design paradigm comes into being when one or more members of a design community 'sees' the design process in a certain way, or believes that the 'essential' nature of design processes is of a certain kind, or feels that it would be fruitful to assume that design processes bear a certain similarity to some other activity. Based on such perceptions a model is then prescribed that encapsulates this particular view, ontology, or analogy. A design paradigm is thus born.

We see, then, that a design paradigm may, like models within a Kuhnian paradigm, be metaphysical in its origins, or it may be of a purely heuristic nature.

Second, by virtue of how it comes into existence, a design paradigm is a model that members of particular community may come to believe in or be committed to. Indeed, a shared belief in, or commitment to, the model may become the reason for an identifiable or distinct community to form. Various 'schools' may become associated with the design paradigm.

Third, design paradigms should not be confused with design methods. A *design method* is a (more or less) explicitly prescribed set of rules which can be followed by the designer in order to produce a design. A paradigm, according to the definition, may – and in general, will – provide a framework or schema for one or more design methods, just as it may serve as a framework or schema for descriptive and automated tools. Conversely, a given design method may be regarded as a concrete and practical embodiment of a design paradigm.

6.4 DESIGN PARADIGMS IN COMPUTER SCIENCE

In its brief life of less than five decades the discipline of computer science has witnessed the emergence of many design paradigms. In the chapters that follow I shall discuss several of these paradigms which for one reason or another appear to be the most important or interesting. It is appropriate then, to introduce these paradigms here so that they may serve in a very preliminary way to illustrate the abstract concept of a design paradigm discussed above.

(A) *The Analysis–Synthesis–Evaluation paradigm* (ASE): Given a set of requirements the design process, according to this paradigm, involves first a stage of *analysis* of the requirements, then one or more stages of *synthesis*, followed by a stage of *evaluation* of the design against the requirements. Nothing in this paradigm is actually stipulated as to how the synthesis stage should proceed or its relationship to the analysis stage or how the evaluation and synthesis stages are related to one another. As will be discussed in chapter 7, ASE is a very widely believed design paradigm in the engineering disciplines.

(B) *The Artificial Intelligence Paradigm*: As the name suggests this design paradigm is, in fact, a special case of a more general model of problem solving and cognition that has served to define an entire Kuhnian paradigm. The artificial intelligence community constitutes the adherents to and the supporters of this larger Kuhnian paradigm. The AI design paradigm is its application to the special problems of design.

In this paradigm, design problems are taken to be *ill-structured* (see chapter 3, section 3.3). The design process involves a symbolic representation of the problem called the *problem space* such that it can describe the initial problem state, the goal or desired problem state, and all other states that may be reached or considered in attempting to reach the goal state from the initial state. Transitions from one state to another are affected by applying one of a finite set of *operators*. The result of applying a sequence of operators is, in effect, a *search* for the solution through the problem space. Precisely which operators to apply and how to control the search so as to reach the desired goal state in an effective way, are determined in part by the designer's *knowledge* of the design domain and in part by a collection of general *heuristics*. This design paradigm is, thus, explicitly founded on the concepts of search, knowledge, and heuristics.

(C) *The Algorithmic Paradigm*: This takes as its main premise the notion that design problems are *well-structured* (see chapter 3, section 3.3). That is, the requirements are taken to be well defined and there are precisely defined criteria for determining whether or not a design meets the requirements. Given these conditions, the design process for a given design problem is characterized as the execution of a *domain-specific algorithm* which, given the requirements, generates a design satisfying the requirements in a finite number of steps.

(D) *The Formal Design Paradigm* (FD): The reader has already been introduced to FD by way of example 5.9 (chapter 5, section 5.4). It is based on the assumption that both the requirements and the design can be represented within the common framework of a *formal mathematical system*. The design, thus, becomes a mathematical proposition or a *theorem* that allegedly solves the *problem* as represented by the specification of the requirements. Furthermore, whether the design actually meets the requirements or not is determined by a formal *proof* using the rules of the underlying formal system. In FD then, the design process is a mathematical activity that uses the traditional methods of mathematical reasoning.

(E) *The Theory of Plausible Designs* (TPD): In contrast to the aforementioned ones, this design paradigm is of very recent origin. TPD is based on two main views of the design act: (i) That the design process is *evolutionary* such that the design and/or the requirements are continually modified so as to attain a state of mutual adaptation (see chapter 5). (ii) That a design at any stage of its development is always a collection of *tentative hypotheses* such that (a) one can at best only attempt to provide evidence in favor of the hypotheses – and thereby establish the *plausibility* of the design – by whatever *objective* means are at one's disposal at any given time, and (b) belief in the design's plausibility may, at a later stage, have to be revised if necessary in the light of new objective evidence.

The design process according to TPD, is a continuous, explicitly evolutionary activity that strives to establish, through objective evidence, the plausibility of the design. While this brief introduction does not make it obvious we shall see in chapter 9 that TPD is based on the view of design as an *empirical scientific* activity in contrast to FD which views design as a mathematical activity.

Chapter 7

The Analysis–Synthesis–Evaluation Paradigm

7.1 CHARACTERISTICS

The analysis–synthesis–evaluation paradigm (ASE) represents a widely held – and, in a sense, is the 'textbook' – view of the design process. Amongst its most influential proponents were Asimow (1962) and Jones (1963), and its prevalence in more recent times can be seen in such diverse fields as structural engineering (Rehak, Howard and Sriram 1985), device design (Middendorf 1986), and software engineering (Boehm 1981, Sommerville 1985).

According to ASE, the design process is thought to consist of three logically and temporally distinct stages: a stage of *analysis* of the requirements, followed by a stage of *synthesis*, followed by a stage of *evaluation*. In general, several instances of this three-stage sequence may be required in order to progress from a more abstract level to a more concrete level (fig. 7.1).

A highly articulated version of the ASE paradigm was formulated by Jones (1963)[1] who, as a general design theorist, proposed ASE as a paradigm applicable to all design and engineering disciplines. In his later book, Jones (1980) refers to the three stages as *divergence, transformation* and *convergence*.

Analysis
Jones (1980, p.64) explains the stage of divergence – as a more extended sense of analysis – in terms of the

> act of extending the boundary of a design situation so as to have a large enough and fruitful enough search space in which to seek a solution.

In his earlier, more detailed, presentation of a specific *method* based on ASE, Jones (1963) describes analysis as involving the identification of all possible factors that

---

[1] Indeed, my selection of a name for this paradigm is largely based on Jones' (1963) identification and naming of the three stages.

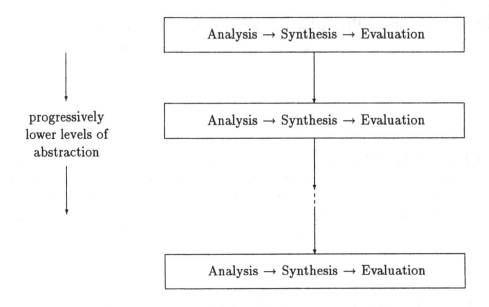

Fig. 7.1 Schematic of the ASE paradigm across several abstraction levels.

may be relevant to the given design situation, determination and resolution of all interactions among the factors and the eventual reduction of these factors to a complete set of specifications.

Synthesis

The act of synthesis – or 'transformation' (Jones 1980) – involves the construction of partial solutions for each of the distinct specifications and the integration of these partial designs into a complete form. According to the proponents of this paradigm, the synthesis stage is the locus of much of the creative aspects of the design process, where most of the imaginative thinking takes place (Jones 1963, 1980).

Evaluation

This stage, also called 'convergence' by Jones (1980), evaluates the design produced by the synthesis step by testing it against the specifications identified during the analysis stage. In the event alternative forms were produced during synthesis, this is also the stage in which a choice may be made between the alternatives as a result of evaluation.

7.2 SOME INSTANCES OF ASE-BASED DESIGN METHODS

Before we discuss more closely the validity of ASE as a design paradigm it is useful to consider some specific instances of design *methods* that appear to follow the paradigm. These examples will also serve to illuminate certain points of discussion later in the chapter.

Example 7.1

One of the seminal works in the 'sciences of the artificial' is Alexander's (1964) monograph which, though primarily addressing an architectural audience, has exercised considerable influence far outside the architectural community. Certainly, many computer scientists (including this author) appear to have been affected by this work in one way or another.[2,3]

For a given design problem (such as designing a kettle or a village, to take his examples) Alexander's method begins by listing all the relevant requirements that the designer can imagine. Let

$$R = \{r_1, r_2, \cdots, r_n\}$$

be the set of these requirements. In the *analysis* stage, the *interactions* between the requirements are first determined. Based on the interactions, a graph $G = \langle V, E \rangle$ is drawn where the elements of R are the vertices of the graph and there exists an edge between a vertex pair if there is an interaction between the corresponding pair of requirements. An edge – called a 'link' by Alexander – may be labeled with a negative sign if the corresponding requirements pair conflict with one another – that is, the satisfaction of one requirement excludes the satisfaction of the other (or makes it difficult to satisfy the other). The edge may be labeled with a positive sign if the corresponding requirements are in mutual agreement – that is, the satisfaction of one requirement supports the satisfaction of the other (or makes it easier to satisfy the other). In the case that there is no noticeable interaction between a pair of requirements, there will be no edge between the corresponding vertices.

Furthermore, the strength of conflict or concurrence can be denoted by numbers or 'weights' attached to the signs. Fig. 7.2 shows the structure of such a labeled graph for a set of eight requirements.[4]

[2,] See, for example, Mills (1976), Brinch Hansen (1977, p.13), Freeman (1980a,b), Zemanek (1980), Simon (1981, p.148), Dasgupta (1984).

[3] It is important for the reader to know however, that somewhat ironically, Alexander later wholly repudiated the particular method he described in this celebrated book. Indeed, in his later writings Alexander has eschewed design methods altogether (Alexander 1971a, 1971b).

[4] The ways by which the interactions between requirement pairs may be determined and the weights computed, are described in (Alexander 1964). Very briefly, interactions between require-

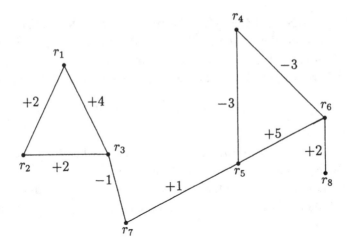

Fig. 7.2 A graph of interacting requirements.

The synthesis stage begins with such a graph $G = \langle V, E \rangle$ and consists of a series of steps of the following kind. In the first step, the most significant and closely interacting subsets of the requirements set are identified from G. Call these, $S_1 = \{s_{11}, s_{12}, \ldots, s_{1p}\}$. The subsets are so identified that the interactions between the subsets are far less significant than those within a subset.[5] Each such subset s_{1j} thus constitutes a (relatively independent) design subproblem which is then solved.

In the next step the subsets in S_1 are clustered into larger subsets $S_2 = \{s_{21}, s_{22}, \ldots, s_{2q}\}$ based on the interactions between the subsets in S_1. The s_{2j}'s thus constitute design problems that are (relatively) independent. These are then solved.

This process continues. In each step i, subsets of the previous step $i - 1$ (for which design solutions have been produced) are clustered into relatively independent subsets

---

ment pairs can be determined by drawing upon the designer's knowledge of, and experience in, the particular design domain, to identify which requirement pairs mutually reinforce one another, which are in conflict, and which have no mutual interaction. The weights are determined from data on past designs of similar artifacts by computing the 'correlation coefficients' for pairwise requirements. This is a probabilistic measure such that for a pair of requirements $\langle r_i, r_j \rangle$, the correlation coefficient $C_{ij} = 0$ if r_i, r_j are independent factors, $0 > C_{i,j} \geq 1$ is a measure of the extent to which r_i, r_j are in concurrence, and $-1 \leq C_{ij} < 0$ is a measure of the extent to which $\langle r_i, r_j \rangle$ are in conflict (Jenkins and Watts 1968, Hadley 1967). For details of the actual computations of the weights, see Alexander (1964, chapter 8 and Appendix 2).

[5] A hierarchical system of components $C_1, \ldots, C_n$ where each C_i is itself an aggregate of more primitive entities such that the interactions between the entities within the C_i's are appreciably stronger than those between the C_i's is called a *nearly decomposable system* (Simon 1981, Courtois 1977).

and are treated as relatively independent design problems which are then solved. Eventually, a single set – i.e., a single problem – will be obtained. The synthesis process is, therefore, hierarchical. For the graph of fig. 7.2, a hypothetical sequence of synthesis steps may be of the form depicted in fig. 7.3.

Steps

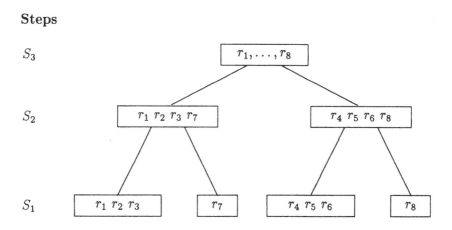

Fig. 7.3 A hierarchy obtained while solving the problem of fig. 7.2.

Clearly, for this synthesis procedure to work it is necessary for the subsets $s_{i1}, s_{i2}, \ldots, s_{ir_i}$ at any level i to satisfy the following two properties:

(a) The design problems represented by the s_{ij}'s must be solvable individually and independently.

(b) Given a set of solutions to the s_{ij}'s at level i it must be possible to solve the problems at the next higher level $i+1$ using the solutions to the s_{ij}'s. That is, the design of the components must be genuinely hierarchical.

Alexander devotes considerable attention to these two issues – in particular, on how to mathematically derive the subsets of the requirements so as to satisfy the above properties. Since we are specifically interested in Alexander's method only insofar as it exemplifies the analysis–synthesis–evaluation paradigm, and not on the design method *per se* I shall not pursue these issues any further here. I shall, however, return to these matters when I later discuss some of the difficulties inherent in ASE as a design paradigm.

The evaluation stage of ASE does not explicitly appear as a separate component in Alexander's method. Nor does he, either in his theoretical discussion or in the context of a worked out example (of an Indian village development) discuss the matter of testing the design against the requirements. [6] Indeed, a tacit assumption appears to be that no distinct evaluation of the design (at any level within the hierarchy of levels) *needs* to be performed: the analysis phase and the subsequent synthesis phase are such that separate evaluation is deemed unnecessary.
End Example

Example 7.2
In software engineering, the most widely adopted (though not the only) model of the software life cycle is the so-called 'waterfall' model (Boehm 1981, Wiener and Sincovec 1984, Sommerville 1985, Ramamoorthy *et al.* 1987). Its general form is shown in fig. 7.4 and, if one interprets the boxes labeled CD and DD as representing what was hitherto called synthesis, and the boxes labeled UT and ST as representing evaluation, it is obvious that the waterfall model is practically a direct embodiment of ASE. Only the box labeled M does not fall into the ASE schema. More will be said about the significance of the maintenance phase in section 7.3.

In fact, regardless of whether one considers large-scale software development or the design of small programs, the development of software design methods has been enormously influenced by the ASE paradigm. We shall consider, as an example, a specific program design method first described in Liskov (1980) and later, in more detail by Liskov and Guttag (1986).

Their method begins with some client requesting a program that is to provide some service. Given an initial, possibly incomplete, imprecise, and poorly understood formulation of the desired service, a requirements analysis phase is first undertaken. The purpose of this phase is to dissect the client's needs and carefully identify the requirements. The output of the analysis phase is a *specification* of the requirements that is, ideally, both *precise* – in that the specification defines the required characteristics of the program unambiguously – and *complete* – that is, the specification encapsulates all relevant characteristics of the program. Typically, the *types* of requirements that are identified and specified belong to the *functional, performance, reliability,* and *modifiability* categories. [7] With regard to the functional requirements, Liskov and Guttag point out that they must characterize how the program is to behave both

---

[6] The application of the method to the design of an Indian village is described fully in Alexander (1963). A part of this paper is reproduced in Alexander (1964, Appendix 1).

[7] See chapter 3 for a detailed discussion of the different types of requirements that characterize design problems.

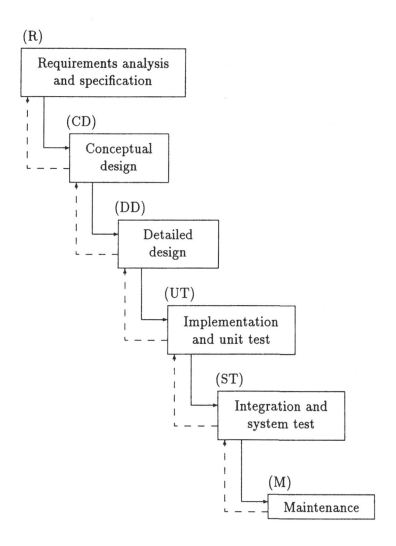

Fig. 7.4 The 'waterfall' model of the software life cycle.

for 'correct' and 'incorrect' inputs. Performance specifications will typically include not only the efficiency requirements for the program itself but also the scheduling constraints on the delivery of the software to the client.

The requirements specification (being a specification of what characteristics the intended program is to exhibit) describes a set of *abstractions*, that is, entities that highlight only those characteristics that are considered to be 'relevant' (in a particular context – in this case, from the perspective of the client) while suppressing others.

Liskov and Guttag recognize, in particular, the following two kinds of abstractions.[8]

(i) The *procedural* abstraction which defines the externally observable characteristics of a procedure without revealing its operational or algorithmic details.

(ii) The *data* abstraction which defines an object and a collection of exactly those operations that are permitted on the object. The operations will, in turn, be specified, as procedural abstractions.

(a) The symbol ST consists of a set of ordered pairs $\langle S, V \rangle$ where $S \in$ SYM, $V \in$ VAL, and SYM, VAL are sets of entities of predefined types. SYM is the set of symbols, VAL is the set of values.

(b) Initially, ST is empty. Notationally, ST = { }

(c) The set of symbols in ST is denoted by **dom**(ST)

(d) The function VALUE(S) is defined as

> **if** $\langle S, V \rangle \in$ ST **then return** V

(e) The operation UPDATE(S, V) is defined by

> **if** $\langle S, V \rangle \notin$ ST **then**
>   **return** ST $\cup$ $\{\langle S, V \rangle\}$

(f) The operation LOOKUP(S) is defined by

> **if** $S \in$ **dom**(ST) **then**
>   **return** VALUE(S)
> **else**
>   **return** errormessage

(g) The operation DELETE(S) is defined by

> **if** $S \in$ **dom**(ST) **then**
>   **return** ST $-$ $\{\langle S, \text{VALUE}(S) \rangle\}$
> **else return** errormessage

Fig. 7.5 Requirements specification for a symbol table.

---

[8] Liskov and Guttag also recognize a third abstraction (for iterations) which is irrelevant to the present discussion.

As a specific instance, consider the design of a symbol table. Its requirements specification (also described earlier in example 3.16) is shown in fig. 7.5. [9] This is a data abstraction in which the object of interest is ST, the symbol table and the allowable operations (as required by the 'user' of the symbol table) are UPDATE, LOOKUP and DELETE. Each of the operations is described by means of procedural abstractions.

Note that the language used to specify this particular abstraction is partly formal and partly informal. Liskov and Guttag's method is independent of any specification language though they are, in fact, strong advocates of *formal specification languages*.

Once the requirements specification has been determined the *design* phase begins. According to Liskov and Guttag, the purpose of the design phase is to define a 'program structure' comprising an integrated set of components which when implemented will satisfy the requirements specification. [10] A design (in their method) is not, however, a compilable/executable program. The latter results when the design is *implemented*.

Recall that the requirements specification is a set of one or more abstractions. The synthesis step selects each of these abstractions one by one. They become in turn, the 'target' abstraction, and for each such target synthesis proceeds according to the following three steps:

(i) Identify *new* abstractions that will help in further refining the target. Such abstractions are called 'helping abstractions' or simply 'helpers'.

(ii) Specify the behavior and other characteristics of each helper.

(iii) Develop a program that will realize the target abstraction in terms of the helper.

As a specific instance, consider the symbol table specified in fig. 7.5. The three operations UPDATE, LOOKUP, and DELETE all involve the need to determine either whether (or not) a given ordered pair $\langle S, V \rangle \in$ ST or whether (or not) a given symbol $S \in \mathbf{dom}($ST$)$. Thus, procedural abstractions for these two functions can be identified as helpers. Similarly, additional helpers for performing the actions

$$\text{ST} \cup \{\langle S, V \rangle\}$$
$$\text{ST} - \{\langle S, \text{VALUE}(V) \rangle\}$$

can be identified.

---

[9] Neither this example, nor the notation used for its specification is taken from or based on Liskov and Guttag (1986). In fact this example is based on Hayes (1985).

[10] The output of what Liskov and Guttag call the design phase is, then, a *form* in exactly the sense I used this word in chapters 3 and 4. Their design phase is thus the synthesis stage of ASE.

The overall structure of a program that will satisfy the requirements specifications can be synthesized in this manner. This program would be complete but for the fact that the helpers have not been designed. In fact, the helpers collectively define an abstract machine on which the program 'runs'. Had the abstract machine been executable the program would be complete. Thus, the next stage is the synthesis of the helper abstractions in terms of more 'primitive' helpers.[11]

As already noted, designs in the Liskov–Guttag method are not executable programs. The form that results from the synthesis step consists of a set of modules and a structure that shows the dependence between the modules. The modules are described by abstractions, and the intermodule structure, by *dependency diagrams*. Fig. 7.6 shows such a dependency diagram in which rectangles A, B, D and E represent procedural abstractions and rectangles C, F and G signify data abstractions. An edge from module i to module j denotes the fact that module i depends on (or uses) module j.

Finally, prior to implementation, the design is evaluated. Liskov and Guttag also refer to this as *design review*. The three main issues that are addressed during this stage are:

(a) Correctness: that is, whether or not the design is correct in the sense that all implementations will satisfy the functional requirements.
(b) Efficiency: that is, whether the program can be implemented so as to meet the efficiency requirements.
(c) Structure: that is, the extent to which the program structure facilitates ease of implementation, testability and modifiability.

Since a Liskov–Guttag design is non-executable, the conventional empirical methods of program testing are inapplicable. Formal (i.e., mathematical) methods could be applied in principle; however, as Liskov and Guttag note, the state of formal verification is not sufficiently advanced as to make this a generally acceptable approach, at least for designs.[12] Thus, design evaluation or review is conducted informally, by

---

[11] Liskov's and Guttag's synthesis process is, in fact, an instance of what is often referred to as *iterative top down design*. An early version of this approach was proposed by Zurcher and Randell (1968) who called it *hierarchical modeling*. A later version which is quite close to the Liskov–Guttag method, is the WELL_MADE program design method of Boyd and Pizzarello (1978). Their method may be summarized as follows: (a) Define an abstract machine M_i; (b) For the program P_i that will run on M_i, identify the data structures to be used by P_i; (c) Develop a functional specification for P_i; (d) Construct a skeleton program for P_i; (e) Refine the program skeleton to obtain P_i. Now machine M_i must be defined by a program P_{i-1} running on a still lower level machine M_{i-1}.
As Liskov (1980) noted, iterative top down design is a variant of *stepwise refinement* (Wirth 1971, Dijkstra 1972) that explicitly recognizes the role of abstractions.

[12] See chapter 8 for further discussion of the formal approach.

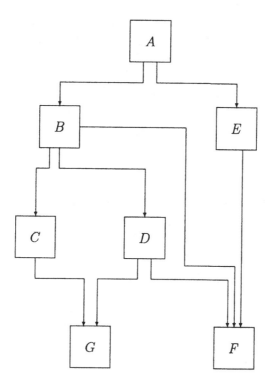

Fig. 7.6 A module dependency diagram.

first systematically examining the description of each module; and then by using test data to invoke traces or paths through the dependency diagram to evaluate how the design as a whole meets the requirements. Quite obviously, such procedures – also called *walkthroughs* – are labor-intensive and potentially imprecise.
End Example

Example 7.3
As a recent and important example of *language design* we shall consider the development of VHDL. This is a hardware design/description language (HDL) designed jointly by Intermetrics, IBM and Texas Instruments in response to the needs established by the U.S. Department of Defense (DoD), as part of their very high speed integrated circuits (VHSIC) program (Barbe 1981), for a DoD-wide standard HDL.[13] Like its older software cousin, Ada,[14] the VHDL design effort is unusual (among language design projects) in two ways: first, its genesis and development

---

[13] 'VHDL' is an acronym for 'VHSIC Hardware Design/Description Language'

[14] Ada is a registered trademark of the U.S. Department of Defense.

have been widely documented in the open literature; and second, it represents the first attempt in the United States to establish a *standard* HDL.[15]

Originally intended to be a DoD standard, VHDL has recently been adopted by the Institute of Electrical and Electronics Engineers (IEEE) as an industry-wide standard.

Strictly speaking, the development of VHDL is an instance of the phylogenic evolutionary process (see chapter 5, sections 5.5 and 5.6). From its inception in 1981 to the present time it has evolved through several versions culminating in the current IEEE standard (IEEE 1988, Coelho 1989, Lipsett, Schaefer and Ussery, 1989). Nonetheless, viewed from a certain perspective, the early development of the language appears to follow quite explicitly the ASE design paradigm and it is this stage of VHDL's life cycle that I shall discuss here.

As already noted, the overall motivation for VHDL stemmed from the DoD's VHSIC program which was concerned with reducing integrated circuit design time and the effective insertion of VHSIC technology into military systems. These concerns revealed a need for a hardware description language that would serve both as a medium of communication and documentation as well as a machine executable design language that would interface with, or serve as a front end of, integrated circuit design automation tools and systems (Dewey 1983).

Based on these considerations, a 'Request for Proposal' (RFP) was initiated by the DoD in early 1983. The RFP included a *requirements document* that specified both a set of broad language design guidelines as well as a set of more specific requirements (U.S. Department of Defense 1983, Dewey 1983). The guidelines included the following:

(1) VHDL is to be a language for the description of *digital hardware systems* ranging from the logic to the highest architectural level. Thus, every construct in the language must be realizable as a digital component and, conversely, any hardware-realizable structure must be specifiable in the language.

(2) VHDL will be used for *design and documentation* purposes. This implies in particular, that there must be adequate software support for the language (compiler, simulator, module library, etc.) capable of interfacing with, and supporting, other integrated circuit design tools.

---

[15] There have been other attempts at establishing a standard HDL. One of these was CONLAN, strictly speaking a family of languages (Piloty *et al.* 1983, Piloty and Borrione 1985), developed between 1973 and 1980 by an international working group, many of whom were associated with Working Group 10.2 (Digital System Description and Design Tools) of the International Federation for Information Processing (IFIP).

(3) The language must not be unnecessarily complex since this would lead to difficulties in implementation, comprehension, learning and use.

The more specific objectives in the requirements document described attributes that the language would have to satisfy. The most important of these attributes pertained to the capacity of VHDL for expressing structural and behavioral characteristics of hardware.

Starting with the DoD requirements document, Intermetrics, IBM and Texas Instruments working cooperatively, derived a more detailed set of language requirements (Intermetrics 1984a). This activity, thus, constituted in a very obvious sense, an *analysis* of the DoD requirements. For convenience, let us call the result of this analysis, the *VHDL requirements*.

The general approach towards the development of the VHDL requirements is stated quite explicitly in Intermetrics (1984a, pp. 1.2–1.4). A collection of *requirements generation guidelines* was first established. These guidelines enunciated desirable characteristics of the VHDL requirements pertaining to conciseness, specificity, preciseness and verifiability.

Given these guidelines, each sentence of the DoD requirements document was examined to determine how it would appear in the VHDL requirements. Requirements were checked against the requirements generation guidelines. If a requirement failed to satisfy the conciseness or preciseness guidelines, it would be decomposed into several requirements. If a requirement failed to satisfy the specificity or verifiability guidelines it would be refined or elaborated thereby generating new requirements. At all times during the VHDL requirements generation phase, the correspondences between the entities in the new document and in the DoD document were recorded. The eventual VHDL requirements – the output of the requirements analysis phase – consist of specifications concerning the overall organization of the language, timing concepts, interface descriptions, behavioral descriptions, structural specifications, and the VHDL design environment.

The development (by Intermetrics, IBM and Texas Instruments) of the VHDL requirements and the subsequent specification of the language itself were completed between July 1983 and July 1984 (Shahdad *et al* 1985, Gilman 1986). The language specification, thus, constituted a *synthesis* phase, in the terminology of the ASE paradigm. The principal document embodying the outcome of the synthesis phase was the VHDL Language Reference Manual, Version 5.0 (Intermetrics 1984b). The *evaluation* or design review was subsequently conducted over a period of two months

by representatives of the DoD, academia, and industry (Nash and Saunders 1986, Gilman 1986, Shahdad *et al.* 1985) and this led to a subsequent version (7.0) of the language (Intermetrics 1985).
End Example

As the above discussion and examples suggest the ASE design paradigm has a wide following in very different areas of engineering. This very observation causes us to raise several questions: What is the logical foundation for ASE? To what extent is ASE, as a prescriptive paradigm, consistent with the characteristics of the design process described in Part I of this book? What are the methodological and practical flaws in ASE? What are its compelling strengths and in what situations can it serve as a genuinely useful design paradigm? These are the questions that I will address in the next few sections.

7.3 INDUCTIVISM AS THE LOGICAL FOUNDATION FOR ASE

At the crudest level, ASE originates in the desire to make design *scientific* and it is the belief that ASE *is*, in some sense, scientific in spirit that is the cause, in my opinion, for the widespread adherence to this paradigm. For, a procedure in which a phase of thorough analysis of the requirements is first performed, followed by the actual creation or synthesis of the design, and then a phase of evaluation or testing the design against the requirements, is, it is widely believed, strongly akin to the 'scientific method'.

Unfortunately, the model of the 'scientific method' implicit in such a belief is an outdated and rather discredited model, viz., *inductivism*. The ASE paradigm is, thus, logically founded on, at best, a *very* limited model of science and, at worst, a model of science that has been held in disrepute for well over a century by scientific methodologists of various persuasions.

Inductivism, or the *inductive model* of science is often mistakenly associated with the name of the late 16th and early 17th century thinker and man of affairs Francis Bacon – to the extent that inductivism is also referred to as the Baconian method. In actual fact inductivism goes back to Aristotle and to such medieval scholars as Roger Bacon, John Duns Scotus, and William of Occam (Losee 1980). Its more modern exponents were the Victorian thinkers John Herschel and, in particular, John Stuart Mill (Losee 1980, Harré 1985). It is discussed at great length by Mill's and Herschel's contemporary, Whewell, in his magisterial two-volume treatise on the 'inductive sciences' (Whewell 1967). Given its two-millennia history it is no wonder that inductivism continues to compel attention!

The central concept underlying inductivism is quite simple:

> Scientific knowledge is obtained by a form of inference called induction in which, from specific data gathered or facts observed, one infers a theory or a law that is a generalization of the facts.

Thus, according to inductivism, one *first* accumulates particular facts and *then* infers a theory or a law that serves as a generalization of the facts. Consider, now, what the ASE paradigm advocates:

> Based on identification and analysis of (all) the requirements that the target artifact is to satisfy, one synthesizes a design that meets the requirements.

That is, one *first* accumulates all the requirements and *then* synthesizes the design to meet the requirements.[16] The correspondence is quite clear (fig. 7.7) and one can see why it is so easy to be seduced into accepting ASE as *the* design paradigm: Adoption of the ASE paradigm implies adoption of inductivism; by adopting inductivism one is pursuing the 'true' model of the scientific method; *ergo*, by adopting ASE one is pursuing a scientific approach to design![17]

Inductivism	ASE
Facts/data	Requirements
Law/theory	Design
Theory testing	Design evaluation

Fig. 7.7 Correspondence between the inductive model of science and ASE.

The difficulty with this entire line of reasoning is, however, twofold. There is, firstly, the fundamental problem of induction as a valid form of reasoning – a problem that has exercised philosophers from the 18th century thinker David Hume (1977) onwards. Stated simply, the 'problem of induction' is the question of whether the derivation of universal statements (such as laws or theories) based on a set of particular statements (such as empirical observations, data, or facts) is at all a valid form of inference. To take a standard example, does the fact that we have observed n cases of white swans allow us to *legitimately* infer the statement that 'all swans are white'?

---

[16] For a recent statement of the 'engineering method' that characterizes it in the form of the ASE paradigm and quite explicitly relates it to the inductive model of science, see Middendorf (1986, p3).

[17] In passing, the reader will note from fig. 7.7 that a correspondence has been identified between designs and scientific theories. This is a matter that will be discussed extensively in Part III.

I shall not address this philosophical issue except to point out that philosophers have, in the main, agreed that there is *no logical* justification for induction (see, e.g., Carnap (1966), Medawar (1969), Popper (1972)) – although it may serve a *psychological* need (and we practice induction all the time in science and in everyday life). Thus induction as a general valid form of inference is no longer a defensible position.

A second problem is whether (regardless of the validity of induction as a form of inference) inductivism actually serves as a 'true' or 'correct' or even reasonably accurate model of how science is conducted. For if one takes inductivism at face value one also presupposes the scientist's mind as a *tabula rasa* – a clean slate – on which sense data impinge, on the basis of which 'facts' are recorded. The scientist then constructs a theory or postulates a law that generalizes or explains these facts. To use a computational phrase borrowed from Langley *et al.* (1987), inductivism is a *data driven* model of scientific discovery.

In fact, through both historical studies of past scientific achievements, and the work of several philosophers of science of the last and (in particular) this century, there is a wide agreement that while induction – in the above sense – may play *a* role in the scientific process, it is by no means the *only* nor even the *primary* mode of scientific thinking. Indeed, to the extent that one talks about 'the scientific process' or 'the scientific method' it is almost entirely in terms other than induction.[18] Inductivism, as a fundamental model of science is, thus, by and large, obsolete.[19]

We are, thus, led to the conclusion that insofar as the ASE paradigm is founded on inductivism it does not really have a logical leg to stand on!

7.4 LIMITATIONS OF THE ASE PARADIGM

The reader may protest that even if inductivism is logically indefensible and that we are fundamentally mistaken in presuming that ASE follows sound scientific methodology, there are other compelling reasons why ASE is an attractive paradigm. For, we *know* that every design activity begins with *some* set of requirements. Such requirements *define* the design problem. Given this fact, if we are sufficiently careful and thorough in identifying and analyzing the requirements prior to commencing

---

[18] See, e.g., Popper (1968, 1972), Hanson (1972), Kuhn (1962), Lakatos (1970), Lakatos and Musgrave (1970), Feyerabend (1978) and Laudan (1977, 1984). For more on the methodology of science and its relationship to design, see Part III.

[19] Yet, there are those who continue to hold on to inductivism as a significant model of science. In particular, it was recently invoked by Langley *et al.* (1987) who constructed a series of computer programs that 'discover' well known scientific laws (Boyle's Law, Ohm's Law, Kepler's third law, and others) from data. For more on this, see chapter 12, section 12.2.

with synthesis, and we defer commencement of synthesis until we are reasonably sure that we have not overlooked all the requirements or their interactions, then surely we are more likely to make informed decisions during the synthesis phase. Furthermore, there will be less likelihood of errors of omission appearing during synthesis thus causing us to return to requirements analysis.

This argument *sounds* unobjectionable, in principle. The problem, however, lies in the assumption that one *can*, in fact, make a clear separation between analysis of requirements, and synthesis of the design; and that one *can* identify, accumulate and analyze 'all' (or even 'most' of) the requirements at the start of the design process. We have already noted (in chapters 3 and 5) that requirements may initially be vague and/or sparse; and that because of bounded rationality, it may simply not be possible to either identify all the requirements or to comprehend or anticipate the interactions amongst the requirements. It was for these reasons that the evolutionary model was suggested (see chapter 5). The very act of synthesizing the form to satisfy a particular set of requirements at any given time will cause additional requirements to surface. Analysis and synthesis are inextricably intertwined in design; they are not distinct phases as the ASE paradigm would have us believe.[20]

Another troublesome issue with ASE is the connection between the evaluation phase and the other two phases. Most statements of the ASE paradigm are, in fact, silent about the precise nature of this connection except for noting, blandly, that there are 'feedback edges' from evaluation back to analysis and synthesis.

According to ASE, the purpose of the evaluation phase is to determine whether or not the design (or form) D meets the requirements R. Suppose this determination reveals a misfit between D and R. The cause of this misfit must then be identified. Essentially, there are two possibilities:

(a) D is found to contain an error (or several errors) in that it fails to satisfy one or more of the requirements in R. D must then be modified. In terms of ASE this means returning to the synthesis phase (fig. 7.8).

(b) D is found to contain one or more errors in the sense that it fails to satisfy one or more *new* requirements (that were not part of R) that surfaced during evaluation. Such new requirements may be generated by virtue of the experiments or from

---

[20] Others in different ways have arrived at similar conclusions. Thus, Rittel and Webber (1973) in their study of planning processes comment that 'problem understanding and problem resolution are concomitant to each other'. Swartout and Balzer (1982), in the context of software design discuss the 'inevitable intertwining of specification and implementation' in which 'specification' refers to the product of requirements analysis and 'implementation' refers to the implementation of the specification – i.e., to synthesis.

the test data used during evaluation. [21] Call these new requirements R'. In order to eliminate the misfit R' must first be integrated with R (producing a set of requirements $R^* = R \cup R'$) and further analysis must be done to ensure the consistency and integrity of R^*. In terms of ASE, this means returning to the analysis phase. The design D must, of course, subsequently be modified in response to the revised set of requirements R^* (fig. 7.9).

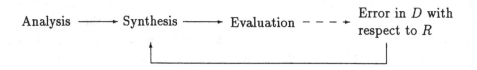

Fig. 7.8 Feedback loop in ASE to synthesis phase.

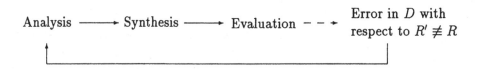

Fig. 7.9 Feedback loop in ASE to analysis phase.

If one accepts the idea that these two scenarios capture *explicitly* the relationships between the evaluation phase and the analysis and synthesis phases (relationships that are only implicit in the ASE paradigm) one further encounters the following implication:

> Evaluation is a distinct activity that *follows* synthesis just as synthesis is a distinct activity that *follows* analysis.

In other words there exists a strict linear order amongst these three phases. Let us, however, consider two of the examples discussed in chapter 5 (section 5.4) and see whether they bear out this supposition. In the following discussion I shall use the subscripted letters R and D to denote requirements and design, respectively and the

---

[21] For example, in developing a piece of software R may have, by oversight, excluded certain boundary conditions and what actions to take for these conditions. The presence of such boundary conditions is revealed by the actual test data used during software testing.

letters A, S, and E to designate, respectively, the activities of analysis, synthesis and evaluation.

Example 7.4
The successive *states* of the design – denoted in terms of ⟨requirements, design⟩ pairs – for the sorting program in example 5.9 can be summarized as follows:

$$(R_0, D_1) \xrightarrow{(1)} (R_1, D_1) \xrightarrow{(2)} (R_2, D_1) \xrightarrow{(3)} (R_2, D_2) \xrightarrow{(4)} (R_3, D_2) \xrightarrow{(5)} (R_3, D_3)$$

where, for $i \neq j$, $R_i \neq R_j$, $D_i \neq D_j$ and, in terms of the notation used in example 5.9,

$$R_2 = \{R_1, R\_int1, R\_int2\}$$
$$R_3 = \{R_1, R\_int1, R\_int2, R\_int3\}$$

The sequence of *activities* that produced this succession of design states can be represented by

$$A \to S \to E_1 \to A \to E_2 \to A \to E_3 \to S \to E_4 \to A \to E_5 \to S$$

where E_1 denotes the evaluation of the pair (R_0, D_1) leading to the pair (R_1, D_1), and so on.
End Example

Example 7.5
The succession of design states for the oil-well logging program (example 5.10) can be depicted as

$$(R_0, D_0) \xrightarrow{(1)} (R_1, D_0) \xrightarrow{(2)} (R_1, D_1) \xrightarrow{(3)} (R_1, D_2) \xrightarrow{(4)} (R_1, D_3)$$
$$(R_1, D_3) \xrightarrow{(5)} (R, D_3) \xrightarrow{(6)} (R, D_4) \xrightarrow{(7)} (R, D_5) \xrightarrow{(8)} (R, D_6)$$
$$(R, D_6) \xrightarrow{(9)} (R, D_7) \xrightarrow{(10)} (R, D_8) \xrightarrow{(11)} (R, D_9) \xrightarrow{(12)} (R, D_{10}) \xrightarrow{(13)} (R, D_{11})$$

where, as before, $i \neq j$ implies $R_i \neq R_j$, $D_i \neq D_j$ and, in terms of the notation used in example 5.10,

$$R = \{R_1, R_2\}$$

The sequence of activities producing this succession of design states is representable as:

$$A \to S \to E_1 \to A \to E_2 \to S \to E_3 \to S \to E_4 \to S \to E_5 \to A \to E_6$$
$$E_6 \to S \to E_7 \to S \to E_8 \to S \to E_9 \to S \to E_{10} \to S \to E_{11} \to S \to E_{12}$$
$$E_{12} \to S \to E_{13} \to S$$

where E_1 denotes the evaluation of the pair (R_0, D_0) leading to the pair (R_1, D_0) and so on.
End Example

As these examples illustrate, the linear order of analysis, synthesis, and evaluation certainly need not be the case in actual design – even in the case of well-structured design problems as these two problems are. Analysis may directly lead to evaluation as often as synthesis leads to evaluation. As the detailed discussions of these examples (in chapter 5, section 5.4) bear out, evaluation is a *tool* that may be used to circumvent bounded rationality or to suggest the direction in which the design should go at each significant moment of time.

Yet another difficulty with ASE is its exclusion or dismissal of the vital role of the designer's *Weltanschauung* or world view in the design process. By this, I refer to the whole complex of facts, assumptions, values, theories, heuristics and examples that the designer possesses and which he or she will bring to bear when required to solve a design problem. This world view – which, in a later chapter I will refer to as the designer's *world knowledge base* – is to the designer what a Kuhnian paradigm is to the scientist (see chapter 6, section 6.2).

As previously noted (in section 7.3), inductivism encourages the notion of the scientist's mind being a *tabula rasa*. The scientist, with no preconceived notions, assumptions or expectations, objectively gathers and records 'facts' from which a theory or law is later inductively generated. By virtue of its implicit adherence to inductivism a similar notion is tacitly contained in the ASE paradigm: the designer, with no prior commitments, assumptions, prejudices or values identifies, collects and analyzes the requirements objectively and a design subsequently emerges based on these requirements.

Modern developments in the philosophy of science have shown how utterly wrong this *tabula rasa* picture – or the 'primacy of data' picture – is (Kuhn 1962, Popper 1965, p. 46, Hanson 1972, chapter 1; see also Part III). Scientists observe or experiment or measure based on *prior theoretical expectations*. Or as an aphorism well known to philosophers of science puts it, *all observations are theory laden*.

So also, the 'primacy of requirements over analysis over synthesis' picture of design is, *in general*, false. When faced with a design problem – a set of requirements – the designer may be influenced by his world view in many ways. He or she may perceive an *analogy* between the problem at hand and others that had been previously solved. This would then suggest a design sketch or a rough form as an immediate initial solution which would then be further elaborated in the course of the design. The process of elaboration not only invokes further identification of requirements and details of the form but also influences the way in which requirements are analyzed.

Alternatively, the designer, on the basis of a few key components of the requirements, may be predisposed towards a particular *style* and it is this style that further drives the design process – by generating new requirements and synthesizing (partial) solutions to meet them (Simon 1975, Dasgupta 1984, chapter 12).[22] In other words, *the designer interprets and explores the design problem according to a particular world view.* Whereas, implicit in ASE is the notion of *deferring* interpretation of the design problem until requirements have been 'fully' analyzed.

Example 7.6

In Dasgupta (1984, chapter 14) the systematic design of a particular computer architecture is described in some detail. I will here recapitulate this design process as an illustration of the ways in which the designer's *Weltanschauung* may strongly dictate the course of design.

The two starting requirements for this problem were the following:

R_f: To design an exo-architecture that would directly support programs written in the C programming language.

R_i: The exo-architecture can be efficiently implemented through emulation on the Nanodata QM-1.[23]

R_f may be viewed as a functional requirement while R_i represents an implementation requirement. The resulting machine is named QM-C.

If we were to follow the ASE paradigm then R_f and R_i would be required to be further analyzed and refined. Consider, in particular, R_f. What would its analysis have entailed?

---

[22] A *style* is a set of characteristics that allows us to distinguish between one group of artifacts and another that may otherwise be functionally equivalent. A style, therefore, represents certain *acts of choice* on the part of the designer, the result of which is the presence of one particular set of features in the artifact rather than another (see also Dasgupta 1984).

[23] *Emulation* is the process in which one computer (termed the 'host') simulates the behavior of another (termed the 'target') through the use of microcode or firmware. Specifically, a target machine's exo-architecture is emulated by developing microcode that is executed by the host machine's micro-architecture so as to interpret object programs that were intended for execution on the target. The Nanodata QM-1 was an instance of a class of computers developed in the 1970s that were specifically designed to support the emulation of a wide range of exo-architectures (Nanodata 1979, Dasgupta 1984, chapter 11). Such machines are called 'universal host machines'. For more on emulation and universal host machines see Neuhauser and Flynn 1988, Dasgupta 1989a, chapter 5.

A computer's exo-architecture is, by definition, the structure and behavior (of the computer) as seen by the systems programmer or the compiler writer (Dasgupta 1984, 1989a). The principal components of an exo-architecture are

(i) The organization of programmable storage
(ii) Data types (and structures) to be directly supported
(iii) Instruction formats
(iv) The instruction set
(v) Addressing modes

Thus, analysis of R_f would have entailed identifying in detail what functional requirements or properties would have to be satisfied by each of the above components in order to meet R_f. For example, given the need to support the representation and execution of C programs, a requirements analysis phase would probably have involved determining the specific data types and the operations available in C, assessing their relative importance and, thereby, producing a collection of such requirements as

R_{f1}: QM-C must directly support integer and character data types;
R_{f2}: QM-C must support the efficient representation and access of array data structures;
R_{f3}: QM-C must provide instructions to execute '++' and '−−' operations in C;

and so on.

The implementation requirement R_i would likewise be further analyzed. Presumably, this would entail an interpretation of the notion of 'efficient implementation' with respect to the QM-1 and would lead to such requirements as

R_{i1}: The instruction formats must be so designed that the QM-1 hardware and firmware can be exploited to efficiently decode instructions and extract the fields of the instruction;
R_{i2}: The most common instructions must be representable in the basic addressable storage unit of the QM-1;
R_{i3}: The most important primitive data types must be representable in the basic addressable storage unit of the QM-1;

and so on.

It is, of course, impossible to attempt to estimate the total size of the requirement set that might emerge from such analysis. The point that *can* be made is that such a collection of requirements exhibits very little *structure* in the sense of neither characterizing the relative importance of the requirements nor revealing the relationships or interactions amongst the requirements. If one were to follow Alexander's approach (see example 7.1) then the relationships or interactions would have to be determined. The problem is that while we can, occasionally, predict (at least qualitatively) interactions between certain *pairs* of requirements, we are in most cases unable to extrapolate such relationships when considering three or more requirements.[24] Worse still, even for requirements taken pairwise, we may be unable to comprehend, *a priori*, their relationship. To take a specific example, consider the following requirements:

R_{fj}: QM-C must provide instructions to execute all the arithmetic, logical, and shift operators available in C.

R_{fk}: QM-C must provide for the efficient support of the three distinct storage classes in C, viz., 'external' variables, 'automatic' variables and registers.

R_{i1}: The instruction format must be so designed that the QM-1 hardware and firmware can be exploited to efficiently decode instructions and extract the fields of the instructions.

In the absence of concrete decisions or solutions with respect to one or more of these requirements – i.e., in the absence of an actual (albeit preliminary) design *solution* to at least one of these requirements – it is, for all practical purposes, impossible to determine *how* these requirements interact (although our knowledge of architectural principles warns us that there will be some interactions). For instance,

(i) If all the arithmetic/logical/shift operators in C are represented by distinct opcodes (R_{fj}), then the opcode field size may be such that the QM-1 hardware is unable to efficiently decode the instruction (R_{i1}); or

(ii) In order to satisfy R_{fk} certain addressing modes would have to be provided which may also impact the satisfiability of R_{i1}.

Let us see how the QM-C design was *actually* pursued. The process is described in Dasgupta (1984) and (in still greater detail) by the QM-C designer, Olafsson (1981). Here, I shall merely sketch the overall profile of this process.

(a) The design process began with the gathering of empirical data regarding the specific nature of C code. The data was obtained by analyzing a large sample of C programs and pertained to the frequencies of occurrences of data types,

---

[24] One may note, in passing, that Alexander's (1964) method is based on the strong assumption that the interaction between any particular pair of requirements is *not* affected by the presence of any other requirement.

operations, expression types and statement types, the lengths of procedures, the usage of the different C storage classes, and so on.

(b) The initial requirements R_f and R_i represent two possibly opposing influences on the architecture-to-come; and the question is, whether the target language (C) or the host computer (QM-1) should be the primary determining influence on the QM-C design. Further consideration indicated that giving primacy to the host provides considerable advantage as far as ease of implementation and performance was concerned. Thus, the overall style of the QM-C architecture would be primarily influenced by its mode of implementation – that is, by the *implementation style*. [25] Because of the specific characteristics of the QM-1 this immediately fixed the QM-C's word length (to 18-bits, the QM-1's word length), determined the basic instruction decoding mechanism that would be used to decode QM-C instructions, and placed restrictions on the instruction formats (7-bit opcodes and specific combinations of 5-, 6-, 11-, 12-, or 18-bit operands). Thus, a *partial design* of the QM-C emerged at this stage.

(c) Decisions concerning the various components of an exo-architecture being mutually interacting, it was decided to establish an ordering on the classes of decisions leading to a *multilevel decision hierarchy* where level i decisions are taken before level $i + 1$ decisions. The decision hierarchy was of the following nature:

At level 1, the storage organization would be determined.
At level 2, decisions regarding addressing modes and data types would be taken.
At level 3, the instruction formats would be determined.
At level 4, the instruction set would be designed.

(d) The design of the storage organization was based on a combination of the *stack machine* and *register machine* styles (Dasgupta 1989a). The choice of this organization was determined by a consideration of the storage classes available in C, the memory organization of the QM-1, and the designer's prior knowledge of the features and capabilities of the register and stack machine styles.

(e) The selection of the storage organization led to the main methods for referencing data objects – i.e., to the identification of the addressing modes.

(f) The empirical analysis of C programs determined which data to support on the QM-C and which to exclude. Representation of the data types (i.e., their mappings onto QM-1 words) was dictated by the basic implementation style, specifically, by the fact that the basic addressable storage entity on the QM-1 was the 18-bit word.

(g) As noted previously, restrictions on the instruction formats had already been established by virtue of the implementation style. The detailed design of the

---

[25] See Dasgupta (1984, chapter 12) for more on implementation style.

formats was further influenced by the insight acquired by analyzing the alternatives (3-, 2- and 1-address instructions, etc.,) in the light of other considerations (such as the addressing modes, the potential size of the opcode field, and the size of the object code, etc.).

(h) The design of the instruction set itself was partly influenced by the implementation style-determined size of the opcode field (7 bits), partly by the statistics gathered about C programs, and partly by two important architectural styles, viz., RISCs, the principles of which had just been published at that time (Patterson and Dietzel 1980, Patterson and Sequin 1981) – and the directly executable language (DEL) machine style of Hoevel and Flynn (Hoevel 1974, Hoevel and Flynn 1977, Flynn 1980).

From this outline we can see the extent to which the designer's *Weltanschauung* played an intimate role in the entire design process. The extent to which analysis of requirements formed a *distinct* phase in the design process was restricted to the empirical study of C programs. And even this analysis was influenced by the designer's knowledge and understanding of language-directed architectural principles. Much of the analysis was driven by prior decisions concerning key aspects of the design, e.g., identification of the design hierarchy, establishing the primacy of the host machine's influence on the architecture, and the adaptation of significant and relevant architectural styles.

End Example

7.5 REMARKS ON REQUIREMENTS ENGINEERING

This chapter has, thus far, been largely a criticism of the ASE paradigm. I have argued that though this paradigm is viewed by many of its proponents as representing a 'scientific' approach to design, the very fact that the logical basis of ASE is inductive renders wholly dubious, any serious claims to ASE being methodologically 'scientific'. I have also pointed out that even if we choose to ignore such theoretical considerations (which, after all, are only likely to be of interest to the more philosophically minded design theorist) there is a serious practical limitation to ASE having to do with whether or not we can, in fact, carry out a design according to the linear ordering of the phases as characterized in ASE. Design is not linear. It is rather, as we have seen through the examples, an interweaving of solutions (designs or forms), problems (requirements) and evaluations in which solutions and evaluations prompt problems as much as problems prompt solutions.

Furthermore, the ASE paradigm strongly suggests an almost mythical state of objectivity (on the part of the designer) in the analysis phase during which requirements are generated and analyzed with no prior commitment to a particular world view.

This neglect of the designer's *Weltanschauung* and the very significant role it actually plays in the design process is another serious defect of ASE.

How, then, is one to reconcile this highly critical perspective of ASE with the development of *requirements engineering*? The main agenda of this subdiscipline of software engineering is the development of sophisticated tools, techniques, and languages, for the analysis, description and modeling of requirements (Yeh *et al.* 1984). Particularly well known and mature examples of such requirements analysis and specification tools include Software Requirements Engineering Methodology or SREM (Alford 1977, 1985) and SADT (Ross 1977, 1985, Ross and Schoman 1977).[26]

In fact, although the emergence of requirements engineering is implicitly supportive of, and takes for granted, the *idea* of the

$$\text{analysis} \to \text{synthesis} \to \text{evaluation}$$

ordering, the development of requirements analysis tools, techniques and languages has *intrinsically* nothing to do with the ASE paradigm. It is obvious that the ability to analyze, model, and describe requirements in a precise, formal and unambiguous manner is not merely highly desirable but imperative. For only then can one attempt to test a design against the requirements and determine unambiguously whether or not the former satisfies the latter. Furthermore, such requirements serve to establish the fundamental interface and contractual document between the client (or user) and the designer. Just as the output of the design process serves as an interface between designer and implementer, so the specification of requirements serves as a medium of communication between designer and client (or, in fact between designer and designer). What is questioned in this chapter is the (very strong) assumption that one can, in fact, conduct such a requirements analysis, specification and modeling to any degree of completeness or usefulness before the synthesis phase actually begins.

7.6 THE USE OF CONCEPTUAL MODELS

An interesting and, in some ways, fruitful way in which the essential limitations of the ASE paradigm can be circumvented – without transgressing its framework and spirit – is to use *conceptual models*. These serve to bridge the schism between analysis and synthesis by creating entities that are part specifications of requirements and part designs or forms.

---

[26] SADT is a trademark of Softech Inc., and is an acronym for 'structured analysis and design technique'. For an example of the use of SADT in the design of a software development system see Freeman (1987).

Recall from the preceding sections that the objections to ASE as a realistic design paradigm are basically threefold: its underlying logical basis of inductivism; the linear ordering and clear separation of the activities of analysis, synthesis, and evaluation; and the neglect of the role of the designer's world view in the design process. Models serve to weaken the extent of these limitations in the following way.

Consider a design problem and assume that, *in broad outline*, the designer posed this problem is an adherent to the ASE paradigm. That is, the designer believes, in principle, in the notion that a separation should exist between the analysis of the problem itself and the development of its solution. He or she, nonetheless, recognizes the limitations that inhere in the paradigm.

Under such circumstances, the designer – in collaboration with the client or user – analyzes the given requirements to the extent that a *conceptual model* can be created such that

(a) The model encapsulates the requirements and their interactions;
(b) It is, in a sense, a highly abstract representation of the target artifact (that is being designed) but expressed in the language of the problem domain;
(c) The task of synthesis becomes one of implementing the conceptual model in the language of the solution domain (i.e., in a design description language); and
(d) The act of evaluation involves matching the designed form (i.e., the implementation of the conceptual model) against the conceptual model.

In other words, the model is a *representation* of the requirements and their interactions. The analysis of requirements is taken as far as is necessary to construct a model which is not only the outcome of analysis but also the first step in synthesis. The model then serves as a basis for communication and discussion between designer and client (or user); and as a basis for refinement and elaboration during synthesis. As the latter goes on and further requirements are determined or prior requirements are revised, the model itself gets modified.

Example 7.7
An example of a design method that explicitly uses conceptual models in the manner just described, is the JSD method for software system design. This method was developed by M.A. Jackson and J.R. Cameron and is described in detail by Jackson (1983).

The JSD development procedure makes a separation between what, in its terminology, are called *specification* and *implementation*. Given the need to design a particular system the designer (or *developer*, in JSD terminology) first constructs a specification of the system and then implements the specification. The act of analysis is contained in the specification step. The act of synthesis is partly embedded in the specification step (as described below) and partly in the implementation step.

JSD Method:
    Develop Specification
        Specify Model of Reality
            Entity action step
            Entity structure step
            Initial model step
        Specify System Specification
            Function step
            System timing step
        Develop implementation
            Implementation step

Fig. 7.10 Organization of the JSD procedure (Jackson 1983).

The overall organization of the JSD method is depicted in fig. 7.10. The boldfaced components constitute the actual steps in JSD. The development process begins with the *entity action step* in which the various *entities* and *actions* of the problem domain – or the *real world*, to use Jackson's term for the latter – are identified. The temporal ordering of the various actions performed by, or on, the entities is next established in the *entity structure step*. The outcome of the entity action and structure steps is an abstract description of the real world including the ordering of actions on the entities. The next step is the *initial model step* in which the abstract description of the real world is specified in the form of a collection of *sequential processes* that simulates the real world entities and their actions. It is this set of sequential processes that constitutes a *model of the real world*; the model serves both to describe the requirements (in the language of the real world) and as the first stage towards the synthesis of a solution.

The remaining steps in specification development further refine the model and carry forward the synthesis process. In the *function step* the actual outputs required to be produced by the system are identified and additional processes are added to the model as necessary. In the *system timing step*, the timing characteristics of, and constraints on, the model processes are further considered and specified so as to ensure the production of correct outputs. Issues such as the ordering of processes for execution and synchronization of processes are considered in this step.

Finally, in the *implementation step*, the developer produces an efficient, cost effective, executable software system as a realization of the specification.
End Example

The interested reader may consult Jackson (1983) for further details of the JSD procedure. The point of interest for our present purposes is the notion of using conceptual models within the ASE framework as a bridge between analysis and synthesis.

A matter of some interest is, clearly, what kind of a *form* models take in such model-based design. In the case of the JSD procedure it was noted that the outcome of the modeling step is a collection of sequential processes. To provide a concrete illustration of how such a 'model' may look, the example below considers the development of a model for a small programming problem. Although the terminology and general approach here are based loosely on the JSD method I have not actually followed the detailed sequence of steps or the detailed methodology of the latter. Thus, the following example should be construed as following the spirit of the JSD method rather than adhering to its letter.

Example 7.8
Consider the development of a software simulator of a vending machine (as a preliminary step, say, in building a prototype of the physical machine). Suppose the initial requirements are as follows:

(i) The machine is to dispense 10 types of candies. Of these, types A, B and C are priced at 50 cents. Types D and E are priced at 65 cents. Types F, G, and H each costs 75 cents. And types I and K are priced at $1.

(ii) The machine will only accept exact amounts for each candy type as combinations of quarters, nickels, and dimes.

(iii) If the correct amount has been inserted for the candy type selected and the candy is in stock the machine issues the requested candy.

(iv) If the amount inserted is not the correct price for the selected candy, the machine displays a lighted message and immediately returns the inserted coins.

(v) If the machine is out of stock for the selected candy, the machine displays a lighted message and immediately returns the inserted coins.

(vi) If, after inserting coins the customer changes his or her mind, the coins can be retrieved by an appropriate button pressed on the machine.

The objective is to develop a program that simulates the 'architecture' of the vending machine so as to exhibit the desired characteristics stated above.

The primary 'real world' entity of interest here is, then, the vending machine. Based on the above requirements, this entity and its actions can be described as follows:

Entity: VENDING MACHINE
Actions: ADD COINS: Compute the total amount inserted by the customer.
OUTPUT CANDY: Issue the selected candy
DISPLAY 'OUT OF STOCK' MESSAGE: Display a lighted message indicating absence of candy.
RETURN COINS: Return the coins inserted by the customer.
DISPLAY 'INEXACT COIN' MESSAGE: Display a lighted message indicating that the coins inserted by the customer is inexact with respect to the selected candy.

The 'environment' in which VENDING MACHINE is to work, consists (for the purpose of this design) of a single entity, viz., the customer which can be characterized as follows:

Entity: CUSTOMER
Actions: INSERT COINS: Customer inserts some combination of quarters, dimes and nickels into the vending machine.
SELECT CANDY: Customer presses a particular candy button from the possible buttons.
PRESS COIN RETURN: Customer presses a button so as to retrieve the coins previously inserted.

Thus far, I have conducted what in the JSD procedure is called the entity action step (see example 7.7). Consider now, the possible timewise orderings of the actions for the two entities. Characterizing these orderings will allow us to capture, in a preliminary way, the dynamic nature of the entities. In the JSD procedure the step that is responsible for identifying the temporal ordering is termed the entity structure step.

Consider, first, CUSTOMER. Clearly, either of (and only) the following sequences of actions are feasible:

(CS1) INSERT COINS; SELECT CANDY
(CS2) INSERT COINS; PRESS COIN RETURN

The customer 'comes alive' (i.e., enters the real world being depicted) by first inserting a coin. He or she may then either select a candy (CS1) or press the coin return button (CS2).

In the case of the vending machine, the possible sequences of actions are as follows:

(VMS1) ADD COINS; OUTPUT CANDY
(VMS2) ADD COINS; DISPLAY 'OUT OF STOCK' MESSAGE; RETURN
         COINS
(VMS3) ADD COINS; DISPLAY 'INEXACT COINS' MESSAGE; RETURN
         COINS
(VMS4) RETURN COINS

(VMS1) represents the normal sequence: the vending machine adds the coins inserted and issues the selected candy. (VMS2) and (VMS3) represent respectively the situations where the selected candy is out of stock or the amount inserted for the selected candy is incorrect. In either case, the coins will be returned. Finally, (VMS4) represents the machine's response to the situation in which the customer, having inserted some coins, presses the coin return button without selecting a candy.

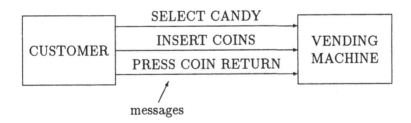

Fig. 7.11 Message connecting CUSTOMER and VENDING MACHINE.

We are now in a position to *connect* the actions of CUSTOMER and VENDING MACHINE (fig. 7.11). The inputs to VENDING MACHINE are *messages* corresponding to the three actions performable by CUSTOMER. VENDING MACHINE *reacts* to these messages. On the other hand there are no messages from VENDING MACHINE to CUSTOMER. The actions of VENDING MACHINE, though obviously significant insofar as its *own* correct functioning is concerned has no relevance whatsoever on the way that CUSTOMER should act. For instance, the real world customer may choose not to pick up the candy issued by the machine, or not to retrieve the coins that the machine returns. Such actions would not violate the correctness of the vending machine itself.

```
VENDING MACHINE:
  seq
    wait for INSERT COIN message;
    wait for SELECT CANDY or PRESS COIN RETURN message;
    sel
      simulate RETURN COINS;
    alt
      seq
        simulate ADD COINS;
        sel
          simulate OUTPUT CANDY
        alt
          seq
            simulate DISPLAY 'OUT OF STOCK' MESSAGE;
            simulate RETURN COINS
          endseq
        alt
          seq
            simulate DISPLAY 'INEXACT COIN' MESSAGE;
            simulate RETURN COINS
          endseq
        endsel
      endseq
    endsel
  endseq
```

Fig.7.12 The VENDING MACHINE process: initial model.

```
CUSTOMER
  seq
    simulate INSERT COINS;
    sel
      simulate PRESS COIN RETURN;
    alt
      simulate SELECT CANDY;
    endsel
  endseq
```

Fig. 7.13 The CUSTOMER process: initial model.

Figs. 7.12 and 7.13 collectively show the *initial model* of the CUSTOMER/VEND-ING MACHINE system in the form of a pair of *communicating sequential processes* (Hoare 1985). The statement form

$$\text{sel } S_1 \text{ alt } S_2 \text{ alt } \ldots \text{ alt } S_n \text{ endsel}$$

denotes that one of the alternative statements $S_1, \ldots, S_n$ will be selected (depending on some condition). Note that the model embodies requirements (ii)–(vi). Since, at this stage of the design exactly how the actions are to be represented has not been specified, requirement (i) is not reflected in this model. Note also that the model is expressed in the language of the real world. Finally, it will be seen that not only can further analysis of the requirements be conducted on the basis of the model; but one may also determine quite exactly how such analysis (and the possible generation of new requirements) may influence the other requirements. For example it may be decided to change the requirements such that when the selected candy is out of stock, the customer should be afforded another choice of selection. The effects of this change on the requirements set as a whole can be clearly localized in the model.
End Example

Example 7.9
The design of the hardware description language (HDL) S*M has been documented in a series of reports (Dasgupta 1984, 1985, Wilsey 1985, Dasgupta and Heinanen 1985, Dasgupta, Wilsey and Heinanen 1986). The details of this language are irrelevant for our present purposes. What *is* important is the method used in designing S*M.[27]

The development of S*M was driven by a single 'high level' objective to construct a language that could be used to specify clocked architectures – in particular , clocked micro-architectures.[28] Such specifications could, then, serve as inputs to design automation systems such as retargetable simulators or microcode compilers (Djordjevic, Ibbett and Barbacci 1980, Damm 1984, Dasgupta, Wilsey and Heinanen 1986). Fig. 7.14 shows the typical structure of a retargetable microcode generation/simulation system and the place of the architectural description in such systems.[29]

More detailed requirements for S*M were then determined based on (a) an analysis of the structure and characteristics of clocked micro-architectures; and (b) a consider-

---

[27] See also, example 5.12, chapter 5 for a discussion of S*M in the context of the phylogenic evolution of designs.

[28] Recall from earlier discussions (e.g., chapter 5, section 5.1) that 'micro-architecture' refers to the architecture of a computer as seen by the microprogrammer.

[29] The term 'retargetable' in the context of microcode generation systems, refers to the ability of the system to produce microcode for arbitrary architectures.

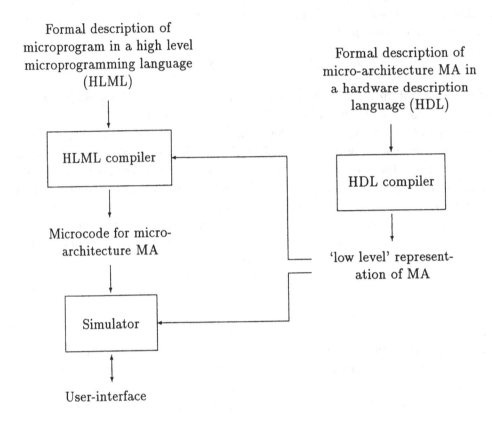

Fig. 7.14 General structure of a retargetable microprogramming system.

ation of the various 'dimensions' of the hardware description space that are relevant
to the problem of describing micro-architectures.

As specific examples of such deliberations it was known from a previously published
analysis of HDLs (Dasgupta 1982) that the primary dimensions of the hardware
description space were

(a) The levels of hardware description that are permitted by the language. Instances of such description (or abstraction) levels include the exo-architectural,
   the micro-architectural, the register-transfer, the logic and circuit levels. A particular HDL may be designed for a specific subset of these levels.
(b) Whether the HDL permits only operational (or algorithmic) specification of hardware systems, or only functional specifications, or some combination of the two.

(c) Whether the language allows procedural descriptions, non-procedural descriptions, or both.[30]

(d) Whether the power of the HDL is to be confined to the specification of structure only, or behavior only, or can be enlarged to include both.

The choice of which aspects of these dimensions are necessary for S*M was based on an analysis and identification of the characteristics of micro-architectures relevant to the application to which micro-architectural descriptions were to be put (fig. 7.14), and by identifying the right 'match' between the dimensional 'values' and the micro-architectural characteristics. A discussion of these choices is presented in some detail in Dasgupta (1985), Dasgupta, Wilsey and Heinanen (1986). In the case of S*M the most significant requirements that emerged from such deliberations were that

(i) S*M must allow for description of behavior (of hardware entities) in an axiomatic functional style.[31]

(ii) S*M will be confined to non-procedural modes of description.

From these and other requirements, a conceptual *model* of clocked architectures was constructed (Dasgupta 1984, 1985, Wilsey 1985). The model showed how an architecture would be viewed when described in S*M so as to satisfy the requirements identified in the previous stage. To give the reader some 'feel' for the model, at the very highest level, it defines a clocked micro-architecture by a 4-tuple:

$$\langle S,\ F,\ C,\ T \rangle$$

where S is a set of *stores*, F is a set of *functional modules*, C is a set of *clocks* and T an entity called the *timekeeper*. Each of these entities and their mutual relationships are further elaborated in the form of other properties. Thus, for example, the

---

[30] In *procedural* descriptions, the textual ordering of statements determines implicitly the ordering of the execution of the actions described by the statements. All programming, microprogramming and hardware description languages in the so called von Neumann style are procedural languages. In contrast, a *non-procedural* description is one in which the textual ordering of statements does not direct their execution ordering. Rather, a statement S_i is selected for execution whenever a specific condition C_i is true. The general form for such statements, then, is $C_i \Rightarrow S_i$. If several conditions $C_1, C_2, \ldots, C_n$ are true at a given time then the corresponding statements $S_1, S_2, \ldots, S_n$ will all be selected for execution. Dataflow graphs represent one such class of non-procedural descriptions (Dennis 1974, Arvind and Gostelow 1982).

[31] A *functional* style of specification is one which prescribes (or describes) the behavior of an entity in terms of its input/output characteristics. A specific instance of the functional style is the *axiomatic* style in which the behavior of the entity being described is expressed in terms of a pair of assertions that characterizes what are true of the entity at the beginning of the activation and at the termination of its activation. These assertions are referred to as the *precondition* and *postcondition* respectively (Dasgupta, Wilsey and Heinanen 1986, Damm 1988).

behavior of all functional modules in F is defined axiomatically, i.e., in terms of precondition/postcondition pairs; each module in F is activated non-procedurally when a particular clock in C is in a particular state; and so on.

The model, then serves as a *bridge* between the requirements and the language-to-be: on the one hand it captured the requirements in a formal, precise way; on the other, the structure and characteristics of the model's components directly represented the required features of S*M. S*M, the language, literally emerged from the model.

It is worth noting that in the course of designing S*M, the model itself underwent modification from an earlier version (as described in Dasgupta (1984, 1985)) to the later and final version described in Wilsey (1985) and Dasgupta, Wilsey and Heinanen (1986). Thus, the model serves as a focus of discussion and criticism.

This same language design method of requirements analysis/model building/synthesis was used to design a successor to S*M called ACE (Wilsey 1987, Wilsey and Dasgupta 1989, 1990).
End Example

7.7 SUMMARY

To sum up, we have seen that the ASE paradigm is widely regarded as constituting a correct model of how design is (or at any rate should be) conducted. The process of design, according to ASE, is composed of three principal and distinguishable phases, viz., analysis, synthesis, and evaluation. Furthermore, analysis precedes synthesis which precedes evaluation. And, while feedback loops to earlier stages of analysis or synthesis are admissible the paradigm by its very nature is strongly committed to the notion of extensive, detailed and comprehensive analysis preceding synthesis.

I have suggested that the ASE paradigm is founded on a now discredited model of science, viz., the inductive model. We have noted that inductivism as a logical foundation of both science and design is seriously deficient.

Even disregarding inductivism, there are other problems with the ASE paradigm. These have to do, firstly, with the idea of clearly separating the intellectual activities of analysis and synthesis; secondly, with the explicit ordering of the three stages; and thirdly, with its exclusion of the role of the designer's world view in the design process. It was shown, however, that one important way in which these fundamental limitations of ASE could be alleviated to some extent is by using conceptual models that serve partly as specifications of requirements and partly as designs.

My criticism of ASE is a criticism of the paradigm *qua* general paradigm. Which is not to say that for specific and restricted classes of design problems it is not a legitimate or even *the* appropriate paradigm. Stated simply, if a design problem is both sufficiently *small* (in the sense of comprising one or two requirements) and *well-structured* (see chapter 3) then it may indeed be possible not only to make a separation between the activities of analysis, synthesis, and evaluation, but also to conduct analysis prior to synthesis and synthesis prior to evaluation; or even to synthesize a form from the requirements specification such that evaluation is not even necessary!

Many instances of algorithm design and small, highly structured or 'toy' programming problems are of this type. In the next chapter we shall consider a paradigm called *formal design* which is a stronger and special version of ASE and which is applicable to precisely these types of design problems.

Chapter 8

The Formal Design Paradigm

8.1 DESIGNS AS FORMAL ENTITIES

A *formal system* consists of a set of *axioms* – that is, formulas or assertions that are assumed or known to be true – and a set of *inference* or *proof rules* that allows one to make deductions. Given a formal system a *formal proof* of an assertion or formula F consists of a finite sequence of formulas

$$F_1 , F_2 , \ldots, F_n = F$$

such that each F_i is deduced from F_{i-1} ($2 \leq i \leq n$) using the set of axioms and the rules of inference. A formula F for which there exists a formal proof is called a *theorem*.

Let us suppose that the requirements R of a design problem and the design D itself are both representable within the common framework of a formal system. In that case the problem of demonstrating that D satisfies R – that there is a fit between D and R – can be addressed by the designer *formally proving* the assertion 'D satisfies R'. The latter assertion becomes, in effect, a theorem.

The notion of treating designs as formal entities so that one may prove (or *verify*) their correctness with respect to a requirements set is at the heart of the *formal design* (FD) paradigm. This paradigm originated some two decades ago in seminal papers by Floyd (1967) and Hoare (1969) which together laid the foundations for proving the correctness of programs. Subsequent developments have been extensive and a vast literature now exists on the theory of formal software design and verification. (See, e.g., Manna 1974, Alagic and Arbib 1978, Dijkstra 1976, de Bakker 1980, C. B. Jones 1980, 1986, Gries 1981, Backhouse 1986, Hoare and Shepherdson 1985, Gordon 1988a).

Since the mid 1970s, the notion of designs as formally verifiable entities has been applied to the domains of firmware (Dasgupta 1988, Damm 1988), computer architectures (Dasgupta 1984) and gate and transistor level hardware circuits (Gordon

1986, 1988b, Hunt 1987, Joyce 1988). It is, therefore, quite meaningful to talk of the existence of a formal design paradigm for computing *systems* in general.

8.2 THE FORMAL APPROACH IN PROGRAMMING

In an inaugural lecture delivered in the University of Oxford, Hoare (1986) enunciated a set of postulates which perhaps most succinctly serve to establish the manifesto of the formalist school of programming:

(a) *Computers are mathematical machines.* That is, their behavior can be mathematically defined and every detail is logically deducible from the definition.

(b) *Programs are mathematical expressions.* They describe precisely and in detail the behavior of the computer on which they are executed.

(c) *A programming language is a mathematical theory.* That is, it is a formal system which helps the programmer in both developing a program and proving that the program satisfies the specification of its requirements.

(d) *Programming is a mathematical activity*, the practice of which requires application of the traditional methods of mathematical understanding and proof.

In this section I shall describe the nature of the FD paradigm in its original context, viz., program development. Later sections will address the role of the paradigm in other types of computing systems.

Consider the problem of programming in an imperative programming language such as Pascal, Occam, or Ada. According to the FD paradigm, a programmer's task begins with a pair of assertions (formulas) expressed in a formal language such as the first order predicate calculus. One of these assertions, called the *precondition* ('PRE') is such that it is always true whenever the program (yet to be developed) begins execution. The second assertion, called the postcondition ('POST') is such that it is always true whenever the program completes execution. The programmer's brief is to develop a program P in a particular programming language L such that a proof for the formula

$$\{PRE\} \ P \ \{POST\} \tag{8.1}$$

can be constructed. This formula is to be read as 'if PRE is true to begin with, the termination of P's execution (providing it does terminate) results in POST being true.'

According to the *FD* paradigm, the formula (8.1) can be proved *formally* since according to Hoare's principles stated above, P is a mathematical entity expressed in a language L that satisfies mathematical laws, and PRE and POST are both, by their very nature, mathematical expressions. Formulas of the form (8.1) were first proposed by Hoare (1969) and, following convention, will be referred to as *Hoare formulas.*[1]

There are essentially two distinct aspects of the formal approach that need to be considered. Firstly, how does one go about *proving* Hoare formulas? Secondly, how is the proof procedure used *during* the program design process?

8.3 HOARE LOGIC

From the perspective of design theory (as discussed in Part I) it will be noted that the $\langle$PRE, POST$\rangle$ pair is a way of specifying the requirements R that the program P must satisfy; therefore, proving a Hoare formula is nothing but a formal demonstration that P satisfies R. In the context of the FD paradigm such an exercise is usually called *program verification* and it is customary to say that the program P has been proved (or verified to be) *correct* with respect to its $\langle$PRE, POST$\rangle$ pair.

Furthermore, a proof of the Hoare formula (8.1) is said to be a proof of *partial correctness* in as far as the postcondition will hold *provided* that P terminates. The interpretation of (8.1) does not guarantee or assert that P *will* terminate. A program P is said to be *totally correct* if (a) it is shown to be partially correct and (b) it is shown that P will terminate. For the purpose of this discussion of the FD paradigm we shall be restricting our attention to issues of partial correctness. Formal systems for proving total correctness are described by Dijkstra (1976) and Gries (1981).

Finally, recalling the evolutionary model of the design process (chapter 5) note that a proof of the correctness of P with respect to $\langle$PRE, POST$\rangle$ is a formal method of conducting a critical test of the fit between design and requirements.

Let us consider, then, the issue of proving Hoare formulas. Consider, in particular, a sequential program.

$$Pl \quad : \quad \textbf{begin } S_1 \text{ ; } S_2 \textbf{ end}$$

Suppose further that (i) the state of Pl's set of variables at the beginning of its execution is such that it always satisfies an assertion A_0 ; and (ii) the termination of Pl's execution leaves its variables in such a state as to always satisfy assertion A_2. The resulting Hoare formula becomes

$$\{A_0\} \quad \textbf{begin } \; S_1 \text{ ; } \; S_2 \; \textbf{ end } \; \{A_2\} \tag{8.2}$$

The way that one can go about proving (the truth of) (8.2) is as follows.

---

[1] The actual notation used by Hoare (1969) was 'PRE $\{P\}$ POST.' The notation of (8.1) is, however, that which is most commonly used in current practice.

An additional assertion A_1 is invented such that we first prove the Hoare formulas

$$\{A_0\} \quad S_1 \quad \{A_1\} \qquad\qquad (8.3)$$

$$\{A_1\} \quad S_2 \quad \{A_2\} \qquad\qquad (8.4)$$

and from this, we attempt to infer that (8.2) is true.

Proving the correctness of programs in this manner demands a formal or deductive system whereby proofs for Hoare formulas can thus be generated; and it was Hoare's significant contribution through his 1969 paper to propose such a system – which, subsequently and for obvious reasons, has come to be known as *Hoare Logic*.[2]

Before explicating the nature of this logic the following points must be made: following de Bakker (1980), it is convenient to collectively refer to assertions such as PRE and POST in (8.1) or to Hoare formulas of the form (8.1) as *correctness formulas*. A correctness formula may be true for some particular state of a program's set of variables, false for other states. A correctness formula is said to be *valid* if it is true for all possible states.

Hoare logic consists of a set of *axioms* that characterize the semantics of the atomic constituents of a programming language (or, as will be seen later, of a microprogramming or a hardware description language), and a collection of *inference rules* or *proof rules* that characterize the semantics of the language's composite statements. Such proof rules will be specified using the notation

$$\frac{F_1 \, , \; F_2 \, , \; \ldots \, , \; F_n}{F} \qquad\qquad (8.5)$$

which is to be read as 'if it can be proved that the formulas $F_1, F_2, \ldots, F_n$ are valid then it may be inferred that the formula F is also valid. $F_1, \ldots, F_n$ are referred to as *premises* or *antecedents* while F is the *conclusion* or *consequence*, respectively. $F_1, \ldots, F_n$ are correctness formulas while F is restricted to being a Hoare formula. Finally, the semantics of a programming language specified in terms of Hoare logic is said to be *axiomatically* defined.

Fig. 8.1 presents a partial description of the axiomatic semantics of the programming language Pascal.[3] It consists of a single axiom, proof rules for three of the executable

---

[2] The term *Floyd–Hoare logic* is also used in this context in recognition of Floyd's (1967) contribution to the topic.

[3] The detailed axiomatic definition of Pascal as constructed originally by Hoare and Wirth (1973) and further enhanced by Alagic and Arbib (1978) contains axioms that characterize data types and the various predefined operations, as well as proof rules for statements not shown in fig. 8.1.

Axiom of Assignment: $\{P[X/E]\}\ X\ :=\ E\{P\}$

Rule of Sequential Composition:

(PR1)
$$\frac{\{P_1\}\ S_1\ \{P_2\},\ \{P_2\}\ S_2\ \{P_3\},\ \dots,\ \{P_n\}\ S_n\ \{P_{n+1}\}}{\{P_1\}\ \textbf{begin}\ S_1;\ S_2;\ \dots;\ S_n\ \textbf{end}\ \{P_{n+1}\}}$$

Conditional Rules:

(PR2)
$$\frac{\{P \wedge B\}\ S\ \{Q\},\ P \wedge \neg B \supset Q}{\{P\}\ \textbf{if}\ B\ \textbf{then}\ S\ \{Q\}}$$

(PR3)
$$\frac{\{P \wedge B\}\ S_1\ \{Q\},\ \{P \wedge \neg B\}\ S_2\ \{Q\}}{\{P\}\ \textbf{if}\ B\ \textbf{then}\ S_1\ \textbf{else}\ S_2\ \{Q\}}$$

Iteration Rules:

(PR4)
$$\frac{\{P \wedge B\}\ S\ \{P\}}{\{P\}\ \textbf{while}\ B\ \textbf{do}\ S\ \{P \wedge \neg B\}}$$

(PR5)
$$\frac{\{P\}\ S\ \{Q\},\ Q \wedge \neg B \supset P}{\{P\}\ \textbf{repeat}\ S\ \textbf{until}\ B\ \{Q \wedge B\}}$$

Rules of Consequence:

(PR6)
$$\frac{\{P\}\ S\ \{R\},\ R \supset Q}{\{P\}\ S\ \{Q\}}$$

(PR7)
$$\frac{P \supset R,\ \{R\}\ S\ \{Q\}}{\{P\}\ S\ \{Q\}}$$

Fig. 8.1 Partial axiomatic semantics of Pascal.

statements in the language, and two additional proof rules the functions of which will be shortly explained.

Consider the assignment statement $X\ :=\ E$ where X is (the identifier of) a variable and E is an arbitrary expression such that X and E are type compatible. The *informal* semantics of the assignment tells us that E is first evaluated and the resulting value assigned to X.

The *axiomatic* semantics of the assignment as shown in fig. 8.1 – the axiom of assignment – is to be interpreted as follows. Let P be an assertion and let $P\,[X/E]$ denote P with all free occurrences of the identifier X replaced by E.[4] Then the axiom of assignment

$$\{P\,[X/E]\,\}\ \ X\ \ :=\ \ E\ \{P\}$$

states that if P is the postcondition of an assignment then its precondition – strictly speaking, the *weakest* precondition (Dijkstra 1976) – is $P\,[X/E]$.

It will be noted that the axiom as stated may be usefully applied as a *backward* rule: given a postcondition P that is required to hold on termination of an assignment, it states what the weakest precondition $R\ =\ P\,[\,X/E\,]$ will be such that

$$\{R\}\ \ X\ \ :=\ \ E\ \{P\}$$

is valid.

The proof rule (PR1) for the sequential block says that if the Hoare formulas $\{P_1\}\ S_1\ \{P_2\}, \{P_2\}\ S_2\ \{P_3\},\dots,\{P_n\}\ S_n\ \{P_{n+1}\}$ are valid, then so is the Hoare formula $\{P_1\}\ \textbf{begin}\ S_1\,;\ S_2\,;\dots;\ \ S_n\ \textbf{end}\ \{P_{n+1}\}$.

Rule (PR2) states that given that P holds on entry to an **if** ... **then** statement, if the premises $\{P \wedge B\}\ S\ \{Q\}$ and $\{P \wedge \neg B\}\ \supset\ Q$ are valid then $\{P\}$ **if** B **then** $S\{Q\}$ is also valid. (PR3) is the corresponding proof rule for the **if** ... **then** ... **else** statement.

In the first of the two iteration proof rules (PR4), the assertion P is called a *loop invariant* as it remains unchanged regardless of the number of times the loop body is executed.

Of the last two rules, (PR6) allows for the *weakening* of a postcondition: if the execution of a statement S ensures that an assertion R is true, it also ensures the truth of an assertion implied by R. (PR7) allows a precondition to be *strengthened*: if an assertion P implies an assertion R such that R is the precondition of a valid Hoare formula involving a statement S and a postcondition Q, then the formula $\{P\}\ S\ \{Q\}$ is also valid.

---

[4] Recall that an occurrence of a variable X in an assertion P is *bound* if it appears within P in the form $\exists\,X\ :\ P'$ or $\forall\,X\ :\ P'$. Otherwise, the occurrences of X in P are *free*. For more on free and bound variables see any text on logic, e.g., Shoenfield (1967). Gries (1981) also discusses the distinction in the context of program verification.

Example 8.1
Let x_0, y_0 be two non-negative integers. We are required to prove the (partial) correctness of the Hoare formula

$$\{X \ = \ x_0 \ \wedge \ Y \ = \ y_0\}$$
$$\textbf{begin}$$
$$\quad S := 0;$$
$$\quad \textbf{while} \ \neg \ (X = 0) \ \textbf{do}$$
$$\quad\quad \textbf{begin}$$
$$\quad\quad\quad \textbf{while} \ \neg \ \mathrm{ODD}(X) \ \textbf{do}$$
$$\quad\quad\quad\quad \textbf{begin}   \qquad\qquad\text{(HF)}$$
$$\quad\quad\quad\quad\quad Y := Y * 2;$$
$$\quad\quad\quad\quad\quad X := X \ \textbf{div} \ 2$$
$$\quad\quad\quad\quad \textbf{end};$$
$$\quad\quad\quad\quad S := S + Y;$$
$$\quad\quad\quad X := X - 1$$
$$\quad\quad \textbf{end}$$
$$\quad \textbf{end}$$
$$\{S \ = \ x_0 \ * \ y_0\}$$

Our general proof procedure will consist of a number of steps. In each step we either generate or identify one or more new Hoare formulas that have to be proved correct or we actually prove such formulas. The overall proof procedure will also follow the *stepwise refinement* style first advocated in the context of program development by Wirth (1971, 1973) – in the sense that if in any given step the proof of a Hoare formula is not possible, the formula will be recursively decomposed into simpler Hoare formulas for which proofs will be attempted and so on.

Step 1F
First key additional assertions are identified and inserted into (HF). This produces the overall *proof outline* shown below

$$\{ X \ = \ x_0 \ \wedge \ Y \ = \ y_0\}$$
$$\textbf{begin}$$
$$\quad S := 0;$$
$$\quad \{X * Y + S = x_0 * y_0\}$$
$$\quad \textbf{while} \ \neg \ (X = 0) \ \textbf{do}   \qquad\qquad\text{(POO)}$$
$$\quad\quad \textbf{begin}$$
$$\quad\quad\quad \text{STMT1}$$
$$\quad\quad \textbf{end}$$

$$\{X * Y + S = x_0 * y_0 \wedge X = 0\}$$
end
$$\{S = x_0 * y_0\}$$

where STMT1 is the identifier for the outermost loop body in (HF).

At the topmost abstraction level, if it can be shown that

$$\{X = x_0 \wedge Y = y_0\}$$
$$S := 0$$ \hfill (HF11)
$$\{X * Y + S = x_0 * y_0\}$$

and

$$\{X * Y + S = x_0 * y_0\}$$
while $\neg(X = 0)$ **do begin** STMT1 **end** \hfill (HF12)
$$\{X * Y + S = x_0 * y_0 \wedge X = 0\}$$

then from proof rules (PR1) and (PR6) (see fig. 8.1) it follows that

$$\{X = x_0 \wedge Y = y_0\}$$
begin
$$\quad S := 0;$$
$$\quad \textbf{while } \neg(X = 0) \textbf{ do}$$ \hfill (HF0)
$$\quad\quad \textbf{begin } STMT1 \textbf{ end}$$
end
$$\{S = x_0 * y_0\}$$

(HF0) is, of course, the desired theorem.

Consider (HF11). Applying the assignment axiom backwards, the weakest precondition for $S := 0$ given its postcondition is

$$X * Y = x_0 * y_0 \hfill (\text{Al1})$$

and since $X = x_0 \wedge Y = y_0 \supset (\text{Al1})$, (HF11) follows by applying (PR7). It remains to be shown that (HF12) is valid.

Step 2F

(HF12) can be refined to the following proof outline:

$$\{X * Y + S = x_0 * y_0\}$$
while $\neg(X = 0)$ **do**
   $\{X * Y + S = x_0 * y_0 \land X \neq 0\}$
   begin   (PO1)
    STMT1
   end
$$\{X * Y + S = x_0 * y_0 \land X = 0\}$$

Thus, in order to prove (HF12) it is required to be shown that

$$\{X * Y + S = x_0 * y_0 \land X \neq 0\}$$
  STMT1   (HF21)
$$\{X * Y + S = x_0 * y_0\}$$

In that case (HF12) may be deduced by applying proof rule (PR4).

Step 3F
(HF21) can be stated in the equivalent form

$$\{X * Y + S = x_0 * y_0 \land X \neq 0\}$$
STMT1 : **begin**
  STMT2 : **while** $\neg$ ODD(X) **do**
    begin
     STMT3   (HF21)$'$
    end;
   $S := S + Y;$
   $X := X - 1$
  end
$$\{X * Y + S = x_0 * y_0\}$$

Thus, if it can be proved that:

$$\{X * Y + S = x_0 * y_0 \land X \neq 0\}$$
  STMT2   (HF31)
$$\{X * Y + S = x_0 * y_0 \land X \neq 0 \land \text{ODD}(X)\}$$

and that

$$\{X * Y + S = x_0 * y_0 \wedge X \neq 0 \wedge \text{ODD}(X)\}$$
$$S := S + Y;$$
$$X := X - 1 \tag{HF32}$$
$$\{X * Y + S = x_0 * y_0 \wedge \neg \text{ODD}(X)\}$$

then by proof rule (PR1) it will follow that

$$\{X * Y + S = x_0 * y_0 \wedge X \neq 0\}$$
$$STMT2;$$
$$S := S + Y; \tag{HF33}$$
$$X := X - 1;$$
$$\{X * Y + S = x_0 * y_0 \wedge \neg \text{ODD}(X)\}$$

and since

$$X * Y + S = x_0 * y_0 \wedge \neg \text{ODD}(X) \supset X * Y + S = x_0 * y_0$$

it will follow from proof rule (PR6) that (HF21) is valid.

Consider (HF32). Applying the axiom of assignment backwards to $X := X - 1$ we first obtain as the latter's weakest precondition

$$(X - 1) * Y + S = x_0 * y_0 \wedge \neg \text{ODD}(X - 1)$$

That is,

$$X * Y + S - Y = x_0 * y_0 \wedge \text{ODD}(X)$$

Using this as the postcondition for $S := S + Y$ and applying the assignment axiom again the weakest precondition

$$X * Y + S + Y - Y = x_0 * y_0 \wedge \text{ODD}(X)$$

that is,

$$X * Y + S = x_0 * y_0 \wedge \text{ODD}(X) \tag{A31}$$

obtains. Since

$$X * Y + S = x_0 * y_0 \wedge X \neq 0 \wedge \text{ODD}(X) \supset (A31)$$

(HF32) follows from proof rule (PR7).

Step 4F
Consider (HF31) with STMT2 refined to its actual form:

$$\{X * Y + S = x_0 * y_0 \land X \neq 0\}$$
$$STMT2: \quad \textbf{while} \neg \text{ODD}(X) \textbf{ do}$$
$$\textbf{begin}$$
$$Y := Y * 2; \qquad\qquad\qquad\qquad\qquad \text{(HF31)}'$$
$$X := X \textbf{ div } 2$$
$$\textbf{end}$$
$$\{X * Y + S = x_0 * y_0 \land X \neq 0 \land \neg \text{ODD}(X)\}$$

To prove this using proof rule (PR4) it must first be established that '$X * Y + S = x_0 * y_0 \land X \neq 0$' is indeed an invariant for the **while** statement. That is, it is required to be proved that

$$\{X * Y + S = x_0 * y_0 \land X \neq 0 \land \neg \text{ODD}(X)\}$$
$$\textbf{begin}$$
$$Y := Y * 2;$$
$$X := X \textbf{ div } 2 \qquad\qquad\qquad\qquad\qquad \text{(HF41)}$$
$$\textbf{end}$$
$$\{X * Y + S = x_0 * y_0 \land X \neq 0\}$$

Applying the assignment axiom backwards to $X := X \textbf{ div } 2$ we obtain as the latter's weakest precondition

$$(X \textbf{ div } 2) * Y + S = x_0 * y_0 \land X \textbf{ div } 2 \neq 0 \qquad \text{(A41)}$$

Applying the same axiom backwards to $Y := Y * 2$ with (A41) as the postcondition leads to the following weakest precondition for $Y := Y * 2$:

$$(X \textbf{ div } 2) * (Y * 2) + S = x_0 * y_0 \land X \textbf{ div } 2 \neq 0 \qquad \text{(A42)}$$

Since

$$X * Y + S = x_0 * y_0 \land X \neq 0 \land \neg \text{ODD}(X) \quad \supset$$
$$(X \textbf{ div } 2) * (Y * 2) + S = x_0 * y_0 \land X \textbf{ div } 2 \neq 0$$

It follows, by applying proof rule (PR7), that (HF41) is valid.

Step 4B
Having proved (HF41), applying rule (PR5) we determine that (HF31) is correct (see step 4F).

Step 3B
Since (HF31) and (HF32) are both correct, the argument given in step 3F leads to the conclusion that (HF21) is valid.

Step 2B
Since (HF21) is valid, (HF12) (see step 2F) is true by application of proof rule (PR5).

Step 1B
Finally, given that both HF11 and HF12 are valid it follows from the argument given in step 1F that HF0 is valid.

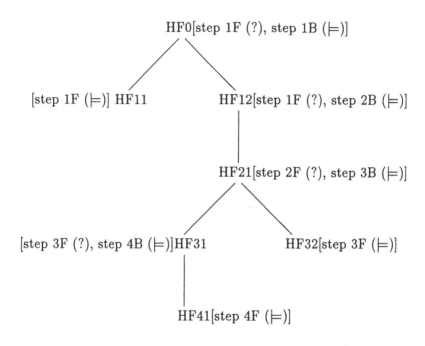

Fig. 8.2 Tree of Hoare Formulas for example 8.1.

Fig. 8.2 shows the tree of the Hoare formulas involved in proving the correctness of the original program. The steps in which a particular formula was generated (but not proved) is indicated alongside the formula with a '?' in parenthesis. The step in which a formula was proved is indicated by a '⊨' in parenthesis.
End Example

8.4 THE FORMAL DEVELOPMENT OF PROGRAMS
The preceding section described the role of formal reasoning in proving the correctness of an *existing* program. However, from the perspective of design paradigms a more interesting issue is whether or how Hoare Logic can serve as a basis for *developing* programs.

This question has, in fact, already been addressed in a different context in chapter 5 (section 5.4, example 5.9). There, I described an approach to program development called the *design-while-verify* (DWV) method.

As noted in example 5.9, the DWV method was first advocated by Dijkstra (1976) and Mills (1975) and further studied by Alagic and Arbib (1978), Jones (1980), Gries (1981) and others. It combines the principle of stepwise refinement with the theory of program correctness. The idea is to develop a program and its proof of correctness together, allowing the proof to guide both refinement and development. The DWV method is, thus, an instance *par excellence* of the FD paradigm.

Example 5.9 also described (in a different context) the development of a sorting program by Alagic and Arbib (1978) based on the DWV method. The reader may profitably review the steps outlined there. In the present section I shall present small examples of the formal development of programs using the DWV method.

Example 8.2
To develop a Pascal program that computes the greatest common divisor (GCD) of two positive integers X and Y. More precisely: let $Z = \mathrm{GCD}(X, Y)$. Then Z is such that (i) Z divides X exactly; (ii) Z divides Y exactly; (iii) Z is the largest integer satisfying (i) and (ii).

Let
$$Z = \mathrm{GCD}(X, Y)$$
denote the assertion

$$X \bmod Z = 0 \wedge Y \bmod Z = 0 \wedge$$
$$\neg \exists Z' : Z' > Z \wedge X \bmod Z' = 0 \wedge Y \bmod Z' = 0 \qquad \text{(A0)}$$

Here, $i \bmod j$ denotes the integer remainder resulting from dividing integer i by integer j.

The pre- and postconditions, then, are

$$\text{PRE}: X > 0 \wedge Y > 0$$
$$\text{POST}: Z = \mathrm{GCD}(X, Y)$$

The nature of PRE and POST suggests the following program form:

Initialize Z to the smallest of X, Y
while Z does not divide exactly into X and Y
do $Z := Z - 1$

Further refinement of this produces the following Pascal program along with its pre- and postconditions:

{PRE: $X > 0 \wedge Y > 0$}
if $X < Y$ then $Z := X$ else $Z := Y$;
while X mod $Z \neq 0 \vee Y$ mod $Z \neq 0$ do   (HF0)
  $Z := Z - 1$
{POST: $Z = GCD(X, Y)$}

Let us *postulate* the following invariant for the loop:

I: $X > 0 \wedge Y > 0 \wedge Z \leq X \wedge Z \leq Y \wedge$
  $\neg \exists Z' : Z' > Z \wedge X$ mod $Z' = 0 \wedge Y$ mod $Z' = 0$

The objective here is to exploit the proof rule for the **while** statement (fig. 8.1, PR4). If it can be shown that I holds on entry to the loop and if further that

{$I \wedge (X$ mod $Z \neq 0 \vee Y$ mod $Z \neq 0)$}
  $Z := Z - 1$ (HF1)
  {I}

then from (PR4) it follows that when the loop terminates

$$I \wedge X \text{ mod } Z = 0 \wedge Y \text{ mod } Z = 0$$

That is,

$$Z = GCD(X, Y)$$

Inserting I into (HF0) produces the following proof outline:

{PRE $: X > 0 \wedge Y > 0$}
> if$X < Y$ then $Z := X$ else $Z := Y$;

{$I : X > 0 \wedge Y > 0 \wedge Z \leq X \wedge Z \leq Y \wedge$ (P00)
  $\neg \exists Z' : Z' > Z \wedge X$ mod $Z' = 0 \wedge Y$ mod $Z' = 0$}
> while X mod Z $\neq$ 0 ∨ Y mod Z $\neq$ 0 do
> $Z := Z - 1$

POST: $Z = GCD(X, Y)$

Consider the formula

$\{\text{PRE}: X > 0 \wedge Y > 0\}$
if $X < Y$ **then** $Z := X$ **else** $Z := Y$ (HF2)
   $\{I\}$

To prove this (using proof rule PR3, fig. 8.1) requires that the following Hoare formulas be shown valid:

$\{\text{PRE} \wedge X < Y\} Z := X \{I\}$ (HF3)
$\{\text{PRE} \wedge X \geq Y\} Z := Y \{I\}$ (HF4)

The weakest precondition for $Z := X$ given I as its postcondition is (applying the axiom of assignment):

$$X > 0 \wedge Y > 0 \wedge X \leq X \wedge X \leq Y \wedge \qquad\qquad\qquad\qquad \text{(A1)}$$
$$\neg \exists Z': Z' > X \wedge X \bmod Z' = 0 \wedge Y \bmod Z' = 0$$

that is

$$X > 0 \wedge Y > 0 \wedge X \leq Y \wedge \qquad\qquad\qquad\qquad\qquad \text{(A2)}$$
$$\neg \exists Z': Z' > X \wedge X \bmod Z' = 0 \wedge Y \bmod Z' = 0$$

Referring to (HF3), given the precondition PRE $\wedge X < Y$, the clause

$$\neg \exists Z': Z' > X \wedge X \bmod Z' = 0 \wedge Y \bmod Z' = 0$$

is obviously true. Hence PRE $\wedge X < Y \supset$ (A2). Thus (HF3) is valid. By a similar argument (HF4) can also be shown to be valid. Hence (HF2) is valid. The assertion I is, therefore, true when the **while** statement first begins execution.

Consider now, the Hoare formula

$\{I \wedge (X \bmod Z \neq 0 \vee Y \bmod Z \neq 0)\}$ (HF5)
   $Z := Z - 1$
    $\{I\}$

Applying the axiom of assignment backwards the weakest precondition for $Z := Z - 1$, given postcondition I is

$$X > 0 \wedge Y > 0 \wedge Z - 1 \leq X \wedge Z - 1 \leq Y \wedge \qquad\qquad\qquad \text{(A3)}$$
$$\neg \exists Z': Z' > Z - 1 \wedge X \bmod Z' = 0 \wedge Y \bmod Z' = 0$$

Now, the actual precondition for $Z := Z - 1$ in (HF5) is

$$X > 0 \wedge Y > 0 \wedge Z \leq X \wedge Z \leq Y \wedge$$
$$\neg\exists\, Z' : Z' > Z \wedge X \bmod Z' = 0 \wedge Y \bmod Z' = 0$$
$$\wedge\ (X \bmod Z \neq 0 \vee Y \bmod Z \neq 0) \qquad\qquad\qquad (A4)$$

In other words, the actual precondition (A4) is such that (i) Z is less than or equal to X and Y; (ii) Z does not divide exactly into X or Y; and (iii) there is no larger integer Z' that divides exactly into both X and Y. (A4) clearly implies (A3) in which case, invoking the rule of consequence (PR7), it may be concluded that (HF5) is valid. In other words, I is indeed an invariant for the loop.

It follows from the proof rule (PR4) that when (and if) the loop terminates, the assertion

$$X > 0 \wedge Y > 0 \wedge X \bmod Z = 0 \wedge Y \bmod Z = 0 \wedge$$
$$\neg\exists\, Z' : Z' > Z \wedge X \bmod Z' = 0 \wedge Y \bmod Z' = 0$$

that is,
$$Z = \mathrm{GCD}(X, Y)$$

is true.

Finally, total correctness of the program (HF0) can be demonstrated by first observing that at the start of the iteration

$$X > 0 \wedge Y > 0 \wedge Z \leq X \wedge Z \leq Y \wedge (Z = X \vee Z = Y)$$

Furthermore, each iteration of the loop body decrements Z by 1 so that *eventually* Z will equal 1 in which case the boolean expression

$$X \bmod Z \neq 0 \vee Y \bmod Z \neq 0$$

will return **false** and the loop will terminate.
End Example

Example 8.3

Write a Pascal program which, given an integer array $A[0 .. N-1]$ for a fixed $N \geq 0$, stores in Z the sum of the elements of A.

The pre- and postconditions for this problem are

$$\text{PRE} : N \geq 0$$
$$\text{POST} : Z = A[0] + A[1] + \cdots + A[N-1]$$

An initial program form suggested by the postcondition is

(a) Initialize Z to 0;
(b) Scan A and add its elements successively to Z until all elements
    of A have been added.   (PG)

Clearly, (b) demands a loop. Moreover, the latter must be such that at the time it is first entered, the condition $Z = 0$ is satisfied and upon its termination the condition POST is satisfied. The following loop invariant and terminating condition are suggested:[5]

$$P : (0 \leq J \leq I - 1 \wedge 0 \leq I \leq N \supset$$
$$Z = \sum A[J] : J) \wedge N \geq 0$$
$$B : I \neq N$$

P states that given that $0 \leq I \leq N$ and $0 \leq J \leq I - 1$, Z will contain the sum of the first I elements of A (i.e., $A[0] + A[1] + \cdots + A[I-1]$).

Using the postulated invariant P and boolean expression B, (PG) is refined to a Pascal form which, with the assertions inserted appropriately, yields the following proof outline:

$\{\text{PRE} : N \geq 0\}$

$\quad Z := 0;$
$\quad I := 0;$

$\{P : (0 \leq J \leq I - 1 \wedge 0 \leq I \leq N \supset$
$\quad\quad Z = \sum A[J] : J) \wedge N \geq 0\}$

---

[5] The notation $\sum X(k) : k$ is used to signify the sum of the elements of X over the range of the variable k. An alternative notation that is also used here is $\sum X(k) : k = i, \ldots, j$ where i, j define the bounds of the range of k.

> while $I \neq N$ do
>   begin
> $Z := Z + A[I]$;
> $I := I + 1$
>   end

(PO1)

$\{\text{POST} : Z = \sum A[J] : J = 0, \dots, N - 1\}$

The weakest precondition for $I := 0$ given P as its postcondition is

$$P' : 0 \leq J \leq -1 \wedge 0 \leq N \supset Z = \sum A[J] : J) \wedge (N \geq 0)$$

and the weakest precondition for $Z := 0$ given P' as its postcondition is

$$P'' : 0 \leq J \leq -1 \wedge 0 \leq N \supset 0 = \sum A[J] : J) \wedge (N \geq 0)$$

Since $0 \leq J \leq -1$ is always **false** the implication in P'' is always **true** so that P'' reduces to $N \geq 0$ which is PRE. Thus the assertion P holds when the loop is first entered. To show that P is also an invariant requires us to prove the formula

$$P \wedge I \neq N$$
$$Z := Z + A[I];$$
$$I := I + 1$$
$$\{P\}$$

(HF1)

The weakest precondition for $I := I + 1$ given P as its postcondition is

$$P^* : (0 \leq J \leq I \wedge 0 \leq I+1 \leq N \supset$$
$$Z = \sum A[J] : J) \wedge N \geq 0$$

The weakest precondition for $Z := Z + A[I]$ given P^* as its postcondition is

$$P^{**} : (0 \leq J \leq I \wedge 0 \leq I+1 \leq N \supset$$
$$Z + A[I] = \sum A[J] : J) \wedge N \geq 0$$

Consider the given precondition in (HF1). Expanding this it is clear that

$$P \wedge I \neq N \supset P^{**}$$

Hence (HF1) is valid. Thus, applying the proof rule (PR4) for the **while** statement we obtain as the latter's postcondition

$$P \wedge I = N \equiv (0 \leq J \leq I - 1 \wedge 0 \leq I \leq N \supset Z = \sum A[J] : J)$$
$$\wedge N \geq 0 \wedge I = N$$

That is, the condition

$$POST: \quad Z = \sum A[J] : J = 0, \ldots, N - 1$$

End Example

As stated in section 8.1, the FD paradigm is also applicable to the design of computing systems other than programs. In the next few sections I shall discuss the nature and use of the FD paradigm in the domains of computer architecture, firmware (microprograms) and hardware, respectively.

8.5 THE FD PARADIGM IN COMPUTER ARCHITECTURE

That computer architecture is a discipline – to which design theory can or should be applied – is a viewpoint that most architectural theorists and practitioners have traditionally ignored. In any case, it is a viewpoint that is of very recent origin. For example, the first systematic treatment of computer architecture as a design discipline appears to be Dasgupta (1984) and my discussion here of the formal design of architectures is largely based on this work.

The question of what *is* computer architecture has been discussed by several authors including Myers (1982), Dasgupta (1984, 1989a) and Hayes (1988). For our present purposes, the following characteristics will suffice to initiate this discussion.[6]

(a) An architecture is *an abstraction of some hardware/firmware system* in the sense that it describes the structure, behavior and performance of the hardware/firmware device viewed as an abstract information processing system.

(b) Architectural attributes include both (i) the externally observable features of the device as visible to the assembly language programmer or compiler writer (the *exo-architecture*) and (ii) its internal organization, structure, and behavior (the *endo-architecture*).

The computer architect is thus, a designer of information processing systems that can be directly realized by a combination of hardware and firmware. Stated in another way, an architectural design may be viewed as *a specification of functional, structural, performance* (and other) *constraints* that are to be met by a system which will be implemented by a combination of hardware and firmware (Aguero and Dasgupta 1987).

---

[6] For a more detailed discussion of 'what is computer architecture' see Dasgupta (1984, chapter 1; 1989a, chapter 1) and Aguero and Dasgupta (1987).

At the heart of the above definition – and the key to applying formal design – is that the architect is a designer of abstract information processing systems in the same sense that the programmer designs information processing systems. The main distinction is that the architect's design is directly *implemented in* hardware/firmware whereas a software design is implemented as (executable) software to be *executed by* a hardware/firmware system.

It is, then, possible to design an architecture (either the exo-architecture alone, the endo-architecture alone, or a highly integrated combination of both) and formally specify it in an *architecture description language* (ADL). ADLs form a subclass of a broader class of languages called *hardware description languages* (HDLs) (Dasgupta 1982; 1989b, chapters 3,4). Like programming languages, an ADL can itself be defined by a set of axioms and proof rules such that one can prove the correctness of an architectural design with respect to its requirements by first specifying the requirements in the form of pre- and postconditions and then proving that the ADL description of the design is correct with respect to the pre-/postconditions.

The first widely studied ADL was ISPS conceived originally by Bell and Newell (1971) and further developed and implemented by Barbacci and his coworkers (Barbacci *et al.* 1978, Barbacci 1981). ISPS has been widely used for the formal description, simulation and evaluation of architectures, especially exo-architectures (Barbacci and Parker 1980, Barbacci and Siewiorek 1982, Siewiorek, Bell and Newell 1982, Djordjevic, Ibbett and Barbacci 1980). However, the semantics of ISPS has never been formally defined and, consequently, the language has never served as the basis for formally designing or verifying architectural descriptions.

As far as is known to this writer, the first ADL for which a proof theory was constructed, was S*A, designed by Dasgupta (1982, 1983) as one of a projected family of languages and implemented in prototypal form by Makarenko (1982).[7] A proof theory for S*A is presented in Dasgupta (1984) and its applications to both proving the correctness of a prior S*A description as well as developing provably correct architectural descriptions (in the DWV style) are illustrated.

S*A is a general purpose, high level, procedural ADL. To a large extent its design was influenced by such programming languages as Pascal and Concurrent Pascal (Brinch Hansen 1977). Of course, as S*A was designed to describe *architectures* its most distinctive features are precisely those constructs appropriate for architectural

---

[7] The prototype implementation consisted of a compiler for S*A that produced a form of executable code and a simulator that interpreted the compiled code on a VAX 11/780 running under UNIX.

(rather than software) specifications. Furthermore, the semantics of the language is defined in terms of what types of hardware components correspond to the constructs.

Stated briefly, an architecture is described in S*A in the form of an entity called a *system* which, in general, would consist of a set of simpler systems so that architectural descriptions can be composed hierarchically. The simplest system consists of a set of global data objects and one or more entities called *mechanisms* where the latter is similar to an abstract data type in the programming sense (Liskov and Guttag 1986). An example of the skeletal composition of a hierarchical system is shown in fig. 8.3.

```
sys MACHINE_X;
  sys INSTRUCTION_CYCLE;
    mech INST_FETCH; ...; endmech;
    mech INST_DECODE; ...; endmech;
    sys INST_EXEC;
      mech FETCH_OPRND; ...; endmech;
      mech EXECUTE; ...; endmech;
    endsys
  endsys
  sys MEMORY;
    mech AUX_MEM; ...; endmech;
    mech MAIN_MEM; ...; endmech;
  endsys
endsys
```

Fig. 8.3 Skeleton of an S*A system.

A mechanism, in fact, is the smallest unit of architectural description; it is composed of a collection of *private* data object declarations and one or more procedures and functions that access, operate on, and update these objects. The *only* access to the private data objects within a mechanism is through the procedures and functions contained in the same mechanism. Mechanisms interact with one another through the global data objects (fig. 8.4).

The basic executional entities from which procedures and functions are composed include the usual statements of imperative languages (e.g., the assignment, sequential composition, **if** statement, **while** statement, etc.) and several additional constructs idiosyncratic to S*A. The data objects are instances of data types that are specific to the architectural context.

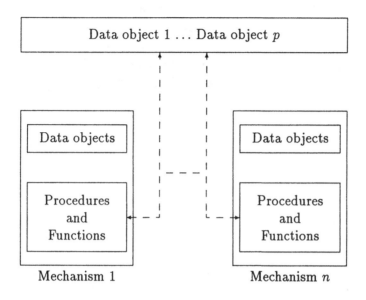

Fig. 8.4 Interaction of mechanisms in S*A.

I shall illustrate the nature of the axioms and proof rules for S*A with several examples of its more distinctive constructs.

Example 8.4
S*A contains the simple data type **bit** and the structured data types sequence, array, tuple and stack. Of these, consider only the **bit** and the sequence.

(1) The data type **bit** consists of the values $\{0, 1\}$. Operations defined on type **bit** consist of the logical operations $\{\wedge, \vee, \neg, \oplus, \neg\wedge, \neg\vee\}$ and the arithmetic operations $\{+, -, *, /\}$

    (1a) Given X, Y of type **bit**, X/Y is undefined for $Y = 0$

    (1b) Given X of type **bit** X represents a binary storage element.

(2) Let T denote a sequence data type: $\mathbf{seq}[i_h \ \ldots \ i_l]$ **bit**

    (2a) $i_h \geq i_l, \quad i_h, i_l \geq 0$

    (2b) Let $i_h \geq i \geq i_l$

        Then $T \ : \ \{i_h, \ \ldots \ , i_l\} \rightarrow$ **bit**. That is, $T(i)$ is an element of type **bit**.

    (2c) Let $\langle bb \ldots b \rangle_{i_l}^{i_h}$ denote a binary string of length $i_h - i_l + 1$. Then,

$$T = \left\{ \langle 00 \ldots 0 \rangle_{i_l}^{i_h} \ \ldots \ \langle 11 \ldots 1 \rangle_{i_l}^{i_h} \right\}$$

That is, a **seq** type is defined both as a mapping function (2b) and as a set of values.

(2d) Logical, arithmetic and shift operations are defined on T so as to satisfy a number of axioms (not stated here).

(2e) Let data object X be of type T. Then X represents any device capable of storing binary strings in the range of values defined by T (2c) such that the elements of the binary string can be accessed in parallel.

End Example

Example 8.5

A synchronizer declaration

$$\textbf{sync } X \; : \; T$$

where T is the type **bit** or **seq**, introduces a data object of type T with the following properties.

The standard procedures **await** X and **sig** X are defined on X according to the following axioms:

(a) $\{X \; = \; x_0 \; > \; 0\}$ **await** X $\{X \; = \; x_0 \; - \; 1 \; \geq \; 0\}$
     $\{X \; = \; x_0 \; = \; 0\}$ **await** X $\{\text{false}\}$
(b) $\{X \; = \; x_0 \; : \; 0 \; \leq \; x_0 \; < \; MAX\}$ **sig** $\{X \; = \; x_0 \; + \; 1 \; > \; 0\}$

where MAX is the maximum integer valued state possible for X and x_0 is a symbolic value.

End Example

Example 8.6

The parallel statement $S_1 \parallel S_2$ specifies the simultaneous execution of S_1 and S_2. The next statement in sequence begins execution when both S_1 and S_2 have terminated. The proof rule is:

$$\frac{\{P_1\} \; S_1 \; \{Q_1\}, \; \{P_2\} \; S_2 \; \{Q_2\}, \; \text{dynamically\_disjoint}(S_1, \; S_2)}{\{P_1 \; \wedge \; P_2\} \; \textbf{do} \; S_1 \parallel S_2 \; \textbf{od} \; \{Q_1 \; \wedge \; Q_2\}}$$

where the predicate *dynamically_disjoint* $(S_1, \; S_2)$ is true if during the period that S_1, S_2 are both in execution their data resource sets are disjoint.

End Example

Example 8.7

await statements are either of the form **await** X **do** S **od** or **await** B **do** S **od** where X is a synchronizer and B a predicate. In the first form, statement S will execute if and only if the synchronizer $X \geq 1$. Thus, **await** X **do** S **od** is formally equivalent to the sequential statement

> **await** X ;
> S

except that the former is an *indivisible* statement.

In the second form, the predicate B is continuously evaluated until it returns **true** at which time S begins execution.

The proof rules for the two statements are

$$\frac{\{Q\}\ S\ \{R\}, \quad \{P\}\ \textbf{await}\ X\ \{Q\}}{\{P\}\ \textbf{await}\ B\ \textbf{do}\ S\ \textbf{od}\ \{Q\}} \tag{AW1}$$

$$\frac{\{P \wedge B\}\ S\ \{Q\}}{\{P\}\ \textbf{await}\ B\ \textbf{do}\ S\ \textbf{od}\ \{Q\}} \tag{AW2}$$

End Example

The concept of physical time is absent from S*A. Thus, the fact that accessing a word from main memory and storing it in a processor register requires a memory clock cycle of 400 nanoseconds (ns), or that the execution of a register-to-register transfer requires 50 ns, cannot be captured in S*A. In this sense S*A is very similar to programming languages. The formal design of an architecture in S*A thus reduces to the problem of describing the architecture in S*A and applying the latter's proof rules to demonstrate the correctness of the description with respect to a given pair of pre-/postconditions.

Example 8.8

Consider an *instruction fetch* process which accesses main memory at some address specified by the program counter (pc), reads the memory word's contents into a 32-bit memory buffer register (mbr) and then transfers this to a 32-bit instruction register (ir). The fetch process is also responsible for updating the pc in preparation for fetching the next sequential instruction.

A second process for *instruction decode* accesses the instruction register (ir) and isolates the operation part of the instruction in preparation for executing the instruction.

The two processes, denoted FETCH and DECODE respectively, are to operate concurrently. Furthermore, at this particular stage of designing the architecture no assumptions are to be made as to the physical times required by the respective processes. Thus, FETCH and DECODE will be required to operate in an asynchronous, parallel fashion.

Assuming the S*A declarations

> **type** word, register = **seq**[31 .. 0] **bit** ;
> **var** mbr, inst_reg : register ;
> **var** mem : **array** [0 .. 64K] **of** word ;
> **var** pc, mar : seq [15 .. 0] **bit**
> **var** opcode_reg : **seq** [7 .. 0] **bit**

(where 'mar' is the memory address register associated with the main memory 'mem'), the pre- and postconditions for FETCH and DECODE are

> PRE(FETCH) : $\{pc = pc_0\}$
> POST(FETCH) :   inst_reg = mem$[pc_0]$ $\wedge$
> $\qquad\qquad\qquad$ pc $= pc_0 + 1$
> PRE(DECODE) : $\{inst\_reg = ir_0\}$
> POST(DECODE) : opcode_reg = op_part_of (ir_0)

(where 'op_part_of' is a function that returns the opcode portion of its argument.)

In the above, pc_0 and ir_0 are *auxiliary variables*. That is, they are required only for correctness proofs and not in the S*A description itself; they typically record some aspect of the state of the 'execution' of the S*A description.

The initial form of the overall process is

$$\textbf{do FETCH } \| \textbf{ DECODE od}$$

Since inst_reg is a shared data object the parallel operation of FETCH and DECODE must guarantee that access or update of inst_reg by one process does not jeopardize its access or update by the other. To ensure this, we define two synchronizers (see examples 8.5 and 8.7):

$$\textbf{sync } F \ : \ \textbf{bit } (1)$$
$$\textbf{sync } D \ : \ \textbf{bit } (0)$$

where the numbers in parenthesis denote the initial values of F and D respectively.

Based on these declarations and the pre-/postconditions, the following S*A description (with the assertions inserted appropriately) eventually emerges:

FD :
  do
    FETCH : **forever do**
        $\{pc = pc_0\}$
      FETCH1 : mar := pc ;
               mbr := mem[mar] ;
               await F **do** inst_reg := mbr **od** ;
               do sig D ‖ pc := pc + 1 **od**
               $\{pc = pc_0 + 1 \wedge \text{inst\_reg} = mem[pc_0]\}$
          od

  ‖
    DECODE : **forever do**
        $\{\text{inst\_reg} = ir_0\}$
      DECODE1 : **await** D **do** opcode_reg :=
                          op_part_of(inst_reg)
               od ;
          sig F
          $\{\text{opcode\_reg} = \text{op\_part\_of}(ir_0)\}$
        od
  od

Note that both FETCH and DECODE are nonterminating loops. It is therefore sufficient to show that the concurrent operation of the loop *bodies* FETCH1 and DECODE1 do not interfere with one another.

The problem of proving the correctness of *parallel systems*, though of more recent vintage than the sequential program correctness problem, has a substantial literature (see, e.g., Milner (1980), Owicki and Gries (1976), Owicki and Lamport (1982), Andrews and Schneider (1983), Soundarajan (1984), Hoare (1985), Chandy and Misra (1988) for its discussion in the software domain, and Damm (1988) in the context of firmware). The particular technique that can be used is one proposed by Owicki and Gries (1976) for parallel programs involving shared variables.[8]

The basic idea of the Owicki–Gries technique is to first prove that each of the individual Hoare formulas

---

[8] Soundarajan (1984) describes an alternate approach to the Owicki–Gries technique for the shared variable model.

$$\{pc = pc_0\}$$
$$\quad \text{FETCH1} \hspace{6cm} \text{(HF1)}$$
$$\{pc = pc_0 + 1 \wedge \text{inst\_reg} = \text{mem}[pc_0]\}$$

and

$$\{\text{inst\_reg} = ir_0\}$$
$$\quad \text{DECODE1} \hspace{5.5cm} \text{(HF2)}$$
$$\{\text{opcode\_reg} = \text{op\_part\_of}(ir_0)\}$$

is correct (ignoring the presence of the other) using the proof rules for the **await** statement, sequential composition, the parallel statement and the axiom of assignment. Note in particular that since the constituents of the parallel statement

$$\textbf{do sig } D \parallel pc := pc + 1 \textbf{ od}$$

are obviously dynamically disjoint, the proof rule presented in example 8.6 will apply in a straightforward manner.

The proof is then completed by showing that (i) the *proof* of (HF1) is not affected by the concurrent operation of DECODE1; and (ii) the *proof* of (HF2) is not affected by the concurrent operation of FETCH1.

More precisely, Owicki and Gries propose the following approach in order to realize the above goal. Firstly, their version of the **await** statement is

$$\textbf{await } B \textbf{ then } S \hspace{5cm} \text{(OGA)}$$

where B is a boolean expression and S is a statement not containing another parallel statement or another **await** statement. The proof rule for (OGA) is identical to the rule (AW2) shown in example 8.7.

Secondly, the proof rule for the parallel statement is proposed as

$$\frac{\{P_1\}\ S_1\ \{Q_1\},\ \ldots,\{P_n\}\ S_n\ \{Q_n\}\ \text{are interference free}}{\{P_1 \wedge \ldots \wedge P_n\}\ \textbf{do}\ S_1 \parallel \ldots \parallel S_n\ \textbf{od}\ \{Q_1 \wedge \ldots \wedge Q_n\}}$$

where the predicate *interference free* is defined as follows:

Given a proof $\{P\}\ S\ \{Q\}$ and a statement T with precondition $\text{PRE}(T)$, we say that T *does not interfere* with $\{P\}\ S\ \{Q\}$ if

(i) $\{Q \land PRE(T)\} \; T \; \{Q\}$

(ii) Let S' be any statement with S but not within an **await** statement. Then $\{PRE(S') \land PRE(T)\} \; T \; \{PRE(S')\}$

Informally, a statement T does not interfere with a proof of $\{P\} \; S \; \{Q\}$ if the former's execution has no effect on the truth of the precondition of S and the final postcondition used in the proof of S.

$\{P_1\} \; S_1 \; \{Q_1\}, \; \ldots, \; \{P_n\} \; S_n \; \{Q_n\}$ are then said to be *interference free* if the following holds: let T be an **await** or assignment statement (that does not appear in an **await**) of S_i. Then, for all $j \neq i$, T does not interfere with $\{P_j\} \; S_j \; \{Q_j\}$.

To actually apply the Owicki–Gries technique to the S*A description above, requires us to first transform the **await** statements into ones that are formally equivalent to the Owicki–Gries version (OGA). Given the S*A **await**

> **await** X **do** S **od**

where X is a **bit** type synchronizer (see example 8.7), this is first transformed to

> **await** X ;
> S

The '**await** X' is further transformed to the equivalent S*A form:

> **await** $X = 1$ **do** $X := 0$ **od**

which is semantically identical to (OGA).

The FETCH–DECODE process previously described (FD) now becomes

```
FD' :
  do
    FETCH' : forever do
        {pc = pc₀}
        FETCH1' : mar := pc ;
                  mbr := mem[mar] ;
                  await F = 1 do F := 0 od;
                  inst_reg := mbr ;
                  do D := 1 ∥ pc := pc + 1 od
                  {pc = pc₀ + 1  ∧  inst_reg = mem[pc₀]}
            od
```

DECODE' : **forever do**
    $\{\text{inst\_reg} = \text{ir}_0\}$
  DECODE1' : **await** $D = 1$ **do** $D := 0$ **od** ;
          opcode_reg :=op_part_of(inst_reg)
          $F := 1$
          $\{\text{opcode\_reg} = \text{op\_part\_of}(\text{ir}_0)\}$
      od

  od

I leave it as an exercise to the reader to prove, using the Owicki–Gries technique that

$\{\text{pc} = \text{pc}_0 \ \wedge \ \text{inst\_reg} = \text{ir}_0 \}$
  do FETCH1' $\|$ DECODE1' **od**
$\{\text{pc} = \text{pc}_0 + 1 \ \wedge \ \text{inst\_reg} = \text{mem}[\text{pc}_0] \ \wedge$
    $\text{opcode\_reg} = \text{op\_part\_of}(\text{ir}_0)\}$

is valid.
End Example

8.6 THE FORMAL DESIGN OF MICROPROGRAMS

A microprogram is, after all, a 'kind of' program. Hence the application of the FD paradigm to microprogramming seems quite natural. In particular, the development of a Hoare logic for microprograms began with the work of Patterson (1976), was further advanced by Wagner and Dasgupta (1983; see also Dasgupta and Wagner 1984), and has most recently culminated in the work of Damm and his colleagues (Damm *et al.* 1986, Damm 1988).[9]

Since microprograms (i.e., firmware) characterize computer behavior at a distinctly lower level of abstraction than either programs or the kinds of architecture descriptions considered in the previous section, the formal design of firmware is not an entirely straightforward matter of transferring the paradigm from one domain to another. Rather, it involves the careful modification and extension of the concepts invented in the software domain so that they are adapted to the idiosyncratic nature of firmware.

The main problem is that microprograms – even those specified in a *high level microprogramming language* (HLML) – are fundamentally *machine specific*. That is, a

---

[9] Formal verification of microprograms is described in detail by Dasgupta (1988). In addition to the axiomatic approach, this reference discusses other techniques including those due to Carter *et al.* (Leeman, Carter and Birman 1974, Carter, Joyner and Brand 1978) and Crocker and his coworkers (Crocker, Marcus and van Mierop 1980, Marcus, Crocker and Landauer 1984).

microprogram is meaningful only in the context of the specific *real* 'host' machine that will execute it. This is to be contrasted to programs such as those written in a high level language in that the latter are designed as entities that are independent of the machine that will execute them.[10,11]

As a result, a proof theory for such a language as Pascal (see section 8.4) is not sufficient for the firmware domain since the various conditions that actually arise in the specific host machine *must* be taken into account when formally developing or verifying firmware.

This is quite strikingly illustrated by considering the axiom of assignment. We have already seen (in section 8.4) that the 'standard' axiom is

$$\{ P[X/E] \} \ X \ := \ E \ \{P\}$$

The axiom says, in effect, that the only distinction between the pre- and postconditions of the assignment lies in the replacement of all (free) occurrences of X in the postcondition P by E in the precondition. Nothing else in P changes.

This however, is hardly the case in the microprogramming domain. The following examples point out the difficulties in the case of one specific but not atypical, host micro-architecture.

Example 8.9
A part of the Nanodata QM-1 (Nanodata 1979) data path is shown in fig. 8.5. The QM-1 is a *universal host machine* – that is, a user-microprogrammable general emulation engine with the capability of implementing and emulating a wide spectrum of target exo-architectures.[12]

In order to investigate the verifiability of QM-1 microcode a proof theory was constructed by Wagner and Dasgupta (1983; Dasgupta and Wagner 1984) for the micro-

---

[10,] This view of the abstract nature of programs is, of course, at the very heart of the FD paradigm as exemplified by Hoare's 'manifesto' (see section 8.2 above). Another version of this view is due to Dijkstra (1976, chapter 26) who makes the point that the central notion in programming is that of specifying computation as exactly as possible; the task of the computer is to execute such programs as efficiently as it can. But see section 8.8 below for more on this.

[11] For discussion of the basic nature of firmware, see Dasgupta (1980a,b), Dasgupta and Shriver (1985).

[12] In addition to Nanodata (1979), Salisbury (1976), Marsland and Demco (1978) and Dasgupta (1984) have detailed descriptions of this machine. For discussions of universal host machines see Flynn and Huck (1984) and Dasgupta (1989a).

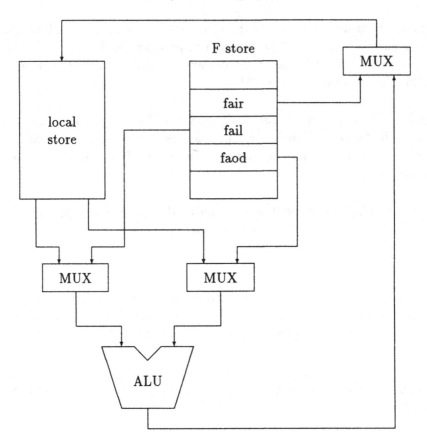

Fig. 8.5 QM-1 data path.

programming language S*(QM-1) (Klassen and Dasgupta 1981, Dasgupta 1984).[13] The present and following examples are based on this proof theory.

Consider the *simple* assignment statement

$$X := Y \tag{AS0}$$

where X, Y both denote local store registers in the QM-1. A particular instance of this construct is the statement

$$\text{local\_store}[15] := \text{local\_store}[14] \tag{AS1}$$

---

[13] S*(QM-1) is a machine-specific *instantiation* of the machine independent microprogramming language *schema* called S* (Dasgupta 1978, 1984) both of which belong to a family of languages developed by Dasgupta and others called the S* family. Other languages in this family include S*A (see section 8.5), S*M (Dasgupta, Wilsey and Heinanen 1986), and the AADL/S* subfamily (Damm *et al.* 1986, Damm 1988). The S* family was discussed in the context of design evolution in chapter 5 (example 5.12).

In the QM-1, local store registers cannot be directly accessed as specified here. They can only be accessed by assigning constants to registers in the F store (see fig. 8.5) which serve as array index variables. Thus, the execution of (AS1) in $S^*(QM-1)$ results, *as side-effects* in the setting of appropriate F store registers to 15 and 14 respectively.

The axiom of the simple assignment (AS0) is, therefore defined as follows:

First, let P be an assertion. Then

$$P\,[X_1/Y_1]\,[X_2/Y_2]\,\cdots\,[X_n/Y_n]$$

signifies the *simultaneous* replacement of $X_1\,\ldots\,X_n$ by $Y_1\,\ldots\,Y_n$ respectively. The axiom of assignment is, then,

$$\{P[X/Y][SEL/V]\}\ X\ :=\ Y\ \{P\}$$

where SEL denotes locations 'side-effected' as a result of the assignment and V denotes the set of corresponding values assigned to the locations in SEL. That is:

$$P[SEL/V]\ =\ P[SEL/V_1][SEL_2/V_2]\,\cdots\,[SEL_n/V_n]$$

End Example

Example 8.10
The second class of assignment statements in $S^*(QM-1)$ is of the form

$$X\ :=\ E \qquad\qquad (AS2)$$

where E is an expression. In executing an $S^*(QM-1)$ microprogram, *the evaluation of an expression can lead to side effects.* As a specific instance, consider the statement

$$\text{local\_store[faod]}\ :=\ \text{local\_store[fail]}\ l\ \ll\ s(5) \qquad\qquad (AS3)$$

Here 'fail' is the F store register used to identify the local store register that will serve as the left input to the ALU and 'faod' is the F store register that identifies the local store register that will serve as the destination of the ALU operation (see fig. 8.5).

The evaluation of the expression in (AS3) causes (i) a left logical shift of 5 positions on local_store[fail], and (ii) a side effect in which the binary encoded values for the 'left logical shift' operation and the shift amount are stored in special registers kshc and ksha that are both part of what in the QM-1 is called the K vector.[14]

---

[14] The reasons for these side effects are not important for the purpose of the present discussion. See, however, Dasgupta 1984 for further details.

Keeping in mind that the side-effects inherent in the simple assignment (AS0) are also invoked in the case of (AS2), the axiom of the assignment form (AS2) is

$$\{\ P[\mathrm{SEL}/V_1][K/V_2][X/E]\ \}\ \ X\ :=\ E\ \{P\}$$

where SEL, as in example 8.9, denotes the F store locations 'side-effected' as a result of performing the assignment and V_1 signifies the corresponding values; and K denotes the registers in the K vector that are set, as side effects, to values V_2 as a result of evaluating the expression E.
End Example

The surprising complexity of the axioms of assignment in S*(QM-1) – and in fact all its proof rules – can be attributed to the fact that concepts such as 'operators', 'expressions' and 'assignments' have to be interpreted somewhat differently in the firmware domain from their connotations in programming. For example, the assignment statements in S*(QM-1) are not assignments at all but are *atomic* (indivisible) *procedures* that modify several locations.

As is well known, microprograms are usually *horizontal*. That is, they involve the parallel execution of micro-operations from the same microinstruction. Thus, microprogramming languages in general, have *parallel* statements for which proof rules have to be constructed. Parallelism in microprograms is a rather complex affair because of the effect of different *timing schemes* by which the executions of the various micro-operations within a microinstruction are controlled (Dasgupta 1979, 1989a, Mueller and Varghese 1988). For instance an entire microinstruction may be executed under the control of a *monophase* (i.e., one-phase) clock cycle, in which case all its constituent micro-operations would execute simultaneously. More commonly the microinstruction's execution may be controlled by a *polyphase* clock such that some micro-operations are activated in the earliest (first) phase, others in the second phase, and so on. In this latter situation the entire microinstruction executes in a single clock cycle although there may not be strict simultaneity amongst the constituent micro-operations.

All this makes the construction of a satisfactory proof rule for a parallel statement in a microprogramming language somewhat nontrivial. In fact it is only with Damm's (1988) recent detailed analysis that really satisfactory proof rules for parallel microprograms have been developed. My example below, however, is taken from S*(QM-1) and is intended to convey the general flavor of such proof rules.

Example 8.11

The general form for the parallel statement in S*(QM-1) is

$$\textbf{cocycle} \ \ S_1 \ \| \ S_2 \ \| \ \dots \ \| \ S_n \ \ \textbf{coend}$$

where the S_i's are simple or composite statements. This indicates that the statements $S_1, \ \dots \ , \ S_n$ begin and end in the same clock cycle. The clock in the QM-1 is monophase. However it is possible for some micro-operations to incur *multiple* clock cycles. Hence in order for a set of statements to appear in a **cocycle** statement, their executions must all begin and end in a single clock cycle. This property is termed COCYCLIC.

Two additional properties of the **cocycle** statement must be noted. First, all the constituent statements must be mappable onto a single microinstruction. Let us call this property COMPILABLE. Notice that COCYCLIC does not imply COMPILABLE nor vice versa – two statements S_i and S_j may be COCYCLIC yet be encoded by the same field in the microinstructions; hence they are not COMPILABLE. Conversely, S_i and S_j may be COMPILABLE – occupying distinct fields of the microinstruction – but S_i may require two or more clock cycles for its execution; hence they are not COCYCLIC.

Secondly, it is necessary for all pairs of statements S_i, S_j in a **cocycle** to be dynamically disjoint – that is, there are no data dependencies between them nor do they require a common set of functional units for their execution. Call this property DISJOINT.

The proof rule for the **cocycle** statement in S*(QM-1) then, is (Dasgupta and Wagner 1984, Wagner and Dasgupta 1983):

$$\frac{\text{For all } (1 \ \leq \ i \ \leq \ n)\{P_i\} \ S_i \ \{Q_i\}, \ \text{COCYCLIC, COMPILABLE, DISJOINT}}{\{P_1 \ \wedge \ \dots \ \wedge \ P_n\} \ \textbf{cocycle} \ S_1 \ \| \ \dots \ \| \ S_n \ \textbf{coend} \ \{Q_1 \ \wedge \ \dots \ \wedge \ Q_n\}}$$

In summary, the studies of Patterson (1976), Dasgupta and Wagner (1984) and Damm (1988) have shed light not only on the nature of the proof theories relevant to microprograms; they have also demonstrated that microprograms can indeed be designed according to the FD paradigm.

Using the proof theory for S*(QM-1), Dasgupta and Wagner (1984) showed how the QM-1 microcode to implement a multiply instruction could be developed and proved using the DWV method. Damm *et al.* used the AADL/S* system as a basis for the rigorous *stepwise design* of firmware. Fig. 8.6 outlines their overall approach.

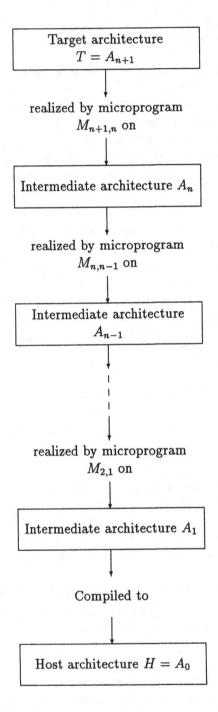

Fig. 8.6 The AADL/S* design method.

The design method begins with a formal specification of both the target (exo-)architecture $T = A_{n+1}$, and the host (micro-)architecture $H = A_0$ in the same architecture description language – in their case AADL (Damm 1985, Damm and Doehmen 1985). The designer's task is to develop a microprogram M that implements T on H. This is carried out by constructing, in top down, hierarchical fashion, one or more *intermediate* architectures, A_n, A_{n-1}, ... , A_1, where A_j is more abstract than A_{j-1} ($n \geq j \geq 2$) and each of the A_j's is expressed in AADL.

Each design step j, then creates a microprogram M_{j+1}, j (in an instantiated version of S^*) that realizes A_{j+1} on A_j. The microprogram M_{j+1}, j refines the data structures and operations of A_{j+1} using the data structures and operations available in A_j and, at the same time, uses the proof systems for AADL$/S^*$ to demonstrate that $M_{j+1,j}$ is correct. The final program $M_{2,1}$ is then compiled into executable microcode for the host machine H.
End Example

8.7 THE FORMAL DESIGN OF HARDWARE STRUCTURES

From the programmer's point of view a computer is a structure with a great deal of plasticity: it provides a set of very abstract commands, the potential for creating an arbitrary large number of abstract data objects and a small set of composition rules. Out of these, an infinite variety of programs can be invented each of which endows the computer with a distinct personality – each creates in fact, a unique new computer out of the old.

This plasticity progressively reduces as one proceeds down the ladder of abstraction levels. At the exo-architectural level one still sees a set of commands, the potential for creating data objects and composition rules. However, they are more concrete than before; they are bound to physical entities. The structure of the computer seen at the exo-architectural level is less plastic, more rigid.

The rigidity of the computing structure becomes still more evident at the microprogramming level. The microprogrammer has some flexibility in that the rules of composition allow considerable variation in the way that commands can be composed; however, the data objects are now fixed and the nature of the commands are determined by these data objects and the transfer paths between them (fig. 8.5) as well as the constraints imposed by physical clocks.

Eventually, at the hardware abstraction level the structure of the computer is revealed in all its invariant detail. At this level, the system has hardly any plasticity; it is a *wired* structure, composed of components (with a given behavior) that are connected

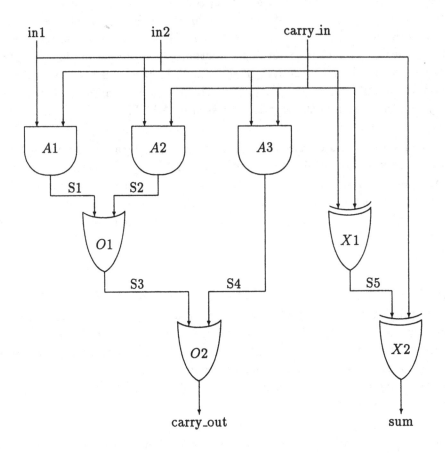

Fig. 8.7 The logic-level structure of a 1-bit full adder.

to one another in a fixed way such that the behavior of the structure as a whole is determined from the behavior of the components and their mutual connectivity relationships. There are no *rules* of composition allowing for plasticity of behavior. The composition is fixed. Thus, for example, fig. 8.7 expresses the fact that there are three AND gates, two OR gates and two EXCLUSIVE OR (XOR) gates (each of which has well defined behavior) and these are wired to one another in a fixed way.

The formal design of hardware is, thus, problematic in the following sense. On the one hand the target design can certainly be described in a *behavioral* way as it is commonly done using many of the hardware description languages (Dasgupta 1982). In other words, the behavioral specification *is* the design. Fig. 8.8 shows such a specification of the 1-bit full adder of fig. 8.7 in a VHDL-like notation.[15]

---

[15] VHDL is a hardware description language the development of which was originally sponsored

---

entity full_adder **is**
  port
    (in1, in2, carry_in: **in bit**;
     sum, carry_out: **out bit**)
  end full_adder;

  architecture behavioral_description **of** full_adder **is**
    begin
      sum <= in1 **xor** in2 **xor** carry_in **after** 30ns;
      carry_out <= ((in1 **and** in2) **or** (in1 **and** carry_in))
                 or (in2 **and** carry_in) **after** 30ns;
    end

Fig. 8.8 Behavioral description of 1-bit full-adder.

---

architecture structure **of** of full_adder **is**
  component and_gate **port** (a, b: **in bit**; c: **out bit**);
  component or_gate **port** (a, b: **in bit**; c: **out bit**);
  component xor_gate **port** (a, b: **in bit**; c: **out bit**);

  − internal signals

  signal S1, S2, S3, S4, S5: **bit**

  begin
    X1: xor_gate(in2, carry_in, S5);
    X2: xor_gate(S5, in1, sum);
    A1: and_gate(in1, in2, S1);
    A2: and_gate(in1, carry_in, S2);
    A3: and_gate(in2, carry_in, S4);
    O1: or_gate(S1, S2, S3);
    O2: or_gate(S3, S4, carry_out);
  end

Fig. 8.9 Structural description of 1-bit full adder.

---

by the U.S. Department of Defense (DoD) as part of their Very High Speed Integrated Circuit (VHSIC) program. Recently VHDL has been adopted (after some modifications) as a standard by the Institute of Electrical and Electronics Engineers (IEEE) and this standard version of VHDL is known as the IEEE-1076 standard (IEEE 1988, Lipsett, Schaeffer and Ussery 1989).

One can, then, adapt Hoare logic to the hardware domain as it has been to the microprogramming arena, and show, for example, that the description of fig. 8.8 satisfies a given pair of pre- and postconditions, using the axiomatic proof theory for the HDL. This approach was used, for example, by Pitchumani and Stabler (1983).

On the other hand, the real objective of hardware design is the creation of wired structures such as the one shown in fig. 8.7. A description of this structure in VHDL-like notation is presented in fig. 8.9. It includes a declaration of the component types (with their respective behavior presumably well defined and known) and the internal wires ('signals', in VHDL terminology); and a specification of the *instances* of the component types including the actual input and output ports for the respective instances.

The task of the formal design here, is to prove that this *structure* exhibits the desired behavior (specified, e.g., in terms of pre- and postconditions).

An adaptation of Floyd's (1967) original inductive assertion technique for the proof of correctness of such structures was proposed by Shostak (1983).[16] In his approach, *input assertions* are attached to each input wire of the circuit, *output assertions* are assigned to each circuit output and additional assertions are attached to arbitrary wires. The latter denote the *initial states* of components (such as the initial value of registers, in the case of sequential circuits). The criterion of correctness is defined as follows: if the inputs satisfy the input assertions, if the initial condition assertions are assumed to hold and if each component behaves according to its defined characteristics then the circuit outputs will satisfy the output assertions. As in Floyd's method the proof procedure involves establishing paths through the structure and establishing and proving invariant assertions at key points in the paths.

Like Floyd's method Shostak's strategy is concerned with proving the correctness of existing circuit designs rather designing provably correct circuits. More recently, Gordon and his coworkers have proposed an elegant method for the specification *and*

---

[16] As noted in section 8.1, Floyd's (1967) paper marked the beginning of the FD paradigm, though its modern form is due to Hoare's (1969) work. Floyd's method involved the representation of programs as *flowcharts* and the association of assertions with certain points in the flowchart. Each such assertion characterizes an invariant condition that is expected to hold when the flow of control reaches that point. The proof strategy is to show that given that an assertion holds at the beginning of a path through the flowchart, the execution of that path leads to an assertion being true at the end of the path. Once this is established for each possible execution path through the flowchart, an inductive argument is used to prove that given an input assertion (pre-condition), the execution of the program will lead to the truth of the output assertion (the postcondition). For more on this the reader may consult Floyd (1967) or Manna (1974).

verification of hardware based on the use of a formalism called *higher order logic* (Camilleri, Gordon and Melham 1987, Gordon 1986, Joyce 1988, Gordon 1988b) and the rest of my discussion below of the FD paradigm in the hardware context is based on their work.[17]

Higher order logic extends first order predicate logic by allowing variables to range over functions and predicates. Thus, functions and predicates can be the arguments and results of other functions and predicates.

The basic advantage is that both behavior and structure of circuits can be represented directly as formulas in higher order logic. Furthermore, the laws of this logic can be used to draw inferences and prove assertions about the circuit. Thus, higher order logic can serve both as a hardware description language and as a proof system for reasoning about hardware structures.

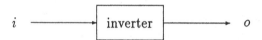

i inverter o

Fig. 8.10 A unit delay inverter.

Consider first, fig. 8.10 which symbolizes an inverter the output of which is the negated value of the input delayed by (say) one time unit (Joyce 1988). Its behavior in higher order logic can be specified as follows. The input (i) and output (o) signals can be represented by functions which map discrete time values to boolean values. Thus, the inverter's behavior can be expressed by the predicate

$$\text{INV}(i, o) \equiv \forall\, t.\; o(t + 1) = \neg\, i(t)$$

Consider now the device shown in fig. 8.11 – a structure composed of two inverters connected by an internal wire p. The behavior of each inverter is characterized by the predicate INV. The behavior of the device as a whole will be constrained by the *conjunction* of the behaviors of its constituents. Thus, the device of fig. 8.11 may be characterized by the predicate

$$\text{INV2}(i, o) \equiv \exists\, p.\; \text{INV}(i, p) \land \text{INV}(p, o)$$

---

[17] The use of higher order logic in the specification and verification of hardware was first proposed and investigated by Hanna (Hanna and Daeche 1985).

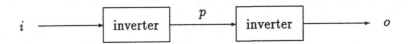

Fig. 8.11 Two inverters connected in series.

Note the use of the existential quantifier to designate the existence of *some* value on the internal wire p such that $INV(i, p)$ and $INV(p, o)$ are both satisfied.

This simple example also illustrates how the specification of a device can be composed hierarchically, from the 'bottom up': given the behavioral specification of 'more' primitive components C_1, ..., C_n, in the form of predicates, a structure S composed out of the components is defined in terms of another predicate that conjoins the given predicates. The newly composed structure S can become the component of another structure, and so on. Furthermore – and herein lies much of the attraction of this method – one can formally infer (using the theory of the logic) the behavior of S from the behavior of the components C_1, ..., C_n and their conjunction. For the inverter example above, this would entail proving that

$$\forall\, i, o\, :\, INV2(i, o)\, \supset\, \forall\, t.\; o(t + 2)\, =\, i(t)$$

that is, the output of the device is identical to its input delayed by two time units.

Example 8.12
Consider the description and verification of a 1-bit full adder with the structure shown in figs. 8.7 and 8.9. The problem with the VHDL specification (fig. 8.9) is the difficulty of proving formally that this structure implies the behavior described in fig. 8.8. We can, however, directly describe the device in the notation of logic and prove that it exhibits the desired behavior as follows.

For the sake of the present discussion, the delays associated with the adder and its components will be ignored. The three component *types* from which the adder is composed can be defined by the following predicates.

$$OR(i_1, i_2, o) \equiv o = i_1 \lor i_2$$
$$AND(i_1, i_2, o) \equiv o = i_1 \land i_2$$
$$XOR(i_1, i_2, o) \equiv o = (i_1 \land \neg\, i_2) \lor (\neg\, i_1 \land i_2)$$

The adder's *structure* can now be characterized in terms of two predicates:

SUM1(in1, in2, carry_in, sum) ≡
    ∃ S5. XOR(in2, carry_in, S5) ∧ XOR(in1, S5, sum)

CARRY_OUT(in1, in2, carry_in, carry_out) ≡
    ∃ S1, S2, S3, S4. AND(in1, in2, S1) ∧ AND(in1,
    carry_in, S2) ∧ AND(in2, carry_in, S4) ∧
    OR(S1, S2, S3) ∧ OR(S3, S4, carry_out)

Now, the *desired* behavior of the 1-bit adder can be defined by the predicates

SUM(in1, in2, carry_in, sum) ≡
    sum = (¬ in1 ∧ ¬ in2 ∧ carry_in) ∨ (¬ in1 ∧ in2 ∧
    ¬ carry_in) ∨ (in1 ∧ ¬ in2 ∧ ¬ carry_in) ∨
    (in1 ∧ in2 ∧ carry_in)

CARRY(in1, in2, carry_in, carry_out) ≡
carry_out = (in1 ∧ in2) ∨ (in1 ∧ carry_in) ∨ (in2 ∧ carry_in)

Note that SUM and CARRY represent the VHDL behavioral description of fig. 8.8 (ignoring the delay factor) while SUM1 and CARRY_OUT represent the VHDL structural description of fig. 8.9.

We are, thus, required to prove that

SUM(in1, in2, carry_in, sum) ≡ SUM1(in1, in2, carry_in, sum)

CARRY(in1, in2, carry_in, carry_out)
    ≡ CARRY_OUT(in1, in2, carry_in, carry_out)

Consider the first of these theorems:

Theorem SUM(in1, in2, carry_in, sum) ≡ SUM1(in1, in2, carry_in, sum)

Proof[18] The proof for this theorem is presented in terms of the following steps.
Step 1

SUM(in1, in2, carry_in, sum) ≡
    ∃ S5. XOR(in2, carry_in, S5)
    ∧ XOR (in1, S5, sum)   [from the definition of SUM1]

---

[18] The proof presented here is based on Camilleri, Gordon and Melham (1987)

$$\equiv$$
$$\exists \, S5. \; (S5 = (\text{in2} \land \neg \, \text{carry\_in}) \lor (\neg \, \text{in2} \land \text{carry\_in}))$$
$$\land \; (\text{sum} = (\text{in1} \land \neg \, S5) \lor (\neg \, \text{in1} \land S5)) \qquad \qquad \text{[by expanding for XOR]}$$

Step 2

Eliminating the existential quantifier:

$$\text{SUM}(\text{in1, in2, carry\_in, sum}) \equiv$$
$$\text{sum} = (\text{in1} \land \neg \, ((\text{in2} \land \neg \, \text{carry\_in}) \lor$$
$$(\neg \, \text{in2} \land \text{carry\_in}))$$
$$)$$
$$\lor \, (\neg \, \text{in1} \land ((\text{in2} \land \neg \, \text{carry\_in}) \lor$$
$$(\neg \, \text{in2}, \land \text{carry\_in})) \qquad)$$

Step 3

The definition of SUM is expanded and the equivalence $\text{SUM}(\ldots) \equiv \text{SUM1}(\ldots)$ is decomposed into two implications:

(I1) $\text{sum} = (\neg \, \text{in1} \land \neg \, \text{in2} \land \text{carry\_in})$
$$\lor \, (\neg \, \text{in1} \land \text{in2} \land \neg \, \text{carry\_in})$$
$$\lor \, (\text{in1} \land \neg \, \text{in2} \land \neg \, \text{carry\_in})$$
$$\lor \, (\text{in1} \land \text{in2} \land \text{carry\_in})$$
$$\supset$$
$$\text{sum} = (\text{in1} \land \neg \, ((\text{in2} \land \neg \, \text{carry\_in}) \lor$$
$$(\neg \, \text{in2} \land \text{carry\_in}))$$
$$)$$
$$\lor \, (\neg \, \text{in1} \land ((\text{in2} \land \neg \, \text{carry\_in}) \lor$$
$$(\neg \, \text{in2} \land \text{carry\_in}))$$
$$)$$

(I2) $\text{sum} = (\text{in1} \land \neg \, ((\text{in2} \land \neg \, \text{carry\_in}) \lor$
$$(\neg \, \text{in2} \land \text{carry\_in}))$$
$$)$$
$$\lor \, (\neg \, \text{in1} \land ((\text{in2} \land \neg \, \text{carry\_in}) \lor$$
$$(\neg \, \text{in2} \land \text{carry\_in}))$$
$$)$$
$$\supset$$
$$\text{sum} = (\neg \, \text{in1} \land \neg \, \text{in2} \land \text{carry\_in})$$
$$\lor \, (\neg \, \text{in1} \land \text{in2} \land \neg \, \text{carry\_in})$$
$$\lor \, (\text{in1} \land \neg \, \text{in2} \land \neg \, \text{carry\_in})$$
$$\lor \, (\text{in1} \land \text{in2} \land \text{carry\_in})$$

Step 4

Consider the implication (I1). Assuming its antecedent to be true, the right hand side of the antecedent equation can be substituted for 'sum' in the consequent, producing

$$(\neg \text{ in1} \wedge \neg \text{ in2} \wedge \text{ carry\_in}) \vee (\neg \text{ in1} \wedge \text{ in2} \wedge \neg \text{ carry\_in})$$
$$\vee (\text{in1} \wedge \neg \text{ in2} \wedge \neg \text{ carry\_in}) \vee (\text{in1} \wedge \text{ in2} \wedge \text{ carry\_in})$$

$=$

$$(\text{in1} \wedge \neg ((\text{in2} \wedge \neg \text{ carry\_in}) \vee (\neg \text{ in2} \wedge \text{ carry\_in})))$$
$$\vee (\neg \text{ in1} \wedge ((\text{in2} \wedge \neg \text{ carry\_in}) \vee (\neg \text{ in2} \wedge \text{ carry\_in})))$$

Step 5

This can be easily proved using the laws of boolean algebra. For the sake of descriptive and manipulative convenience, let us use $\overline{X}$ for $\neg X$, $X \cdot Y$ for $X \wedge Y$ and $X + Y$ for $X \vee Y$. The above equation can then be stated as

$$\overline{\text{in1}} \cdot \overline{\text{in2}} \cdot \text{carry\_in} + \overline{\text{in1}} \cdot \text{in2} \cdot \overline{\text{carry\_in}} +$$
$$\text{in1} \cdot \overline{\text{in2}} \cdot \overline{\text{carry\_in}} + \text{in1} \cdot \text{in2} \cdot \text{carry\_in}$$

$=$

$$\text{in1} \cdot \overline{(\text{in2} \cdot \overline{\text{carry\_in}} + \overline{\text{in2}} \cdot \text{carry\_in})}$$
$$+ \overline{\text{in1}} (\text{in2} \cdot \overline{\text{carry\_in}} + \overline{\text{in2}} \cdot \text{carry\_in})$$

The right hand side $=$

$$\text{in1} \cdot \overline{((\text{in2} \cdot \overline{\text{carry\_in}}) \cdot \overline{(\overline{\text{in2}} \cdot \text{carry\_in})}} +$$
$$\overline{\text{in1}} \cdot \text{in2} \cdot \overline{\text{carry\_in}} + \overline{\text{in1}} \cdot \overline{\text{in2}} \cdot \text{carry\_in}$$
$$= \text{in1} \cdot (\overline{\text{in2}} + \text{carry\_in}) \cdot (\text{in2} + \overline{\text{carry\_in}}) +$$
$$\overline{\text{in1}} \cdot \text{in2} \cdot \overline{\text{carry\_in}} + \overline{\text{in1}} \cdot \overline{\text{in2}} \cdot \text{carry\_in}$$
$$= (\text{in1} \cdot \overline{\text{in2}} + \text{in1} \cdot \text{carry\_in}) \cdot (\text{in2} + \overline{\text{carry\_in}}) +$$
$$\overline{\text{in1}} \cdot \text{in2} \cdot \overline{\text{carry\_in}} + \overline{\text{in1}} \cdot \overline{\text{in2}} \cdot \text{carry\_in}$$
$$= (\text{in1} \cdot \text{in2} \cdot \text{carry\_in} + \text{in1} \cdot \overline{\text{in2}} \cdot \overline{\text{carry\_in}} +$$
$$\overline{\text{in1}} \cdot \text{in2} \cdot \overline{\text{carry\_in}} + \overline{\text{in1}} \cdot \overline{\text{in2}} \cdot \text{carry\_in}$$
$$= \text{the left hand side.}$$

Step 6

Steps similar to steps 4 and 5 can be carried out for the implication (I2) and the resulting boolean identity proved.

This completes the proof of the theorem. Following a similar argument, the second theorem

$$\text{CARRY(in1, in2, carry\_in, carry\_out)}$$
$$\equiv \text{CARRY\_OUT(in1, in2, carry\_in, carry\_out)}$$

can be proved, thus completing the demonstration that the structure of the 1-bit adder exhibits the desired behavior.
End Example

8.8 LIMITS TO THE UNIVERSALITY OF FORMAL DESIGN

This chapter has, thus far, sought to explain and show how the abstract notion of *designs as formal entities* has been effectively employed across the main abstraction levels at which computing systems are conceived and designed. The general situation is, perhaps, most appropriately summed up by fig. 8.12 which shows the correspondences between the key concepts in mathematical practice and design. The FD paradigm then, treats designs along with its specification of requirements as theorems, and the proofs of correctness of such complexes as proofs of the theorems. Thus, as a specific example, given the requirement, to construct a program such that if it begins with precondition $X \geq 0 \wedge Y \geq 0$, it will terminate so as to satisfy the postcondition $Z = \text{GCD}(X, Y)$, the theorem to be proved, given some proposed program P, is the Hoare formula

$$\{X \geq 0 \wedge Y \geq 0\}$$
$$P$$
$$\{Z = \text{GCD}(X, Y)\}$$

In fact, recalling Hoare's four postulates (section 8.2) the relationship between mathematics and design, according to the FD paradigm, must be construed as *more* than a mere correspondence or an analogy. The design/requirements complexes *are* theorems in the context of an axiomatic (formal) system; and their verifications demand nothing less than deductive proofs using the axioms and the inference rules of the formal system.

Mathematics	Design
Problem definition	Specification of requirements
Theorem	Design/requirements complex
Proof	Proof

Fig. 8.12 Correspondences between design and mathematics.

The intellectual appeal of the FD paradigm is, obviously, considerable: if a design problem can be couched in formal terms then one can bring to bear on it the entire apparatus of mathematical reasoning in order to derive a provably correct solution.

There are, however, two quite fundamental limits to formal design; the first of these has significant practical implications for the universality of the FD paradigm and is discussed in this section. The other is of considerable theoretical importance and is the subject of section 8.9.

Firstly, the FD paradigm ignores those situations of design that begin with incomplete or imprecise requirements. As I noted at the end of chapter 7, the FD paradigm is meaningful only in the context of very well-structured design problems. The examples discussed in this chapter amply illustrate this fact. With respect to the discussion of the nature of the design problems in chapter 3, the requirements must not merely have to be empirical to qualify as a formal design problem; they must also be expressible in the language of a formal system. A problem that cannot be expressed in such terms cannot be solved by the FD paradigm.

Thus, as an example, a project for designing a user-interface could have as a requirement the objective that the interface must cater for both novices and experts. What constitutes a 'novice' or an 'expert' may certainly be unclear at the onset of design and may remain so for a considerable part of the design process. Obviously, one must have recourse to other, more relevant, paradigms until subproblems emerge that *are* expressible in the language of formal systems – at which time the FD paradigm *can* be adopted.

Secondly, the FD paradigm, by its very nature, does not admit any form of evidence for supporting the claims that a designer may make about a design other than mathematical proofs of correctness. Notice that the question of *evidence* is related to what kinds of arguments and knowledge one brings to bear on demonstrating that a design does (or does not) satisfy its requirements. This issue is not intrinsically related to the possible impreciseness or incompleteness of requirements. For, even where the requirements are precise and complete, the designer may be forced to invoke evidence other than proofs, both as justifications for design decisions and during the critical testing of the design.

Such evidence may be *experimental* data, gathered by the designer using simulation or other test procedures; or it may be the evidence of *prior research* on the relevant topic conducted by others using other techniques such as analytical modeling, graph theory and so on, and reported in the literature. While such forms of evidence may not be as *certain* as proofs they may well provide the designer with a high level of confidence as to the validity of the design. More importantly, they may be the *only* kinds of evidence that are available.

Example 8.13
Consider the design of a cache memory. This basically involves the identification of the following parameters (Smith 1982, Hayes 1988, Dasgupta 1989a):

(a) The placement policy, which determines how main memory words are to be mapped onto cache memory words.
(b) The size of the blocks to be transferred between main memory and cache.
(c) The size of the cache.
(d) The replacement policy which determines which blocks are to be removed from the cache to make room for new, incoming blocks.

Now, a significant – perhaps the most important – objective in cache design is to minimize (in some practical, satisficing sense) the *cache miss ratio* – that is, the proportion of memory requests that cannot be successfully serviced by the cache and for which main memory access must be made. The cache designer may thus be required to examine the extensive data (gathered empirically or through simulation) on the effect of varying the different cache parameters on the miss ratio. Such data has been published, for example, by Smith (1982). Based on such analysis, the designer may establish the specifics for the aforementioned parameters in the context of his particular design problem.

Note that (at least in the current state of our knowledge of cache behavior) it is impossible for the designer to *prove* that his design satisfies the given requirement of not exceeding a certain miss ratio. He can, however, invoke the evidence of the published data *in support of* and *as justification for* his design decisions.
End Example

8.9 ON THE DISTINCTION BETWEEN PROOFS OF DESIGN CORRECTNESS AND MATHEMATICAL PROOFS

The limits to formal design discussed above reflect the facts that (a) design problems are frequently ill-structured and, therefore, are not directly amenable to formalization; and (b) the specification of requirements and design may be such that it is simply not possible to deductively prove that the design satisfies the requirements.

There is yet another problem; and this is the issue of the *validity* of the very idea of designs as formal entities – or, equivalently, the notion that a design/requirements complex is a theorem the truth of which can be deduced according to the laws of mathematics and logic.

This issue was actually raised in the context of programming and it is in this context that I shall discuss it here. Its relevance to other classes of computing systems will be briefly touched upon later.

The issue at hand is the parallel between programming and mathematics. In an important critique, de Millo, Lipton and Perlis (1979) pointed out that in the case of mathematical practice, the mere *existence* of a proof of some theorem may not suffice; the proof must be *accepted* by the practitioners in the relevant domain in order to become a part of mathematical knowledge. And, acceptance of a proof depends on *social processes* – in the sense that the proof is studied, discussed, and criticized by members of the relevant community. As a result of such processes the proof may either be believed and the theorem assimilated into the mathematical *Weltanschauung* or it may be rejected. A theorem may even be only *tentatively* accepted and later discarded because of an error being detected in the proof.[19] De Millo *et al.* further point out that the proofs of the mathematicians are seldom long chains of formal logical deductions – for, if they were it would be quite unlikely that such proofs would ever get read and be accepted. Rather, mathematical proofs are most often *proof sketches*.

The process of proving programs, according to de Millo *et al.*, is of quite a different nature. Program proofs – specially those generated by machine – are long tedious sequences of logical deduction that look and are very different from mathematical proofs. For, most certainly, they are not subject to the same social processes that mathematical proofs undergo. Consequently, their acceptance or otherwise through the process of criticism, argument and analysis can never happen. As de Millo *et al.* put it, one either believes program proofs as an act of faith or one does not.

As one might expect the position taken by de Millo, Lipton and Perlis generated considerable discussion.[20] As one aspect of this debate, Scherlis and Scott (1983) while not repudiating the social aspect of mathematics objected to the proposition that computer generated proofs are not – or cannot be – subjected to the same kind of social processes. They cited as an example, the four-color problem and the computer-aided proof discovered by Haken, Appel and Koch (1977) for this theorem.[21] Scherlis and Scott have documented how this proof underwent exactly the same kind of public debate that traditional mathematical proofs go through – to the extent that a flaw in the original Haken–Appel–Koch proof was discovered and subsequently corrected.

A very different aspect of the de Millo–Lipton–Perlis paper was very recently artic-

---

[19] See also Lakatos(1976) for what is now the classic discourse on the nature and logic of mathematical discovery.

[20] See, in particular, the ACM Forum Section of the *Communications of the ACM*, Nov. 1979, pp. 621–630 and the review by C. A. R. Hoare in *ACM Computing Reviews*, vol. 20, No. 1, August 1979.

[21] The four-color problem is: Can a finite planar map be colored with four colors so that no two adjacent regions have the same color? For a discussion of the nature of the proof strategy used for this theorem, see Appel (1984). The proof itself necessitated some 1800 computer runs and the generation of over 400 pages of checklists.

ulated by Fetzer (1988). Fetzer admits that whether or not a community accepts a proof of some theorem as valid or not does not make it so. Similarly, the presence or otherwise of a social process for program proofs does not ensure the validity of the proof or otherwise. The problem is whether there are *logical* grounds for presuming that programs are mathematical entities – in the sense of Hoare's postulates (section 8.2) – or whether, in fact, mathematical theorems (and their proofs) and programs (and their proofs) are altogether different kinds of entities.

The main argument presented by Fetzer (1988) can be summarized as follows:

(1) The term *verification* is used in two different ways. In the realm of pure mathematics and logic, a verification – or proof – is a demonstration that a given theorem or proposition can be deduced from some basic set of axioms. Such propositions are termed *absolutely verifiable*.

In contrast, in the realm of scientific discovery or ordinary reasoning, verification refers to the situation where certain conclusions follow from some given set of premises where the validity of the premises themselves may be subject to doubt or may be unverifiable. Conclusions of this sort are termed *relatively verifiable*.

(2) A theorem – being a string of symbols or 'markings' that is deducible from some basic set of axioms by the application of a series of inference rules – has no semantic significance. It is a purely *syntactic* entity. In contrast, a program has a *meaning*; it specifies a sequence of operations that can be or are required to be performed by a computer.

A program is to be distinguished from an *algorithm* in the following sense: an algorithm is an abstract logical structure that specifies a function to compute outputs from some given inputs. Insofar as an algorithm is an executable entity, its target computer is an *abstract machine* which has no physical significance. A program, on the other hand, is a *causal model* (of some algorithm) in that it requires the existence of a real processor or device that occupies physical space, the operation of which consumes physical time, and which is subject to causal relationships.

Algorithms – or even programs viewed as the encodings of algorithms for execution on abstract machines – are not causal models as they neither occupy physical space/time nor are subject to causal relationships. Thus, while algorithms may indeed be of the same type as theorems, programs as construed above, are not.

(3) It follows from the above that algorithms may indeed be absolutely verifiable (see (1) above). Programs – being causal models – can at best be subject to *relative* verification since the premises underlying such verification are in the

final analysis dependent on *empirical justification* involving the physical system that would execute the program.

More precisely, given a program P and pre-/postconditions PRE and POST, if P is a program for an abstract machine – that is, is really an (encoded version of an) algorithm – the formula

$$\{\text{PRE}\}\ P\ \{\text{POST}\}$$

can be absolutely verified from the axioms and proof rules governing the language in which P is expressed. If, however, P is an encoding of an algorithm that will be compiled and executed on a physical computer, the above Hoare formula will only be relatively verifiable as the validity of the very axioms and proof rules will depend on the causal properties of the physical target computer – that is, in the latter's hardware and firmware – and *that* can only be determined through empirical means, not through formal arguments.

(4) In the light of the foregoing argument, programs – that is, programs constructed as encodings of algorithms that are to be compiled and executed on physical systems subject to causal laws – can at best be treated as *conjectures* that can be *refuted* conclusively but never verified *absolutely*.

The notions of conjectures and refutations are, of course, at the very heart of Popper's (1965, 1968) well known theory of the scientific method and Fetzer's conclusion suggests that programs bear a correspondence with the propositions of the empirical sciences rather than with mathematical theorems. This correspondence has also been suggested contemporaneously and independently by Dasgupta (1989c) in the context of designs (of computing systems) in general and I shall discuss the relationship between design and science in much greater detail in Part III of this book.

We may, then, conclude this section (and the chapter) as follows: The FD paradigm rests on the fundamental notion of designs as formal entities; programs, microprograms, computer descriptions and hardware, are all representable within the framework of a formal axiomatic system such that the correctness of the design of such a computing system can be proved deductively using the apparatus of the formal system.

However, the question has been raised as to whether computing systems do, in general, correspond to mathematical entities. Fetzer (1988) has pointed out that given that programs are causal models, they are not absolutely verifiable in the sense that theorems are. And if programs are causal models, then systems such as architectures, firmware and hardware are decidedly so.[22] Programs, microprograms and hardware designs can, then, only be regarded as conjectures subject to empirical refutation at best.[23]

---

[22] Recall from section 8.6 that one of the concerns that led to the development of proof rules for microprogram verification was the recognition of the causal properties associated with the underlying host machines that execute microprograms.

[23] As in the case of the paper by de Millo *et al.*, Fetzer's (1988) thesis spawned considerable, even violent, reaction mostly from the advocates of the FD paradigm. See in particular, the ACM Forum and Technical Correspondence sections of *Communications of the ACM*, Vol. 32, No. 3, March 1989.

Chapter 9

The Theory of Plausible Designs

9.1 INTRODUCTION

Let us recapitulate some of the very basic features of the design process as articulated in Part I of this book.

(a) The requirements constituting the specification of a design problem may (initially) be neither precise nor complete; hence the elaboration of requirements becomes an integral part of the design process. Requirements may, furthermore, be of an empirical or a conceptual nature.

(b) A design is an abstract description of the target artifact that serves as a blueprint for implementation, and as a medium for criticism, experimentation and analysis.

(c) The designer is constantly faced with the problem of bounded rationality – the fact that designers and their clients are limited in their capacities to make fully rational decisions, or are limited in their ability to grasp the full implications of such decisions.

(d) Design decisions are more often than not satisficing procedures.

As a consequence of all of the above design can be naturally viewed as an evolutionary process possessing the following characteristics: at any stage of its development the design is viewed as a *tentative* or *conjectural* solution to the problem posed. The designer's task in each evolutionary cycle is to elaborate either the design or the requirements so as to establish or converge towards a fit between the two. Thus, an integral part of each evolutionary cycle is the critical testing of the 'current' design against the 'current' requirements (see chapter 5, especially section 5.3).

Given this evolutionary model and, in particular, the conjectural nature of designs, it is reasonable to suggest that (in general) the best that one can do during the design process is to advance the design so as to enhance its *plausibility* or believability. Furthermore, the plausibility of a design – the extent to which the designer or the client (or anyone else for that matter) has grounds for believing that the design indeed does satisfy the requirements – will depend on the following two types of information recorded by the designer:

(a) The *history* of the design, where 'history' refers to the documented sequences of design decisions and the cause–effect relationships between such decisions.

(b) The *nature of the evidence* used by the designer to justify design decisions and/or establish the fact that a particular set of design features satisfies a particular set of requirements.

The *theory of plausible designs* (TPD) is a design paradigm proposed recently by Aguero and Dasgupta (1987) that addresses both these issues. [1] As I shall show below a design method based on TPD – a *plausibility-driven design method* – will not only be an instrument of design but will also (i) generate and document explicitly the causal structure of the design decisions and thus provide an explanation of why a particular design evolved the way it did; and (ii) document explicitly the nature and source of the evidence invoked by the designer in support of his or her claim about the plausibility of the design.

9.2 CONSTRAINTS

A central notion in TPD is that a design (of some target artifact) is a specification of various functional, behavioral, structural, performance, reliability, aesthetic, or other characteristics or features that are to be present in the physically implemented artifact. [2]

In TPD, the generic term *constraint* is used to designate all such features. A design at any particular abstraction level is, then, a specification of any organized, mutually consistent collection of constraints which a future implementation must satisfy. The constraints are so called because they signify *constraints on the implementation*. In TPD, the constraints collectively *are* the design.

Constraints are essentially of two types. A *first order* constraint is any feature that serves as (or is a part of) the blueprint for implementation. A *higher order* constraint is a property, assertion or predicate that is satisfied by a lower order constraint. For the present we shall consider only first and second order constraints. A certain type of third order constraint will be introduced in section 9.9.

---

[1] See also Dasgupta and Aguero (1987), Hooton, Aguero, and Dasgupta (1988) and Patel and Dasgupta (1989).

[2] A *physical implementation* is an operational version of an artifact. In addition to circuits, computers, bridges or buildings which are physical implementations in an obvious way, a program that has been compiled and loaded for execution is also a physical implementation in this sense. See also the discussion in section 8.9, chapter 8.

Example 9.1
Consider the following Pascal program fragment:

P: if $X < Y$ then $Z = X$ else $Z = Y$;
   while X mod $Z \neq 0 \vee Y$ mod $Z \neq 0$ do
   $Z := Z - 1$

The program itself constitutes a first order constraint: it is intended to serve directly as the input to, or the blueprint for, the implementation step. The constraint in this case is of a structural–behavioral nature in that it says something about both the structure and the behavior of the yet-to-be-implemented form.

The assertion '*P* computes the GCD of two non-negative integers X and Y' or, more succinctly, the Hoare formula

$$\{X > 0 \wedge Y > 0\}\ P\ \{Z = \mathrm{GCD}(X, Y)\}$$

is an instance of a second order constraint that asserts a property that P must satisfy – and, by implication, a property that an implementation of P must satisfy. This particular constraint happens to be *functional* in nature in that it says something about a functional property of P.
End Example

Example 9.2
Consider the VHDL description of a 1-bit full adder shown in fig. 9.1 (see also section 8.7, chapter 8). This specification serves as a blueprint for implementing a full adder circuit such that the implementation satisfies the facts that

(i) the components of the circuit are to satisfy the functional properties of the and-gate, or-gate and xor-gate components and
(ii) the structural relationships between the circuit components must satisfy the relationships shown in the *architecture* part of this description.

This VHDL description constitutes an organized collection of first order constraints. In contrast, the predicates

SUM(full adder) $\equiv$
sum = $(\neg$ in1 $\wedge \neg$ in2 $\wedge$ carry_in$) \vee$
$(\neg$ in1 $\wedge$ in2 $\wedge \neg$ carry_in$) \vee$
$($in1 $\wedge \neg$ in2 $\wedge \neg$ carry_in$) \vee$
$($in1 $\wedge$ in2 $\wedge$ carry_in$) \vee$

CARRY(full_adder) $\equiv$
carry_out = $($in1 $\wedge$ in2$) \vee ($in1 $\wedge$ carry_in$) \vee$
$($in2 $\wedge$ carry_in$)$

```
entity full_adder is
   port (in1, in2, carry_in: in bit;
         sum, carry_out: out bit)
end full_adder;

architecture structure of full_adder is
   component and_gate port(a, b: in bit; c: out bit);
   component or_gate port(a, b: in bit; c: out bit);
   component xor_gate port(a, b: in bit; c: out bit);

   - internal signals
   signal S1, S2, S3, S4, S5: bit

   begin
      X1: xor_gate(in2, carry_in, S5);
      X2: xor_gate(S5, in1, sum);
      A1: and_gate(in1, in2, S1);
      A2: and_gate(in1, carry_in, S2);
      A3: and_gate(in2, carry_in, S4);
      O1: or_gate(S1, S2, S3);
      O2: or_gate(S3, S4, carry_out);
   end
```

Fig. 9.1 VHDL description of a full adder structure.

characterize the desired behavior of the full adder. These predicates constitute second order behavioral (or functional) constraints that are part of the full_adder design. Note that SUM and CARRY are irrelevant as far as the implementer (whether an engineer or silicon compiler) is concerned. Nonetheless, from the perspective of TPD, they are an integral part of the design in that it is required that the circuit implementation satisfies these predicates as much as the structural VHDL description of fig. 9.1.

End Example

Example 9.3

Consider the Pascal program shown in fig. 9.2 and the following assertions associated with it:

$C1(MPY)$: $\{x = x_0 \wedge y = y_0\}$ MPY $\{S = x_0 * y_0\}$
$C2(MPY)$: is_well_structured (MPY)

Here, MPY itself is a first order constraint while $C1$ and $C2$ are second order constraints. $C1$ is functional in nature while $C2$ may be regarded (depending on one's view) as a structural or an aesthetic constraint.
End Example

```
MPY : begin
          S := 0;
          while ¬ (x = 0) do
              begin
                  while ¬ ODD(x) do
                      begin
                          y := y * 2;
                          x := x div 2
                      end
                  S := S + y;
                  x := x − 1
              end
      end
```

Fig. 9.2 A multiplication program.

Example 9.4
Let INST_SET denote a specification of the format and semantics of an instruction set. INST_SET then, constitutes a collection of first order constraints that is to be satisfied by a computer (yet to be implemented, say). In addition, consider the following predicate:

Eff (INST_SET) ≡
  $\forall\, p \in$ BENCHMARKS:
      Size(Obj_code(p, INST_SET)) $\leq$ LOWSIZE
  $\land$ Exec_time (Obj_code(p, INST_SET)) $\leq$ LOWTIME

Eff is a predicate which is true for INST_SET if every program p from a given set of benchmark programs BENCHMARKS is such that (a) the size of the object code for p using INST_SET is less than some constant LOWSIZE and (b) the execution time for the object code is less than some constant LOWTIME.

The predicate Eff constitutes a second order *performance* constraint that is to be satisfied by any implementation of INST_SET.
End Example

9.3 THE PLAUSIBILITY OF A CONSTRAINT

In the TPD paradigm, then, a design is viewed as an organized collection of constraints that an implementation must directly or indirectly satisfy. Given a constraint, its *plausibility* refers to the extent to which we believe that an implementation of the artifact satisfies (or a future implementation will satisfy) the constraint.

Furthermore, the extent of our belief will be determined by the nature of the *evidence* at our disposal. Thus, a constraint's plausibility is determined by the nature and strength of the evidence invoked in support of the claim that an implementation does or will satisfy that constraint.

Recall that a *first order* constraint is a blueprint (or part thereof) that informs the implementer about the structural form that is to be met by the implementation. The description of first order constraints must, therefore, be in a language common to the designer and implementer; furthermore, a fundamental assumption underlying the use of such a language is that any design expressed in that language *is implementable*. That is, given a constraint described in that language the implementer knows exactly how to implement the constraints.

For example, the Pascal program for computing the GCD function is known to be implementable under the assumption that there exist Pascal compilers that will produce executable code from that program for different target machines. Similarly the VHDL description of fig. 9.1 is implementable under the assumption that the implementer can translate this description into a full adder circuit.

The only kind of evidence one needs, then, to establish the plausibility of a first order constraint is that *the latter be expressed in a language that is known to be implementable*. We believe that a future implementation of the adder can satisfy the description in fig. 9.1 because the latter is specified in an implementable language, VHDL. Thus the constraints expressed in fig. 9.2 are indeed plausible.

The situation with *second order* constraints is more problematic. The plausibility of a full adder circuit satisfying the predicates SUM and CARRY (example 9.2) is a function, partly of the plausibility of the first order full adder constraint of fig. 9.1; and partly of the grounds (evidence) we have in believing that the full adder constraint satisfies SUM and CARRY. The evidence we might invoke in the latter case might be a *formal proof* that SUM(full_adder) and CARRY(full_adder) are true (see section 8.7, chapter 8); or an *experimental demonstration* (using a simulator for VHDL) which allows that for all anticipatable sets of values for in1, in2 and carry_in the outputs sum and carry_out of the VHDL full adder are such that SUM(full_adder) and CARRY(full_adder) are satisfied; or in the absence of our ability to do either – for instance, neither a proof theory nor a simulator for VHDL may exist – the evidence may take the shape of a *prototype* circuit on which experiments are conducted. Clearly, the strength of our belief in (and therefore the plausibility of) the constraints SUM and CARRY will depend on which kind of evidence we decide to use, and the details of that evidence.

9.4 PLAUSIBILITY STATES

Henceforth, the terms 'plausibility' or 'is plausible' when applied to a constraint C will be used as an abbreviation for the proposition 'C can be, or has been (depending on the context) satisfied by an implementation'.

At any stage of a TPD based design process, a constraint C can be in exactly one of four *plausibility states*:

(a) **Assumed:** when there is *no evidence against* C's plausibility.
(b) **Validated:** when there is *significant evidence in favor of* and *no evidence against* C's plausibility.
(c) **Refuted:** when there is *evidence against* C's plausibility.
(d) **Undetermined:** when it is *not known* what counts (or may count) as evidence for or against C's plausibility (or where to look for that evidence).

The plausibility state of a constraint C, then, is a function of the *design stage k* at which the state is being asserted to hold, and the *available evidence* at that stage. The form, source, or nature of the evidence will be explicated shortly. For the present, it is important to note that the definition of the plausibility states causes us to draw a strong, initial analogy between TPD and *science*. Fig. 9.3 shows the main features of this analogy.

The analogy itself is no coincidence. The TPD paradigm is as much based on contemporary ideas about the method of science as the FD paradigm was based on the mathematical–logical enterprise. In the FD paradigm, a design is viewed as a theorem (or a complex of theorems) the truth or falsehood of which is established using proof procedures. In TPD, a design is viewed as a complex of hypotheses or conjectures the plausibility of which is to be established according to the evidence at hand.[3]

---

[3] The methodology of science (i.e., of the natural sciences) has already appeared in several different contexts in this book. See e.g. chapter 8, section 8.9 (especially the last part of the discussion of Fetzer's work). The relationship between design processes and the method of science is systematically explored in Part III. For the present the reader may merely note that TPD is indeed based on this analogy.

TPD	Science
A constraint (or an organized collection of constraints)	A proposition, hypothesis or conjecture (or a complex thereof)
undetermined constraint	A conjecture for which it is not known what counts as evidence *pro* or *contra*
assumed constraint	A testable (but possibly untested) conjecture for which there is as yet no evidence for its falsification.
validated constraint	A tested conjecture for which there is significant supporting evidence and no falsifying or refuting evidence.
refuted constraint	A tested conjecture that has been falsified or refuted based on the available evidence.

Fig. 9.3 Correspondences between plausibility states in TPD and states of hypotheses/conjectures in science.

9.5 THE NATURE OF EVIDENCE IN TPD

In general, a designer will wish to invoke the strongest possible evidence in support of his or her claims regarding a proposed design. But the strongest possible evidence may not be forthcoming due to, say, a gap in the knowledge or understanding of the particular domain of interest. The designer may be forced, instead, to use weaker forms of evidence or arguments. In general, then, designers have a *range* of types of arguments or evidence at their disposal which they draw upon in the best way that they can.

Accordingly, in TPD, the nature of the evidence may be any combination of the following:

(a) **Formal proofs**: the use of logic to demonstrate that the plausibility state of a constraint is implied from given premises according to the rules of some formal system.

(b) **Experiments**: where the evidence takes the form of conclusions drawn from repeatable experiments. These may involve simulation, prototype implementation and the systematic testing thereof, or *thought* experiments (see footnote 43, chapter 5).

(c) **Knowledge base**: where the evidence is reference to the data, analyses, theories, models or experimental/experiential observations reported in the research and technical literature.

(d) **Heuristics**: that is, arguments based on the use of heuristics or commonsense reasoning.

9.6 PLAUSIBILITY STATEMENTS

In the course of the design process each new constraint is introduced into the design in the form of a *plausibility statement*. This is defined as a 5-tuple:

$$S = \langle C, A, R, V, P \rangle$$

where

C is a specific constraint the plausibility of which is being (or is to be) determined.

A is the *knowledge base* used to *assist* in establishing C's plausibility. This includes facts, theories, principles, tools, research results, as well as other constraints belonging to the current design.

R is a *logical relationship or assertion* the plausibility of which implies the plausibility of C. R is specified in the predicate calculus.[4]

V denotes the *means of verification* (that is, the nature of the evidence) used to establish C's plausibility.

P is the plausibility state in which C is being (or is to be) placed.

A plausibility statement S signifies two things. Firstly, it defines the constraint C in terms of a logical relationship or assertion R. In the case C is a first order constraint, R will simply stipulate C itself. In the case C is a second order constraint, R will be a relationship involving other constraints. In either case, the connection between C and R is that if it is known that R is in plausibility state P then so will be C.

Secondly, S asserts that using the verification means V it can be shown that C is indeed in plausibility state P. In this case, S is said to have been *verified*. The admissible means of verification – the nature of the evidence – can be any one or a combination of the types stated in section 9.5.

In sum, then, a given plausibility statement S is interpreted as stipulating that it has been (or can be) verified that C is in state P because, using the verification means V, it has been (or can be) established that R is in plausibility state P.

---

[4] Precisely what it means for an assertion or a logical relationship R to be in a plausibility state is explained later.

Example 9.5

Recall example 9.4 which described a first order constraint 'INST_SET' and a second order constraint 'Eff(INST_SET)'. A plausibility statement for the former is as follows:

($S1$) $C1$:   INST_SET specified in the architecture description language S*M.

          $A1$:   Language Report and User Manual for S*M.

          $R1$:   INST_SET specified in S*M.

          $V1$:   Inspection of INST_SET with respect to the Report/User Manual for S*M.

          $P1$:   **Validated**

Since INST_SET is a first order constraint its plausibility can be directly assessed by examining its specification and determining whether it is expressed in an implementable language – in this case, S*M (see section 9.3). Hence the R field of ($S1$) simply re-states the constraint itself. ($S1$), then, states that INST_SET is placed in the **validated** state if inspection of the S*M description of INST_SET shows that (by expanding the meaning of **validated**) there is significant evidence in favor of and no evidence against INST_SET's plausibility – that is, that INST_SET has indeed been correctly specified in S*M.

($S2$) below, is a plausibility statement for the second order constraint 'Eff':

($S2$) $C2$:   Eff(INST_SET)

          $A2$: $C1$, BENCHMARKS, Compiler for BENCHMARK to INST_SET.

          $R2$: $\forall\, p \in$ BENCHMARKS:
                   Size(Obj_code(p, INST_SET)) $\leq$ LOWSIZE
                   $\wedge$ Exec_time(Obj_code(p, INST_SET)) $\leq$ LOWTIME

          $V2$:   Experiments using compiler for BENCHMARKS to INST_SET.

          $P2$:   **Refuted**

($S2$) tells us that the constraint Eff(INST_SET) is in the plausibility state **refuted** – that is, there is evidence against this constraint – because it has been (or can be) shown using experiments ($V2$) that there is evidence against the plausibility of the assertion specified in $R2$. Note that the efficiency constraint 'Eff' has been defined in terms of the assertion $R2$.

Suppose at the design stage k that ($S2$) is constructed, INST_SET has not been fully developed. In that case, we could neither be able to invoke significant evidence in favor of $R2$'s plausibility nor could we invoke evidence against it. ($S2$) itself would not be verifiable. We could, however, claim that there is *no evidence against $R2$'s* plausibility in which case the following plausibility statement $(S2')$ can be stated and verified.

$(S2')$	$C2'$:	Eff(INST_SET)
	$A2'$:	Knowledge base (KB) regarding instruction set design.
	$R2'$:	$\forall\, p \in$ BENCHMARKS:
		$\quad$ Size(Obj_code(p, INST_SET)) $\leq$ LOWSIZE
		$\quad \wedge$ Exec_time(Obj_code(p, INST_SET)) $\leq$ LOWTIME
	$V2'$:	Approximate reasoning based on KB.
	$P2'$:	**assumed**

The **assumed** plausibility state is thus, a state of 'hopefulness' on the part of the designer; it signifies that in the absence of stronger evidence one way or another at a particular design stage, there is no ground for doubting the plausibility of the constraint.
End Example

Example 9.6

$(S3)$	$C3$:	VHDL description of full adder
	$A3$:	VHDL User Manual
	$R3$:	VHDL description of full adder
	$V3$:	Inspection of the full adder description with respect to the VHDL User Manual
	$P3$:	**Validated**

$(S4)$	$C4$:	is_correct($C3$)
	$A4$:	$C3$; Proof theory for VHDL.
	$R4$:	sum $= (\neg$ in1 $\wedge \neg$ in2 $\wedge$ carry_in) $\vee$ $(\neg$ in1 $\wedge$ in2 $\wedge \neg$ carry_in) $\vee$
		$\quad$ (in1 $\wedge \neg$ in2 $\wedge \neg$ carry_in) $\vee$ (in1 $\wedge$ in2 $\wedge$ carry_in)
		carry_out $=$ (in1 $\wedge$ in2) $\vee$ (in1 $\wedge$ carry_in) $\vee$
		$\quad$ (in2 $\wedge$ carry_in)
	$V4$:	formal proof.
	$P4$:	**Validated**

$(S3)$ is a plausibility statement for the first order constraint 'full adder' described in VHDL. $(S4)$ is a plausibility statement for the second order constraint 'is_correct $(C3)$'; note that $C4$ is defined in terms of assertion $R4$ involving the input and output parts specified as part of $C3$. $(S4)$ will be verified if it can be formally proved (using a proof theory for VHDL) that R4 is plausible – or, in this particular case, true.
End Example

Example 9.7

Finally, consider the design of an airline reservation system and suppose the (first order) constraints expressed in some programming language are denoted by ARS. Suppose further that one of the requirements initially postulated for this system is that 'user satisfaction is very high'. This can be denoted by the predicate USER_SAT (ARS).

At the time this constraint enters the design the designer has no sense of what criteria to use to determine the plausibility of USER_SAT(ARS). That is, it is not known, what would count as evidence for or against the plausibility of this constraint. In that sense, *at this particular stage* of the design process, the plausibility state of USER_SAT(ARS) should be undetermined:

($S5$)	$C5$:	USER_SAT(ARS)
	$A5$:	?
	$R5$:	?
	$V5$:	?
	$P5$:	**undetermined**

At some later stage in the design further understanding or information may lead the designer to define USER_SAT in terms of other constraints, e.g., response time to user requests or a fair reservation strategy, etc., in which case ($S5$) would be revised accordingly, the A, R, V fields completed and the P field changed from **undetermined** to some other state.

End Example

9.7 THE LOGIC OF PLAUSIBILITY STATES

The plausibility state of a constraint is based on the evidence E_k at hand at a particular step k in the design process. Starting from this simple notion a logic of plausibility states was developed by Aguero (1987) (see also Aguero and Dasgupta (1987)) as follows.

Consider, first, the following functions:

($E1$) **evid_fav**(E_k, C)

$\qquad = 1$ if E_k contains evidence in favor of C's plausibility

$\qquad = 0$ if E_k contains no evidence in favor of C's plausibility

$\qquad = 0.5$ if it is not known what counts as evidence in favor

$\qquad\qquad$ of or against C's plausibility.[5]

---

[5] The value of 0.5 is quite arbitrary. All that is required is some value V returned by **evid_fav** (in this particular situation) such that $0 < V < 1$. A similar remark holds for **evid_ag** function defined above.

(E2) **evid_ag**(E_k, C)

     $= 1$ if E_k contains evidence against C's plausibility

     $= 0$ if E_k contains no evidence against C's plausibility

     $= 0.5$ if it not known what counts as evidence for or against C's plausibility.

(E3) **sig_evid_fav**(E_k, C)

     $= 1$ if **evid_fav**$(E_k, C) = 1$ and the evidence is assessed to be significant

     $= 0.5$ if **evid_fav**$(E_k, C) = 0.5$ or if **evid_fav**$(E_k, C) = 1$ but it is unknown whether or not the evidence is significant

     $= 0$ otherwise

(E4) **sig_evid_ag**(E_k, C)

     $= 1$ if **evid_ag**$(E_k, C) = 1$ and the evidence is assessed to be significant

     $= 0.5$ if **evid_ag**$(E_k, C) = 0.5$ or if **evid_ag**$(E_k, C) = 1$ but it is unknown whether or not the evidence is significant

     $= 0$ otherwise

It is important to note that whether or not E_k contains evidence in favor of or against a constraint's plausibility, or whether the evidence is deemed significant or not, are matters on which TPD is silent. These are empirical matters that are determined by the knowledge base surrounding the design, the designer's *Weltanschauung*, the precise rules to interpret the evidence and so on.

The plausibility state of a constraint C can now be formally defined as follows:

Let the functions **ass**(k, C), **val**(k, C), **ref**(k, C) and **und**(k, C) return 1 if C qualifies to be in the **assumed, validated, refuted** and **undetermined** states respectively in design step k, and let them return 0 otherwise. Then

(A1) **ass**$(k, C) = 1$ iff **evid_ag**$(E_k, C) = 0$

(A2) **val**$(k, C) = 1$ iff **evid_ag**$(E_k, C) = 0 \wedge$ **sig_evid_fav**$(E_k, C) = 1$

(A3) **ref**$(k, C) = 1$ iff **evid_ag**$(E_k, C) = 1$

(A4) **und**$(k, C) = 1$ iff **evid_ag**$(E_k, C) = 0.5$

The following 'laws' of plausibility states can easily be verified to follow from (A1)–(A4):

$(L1)$ **val**$(k, C) = 1 \rightarrow$ **ass**$(k, C) = 1$
$(L2)$ **ass**$(k, C) = 1 \rightarrow$ **ref**$(k, C) = 0$
$(L3)$ **ref**$(k, C) = 0 \wedge$ **und**$(k, C) = 0 \rightarrow$ **ass**$(k, C) = 1$
$(L4)$ **ref**$(k, C) = 0 \nrightarrow$ **val**$(k, C) = 1$
$(L5)$ **val**$(k, C) = 0 \nrightarrow$ **ref**$(k, C) = 1$
$(L6)$ **ass**$(k, C) = 1 \nrightarrow$ **val**$(k, C) = 1$
$(L7)$ **und**$(k, C) = 1 \rightarrow$ **val**$(k, C) = 0 \wedge$ **ass**$(k, C) = 0 \wedge$ **ref**$(k, C) = 0$

Proofs for these laws can be found in Aguero (1987).

Consider now, the plausibility statement $S = \langle C, A, R, V, P \rangle$ where C is defined in terms of R. Using the functions introduced in $(E1)$, $(E2)$ and $(E3)$ and the functions **ass**, **val**, **ref** and **und** over R, the plausibility states of R can be specified according to:

$(B1)$ **ass**$(k, R) = 1$ **iff evid_ag**$(E_k, R) = 0$
$(B2)$ **val**$(k, R) = 1$ **iff evid_ag**$(E_k, R) = 0 \wedge$ **sig_evid_fav**$(E_k, R) = 1$
$(B3)$ **ref**$(k, R) = 1$ **iff evid_ag**$(E_k, R) = 1$
$(B4)$ **und**$(k, R) = 1$ **iff evid_ag**$(E_k, R) = 0.5$

The plausibility states of the constraint C in statement S can be computed according to the assertions

$(C1)$ **ass**$(k, C) = 1$ **if ass**$(k, R) = 1$
$(C2)$ **val**$(k, C) = 1$ **if val**$(k, R) = 1$
$(C3)$ **ref**$(k, C) = 1$ **if ref**$(k, R) = 1$
$(C4)$ **und**$(k, C) = 1$ **if und**$(k, R) = 1$

$(B1)$–$(B4)$ tells us how to determine the plausibility states of R from the values returned by the functions **evid_ag** and **sig_evid_fav**. Consider now, how these functions compute values for R. Recall that R is expressed as a well formed formula (wff) in the predicate calculus.

If R is an *atomic* wff then **evid_ag**(E_k, R) and **evid_fav**(E_k, R) returns 0.5, 1 or 0 according to the definitions $(E1)$ and $(E2)$ and the plausibility states of R are determined accordingly. In the case of R being a *non-atomic* wff composed of more primitive wff's A and B the following relationships hold.

(D11) **evid_ag**$(E_k, A \lor B)) = \text{MIN}(\textbf{evid\_ag}(E_k, A), \textbf{evid\_ag}(E_k, B))$
(D12) **evid_fav**$(E_k, A \land B) = \text{MAX}(\textbf{evid\_fav}(E_k, A), \textbf{evid\_fav}(E_k, B))$
(D21) **evid_ag**$(E_k, \neg A) = \textbf{evid\_fav}(E_k, A)$
(D22) **evid_fav**$(E_k, \neg A) = \textbf{evid\_ag}((E_k, A)$
(D31) **sig_evid_fav**$(E_k, \neg A) = \textbf{sig\_evid\_ag}(E_k, A)^6$
(D32) **sig_evid_ag**$(E_k, \neg A) = \textbf{sig\_evid\_fav}(E_k, A)$

The identities

$$A \land B \equiv \neg (\neg A \lor \neg B)$$
$$A \rightarrow B \equiv \neg A \lor B$$

lead to

(D41) **evid_ag**$(E_k, A \land B) = \text{MAX}(\textbf{evid\_ag}(E_k, A), \textbf{evid\_ag}(E_k, B))$
(D42) **evid_fav**$(E_k, A \land B) = \text{MIN}(\textbf{evid\_fav}(E_k, A), \textbf{evid\_fav}(E_k, B))$
(D51) **evid_ag**$(E_k, A \rightarrow B) = \text{MIN}(\textbf{evid\_fav}(E_k, A), \textbf{evid\_ag}(E_k, B))$
(D52) **evid_fav**$(E_k, A \rightarrow B) = \text{MAX}(\textbf{evid\_ag}(E_k, A), \textbf{evid\_fav}(E_k, B))$

Let $D = \{d_1, \ldots, d_n\}$ be the domain of values for a variable x and let $V \in D$. Define the notation

$$\bigwedge_{V \in D} A(V) \equiv A(d_1) \land \ldots \land A(d_n)$$
$$\bigvee_{V \in D} A(V) \equiv A(d_1) \lor \ldots \lor A(d_n)$$

Then

(D61) **evid_ag**$(\forall x \; A(x)) = \textbf{evid\_ag}(\bigwedge_{V \in D} A(V))$
(D62) **evid_fav**$(\forall x \; A(x)) = \textbf{evid\_fav}(\bigwedge_{V \in D} A(V))$
(D71) **evid_ag**$(\exists x \; A(x)) = \textbf{evid\_ag}(\bigvee_{V \in D} A(V))$
(D72) **evid_fav**$(\exists x \; A(x)) = \textbf{evid\_fav}(\bigvee_{V \in D} A(V))$

Finally, the following laws are pertinent to the conjunction and disjunction of wffs A and B.

(F11) **val**$(k, A) = 1$ and **val**$(k, B) = 1$ implies **val**$(k, A \land B) = 1$
(F12) **ass**$(k, A) = 1$ and **ass**$(k, B) = 1$ implies **ass**$(k, A \land B) = 1$
(F13) **ref**$(k, A) = 1$ or **ref**$(k, B) = 1$ implies **ref**$(k, A \land B) = 1$

---

[6] Note that the **sig_evid_ag** function defined in $(E4)$ is relevant only in the case of $(D31)$ and $(D32)$.

(F21) **val**$(k, A) = 1$ or **val**$(k, B) = 1$ implies **val**$(k, A \lor B) = 1$

(F22) **ass**$(k, A) = 1$ or **ass**$(k, B) = 1$ implies **ass**$(k, A \lor B) = 1$

(F23) **ref**$(k, A) = 1$ and **ref**$(k, B) = 1$ implies **ref**$(k, A \lor B) = 1$

Given a plausibility statement $S = \langle C, A, R, V, P \rangle$, the laws (F11)–(F23) are useful for establishing R's plausibility state when R is partitioned into two or more wffs. (F11)–(F23) may, thus, be referred to as *rules or laws of partitioning*.

Example 9.8

Consider the plausibility statement $S2$ from example 9.5. This tells us that **ref**$(k, C2)$ $= 1$ if **ref**$(k, R2) = 1$ for some design step k. By definition, **ref**$(k, R2) = 1$ if **evid_ag** $(E_k, R2) = 1$. Let $B1, \ldots, Bn$ be the set of programs in BENCHMARKS. Then

> **evid_ag**$(E_k, R2) = 1$ if
>> **evid_ag** ((Size(obj_code(B1, INST_SET)) $\leq$ LOWSIZE
>> $\land \ldots$
>> $\land$ Size(obj_code(Bn, INST_SET)) $\leq$ LOWSIZE
>> $\land$ Exec_time(obj_code(B1, INST_SET)) $\leq$ LOWTIME
>> $\land \ldots$
>> $\land$ Exec_time(obj_code(Bn, INST_SET)) $\leq$ LOWTIME
>>) $= 1$

that is, if

> MAX(**evid_ag**(Size(obj_code(B1, INST_SET)) $\leq$ LOWSIZE,
>
> $\ldots$
>
> **evid_ag**(Size(obj_code(Bn, INST_SET)) $\leq$ LOWSIZE,
> **evid_ag**(Exec_time(obj_code(B1; INST_SET)) $\leq$ LOWTIME,
>
> $\ldots$
>
> **evid_ag**(Exec_time(obj_code(Bn, INST_SET)) $\leq$ LOWTIME
>) $= 1$

Thus, if the MAX functions evaluates to 1 there is some evidence against the plausibility of $R2$, hence against the plausibility of $C2$. The plausibility statement will then have been *verified*.

End Example

9.8 THE STRUCTURE OF PLAUSIBILITY-DRIVEN DESIGN

The general structure of a *plausibility driven* design process can now be characterized as follows:

(A) A design D_k at any stage k of its development is an organized set of constraints. Each constraint may be stated formally (in a design language or as a set of logical propositions) or in the semi-formal language of scientific discourse.

(B) The plausibility of D_k is captured by a collection of plausibility statements. Since a design should not include any constraints that may have been **refuted** – these should have been removed from the design – the plausibility state of each constraint in D_k will be in the **assumed, validated,** or **undetermined** state.

(C) The constraints in D_k will, in general, have *dependencies* among them. Let $S_i = \langle C_i, A_i, R_i, V_i, P_i \rangle$ be the plausibility statement for C_i and let C_j be a constraint appearing in R_i. This means that the plausibility state of C_i *depends* (at least in part) on the plausibility state of C_j.

Dependencies between constraints within a design D_k are explicitly represented by a directed acyclic graph called a *constraint dependency graph* (CDG) an example of which is shown in fig. 9.4. The nodes or vertices of a CDG denote constraints C_i, C_j, etc. A directed edge from C_i to C_j indicates that the plausibility of C_i depends upon the plausibility of C_j. The node corresponding to C_i is termed a *consequent* node and that corresponding to C_j is termed an *antecedent* node.

In constructing CDGs, the further convention is adopted that edges originating from the same point on the consequent node represents a conjunction, while edges originating from different points denote a disjunction (see fig. 9.4). A CDG at any stage k of a design will also contain nodes without dependencies. These are referred to as *unsupported* nodes.

In fig. 9.4, $C5$ is the consequent node with respect to C_6, C_7 and C_8 and the latter are C_5's antecedents. C_6, C_7 form a conjunction while C_8, C_{11}, C_{12} and C_{13} are the unsupported nodes.

(D) Given D_k, the design further evolves by the designer's attempt to (i) change an **assumed** constraint to a **validated** one, or (ii) place an **undetermined** constraint in the **assumed** or **validated** state.

In order to do either, the original constraint C may have to be *refined* or *partitioned* into a set of new constraints C_i, C_j, ...,, such that some relationship between these constraints can be used to demonstrate the desired plausibility state for C. The laws of partitioning (F11)–(F23) stated in Section 9.7 can be used for this purpose.

(E) A design may evolve in other ways also. For instance, in the process of attempting to change the plausibility state of a constraint C_j from **assumed** to **validated**

($S5$) $C5$: ...
     $A5$: ...
     $R5$: $(C6 \wedge C7) \vee C8$
     $V5$: ...
     $P5$: ...

($S6$) $C6$: ...
     $A6$: ...
     $R6$: $(C11 \wedge C12)$
     $V6$: ...
     $P6$: ...

($S7$) $C7$: ...
     $A7$: ...
     $R7$: $(C11 \wedge C13)$
     $V7$: ...
     $P7$: ...

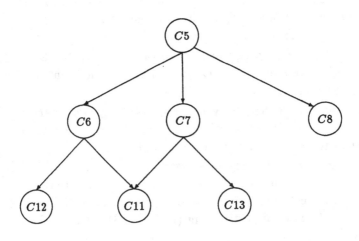

Fig. 9.4 Skeletons of three plausibility statements and the corresponding CDG.

it may happen that the evidence E_k is such that C_j is found to be **refuted**. In that case, C_j must be eliminated from the design and, if some other constraint C_i is dependent on C_j, then C_i's plausibility state will have to be *revised* in the light of this new state of affairs.

In other words, the plausibility states of constraints in a design *may have to be revised* when new constraints are introduced, the states of one or more constraints are reassigned or when new evidence is at hand. Plausibility driven design is, thus, *non-monotonic* in nature (Reiter 1987).

Example 9.9

Consider the situation depicted in fig. 9.4 and assume that at the start of the design step k the following plausibility states have been assigned to the unsupported constraints:

$C8$:   **undetermined**
$C11$: **validated**
$C12$: **validated**
$C13$: **assumed**

Consequently, the remaining constraints have the states

$C6$: **validated**
$C7$: **assumed**
$C5$: **assumed**

Suppose that in step k it is established that there is significant evidence in favor of and no evidence against $C8$'s plausibility. $C8$ is made **validated** as a result of which, the plausibility state of $C5$ is revised to **validated** also, according to the logic of plausibility states described earlier.

In the next step, $k+1$, suppose that new evidence reveals that $C13$ has to be **refuted**. As a result $C7$ must also be **refuted** and both $C7$ and $C13$ are to be eliminated from the design. Notice that $C5$ will remain **validated** (because of $C8$). The plausibility statement ($S5$) must, however, be reconsidered as the conjunction $C6 \wedge C7$ will be **refuted** in which case the $R5$ field does not make *empirical* sense (although it is still *logically* valid).

The designer may decide to revise $R5$ to simply $C8$ in which case, the CDG will correspondingly have to be modified to consist only of $C5$ and its antecedent node $C8$; or after careful consideration, the designer may decide that $R5$ should be $C6 \vee$

$C8$ in which case the CDG will be identical to fig. 9.4 save for the absence of $C7$ and $C13$ and the plausibility states of $C6$, $C11$ and $C12$ will remain unchanged.
End Example

9.9 JUSTIFICATION CONSTRAINTS

In section 9.2 it was pointed out that constraints may be of an order higher than two. Here, I shall introduce a particular type of third order constraint called *justification* constraints.

Consider the (second order) constraint

$C0$: message_based(M)

where M is a parallel, object-oriented (hardware or software) system specified in an appropriate implementable language. M is, then, a first order constraint. Suppose a plausibility statement $S0$ is constructed for $C0$ as follows.

($S0$)	$C0$:	message_based(M)
	$A0$:	...
	$R0$:	$\forall \mathrm{obj}_i, \mathrm{obj}_k \in M$: send_receive_comm($\mathrm{obj}_i, \mathrm{obj}_k$)
		$\wedge \neg$ shared_mem_comm($\mathrm{obj}_i, \mathrm{obj}_k$)
	$V0$:	...
	$P0$:	**validated**

Here $C0$ is defined in terms of $R0$ such that $C0$ is **validated** if $R0$ is validated. There is, however, another aspect to $C0$: and that is, the question as to *why* this constraint was established at all for the system M. In TPD, third order constraints called *justification* constraints are admissible precisely for the purpose of answering such questions.

Justification (J-) constraints are of the form 'is_desirable', 'is_good', or 'is_valuable' and apply to second order constraints. In the case of $C0$ we may want to explicitly document the justification for selecting or desiring this constraint; in which case, the following plausibility statement may be constructed.

($S0_j$)	$C0_j$:	is_desirable($C0$)
	$A0_j$:	knowledge base for multiprocessing, parallel processing and distributed processing systems.
	$R0_j$:	$\forall\, o \in$ object_oriented_systems: parallel_computational_model(o) = 'message_based'
	$V0_j$:	Approximate reasoning based on the knowledge base.
	$P0_j$:	**validated**

That is, (SO_j) stipulates that the desirability of the constraint 'message_based(M)' is justified by the fact that for all instances of object-oriented systems the underlying parallel computational model is the message based model. If, RO_j can be **validated** using the relevant knowledge base then $C0_j$ will also be **validated**. By convention, plausibility statements for justification constraints will be identified by the subscript j as shown above.

9.10 EXERCISES IN PLAUSIBILITY-DRIVEN DESIGN

Originally, the TPD paradigm was conceived in the context of computer architecture (Aguero and Dasgupta 1987). As is well known, the 'architecture' of a computer refers to certain abstract properties of the computer. Thus, the computer architect – the designer of architectures – is faced with the problem of designing *abstractions*. Such abstractions – consisting of instruction sets, addressing modes, instruction formats, the organization and control of storage and functional modules, etc. – are intended to serve as specifications of constraints (properties or features) that are to be satisfied by a hardware/firmware implementation. The 'goodness' of the architecture must, *in the final analysis*, be determined after implementation. All that the architect can do at the time of design is to establish the plausibility of the architecture using the strongest evidence at his or her disposal.

In spite of its origins, TPD is a very general design paradigm which appears to be applicable to many different kinds of computing systems regardless of whether such systems are intended to be implemented in silicon or with symbols.

In this section I shall illustrate the application of TPD to two fragmentary design problems. The operative word here is 'fragmentary' since limitation of space (and readability) forces one to limit the sizes of the examples. Yet the design problems considered here are nontrivial, 'real world' problems with all the complexities attendant therein.

Example 9.10
The first detailed example of a plausibility-driven design was undertaken by Aguero (1987). This pertained to the design of an architecture based on the RISC or *reduced instruction set computer* style.[7] The following discussion is based on Aguero(1987) but deviates somewhat in detail from the latter.

---

[7] The principle of the reduced instruction set computer (RISC) originated in the work of Patterson, Hennessy, Cocke and their colleagues in response to essentially two distinct forces: the fact that most of the contemporary programming is done in high level languages rather than assembly languages; and the advent of very large scale integration (VLSI) technology. For discussions of the RISC style see Patterson(1985), Hennessy (1984), Katevenis (1985), Dasgupta (1989a).

The overall objective is the development of an instruction set that can efficiently support the execution of the most frequent and the most time consuming types of operations found present in programs written in such languages as Pascal or C.

Clearly, to establish the plausibility of such an instruction set design, certain clarifications of the above goal must be done. This led to the following set of initial constraints.

(1) *Inst_set*: an instruction set, to be specified formally in the architecture description language S*M. This is a first order constraint.

(2) *Eff(inst_set)*: a predicate that is true if the instruction set is efficient. This is a second order constraint.

(3) *Op_supporting(inst_set, BENCHMARKS)*: a predicate that is true if the instructions support the most frequent and time consuming operations found in BENCHMARKS, a set of predetermined benchmark programs written in a predetermined set of languages. This is a second order constraint.

Further consideration led to the following plausibility statements.

$(S1)$ $C1$:   Eff(inst_set)

         $A1$:   inst_set; BENCHMARKS; Knowledge base(KB) regarding instruction set design; compiler for instruction set.

         $R1$: $\forall\, p \in$ BENCHMARKS :

                 Size(obj_code(p,inst_set)) $\leq$ LOWSIZE(p)

                 $\wedge$ Exec_time((obj_code(p,inst_set)) $\leq$ LOWTIME(p)

         $V1$:   Approximate reasoning based on KB.

         $P1$:   **assumed**

---

where:

(i) Size(obj_code(p,inst_set)) = the size of the object code (measured in bytes) produced from p using inst_set.

(ii) Exec_time((obj_code(p,inst_set)) = the execution time of the object code (measured in some convenient unit such as processor cycles) produced from p using inst_set

(iii) LOWSIZE(p), LOWTIME(p) are constants establishing bounds for program size and execution time respectively for each program p.

(S2)	C2:	Op_supporting(inst_set, BENCHMARKS)
	A2:	inst_set; BENCHMARKS; Knowledge base(KB) regarding frequency and time complexity of operations in BENCHMARKS.
	R2:	∀ op ∈ supports(inst_set, BENCHMARKS): Frequent(op) ∨ Time_consuming(op)
	V2:	Empirical analysis based on KB; Approximate reasoning involving inst_set.
	P2:	**assumed**

where:

(i) supports(inst_set, BENCHMARKS) = the set of operations such that each operation op in this set (a) occurs in at least one of the BENCHMARKS programs, and (b) either is a member of inst_set or can be demonstrably synthesized by members of inst_set.

(ii) Frequent(op) is a predicate that is true if operation op occurs frequently in BENCHMARKS

(iii) Time_consuming(op) is a predicate that is true if op's execution consumes a large amount of time

In (S1), the constraint $C1 = $ Eff(inst_set) has been characterized in terms of the assertion stated in R1. The means of verifying R1 has also been identified. Thus, it is now known, or has been established as to what would count as evidence for or against C1's plausibility. However, at this stage of the design it is obviously impossible to provide significant evidence in favor of C1; nor is it possible for us to refute C1. C1 is thus assigned the state **assumed**. (S1) can now be 'read' as saying that: 'At this stage of the design process, C1 is in plausibility state **assumed** since given that we are to employ the kind of evidence stated in V1, there is (as yet) no evidence against R1's plausibility.

At a (much) later stage in the design when 'inst_set' is available, it would be expected that using V1 we would be able to obtain significant evidence for R1's plausibility (and no counter-evidence), in which case the P1 field would be changed to **validated**.

The statement (S2) can be interpreted in a similar fashion. There is, however, a notable difference between the constraints C1 and C2: once inst_set is available the plausibility of C1 can be strengthened (to **validated** or **refuted**) and the resulting form of (S1) verified directly on the basis of R1. C2, however, is defined (according to R2) in terms of the predicates Frequent(op) and Time_consumption(op) which are, themselves, specified in such a way that we would not be able to **validate** or

refute $R1$ (hence $C1$) even if inst_set was available. The constraint described in $R2$ is, accordingly amplified in the following plausibility statement.

$(S3)$ $C3$:   ∀ op ∈ supports(inst_set, BENCHMARKS):
                    Frequent(op) ∨ Time_consuming(op)

         $A3$:   inst_set; BENCHMARKS; Statistical data on BENCHMARKS;
                    Compiler for inst_set; related literature
                    on programming language usage.

         $R3$:   ∀ op ∈ supports(inst_set, BENCHMARKS):
                     mean_stat_freq(op) ≥ STATFREQ
                   ∨ mean_dyn_freq(op) ≥ DYNFREQ
                   ∨ mean_time_weighted_dyn_freq(op) ≥ TW_DYNFREQ

         $V3$:   Empirical analysis of BENCHMARKS statistics;
                    review of related literature; approximate reasoning.

         $P3$:   **assumed**

---

where

- (i) mean_stat_freq(op) = the mean frequency of occurrence of 'op' in the texts of BENCHMARKS programs
- (ii) mean_dyn_freq(op) = the mean frequency of occurrence of 'op' during the execution of BENCHMARKS programs
- (iii) mean_time_weighted_dyn_freq(op) = mean_dyn_freq(op) * est_time(op)
- (iv) est_time(op) = estimated time (in processor cycles) consumed for execution of 'op'.
- (v) STATFREQ, DYNFREQ, TW_DYNFREQ are constants identifying lower bound values for the functions (i)–(iii) respectively.

Given $(S3)$, members of the set 'supports(inst_set, BENCHMARKS)' satisfying the $R3$ field must next be identified. This necessitated analysis of the statistical data on the static and dynamic frequencies of statements appearing in BENCHMARKS programs, possibly corroborated by data reported in the literature for other programs and/or programming languages. It also necessitates determining the weights of 'est_time(op)' to attach to each 'op'. These weights will be proportional to the number of machine instructions (or number of processor cycles) that will actually be executed in order to execute 'op'. In the absence of inst_set itself, approximate reasoning will have to be used at this stage of the design.[8]

---

[8] In the specific case of the Berkeley RISC project, 'typical' machine code sequences for each operation were generated based on prior studies of compilers for other architectures (Patterson and Sequin 1981).

Such analysis leads to the identification of the following classes of operation.

(a) Let ASSIGNSET denote the set of operations appearing in the following types of assignments

$$A := B$$
$$A := A \text{ op } B$$
$$A := k$$
$$A := A \pm k$$

where A, B are simple or subscripted variables, k is a constant, and op $\in$ {integer add, integer subtract, AND, OR, EXCLUSIVE OR}. The above assignments correspond to the most frequently encountered types of assignments in high level language programs (Dasgupta 1984, chapter 13; Dasgupta 1989a, chapters 4 and 7; Katevenis 1985, chapter 2). We will suppose that ASSIGNSET includes MOVE, integer ADD and SUBTRACT, AND, OR, EXCLUSIVE OR, INCREMENT and DECREMENT.

(b) Let CALLSET denote the set of operations CALL and RETURN corresponding to procedure call and return statements where (i) the number of parameters passed between procedures ≤ 6; and (ii) the number of local variables in the procedures ≤ 10. CALLSET is so identified because the data reveals that (a) procedure calls and returns are the most time consuming of operations and (b) the bounds on the number of parameters and local variables account for a majority of procedures (Katevenis 1985, chapter 2).

(c) Finally, let JUMPSET denote the set of operations implicitly or explicitly present in **if** statements. We will suppose that JUMPSET consists of the unconditional JUMP and a small set of conditional JUMPS.

Based on the above analysis, the following plausibility statement is proposed.

(*S4*) *C4*: ∀ op ∈ supports(inst_set, BENCHMARKS):
        mean_stat_freq(op) ≥ STATFREQ
        ∨ mean_dyn_freq(op) ≥ DYNFREQ
        ∨ mean_time_weighted_dyn_freq(op) ≥ TW_DYNFREQ

   A4: inst_set; BENCHMARKS; Statistical data on BENCHMARKS;
        related literature on programming language usage;
        related literature on code generation strategies.

   R4: ∀ op ∈ ASSIGNSET:
          op ∈ supports(inst_set, BENCHMARKS) ∧
          (mean_stat_freq(op) ≥ STATFREQ
          ∨ mean_dyn_freq(op) ≥ DYNFREQ)
        ∧

        ∀ op ∈ CALLSET:
          op ∈ supports(inst_set, BENCHMARKS) ∧
          mean_time_weighted_dyn_freq(op) ≥ TW_DYN_FREQ
        ∧
        ∀ op ∈ JUMPSET:
          op ∈ supports(inst_set, BENCHMARKS) ∧
          (mean_stat_freq(op) ≥ STATFREQ
          ∨ mean_dyn_freq(op) ≥ DYNFREQ)

  $V4$:   Analysis of statistical data on BENCHMARKS;
         approximate reasoning.
  $P4$:   **assumed**

The design at this point consists of the plausibility statements $(S1)$–$(S4)$. In the case of $(S1)$, note that $C1$ is defined in terms of the conjunction of two constraints which we will label $C5$ and $C6$:

$C5$: ∀ p ∈ BENCHMARKS:
    Size(obj_code(p, inst_set)) ≤ LOWSIZE(p)

$C6$: ∀ p ∈ BENCHMARKS:
    Exec_time(obj_code(p, inst_set)) ≤ LOWTIME(p)

In the case of $(S4)$, $C4$ is defined in terms of the conjunction of three constraints which we will label $C7$, $C8$ and $C9$:

$C7$: ∀ op ∈ ASSIGNSET:
    op ∈ supports(inst_set, BENCHMARKS) ∧
    (mean_stat_freq(op) ≥ STATFREQ ∨
    mean_dyn_freq(op) ≥ DYNFREQ)

$C8$: ∀ op ∈ CALLSET:
    op ∈ supports(inst_set, BENCHMARKS) ∧
    mean_time_weighted_dyn_freq(op) ≥ TW_DYNFREQ

$C9$: ∀ op ∈ JUMPSET:
    op ∈ supports(inst_set, BENCHMARKS) ∧
    (mean_stat_freq(op) ≥ STATFREQ ∨
    mean_dyn_freq(op) ≥ DYNFREQ)

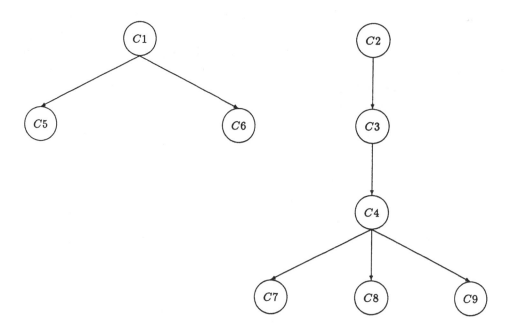

Fig. 9.5 A first snapshot of the CDG.

The corresponding CDG is depicted in fig. 9.5.

At this point it is decided to pursue further, the constraints $C5$ and $C6$. Now, one of the architectural principles that is widely believed to be true is that *register oriented* instruction sets are more time-efficient than *memory based* instruction sets.[9]

This principle – a heuristic law, one might say – is obviously relevant to $C6$ though its relevance to $C5$ is by no means clear (Dasgupta 1989a, chapter 4). Accordingly leaving $C5$ aside, suppose the following plausibility statement is constructed for $C6$.

$(S6)$	$C6:$	$\forall\, p \in$ BENCHMARKS:
		Exec_time(obj_code(p,inst)) $\leq$ LOWTIME(p)
	$A6:$	KB on instruction set design.
	$R6:$	reg_oriented(inst_set)
	$V6:$	review of the literature.
	$P6:$	**assumed**

where reg_oriented(inst_set) – call this constraint $C10$ – is true if most of the instructions can access operands and leave results in registers.

---

[9] For more on this, see Dasgupta (1989a, chapter 4)

On further reflection ($S6$) is clearly seen to be unsatisfactory. For, ($S6$) implies that $C6$ is *only* dependent on $C10 \equiv$ reg_oriented(inst_set) whereas the very nature of $C6$ indicates that, if inst_set is available, we should be able to determine its plausibility by conducting experiments involving inst_set and BENCHMARKS using emulation, simulation or prototyping techniques. In other words, the following plausibility statement seems far more legitimate for $C6$:

($S6'$) $C6'$: $\forall p \in$ BENCHMARKS:
                    Exec_time(obj_code(p,inst)) $\leq$ LOWTIME(p)
          $A6'$:   inst_set; BENCHMARKS.
          $R6'$: $\forall p \in$ BENCHMARKS:
                    Exec_time(obj_code(p,inst_set)) $\leq$ LOWTIME(p)
          $V6'$:   Experiments (through emulation, simulation, or
                    prototyping) using inst_set, BENCHMARKS.
          $P6'$:   **assumed**

Making $R6'$ identical to $C6'$ merely indicates that the constraint can be directly verified to be in the given plausibility state.

($S6'$) is not, however, helpful in determining *how C6 can be achieved* through design; whereas ($S6$) *is* directed towards that objective.

The situation, then, is this: ($S6$) is patently incorrect; it paints a false picture regarding what kind of evidence counts for establishing the time-efficiency of the instruction set. Yet, it seems that a register-oriented instruction set will *very likely* contribute to the goal of achieving a time-efficient instruction set.

This suggests revisiting the plausibility statement ($S1$) for constraint $C1 \equiv$ Eff(inst_set) and adding $C10 \equiv$ reg_oriented(inst_set) to its R field. The revised version of ($S1$) is now

---

($S1'$) $C1'$:   Eff(inst_set)
          $A1'$:   inst_set; BENCHMARKS; KB on instruction set
                    design; Compiler for inst_set.
          $R1'$:   reg_oriented(inst_set) $\wedge$ ($\forall p \in$ BENCHMARKS :
                        Size(obj_code(p,inst_set)) $\leq$ LOWSIZE(p))
                    $\wedge$ Exec_time((obj_code(p,inst_set)) $\leq$ LOWTIME(p)
          $V1'$:   Approximate reasoning based on KB; Experiments.
          $P1'$:   **assumed**

The CDG is accordingly modified to the form shown in fig. 9.6. Note that if at a later stage of the design process we wish to **validate** C1 and if inst_set is register oriented but one of the efficiency constraints is not yet met then the validation of C1 will fail. Similarly, if the inst_set is not register oriented yet the efficiency constraints are met then also we will have failed to **validate** C1. In either case the designer may choose to *weaken* the claim made about the design or to start a new round of redesign.

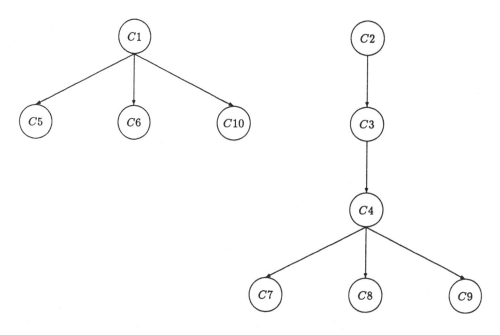

Fig. 9.6 Second snapshot of the CDG.

At this point several modifications are made to the current design. Firstly, a plausibility statement is created for C10. This takes the form

(S10)	C10 :	reg_oriented(inst_set)
	A10 :	inst_set.
	R10 :	for most $i \in$ inst_set:
		registers(operands(i)) $\wedge$
		registers(results(i))
	V10 :	Empirical evaluation of inst_set.
	P10 :	assumed

where

operands(i) = the set of inputs (operands) to instruction i

results(i) = the set of outputs (results) of instruction i

registers(x) = true if information x is stored in a processor register

Note the imprecise form of $R10$ since a decision as to exactly which instructions or what proportion of the instruction set must have its operands and results in registers is postponed for the present. Denote the constraint introduced in $R10$ as $C11$.

Secondly, the *reasons* for selecting a register-oriented style are documented as part of the design. This is effected by creating a plausibility statement for a J-constraint (see section 9.9) $C10j$ corresponding to $C10$:

($S10j$)	$C10j$:	is_desirable($C10$)
	$A10j$:	KBs on architecture and integrated circuit technology.
	$R10j$:	access_time(register) < access_time(memory)
		$\wedge$ no_of_address_bits(register) <
		no_of_address_bits(memory)
	$V10j$:	Approximate reasoning based on KBs.
	$P10j$:	**Validated**

In other words, the choice of a register-oriented instruction set is justified on the grounds that (i) register access times are less than memory access times; and (ii) the number of bits required to address registers is smaller than that required to address memory. ($C10j$) can be verified to be in the **validated** state as the relevant knowledge on architecture and technology reveals significant evidence in favor of both (and no evidence against either) propositions.

Finally, while it is certainly the case that register-oriented instructions are conducive to efficiency other architectural features also contribute to this same goal. These include, in particular

$C12$: small_number_of(inst_formats)

$C13$: fixed_size(inst_set)

$C14$: small_size(inst_formats)

$C15$: overlap(inst_fetch, inst_execute)

$C12$ is a predicate that is true if the number of distinct instruction formats is small; $C13$ is true if all members of inst_set are identical in size; $C14$ is true if all the instruction formats are small in size; and, finally, $C15$ is a predicate that is true if the architectural components for fetching and executing instructions are overlapped.

Note that in addition to $C12$–$C15$, the constraints inst_formats, inst_fetch, and inst_execute have been introduced into the design. The latter three are all (likely to be) first order constraints.

The plausibility statement ($S1'$) for $C1$ must now be revised to reflect the introduction of $C12$–$C15$. The revised statement is

($S1''$)	$C1''$:	Eff(inst_set).
	$A1''$:	inst_set; BENCHMARKS; KB on instruction set design;
		compiler for instruction set; inst_formats; inst_fetch; inst_execute.
	$R1''$:	reg_oriented(inst_set) $\wedge$
		small_number_of(inst_formats) $\wedge$
		fixed_size(inst_formats) $\wedge$ small_size(inst_formats)
		$\wedge$ overlap(inst_fetch, inst_execute)
		$\wedge$ ($\forall\, p \in$ BENCHMARKS:
		Size(obj_code(p,inst_set)) $\leq$ LOWSIZE(p)
		$\wedge$ Exec_time((obj_code(p,inst_set)) $\leq$ LOWTIME(p))
	$V1''$:	Approximate reasoning based on KB; Experiments.
	$P1''$:	**assumed**

The revised CDG incorporating these several modifications is shown in fig. 9.7. Note that a dotted edge connects the constraint $C10$ to its associated J-constraint $C10_j$. The design at this stage, consists of this CDG along with the plausibility statements ($S1''$), ($S2$)–($S4$), ($S10j$) and ($S10$). The unsupported constraints are $C5$, $C6$, $C11$, $C12$–$C15$, $C7$–$C9$. Note also that only $C10_j$ has been **validated** thus far.

I will not pursue the development of this architecture any further except to note the following. Eventually, the design of inst_set and other first order constraints such as inst_formats will begin. Suppose inst_set is specified completely in a formal architecture description language such that inst_set is implementable. Then, by hypothesis (see section 9.3) inst_set will have been **validated**. The process of strengthening the plausibility states of all second order constraints that are still in the **assumed** state and which depend on inst_set can, then, begin; these constraints will be either **validated** or **refuted**. In the latter case the **refuted** constraints are removed from the design and the consequences of such removal must be traced through the design using the CDG to determine the dependencies, and the design revised accordingly.

Consider, for instance the following plausibility statements for $C5$ and $C6$ which are to be verified:

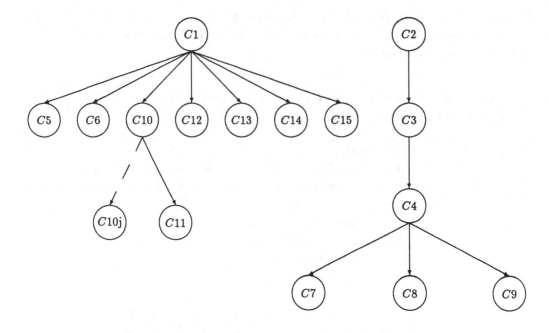

Fig. 9.7 Third snapshot of the CDG.

$(S5)$	$C5:$	$\forall\, p \in$ BENCHMARKS:
		Size(obj_code(p, inst_set)) $\leq$ LOWSIZE(p)
	$A5:$	inst_set; compiler; simulator for the architecture
		description language; BENCHMARKS.
	$R5:$	$C5$
	$V5:$	Experiments.
	$P5:$	**Validated**

$(S6)$	$C6:$	$\forall\, p \in$ BENCHMARKS:
		Exec_time(obj_code(p, inst_set)) $\leq$ LOWTIME(p)
	$A6:$	inst_set; compiler; simulator for the architecture
		description language; BENCHMARKS.
	$R6:$	$C6$
	$V6:$	Experiments.
	$P6:$	**Validated**

Note that in each of the statements, the content of the R field is the constraint itself. The verification of $(S5)$ and $(S6)$ has to wait till inst_set has been completely specified in an implementable architecture description language. When the latter is available, verification of $(S6)$ is found to be successful: experiments using compiled

BENCHMARKS programs running on a simulated implementation of inst_set reveal that $C6$ is indeed true; it is, therefore, **validated**. On the other hand, $C5$ is found not to hold for all the BENCHMARKS programs. The plausibility state of $C5$ is changed to **refuted** and the *resulting* statement is verified. Thus $C5$ is no longer part of the design. Since $C1$, 'Eff(inst_set)', depends on $C5$ (as well as other constraints), its plausibility state would also have to be **refuted** according to $(S1'')$.

At this stage, the architect may determine that as all the other constraints appearing in $R1''$ have been satisfied – that is, are in the **validated** state – the criteria for efficiency should be weakened to exclude $C5$. The plausibility statement for $C1$ is revised as follows:

$(S1''')$	$C1'''$:	Eff(inst_set).
	$A1'''$:	inst_set; BENCHMARKS; KB on instruction set design;
		compiler for instruction set; inst_formats; inst_fetch; inst_execute.
	$R1'''$:	reg_oriented(inst_set) $\wedge$
		fixed_size(inst_formats) $\wedge$ small_number_of(inst_formats)
		$\wedge$ overlap(inst_fetch, inst_execute)
		$\wedge$ ($\forall\, p \in$ BENCHMARKS:
		Exec_time((obj_code(p,inst_set)) $\leq$ LOWTIME(p)
	$V1'''$:	Approximate reasoning based on KB;
		Empirical analysis and Experiments.
	$P1'''$:	**validated**

$(S1''')$ is now verified. The revised characterization of the R field represents the strongest claim that the architect can make about the efficiency of the instruction set.

End Example

Example 9.11
This example is taken from a plausibility-driven design of a user-interface to UNIX for use in a workstation environment (Landry *et al.* 1988). The user-interface was named PDI and the requirements *as originally established* were the following:

(i) PDI is to provide full coverage of, or access to, all facilities on the Berkeley 4.2 and 4.3 BSD Unix operating systems.
(ii) PDI is to provide an easy-to-use interface to Unix for use on workstations with good window management facilities.
(iii) PDI must be adaptable to the user's skill level.
(iv) PDI must be adaptable to the user's task.

  (v) PDI will utilize a vocabulary that is either task domain dependent or user-customized.

  (vi) Guidance, training, and practice are an integral part of PDI.

  (vii) PDI must be internally consistent.

The ultimate output of the design process is to be a specification of PDI in an appropriately agreed upon design language. This may be an Ada-like psuedocode or the Ada programming language itself. This specification will thus constitute the set of first order constraints.

In the present discussion we shall follow one strand of the overall design. This particular strand originated in requirement (vi) and appears in PDI as the constraint[10]

$C7$: PDI provides guidance to the user and allows the user to practice.

The development of, and refinement to $C7$ as described below, is due to Levy and Pollacia (1988).

The plausibility statement for $C7$ is

$(S7)$	$C7$:	PDI provides guidance to the user and allows the user to practice.
	$A7$:	PDI specification in pseudocode; KB on user interface design.
	$R7$:	$C25 \wedge C28$ where
		$C25$: PDI provides guidance to the user and allows the user to practice at each PDI-defined skill level and at each PDI-defined task domain
		$C28$: PDI provides guidance to the user and allows the user to practice in the use of the interface itself.
	$V7$:	Empirical analysis; approximate reasoning based on the PDI specification and the KB.
	$P7$:	**assumed**

---

[10] As the reader will see, the constraints in this example are stated mostly in English language statements. This was exactly how the design of PDI was constructed and I have retained the original form of the constraints as far as possible.

($S7$) is verified as there is no evidence against $C7$'s plausibility. The constraint $C25$ is defined according to

---

($S25$)	$C25$:	PDI provides guidance to the user and allows the user to practice at each PDI-defined skill level and in each PDI-defined task domain.
	$A25$:	PDI specification in psuedocode; KB on user interface design.
	$R25$:	$C14 \land C29 \land C30 \land C35 \land C808$ where
		$C14$: PDI supports distinct PDI-defined task domains.
		$C29$: For each PDI-defined task domain there exists an on line tutorial.
		$C30$: Printed documentation provides guidance for each skill level in each task domain.
		$C35$: For each skill level in each task domain there exists an online help facility.
		$C808$: PDI provides feedback appropriate to the skill level of the user in the given task domain.
	$V25$:	Approximate reasoning and empirical analysis based on the PDI specification and the KB.
	$P25$:	**assumed**

($S25$), thus, establishes what it means for $C25$ to hold. The constraints $C14, \dots, C808$ are identified based on the KB on user-interface design. It may be noted that a critic or the client may, based on the same KB, regard $C14, \dots, C808$ as insufficient to satisfy *their* interpretation of $C25$. In which case additional constraints may serve to augment $R25$. Note further that in the absence of the actual PDI specification one can neither **refute** nor **validate** R25 (hence $C25$); yet the nature of the evidence is known. Hence $C25$ is placed and verified to be in the **assumed** state. The basis for such verification is approximate reasoning about the nature of the $R25$ field on the basis of the KB on user interface design.

Fig. 9.8 shows the relevant part of the CDG at this stage of development.

Let us now pursue the development of $C35$ which is concerned with the design of an online 'Help' facility. In a separate region of the PDI project three user *skill levels* have been identified: 'novice', 'experienced' and 'expert'. The set of skill levels is denoted by SL. In yet another region of the project the *task domains* supported by PDI

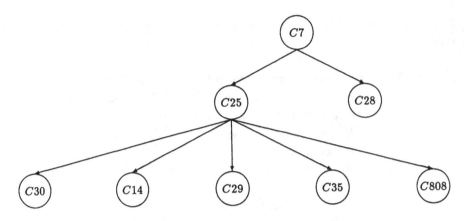

Fig. 9.8 A first (partial) snapshot of PDI's CDG.

have been identified. There are five such task domains, viz., 'program development', 'text processing', 'systems administration', 'systems programming' and a set of 'core tasks'. The last consists of frequently performed tasks such as creating, deleting, copying files and directories, editing, viewing and printing textfiles, and so on. Core tasks are shared among the other task domains. The set of task domains is denoted by TD.

The plausibility statement for $C35$ (stated in more concise form) is developed as follows:

$(S35)$	$C35:$	$\forall \langle s,t \rangle \in SL \times TD$: online_help(s,t)
	$A35:$	PDI specification; KB on user interfaces.
	$R35:$	$C36 \wedge C37 \wedge C38$ where:
		$C36: \forall \langle s,t \rangle \in SL \times TD$: there exists information for all relevant interface features, commands, parameters, and their consequences.
		$C37: \forall \langle s,t \rangle \in SL \times TD$: PDI provides help with displayed PDI prompts upon user request.
		$C38: \forall \langle s,t \rangle \in SL \times TD$: user may request help with displayed PDI error messages.
	$V35:$	Empirical analysis of PDI; Experiments with PDI; Approximate reasoning based on the KB.
	$P35:$	**assumed**

The constraint $C37$ is further developed in terms of a series of plausibility statements. These statements are presented below. The plausibility states shown in these statements are the *final* states as explained shortly. The initial postulated state assignments for $C37$, $C145$, $C146$, $C147$ and $C148$ were **assumed**. The final states are the outcome of revising the plausibility statements after the module $M145$ has been described in pseudocode.

$(S37)$	$C37:$	$\forall \langle s,t \rangle \in$ SL $\times$ TD: PDI provides help with displayed prompts upon user request.
	$A37:$	PDI specification.
	$R37:$	$C145 \wedge C146$
		$C145: \forall \langle s,t \rangle \in$ SL $\times$ TD: if the user requests help with a system generated prompt, PDI will return an explanation or syntax description of the prompt.
		$C146:$ The text of the explanation of each displayed PDI prompt is appropriate to the user's skill level.
	$V37:$	Empirical analysis of PDI; Experiments with PDI.
	$P37:$	**validated**

$(S37j)$	$C37j:$	$C37$ is desirable.
	$A37j:$	KB on online Help facilities.
	$R37j:$	Cond37a $\wedge$ Cond37b, where
		Cond37a: A good Help facility allows the user to switch easily to and from Help mode.
		Cond37b: Help should be provided to explain system-generated prompts.
	$V37j:$	Analysis of the KB.
	$P37j:$	**validated**

$(S145)$	$C145:$	$\forall \langle s,t \rangle \in$ SL $\times$ TD: If the user requests help with a system generated prompt PDI will return an explanation or syntax description of the prompt.
	$A145:$	PDI specification.
	$R145:$	$C147 \wedge C148$ where:
		$C147: \forall \langle s,t \rangle \in$ SL $\times$ TD: if the user does not enter the full command PDI prompts the user for the necessary parameters.
		$C148: \forall$ PDI-displayed prompts: the user has the option to enter a '?' to receive explanation of the prompt followed by the prompt again.
	$V145:$	Empirical analysis of PDI; Experiments with PDI.
	$P145:$	**validated**

$(S146)$	$C146:$	The text of the explanation of each displayed PDI prompt is appropriate to the user's skill level.
	$A146:$	PDI specification of pseudocode module $M145 \equiv$ COMMAND_PROMPTS.
	$R146:$	Help_explanation_part_of($M145$) is appropriate to user's skill level.
	$V146:$	Analysis of $M145$.
	$P146:$	**validated**

$(S147)$	$C147:$	$\forall \langle s,t \rangle \in$ SL $\times$ TD: if the user does not enter the full command PDI prompts the user for necessary parameters.
	$A147:$	PDI specification of pseudocode module $M145 \equiv$ COMMAND_PROMPTS.
	$R147:$	If the user does not enter the full command, M145 generates a prompt for necessary parameters.
	$V147:$	Analysis of $M145$.
	$P147:$	**validated**

$(S148)$	$C148:$	$\forall$ PDI_displayed prompts: the user has the option to enter a '?' to receive an explanation of the prompt again.
	$A148:$	PDI specification of pseudocode module $M145 \equiv$ COMMAND_PROMPTS.
	$R148:$	$\forall$ PDI_displayed prompts: $M145$ accepts a '?' from user, produces explanation of the prompt and then displays the prompt again.
	$V148:$	Analysis of $M145$.
	$P148:$	**validated**

At this stage of the design the relevant portion of the CDG is as shown in fig. 9.9. Note the justification constraint $C37j$ associated (through a dashed edge) with $C37$. As $(S37j)$ stipulates, $C37j$ is in the **validated** state.

Considering $(S147)$ and $(S148)$, their respective R fields are sufficiently well structured that the designer can attempt to **validate** or **refute** them. (In fact $R147$ and $R148$ *could* both be stated in the style of Hoare formulas). The verification of $(S147)$ and $(S148)$ proceeds by empirical analysis of, and approximate reasoning based on, a code module called $M145$ (not shown here). It is assumed (through a prior design

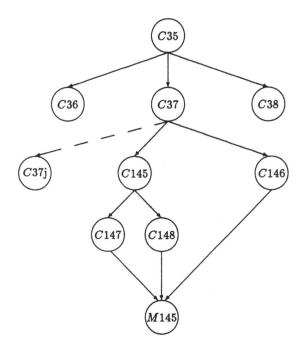

Fig. 9.9 A second (partial) snapshot of PDI's CDG.

decision) that the design language for specifying PDI will be an appropriate psue-docode. Hence $(S147)$ and $(S148)$ cannot be *formally* verified using a proof theory – as would be possible if the design language was to be a programming language. The verifications of $(S147)$ and $(S148)$ are, then, based on empirical analysis and approximate reasoning. The constraint $C146$ is also defined as being dependent directly on $M145$ in which case one might expect that $(S146)$ can be directly verified by analyzing $M145$. It will be noticed, however, that R146 states that the 'help-explanation-part-of' $M145$ is *appropriate* to the user's skill level. Since this attribute has not been further defined in an *objectively testable* form, the evidence in favor of or against $C146$ may have to rely entirely on *subjective* analysis of $M145$. Indeed at the design stage such an assessment is all that probably *can* be done! The alternative is to defer verification of $C146$ (and merely place it, temporarily, in the **assumed** state) until actual experiments can be conducted with users. The evidence in that case would be empirical and take the form of user feedback at different skill levels.

Assuming that only subjective analysis of $M145$ is used as evidence, $C146$ can be verified to be in the **validated** state. As a result of this, $C37$ can also be **validated**. *End Example*

9.11 DISCUSSION, CONTRASTS AND COMPARISONS

The theory of plausible designs is a paradigm which, in the final analysis, is founded on a simple unifying notion: that a design is to be viewed as a complex of hypotheses, the plausibility of which is to be established and which is determined according to the evidence at hand. As was noted in section 9.4, TPD is grounded in an analogy between design and the method of science (fig. 9.3). This analogy will be explored in much greater detail in chapter 12. For the present it will perhaps be more illuminating to identify or establish other more practical features of TPD and to contrast and compare it to the other paradigms discussed in this book.

(A) Unification of design and requirements

We can first note that in TPD the concepts of 'requirements' and 'design' are unified into the single notion of 'constraints'. This is in response to some key observations made in chapter 5: that in the course of the design, both the design itself and the set of requirements evolve; that the distinction between 'design' and 'requirements' is quite frequently blurred; and consequently, the separation of analysis (of requirements) from synthesis (of design) is frequently meaningless.

In TPD, the design process begins with some set of *goal* constraints. It becomes the designer's task to make these constraints matters of *fact*. In the case of the PDI problem (example 9.11) an initial requirement was that 'guidance, training and practice are [to be] an integral part of PDI'. This requirement becomes one of the top level constraints ($C7$) in the PDI design effort. In the case of the RISC problem (example 9.10) the requirement was 'the development of an instruction set that can efficiently support the execution of the most frequent and/or time consuming types of operations found in programs written in such languages as Pascal or C'. This requirement was assimilated into the RISC design in the form of two constraints ($C1$) and ($C2$).

One might argue that in both ASE and FD, requirements are also assimilated into the design process. The difference lies in that in both these paradigms a clear distinction is made between requirements and design. This is perhaps most clearly realized by noting the language used in these paradigms: in both ASE and FD a design is intended to *satisfy* the requirements. Even in the case of FD where an instance of the Hoare formula

$$\{\text{PRE}\}\ P\ \{\text{POST}\}$$

is viewed as a single entity for the purpose of correctness proving, P (a program, microprogram, circuit specification or whatever) is, nonetheless, distinct from the PRE/POST collective requirement – in the sense that it is taken for granted that PRE/POST will remain fixed while P itself may evolve in the course of the design.

The reader might argue that TPD does, in fact, distinguish between 'first order' and 'higher order' constraints; and that the former concept corresponds to the ASE/FD notion of 'design' while the latter to the notion of 'requirements'. However, the distinction between first order and higher order constraints is *only* to establish what would count as evidence for the plausibilities of these two types of constraints (section 9.2).

(B) The broad view of design form

A closely related feature of TPD is that the entire complex of constraints, their dependencies and the associated plausibility statements constitute the design. This is entirely consistent with, and supportive of, the idea that the form of a design must serve several different functions: as a blueprint for implementation; as a user's guide; and as a medium for criticism, change and experimentation (chapter 4). Thus TPD takes a considerably *richer* view of the form of the design solution than either ASE or FD.

(C) Plausibility and evidence

Perhaps one of the most distinct features of TPD is its explicit attention to the role and nature of the evidence in establishing a design's plausibility. Stated simply, the plausibility of a design as claimed by the designer is determined by the kind of evidence invoked in support of the claims. The evidence in turn, involves relevant *knowledge* of the design domain; *tools* (compilers, simulators, prototypes etc.); the *techniques of verification* (empirical analysis, approximate reasoning, experiments, formal proofs, etc.); and the *causal history* of the individual constraints as illuminated by the constraint dependency graph and the plausibility statement of the corresponding constraints. The plausibility of each constraint is determined by *all* these factors.

Furthermore, a design's plausibility is not only gauged in terms of its **validated** or **assumed** constraints. One might as such wish to attempt to **refute** a constraint.

Thus, a design and its plausibility are determined by an entire *Weltanschauung* that is shared by the relevant design community. This, we recall, was a crucial missing feature of the ASE paradigm (chapter 7, section 7.4).

In this context, it will also be noted that in a very real sense the FD paradigm may be regarded as being subsumed by TPD. Consider, for example, the following pair of plausibility statements (taken from example 9.6) which we assume were constructed in the course of designing an ALU circuit.

(S3)	C3 :	Full adder: specified in VHDL.
	A3 :	VHDL User Manual.
	R3 :	Full adder: specified in VHDL.
	V3 :	Inspection of the full adder description for syntactic correctness with respect to VHDL.
	P3 :	**Validated**

(S4)	C4 :	is_correct($C3$)
	A4 :	$C3$; Proof theory for VHDL.
	R4 :	sum $= (\neg$ in1 $\wedge \neg$ in2 $\wedge$ carry_in) $\vee$ ($\neg$ in1 $\wedge$ in2 $\wedge \neg$ carry_in) $\vee$ (in1 $\wedge \neg$ in2 $\wedge \neg$ carry_in) $\vee$ (in1 $\wedge$ in2 $\wedge$ carry_in) carry_out $=$ (in1 $\wedge$ in2) $\vee$ (in1 $\wedge$ carry_in) $\vee$ (in2 $\wedge$ carry_in)
	V4 :	formal proof.
	P4 :	**Validated**

$C4$ is therefore dependent on $C3$. To verify that $C4$ is **validated** requires us to prove formally, using VHDL's proof theory (provided that there is one) that $R4$ is **validated**. Such a verification process is, of course, simply an exercise in formal design.

(D) Evolutionary aspects of TPD

The evolutionary nature of the TPD paradigm (with respect to the evolutionary schema described in chapter 5, section 5.3) is quite explicit. In TPD, the *objects* that evolve are the constraints constituting a design/requirements complex; the *direction* of evolution is towards the attainment of **validated** constraints; and the *mechanism* of evolution is the attempt to verify the plausibility states of existing constraints and, as a consequence, the removal of **refuted** constraints, possible revision of the plausibility states of other existing constraints and the introduction of new constraints. The correspondence between TPD and the steps of the evolutionary model of fig. 5.5 is depicted in fig. 9.10.

(E) Belief revision in TPD

The very fact of evolution focuses attention on another aspect of TPD already noted in section 9.8: the plausibility of a design *is constantly subject to revision*. The underlying reasoning is non-monotonic in nature (Reiter 1987, Genesereth and Nilsson 1987). There is nothing sacrosanct about a design (or claims made about it). The designer's belief in the design at a given time t_1, is determined by the evidence

Evolutionary model	TPD
Design + Requirements	Set of constraints with associated plausibility statements
Critical test	Attempt to assign and verify plausibility statements based on evidence at hand
Misfit identification	Identification of constraints that cannot be **validated**; or constraints that are **refuted**
Misfit elimination	Removal of **refuted** constraints; revision of plausibility states of existing constraints; generation of new constraints

Fig. 9.10 Evolutionary features of TPD.

available at t_1 and his or her interpretation of that evidence. At some (possibly much) later time t_2 any one of a number of things can happen. New evidence may come to the designer's attention; the designer may realize that a wrong interpretation had been put on some piece of data; or the experiments previously used to verify a plausibility statement were erroneous and fresh experiments simply contradicted the results of the previous ones. Whatever be the reason the plausibility states of constraints may have to be revised as a result of some change in the plausibility state of a particular constraint. This is, of course, a further manifestation of bounded rationality.[11]

Consider a CDG with plausibility states assigned to each of its constituent constraints. A constraint C either has just been introduced into the design or is an existing constraint the plausibility state of which has just been altered. The problem of systematically revising the plausibility states of all constraints that may be affected by the state of C is similar to the belief revision or truth maintenance problem in Artificial Intelligence. And, just as automatic *truth maintenance systems* (TMSs) or *belief revision systems* (BRSs) have been implemented in the context of AI systems (Doyle 1979a, 1979b; de Kleer 1986a, 1986b, 1986c, 1988), a system called TPD-BRS for automatically revising the plausibility states of constraints in a CDG has been recently constructed by Patel (1990; See also Patel and Dasgupta 1989).

---

[11] As I shall further discuss in chapter 12, this establishes yet another link between design and science; in science one also revises one's belief about what is true or not based on changing evidence. We must also note, however, that similar evidence-based revisions of beliefs of what is or is not the case appear in other areas of human activity. Consider, in particular, legal verdicts (Dworkin 1986).

(F) The goal-directed nature of constraint generation in TPD

Finally, we note the following feature of the paradigm. Plausibility driven design begins with one or more top level constraints that serve as the ultimate goals to be achieved. Call these $\{C_g\}$. The designer then proceeds to identify other constraints $\{C_1\}$ which, if found to be plausible will entail the plausibility of $\{C_g\}$. These in turn lead to still further sets of constraints $\{C_2\}$ which will entail the plausibility states of $\{C_1\}$ and so on, until a design in terms of first order constraints $\{C_n\}$ is reached. Solving a problem beginning with a set of goals, identifying subgoals which when achieved realize the goals, then further identifying sub-subgoals that entail the subgoals, and so on, goes by several names in the computer science, cognitive science and AI literatures, notably, *goal directed* problem solving, the method of *stepwise refinement*, and *backward chaining* (Alagic and Arbib 1978, Charniak and McDermott 1985, Newell and Simon 1972, Johnson-Laird 1988). Constraint generation in TPD is, thus, goal directed in nature.

Chapter 10

Design and Artificial Intelligence

10.1 THE AUTOMATION OF DESIGN

Thus far, the discussion of design paradigms has been basically devoted to the significance of design theory for computing systems design. Furthermore, the implicit focus has been on design as an intellectual, cogitative, human activity. In this and the next chapter I shall examine the obverse side of the coin – that is, the implications of computer science for design theory.

This is an issue that becomes rather relevant if we are interested in the *automation of design*. Specifically, we may ask the following types of questions: does the goal of automation cause us to expand our understanding of the design process (with respect to the architectonics discussed in Part I)? Given the desire to automate design, what are the characteristics of the relevant design paradigms?

The 'classical' response to the need to automate any task is to devise *algorithms* to perform the task. From a 'classical' perspective then, we are led to the *algorithmic design paradigm*. According to this paradigm, given a design problem one constructs algorithms that produce the design form. An algorithmic approach to design automation has the same kind of compelling appeal exhibited by the formal design paradigm: algorithms are formal, objective procedures with well defined, understandable behavioral characteristics. The problem with this paradigm is essentially twofold: firstly, the design problem must itself be sufficiently *well-structured* (see chapter 3, section 3.3) as to allow the algorithm to contain well defined conditions for its own termination; that is, in order to generate a solution to the design problem, the algorithm must 'know' what constitutes a solution and how to recognize the attainment of a solution. And, secondly, whatever knowledge is required about the design task domain must be entirely embedded in the algorithm itself.

These conditions quite obviously place severe limitations on the *scope* of the algorithmic paradigm. A bolder response to the design automation problem is to attack the problem in its full generality, by recognizing that most interesting design problems are ill-structured and imprecise, and often poorly understood (see chapter 3, sections 3.3 and 3.4), and that the process of design involves access to a wide variety and complex types of knowledge. The interesting paradigm for design automation in this setting, is based on techniques of Artificial Intelligence (AI). We may call it the *AI design paradigm.*

The AI paradigm is the focus of the present chapter. This discussion will allow us to establish a rather detailed picture of what design automation in its most general form will realistically entail. In chapter 11, I shall then discuss somewhat more briefly what is probably the most successful version of the algorithmic paradigm, viz., the *compilation* approach.

10.2 GENERAL STRUCTURE OF THE AI DESIGN PARADIGM

At the time of writing it would certainly be inaccurate to claim that the discipline of AI is securely grounded on a single, commonly agreed upon, unified set of concepts – that is, there is a single Kuhnian paradigm that dominates AI.[1] As Papert (1988) has pointed out, the problem space/heuristic search based model (discussed below) which for so long has been *the* K-paradigm in AI has in recent times been challenged by the so-called connectionistic model – to the extent that the latter is now being regarded by many as a serious contender for the status of dominant paradigm.[2]

In the context of design, however, connectionism has yet to exercise any influence; thus when we talk of the AI *design* paradigm there is as yet little disagreement as to what is being referred to.

The AI (design) paradigm is based on a model of human problem solving and intelligence that reaches back to the earliest days of AI in the 1950s, and that is largely the work of Newell, Simon and their coworkers (Ernst and Newell 1969, Newell, Shaw and Simon 1960, Newell and Simon 1972, 1976, Laird, Newell and Rosenbloom 1987). This model goes by several names including 'symbolic state space', 'heuristic search', 'problem space' and 'information processing'. For the purpose of this discussion I shall refer to it as the *problem space/heuristic search* model; and it is this that provides the foundation for the AI paradigm.

According to this model (fig. 10.1) a problem is solved by first creating a symbolic representation of the problem in a state space called the *problem space*. The problem

---

[1] Recall from chapter 6 that I shall make when necessary a distinction between the concepts of the *Kuhnian* (or *K-*) *paradigm* and that of the *design* paradigm.

[2] See, for example, the Winter 1988 special issue of *Daedalus* (the Journal of the American Academy of Arts and Sciences) on AI which is largely dominated by articles on connectionism.

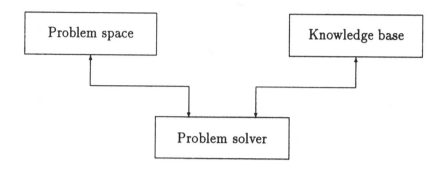

Fig. 10.1 An abstract view of the problem/heuristic search model.

representation in this space may typically denote the *initial state* which is what the problem solver is given and the *goal state* which designates a solution to the problem. In addition the problem space must be capable of representing all possible states that might be attained or reached in the effort to go from the initial to the goal state.

Transitions from one state to another are effected by applying a finite sequence of *operators* selected from a repertoire of operators residing in the *knowledge base* (KB). The application of such operators in effect results in the problem solver conducting a *search* for a solution path through the problem space. The problem is said to be solved when either (i) the application of a sequence of operators results in the goal state being reached from the initial state; or (ii) a sequence of operators has been identified such that given the initial state, the successive application of the operators in this sequence is guaranteed to lead to the goal state.[3]

Since a problem space might be arbitrarily large, the search through it should not be randomly conducted. Rather, the problem solver uses *heuristics* – 'rules of thumb' – to control the amount of search and thereby converge to a solution (or solution plan) as rapidly as possible.[4]

The heuristics that may participate in the problem solving process may range from the very general – that is, they are quite independent of the nature of the problem or task domain – to being very specific to the task domain. In general when less is

[3] Strictly speaking situation (i) represents an actual solution to the problem whereas situation (ii) corresponds to the function of a *plan* for solving the problem. For a formal discussion of planning see Genesereth and Nilsson (1987, chapter 12). See also example 10.9 below.

[4] The classic introduction to heuristic problem solving is Pólya (1945). A modern discussion of the nature of heuristics from an AI perspective is Lenat (1982).

known about the task domain or the problem solver has less experience in solving a particular type of problem, general or *domain-independent* heuristics are more appropriately evoked. When the task domain is known in relative detail or relatively low level or detailed decisions are to be made, *domain-specific* heuristics are more likely to be used.

Problem solving methods based essentially on domain-independent heuristics are also often called *weak methods*; those based primarily on task-domain-specific knowledge are also termed *strong methods* (Newell and Simon 1976, Langley *et al.* 1987). The so-called 'expert systems' are instances of automatic problem solvers that rely very heavily on domain-specific heuristics ('expert knowledge').

This problem space/heuristic search model of AI, then, constitutes the AI design paradigm. It provides the underpinning for many of the automatic or computer-aided design systems developed in recent years. The rest of this chapter articulates the detailed, fine structure of this paradigm.

10.3 REPRESENTING KNOWLEDGE USING PRODUCTION RULES

Our discussion of TPD (chapter 9) revealed quite explicitly the role of and the extent to which *knowledge* is important to the design process. In the context of TPD knowledge participates in two ways. Firstly, for a given constraint C it determines the choice of other constraints C_1, ..., C_n such that the plausibility state of C is believed to be determined by the plausibility states of C_1, ..., C_n. In other words, knowledge is used to explicitly elaborate and refine a plausibility driven design. Secondly, knowledge determines the selection of the evidence that is invoked in verifying a constraint's plausibility state.

However, the specific *form* of knowledge is not explicated in TPD except to note that it consists of 'facts, theories, principles, tools and research results' (chapter 9, section 9.6). This is because TPD was conceived as a paradigm for *human-conducted* design.

In contrast the AI paradigm is explicitly concerned with *automatic* (or at least *computer assisted*) design; thus the problem of organizing and representing knowledge in the KB (fig. 10.1) becomes of paramount importance in order that the design system can access the KB, extract relevant knowledge and modify the KB efficiently. In particular, when the design system is to rely heavily on large amounts of domain-specific heuristics the issue of *knowledge representation* assumes still greater significance.

The problem of knowledge representation is, in a very real sense, at the very heart of the agenda of the AI discipline. The extent to which this is the case is exemplified by what Smith (1985) called the *knowledge representation hypothesis*; this says, roughly, that any process or system capable of reasoning intelligently must contain within it an explicit *representation* of the knowledge and beliefs that the system may be said to possess about the world.

Various alternative knowledge representational forms have thus been proposed.[5] In the present discussion of the AI design paradigm, I shall concentrate almost entirely on the representation of knowledge by entities called *production rules* since this form has, for several reasons, dominated systems based on the AI paradigm. Problem solving systems based on the use of production rules are also referred to as *production* or *rule based* systems.

A production rule (or simply *rule*) is an entity of the form

IF condition **THEN** action

which states that if the 'current' state of affairs in a particular act of cognition, problem solving, design, etc., is such that 'condition' is satisfied then the corresponding 'action' may be performed.

It is important to note that a production rule is not an imperative statement in the sense that an **if** ... **then** statement in a conventional (or von Neumann style) program constitutes an imperative. Rather, a rule states that if the specified condition is satisfied then the corresponding action is an appropriate one to take.[6]

A production system has the general organization shown in fig. 10.2. The set of rules each of the form

IF condition **THEN** action

is held in *rule memory*; a *working memory* (also called a *context*) holds or represents the current state of the design (or more generally, problem solution); and an *interpreter* (or *inference engine*) decides (based on the current state of the working

---

[5] For an anthology of some of the seminal papers on this topic, see Brachman and Levesque (1985). For concise and well integrated surveys of knowledge representation, the reader is referred to Winston (1977) and Barr and Feigenbaum (1981).

[6] The origins of production rules reach back to the logician, Emil Post's (1943) concept of productions for the formal (syntactic) manipulation and transformation of symbolic structures (Minsky 1967). This same work may have led to the idea of defining the grammar of a formal or natural language in terms of rewriting rules (Chomsky 1957) or productions (Floyd 1961). The use of production rules to represent domain-specific knowledge in the AI context and as a basis for modeling cognitive behavior, appears to be due to Newell in the early 1960s (see Newell and Simon (1972), Anderson (1983)).

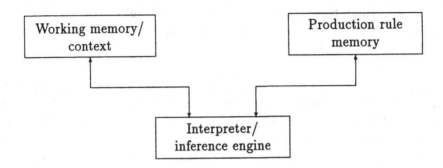

Fig. 10.2 Organization of a production system.

memory) which rule to select next from rule memory and causes that rule to *fire* –
that is, it executes the action part of the selected rule.

The result of rule firing is to effect a change in the state of the working memory. As
a result one or more other conditions may be found to be satisfied by the state and
the cycle of rule selection, firing and working memory state change begins anew. The
cycle will continue to be activated until and unless the working memory state is such
that it does not satisfy the condition part of the rules.

The correspondence between the problem space/heuristic search schema of section
10.2 (see fig. 10.1) and production systems will be noted. The problem space itself is
represented by the working memory. The rule memory constitutes the KB. Operators
in the problem space/heuristic search schema are represented by the actions contained
in the rules. And the conditions that determine which rule will be selected for firing,
correspond (in part) to the heuristics of the problem space/heuristic search schema.
It can be seen that the interpreter is basically a state machine that can be in one of
three states, match, select and execute.

> **match:** Identify all rules in the rule memory the condition parts of which satisfy
> the state of the working memory; collect these rules into a *conflict set*.
> Go to the select state.
>
> **select:** Select a preferred rule from the conflict set to fire. Go to the execute
> state.
>
> **execute:** Fire the selected rule. Go to match.

The selection from (or the conflict resolution among) members of the conflict set
will be determined by some *problem solving strategy* inherent to the interpreter itself.

Such strategies may themselves be constituted as rules but at a more abstract level than the rules that are selected by the interpreter from the rule memory: they are, so to speak, rules for selecting rules and may therefore be called *metarules*.

In the next section I shall discuss in some detail, a small but interesting example of a production rule based approach to design. The example will also help surface several additional issues pertinent to the AI design paradigm. Prior to that exercise I present below a small number of examples of production rules from diverse design domains in order to illuminate the general nature of this form of knowledge representation.

Example 10.1

    IF a current goal is volumetric analysis
        THEN separate the solid and fluid analysis parts

    IF a current goal is fluid analysis
        THEN first compute water saturation

These examples, taken from Barstow (1985) are instances of *domain-specific* metarules relevant to the domain of oil well logging. Barstow shows how such rules are used in the design of programs for computing geological characteristics from oil well logs (measurements).
End Example

Example 10.2

    IF signal(CTL) = 'high' at time t
        THEN signal(OUT) = signal(IN) at time $t + 1$

This example taken from Brown, Tong and Foyster (1983) expresses the behavior of a unidirectional pass transistor with ports IN, OUT and CTL. Such rule based definitions of behavior are used in the Palladio VLSI Circuit design environment (Brown, Tong and Foyster 1983).
End Example

Example 10.3

    IF the goal is to make the postcondition
        Rout = Rin1 + Rin2
    THEN generate the micro-operation sequence
        Aout := Ail + Air;
        Rout := Aout
    and generate a new goal
        Ail = Rin1 $\wedge$ Air = Rin2

This rule, based on Mueller and Varghese (1985) specifies a piece of knowledge relevant to the automatic synthesis of microprograms.
End Example

Example 10.4
>   IF the intended function of the module is to convert
>   a serial signal to a parallel form
>   THEN use a shift register

This is an instance of a domain specific rule used in the VEXED system for VLSI circuit design (Mitchell, Steinberg and Shulman 1985).
End Example

Example 10.5
>   IF the current context is assigning a power supply
>   **and** an SBI module of any type has been put in a cabinet
>   **and** the position it occupies in the cabinet is known
>   **and** there is space available in the cabinet for a power supply for that position
>   **and** there is no available power supply
>   **and** the voltage and frequency of the components on the order is known
>   THEN find a power supply of that voltage and frequency and
>   add it to the order.

>   IF the current context is assigning a power supply
>   **and** an SBI module of any type has been put in a cabinet
>   **and** the position it occupies is known
>   **and** there is space available in the cabinet for a power supply for that position
>   **and** there is an available power supply
>   THEN put the power supply in the cabinet in the available space

These examples, taken from McDermott (1982) are instances of rules from R1 – a program that configures VAX-11/780 systems.
End Example

Example 10.6
>   IF current state has a room-A and right-wall-of(room-A)
>   is clear
>   THEN conjoin right-wall-of(room-A) with a room-C such
>   that top-wall-of(room-C) is clear and right-wall-of(room-C)
>   is clear and left-wall-of(room-C) is clear.

IF current context is to satisfy room configuration goal
  and site context goal
THEN achieve room configuration goal first

These examples are based on Gero and Coyne (1987). The first instance is an example of a domain-specific rule relevant to the configuration of rooms in the context of building design. The second rule is an instance of a metarule that may be used to resolve conflict between the coexisting goals of room configuration and meeting site constraints.
End Example

Example 10.7
  IF actual stress $\leq$ allowable stress
  THEN stress constraint satisfied

  IF section is compact and not hybrid girder or made of A514 steel
  THEN allowable stress in bending $F_{\mathrm{b}} = 0.66F_{\mathrm{y}}$

  IF analysis of structure is complete
    and detailed design is required
  THEN activate the knowledge module for detailed design

These rules, taken from Sriram, Maher and Fenves (1984) (see also Maher 1988), exemplify knowledge and heuristics relevant to structural design. The first two embody constraints on the design of structures while the last is a metarule.
End Example

10.4 THOUGHT EXPERIMENTS IN RULE-BASED DESIGN

Let us consider a highly simplified version of *data path design*. The issue is as follows:

The *micro-architecture* of a single processor computer consists of two major components: the data path and the control unit (fig. 10.3). The *data path* itself is a structure consisting of special and general purpose registers, functional units (e.g., arithmetic-logic units, shifters and counters) and pathways that link functional units and registers to one another. The *control unit* is essentially a finite state machine that executes partially ordered sets of primitive actions called *micro-operations*. Each such micro-operation when executed causes one or more control signals to be issued from the control unit to defined parts of the data path thereby enabling specific events to take place in the latter. For example, a micro-operation represented by the symbol

$$R1 \;\leftarrow\; R2$$

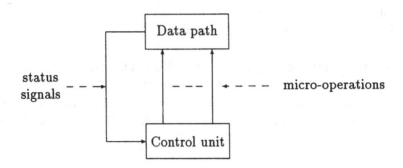

Fig. 10.3 Components of micro-architecture.

when executed by the control unit causes control signals to be issued which in turn causes the content of the specified register $R2$ to be gated to the register $R1$.

Each micro-operation represents a potential primitive action in the data path. The repertoire of micro-operations, thus, constitutes not only the interface between the data path and the control unit but also establishes or defines constraints that the data path structure must satisfy in the following sense: the data path must be such as to enable the action specified by each micro-operation to occur as a primitive action. For instance, given the micro-operation

$$R2 \quad \leftarrow \quad R1$$

the data path is constrained to having a path from $R1$ to $R2$ that is evoked by the execution of the micro-operation.[7]

Let us suppose that a rather high level problem-solving strategy has been established according to which the design process is to conform to the following metarule.

(MR1) IF the goal is to design a micro-architecture
       THEN 1. first establish the micro-operation repertoire
            2. then identify the registers in the data path
            3. then design the rest of the data path
            4. then design the control unit

We shall further suppose that the micro-operation repertoire is established by analyzing an already designed exo-architecture (Dasgupta 1989a) – that is, the instruction

---

[7] The constraint that the micro-operation as a whole must satisfy is that it should provide efficient and reliable support for the execution of a computer's instruction set. For more details on micro-architecture, see, e.g., Dasgupta (1989a, chapter 5).

set, storage organization, addressing modes, etc., that are to be visible to the compiler writer and operating systems designer. Such an analysis reveals what types of operations will be necessitated at the level of the micro-architecture. Based on the micro-operation repertoire the principal registers in the data path can also be identified.

Assume now that subgoals 1 and 2 of (MR1) have been achieved. The architect is now faced with the following design problem.

Current Data Path

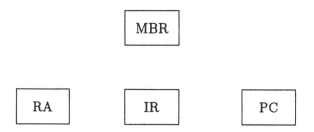

Current Goals: Enable (M1), (M2), (M3), (M4), (M5), (M6)

Fig. 10.4 Initial design problem state.

Example 10.8
Given the 'current' data path shown in fig. 10.4 generate a data path that is able to execute the following set of micro-operations:

(M1) IR ← MBR
(M2) RA[k] ← RA[i] + RA[j]
(M3) RA[i] ← MBR
(M4) RA[k] ← RA[i] ∧ RA[j]
(M5) PC ← PC + 1
(M6) PC ← IR

In fig. 10.4, RA signifies a *register array*. It is assumed that RA is associated with two output ports (OUT1 and OUT2) and one input port (IN). Each of the other registers is associated with a single output port (OUT) and a single input port (IN). The meaning of most of the micro-operations (M1)–(M6) should be clear. The two operations (M2) and (M4) stipulate that any pair of registers from RA can serve as inputs to the respective 'add' or 'and' operations and any register in RA can serve as the destination of the result.

By adding the current goal to the current data path, fig. 10.4 shows the state of the working memory (or equivalently, problem state) at the onset of the design activity.

A portion of the domain-specific knowledge relevant to this aspect of micro-architecture design is expressed in terms of the rules presented in fig. 10.5. The rules (R1)–(R10) embody knowledge pertaining to specific, common classes of micro-operations. The rules (R11)–(R16) specify heuristic knowledge that may be useful in 'optimizing' data paths.

As stated above the task at hand is to produce a data path that satisfies the requirement that micro-operations (M1)–(M6) must be executable or realizable. The designer (or design system) must search through the problem space for a pathway from the initial state of the data path shown in fig. 10.4 to some state of the data path such that the goal 'Enable (M1), ..., (M6)' is achieved.

Recall from section 10.2 that among the heuristics used to effect such a search are the *weak methods*: strategies that are general or domain independent. An important instance of such a strategy is called *forward chaining* in which the designer/problem solver proceeds *from* the initial state *to* the goal state (if possible). The converse of this strategy is called *backward chaining*. Here the strategy is to begin with the goal state and decompose this recursively into subgoals until, eventually a set of goals are obtained that are sufficiently simple as to be immediately attainable.[8]

In attempting to solve our goal let us assume that forward chaining will serve as the problem solving strategy. In the context of production systems this strategy will be embedded in the interpreter/inference engine.

---

[8] Recall from chapter 9, section 9.11 that TPD and FD (the latter when combined with stepwise refinement) both use backward chaining as the overall strategy.

(R1) IF current goal is to enable $R_j \leftarrow R_i$
    and there is no link from OUT(R_i)
    and there is no link to IN(R_j)
    THEN Create link from OUT(R_i) to IN(R_j)

(R2) IF current goal is to enable RA $\leftarrow R_i$
    and there is no link from OUT(R_i)
    and there is no link to IN(RA)
    THEN Create link from OUT(R_i) to IN(RA)

(R3) IF current goal is to enable $R_j \leftarrow R_i$
    and there is a link from OUT(R_i) to IN(RA)
    and there is a link to IN(R_j)
    THEN Delete link from OUT(R_i) to IN(RA)
        and Create Bus
        and Create link from OUT(R_i) to Bus
        and Create link from Bus to IN(RA)
        and Create link from Bus to IN(R_j)

(R4) IF current goal is to enable RA $\leftarrow R_i$
    and there is a link from OUT(R_i) to some IN(R_j)
    and there is no link to IN(RA)
    THEN Delete link from OUT(R_i) to IN(R_j)
        and Create link from OUT(R_i) to Bus
        and Create link from Bus to IN(RA)
        and Create link from Bus to IN(R_j)

(R5) IF current goal is to enable $R_j \leftarrow R_i$
    and there is a link $L1$ to IN(R_j) from some source S
    and there is no link from OUT(R_i)
    THEN Delete $L1$
        and Create Multiplexer
        and Create link from S to Multiplexer
        and Create link from OUT(R_i) to Multiplexer
        and Create link from Multiplexer to IN(R_j)

Fig. 10.5 Some rules for data path design.

(R6) IF current goal is to enable RA ← RA + RA
     and there is no adder
     and there is no link from OUT1(RA)
     and there is no link from OUT2(RA)
     and there is no link to IN(RA)
   THEN Create Adder
       and Create link from OUT1(RA) to LEFT_IN(Adder)
       and Create link from OUT2(RA) to RIGHT_IN(Adder)
       and Create link from OUT(Adder) to IN(RA)

(R7) IF current goal is to enable RA ← RA ∧ RA
     and there is no logic unit
     and there is no link from OUT1(RA)
     and there is no link from OUT2(RA)
     and there is no link to IN(RA)
   THEN Create logic unit
       and Create link from OUT1(RA) to LEFT_IN(Logic Unit)
       and Create link from OUT2(RA) to RIGHT_IN(Logic Unit)
       and Create link from OUT(Logic Unit)to IN(RA)

(R8) IF current goal is to enable RA ← RA + RA
     and there is no adder
     and there is no link from OUT1(RA)
     and there is no link from OUT2(RA)
     and there is a link from some OUT(R_i) to IN(RA)
   THEN Create Adder
       and Create link from OUT1(RA) to LEFT_IN(Adder)
       and Create link from OUT2(RA) to RIGHT_IN(Adder)
       and Delete link from OUT(R_i) to IN(RA)
       and Create Multiplexer
       and Create link from OUT(R_i) to Multiplexer
       and Create link from OUT(Adder) to Multiplexer
       and Create link from Multiplexer to IN(RA)

Fig. 10.5 (continued).

(R9) IF current goal is to enable RA ← RA ∧ RA
    and there is no logic unit
    and there is a link $L1$ from OUT1(RA) to some
       destination $D1$
    and there is a link $L2$ from OUT2(RA) to some
       destination $D2$
    and there is a link $L3$ from some source S to
       IN(RA)
   THEN Delete $L1$, $L2$, $L3$
      and Create Bus1, Bus2, Multiplexer, Logic Unit
      and Create link from OUT1(RA) to Bus1
      and Create link from OUT2(RA) to Bus2
      and Create link from Bus1 to $D1$
      and Create link from Bus2 to $D2$
      and Create link from Bus1 to LEFT_IN(logic Unit)
      and Create link from Bus2 to RIGHT_IN(logic Unit)
      and Create link from S to Multiplexer
      and Create link from OUT(Logic Unit) to Multiplexer
      and Create link from Multiplexer to IN(RA).

(R10) IF current goal is to enable R_i ← $R_i + 1$
    and there is an Adder
    and there is a link $L1$ from OUT1(RA) to LEFT_IN(Adder)
    and there is a link $L2$ from OUT2(RA) to RIGHT_IN(Adder)
    and there is a link $L3$ from OUT(Adder) to some
       destination D
    and there are no links from OUT(R_i) or to IN(R_i)
   THEN Create Read Only Constant $C1$
      and Delete links $L1$, $L2$, $L3$
      and Create Multiplexer1, Multiplexer2, Bus
      and Create link from OUT1(RA) to Multiplexer1
      and Create link from OUT(R_i) to Multiplexer1
      and Create link from Multiplexer1 to LEFT_IN(Adder)
      and Create link from OUT2(RA) to Multiplexer2
      and Create link from OUT($C1$) to Multiplexer2
      and Create link from Multiplexer2 to RIGHT_IN(Adder)
      and Create link from OUT(Adder) to Bus
      and Create link from Bus to D
      and Create link from Bus to IN(R_i)

Fig. 10.5 (continued).

(R11) IF current goal is to maximize parallelism
        and there is a link from OUT(PC) to some Bus1 or
        Multiplexer1
        and there is a link from Constant $C1$ to some Bus2 or
        Multiplexer2
        and there is a link from Bus1/Multiplexer1 to LEFT_IN(adder)
        and there is a link from Bus2/Multiplexer2 to RIGHT_IN(adder)
     THEN Delete link from OUT(PC) to Bus1/Multiplexer1
        and Delete link from $C1$ to Bus2/Multiplexer2
        and Delete link to IN(PC)
        and Recreate PC as counter

(R12) IF current goal is to reduce component count
        and there is a link $L1$ from some source S to a
        Multiplexer
        and there are no other links to Multiplexer
        and there is a link $L2$ from some Multiplexer to some
        destination D
     THEN Delete links $L1$, $L2$, Multiplexer
        and Create link from S to D

(R13) IF current goal is to reduce component count
        and there is a link $L1$ from some source S to a Bus
        and there are no links to Bus
        and there is exactly one link $L2$ from Bus to some
        Destination D
     THEN Delete links $L1$, $L2$, Bus
        and Create link from S to D

(R14) IF current goal is to reduce component count
        and there is a component with no links to it and no
        links from it
     THEN Delete Component

Fig. 10.5 (continued).

(R15) IF current goal is to reduce component count

      and there are an Adder and a Logic Unit with

      identical sources $S1$, $S2$ and destination D

  THEN Delete links LEFT_IN(Adder), RIGHT_IN(Adder)

      from $S1$, $S2$ respectively

      and Delete links to LEFT_IN(Logic Unit), RIGHT_IN(Logic Unit)

      from $S1$, $S2$ respectively

      and Delete links from OUT(Adder), OUT(Logic Unit)

      to D respectively

      and Create ALU

      and Create links from $S1$, $S2$ to LEFT_IN(ALU),

      RIGHT_IN(ALU) respectively

      and Create link from OUT(ALU) to D

(R16) IF current goal is to reduce component count

      and there are two multiplexers $M1$, $M2$ in series

      and the inputs to $M1$ are links $L11$, $L12$ from source

      $S11$, $S12$ respectively

      and the inputs to $M2$ are links $L21$, $L22$ from $M1$

      and some other source $S2$ respectively

      and there is a link L from $M2$ to some destination

  THEN Delete links $L11$, $L12$, $L21$, $L22$, L

      and Delete multiplexers $M1$, $M2$

      and Create next larger multiplexer M

      and Create links from $S11$, $S12$, $S2$ to M

      and Create link from M to D

Fig. 10.5 (continued).

Fig. 10.6 shows the *search tree* generated in the course of searching for a solution to the data path problem. At each step of the search the condition parts of the rules (fig. 10.5) are matched against the 'current' state of the design – the latter comprising both the 'current' data path and the (remaining) 'current' goals. Since many rules may match the current state additional (meta)rules will determine the preferred rule. In this particular example the metarule for rule preference is

(MR2)

      1. **Make** as preferred rule the rule that matches the

        first of the subgoals of the (remaining) 'current' goal

2. **While** preferred rule leads to failure
   Make as preferred rule the rule that matches
   the next of the subgoals of the (remaining)
   'current' goal.

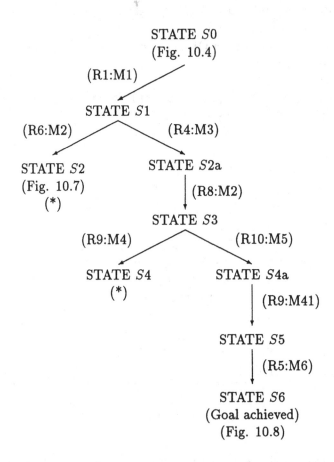

Fig. 10.6 Search tree for data path synthesis using forward chaining.

The labels of the edges in fig. 10.6 announce which rule is being fired and the relevant subgoal that led to the rule being selected. The '*' designates 'failure' states – that is, states at which no further progress could be made.

Fig. 10.7 shows the data path and current goal corresponding to state $S2$ of fig. 10.6. This is a failure state since none of the rules in fig. 10.5 matches this state.[9] The

---

[9] Note that $S2$ is a failure state with respect to the knowledge base as represented by the rules

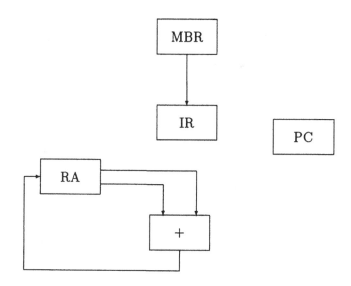

Current Goal: Enable (M3), (M4), (M5), (M6)

Fig. 10.7 The data path at state $S2$.

search continues but reaches another failure state $S4$. Backtracking and resuming the search eventually leads to state $S6$ in which the problem is solved. The data path corresponding to this state is shown in fig. 10.8.
End Example

Consider now the following:

Example 10.9
Given the state of the data path shown in fig. 10.4 generate a data path which (i) can execute the set of micro-operations (M1)–(M5); (ii) facilitate parallelism where possible; and (iii) otherwise, 'minimize' the component count.

In this problem, not only must the design meet multiple goals of the same type as in example 10.8, but also goals of different types:

(G1) Enable micro-operations (M1)–(M5)
(G2) Facilitate parallelism
(G3) Minimize/reduce component count

in fig. 10.5. This KB may, of course, be augmented with additional rules in which case further progress from $S2$ may well be possible.

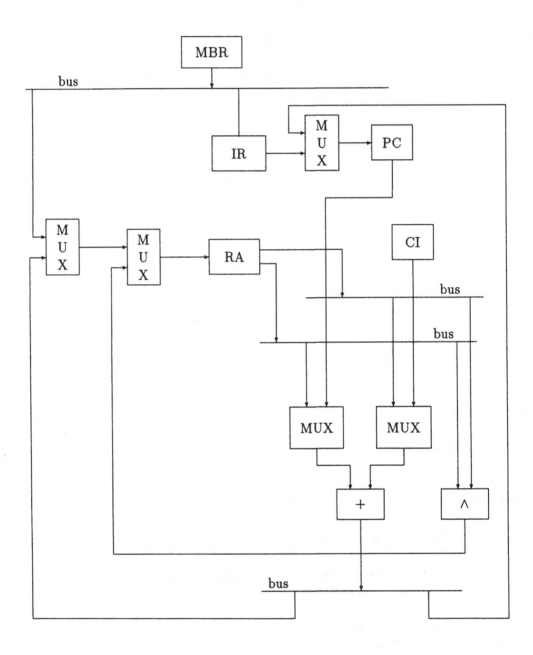

Fig. 10.8 Final data path corresponding to state $S6$.

Note that the rule set in fig. 10.5 includes rules (R11–R15) relevant to goals (G2) and (G3). However, the designer/design system is faced with the question of whether the above goals are to be treated alike when searching for a solution. While such a policy can indeed be enacted, the resulting search may turn out to be rather inefficient. For example, if no distinction is made between the *relative importance* of the goals (G1), (G2), (G3), the search may attempt to satisfy the component count requirement (G3) before all the micro-operation subgoals in (G1) have been achieved. The effort expended in meeting (G3) may turn out to be wasted due to the subsequent design modifications required to satisfy the remaining subgoals in (G1).

The designer/system must therefore formulate a *plan of actions* that helps to control the extent of search and backtracking in the presence of such multiple goals.[10]

An example of a domain-independent planning heuristic is

(PR1) IF the goal is to achieve a conjunction of subgoals
$(G1), \ldots, (G_n)$
THEN order $(G1), \ldots, (G_n)$ in any arbitrary way.

This rule, originally formulated by Sussman (1975, chapter VIII) and called the *linear assumption heuristic* assumes that goals $(G1), \ldots, (G_n)$ can be treated *as if* they are non-interacting. (PR1) was, in fact, implicitly used in conducting the search for a solution to the problem in example 10.8 where the goals (M1)–(M6) were ordered arbitrarily.

The linear assumption heuristic will not work for the current problem as the subgoals (G1), (G2), (G3) are not non-interacting. In this case the following planning rule more specific to the domain of computing systems design may be invoked.

(PR2) IF the goal is to achieve a conjunction of a functional
subgoal (F) and a nonfunctional subgoal (N)
THEN achieve (F) before (N).

Invoking this metarule results in an initial plan of the form

(P1): Achieve (G1)
(P2): Achieve (G2) $\wedge$ (G3)

---

[10] The literature on planning from an AI perspective is extensive. For an excellent review of the topic see Cohen and Feigenbaum (1982, chapter XV). For other perspectives see also, Genesereth and Nilsson (1987, chapter 12) and Charniak and McDermott (1985, chapter 9). An important earlier monograph on the topic is Sacerdoti (1977). The classic work on planning from a cognitive science perspective is Miller, Galanter and Pribram (1960).

Resolution between (G2) and (G3) can be obtained from the statement of the problem itself: this requires that parallelism should not be sacrificed in the interest of component count reduction: (G2) is more important or critical than (G3). The resulting plan is, therefore, the sequence of steps

(P1): Achieve (G1)
(P2): Achieve (G2)
(P3): Achieve (G3)

Beginning with the data path shown in fig. 10.4, plan step (P1) generates the search tree of fig. 10.6 up to and including the state $S5$.[11] Fig. 10.9 shows the corresponding data path. Plan step (P2) is now invoked. In fact, the rule memory contains only one rule (R11) relevant to the goal of parallelism enhancement and since the condition part of (R11) matches the state $S5$ of the data path the corresponding action is executed producing a new state $S7$. Plan step (P2) is terminated and (P3) takes over. It turns out that beginning with state $S7$, the sequence of rules:

$$(R14), (R12), (R13), (R16), (R15), (R13)$$

can be fired until a data path state is produced to which no rules can be further applied. This final data path is shown in fig. 10.10. Note the elimination of several of the buses and multiplexers that were present in fig. 10.9.
End Example

The method of forward chaining described here, and rules of the type depicted in fig. 10.5 (but far greater in number and variety) were used in the Design Automation Assistant (DAA) – a system for data path synthesis developed by Thomas, Kowalski and their collaborators (Thomas *et al.* 1983, Kowalski and Thomas 1984, Kowalski *et al.* 1985, Kowalski 1985, 1988).

10.5 WEAK METHODS REVISITED

Recall that *forward chaining* is an instance of what Newell and Simon (1976) called *weak methods*: domain-independent problem solving strategies that provide direction to and impose control on, the search process. We also saw, in the 'experiments' described above, the use of a *match and select* policy by the rule interpreter to determine which operator to next apply and the construction of plans as represented by plan heuristics (PR1) and (PR2). These are additional instances of weak methods. As the data path examples illustrated, two or more weak methods may be *combined* to establish a 'grand' problem solving strategy for the designer or design system.

---

[11] Note that in this problem, enabling the micro-operation (M6) is *not* part of the goal.

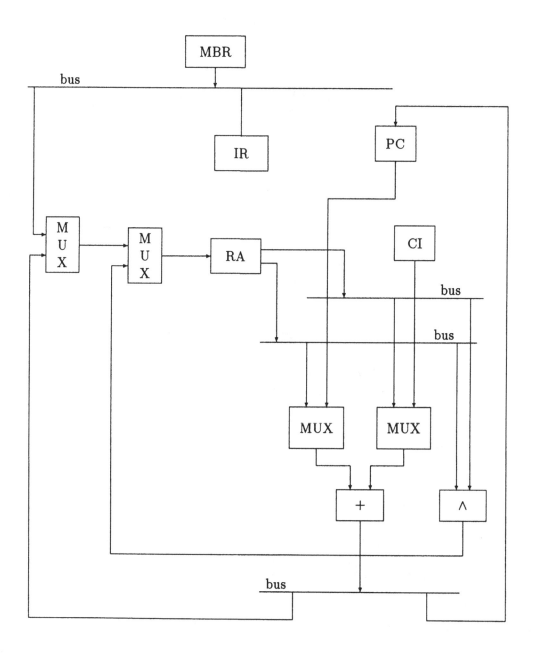

Fig. 10.9 Data path in state $S5$.

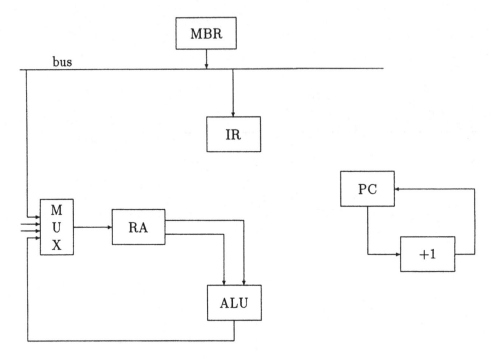

Fig. 10.10 The final data path solution for example 10.9.

Forward chaining is almost invariably contrasted with *backward chaining* in which the search process begins with the goal state. The preconditions to the attainment of the goal state are identified and these become subgoals. The search process is then applied recursively on the subgoals until eventually a set of goals are identified that correspond to the initial state or are otherwise known to be achievable.

Example 10.10

Consider the following problem in automatic *program synthesis*. The state of such a design at any stage will consist of the program fragment synthesized up to that point, a goal state and an initial state.

Let us suppose that the goal state is the identity

(GS) $GR1 = a + b$

where GR1 is a general register, and a, b are symbolic values. Let the initial state be defined by the assertion

(IS) $X = a \wedge Y = b$

where X, Y are memory variables.

In this example, the domain-specific knowledge is about the instruction set for the computer for which the object program is being synthesized. We suppose that this knowledge is rule based and includes the pair of rules shown in fig. 10.11.

(R1) IF the goal is to make Reg = p OP q
     THEN Select a register $R1$
        and generate the instruction
          OP Reg, Reg1 (Reg ← Reg OP Reg1)
        and establish as subgoal
          Reg1 = p ∧ Reg = q

(R2) IF the goal is to make Reg = p
     THEN Select a memory variable X
        and generate the instruction
          LOAD Reg, X (Reg ← X)
        and establish as subgoal
          $X = p$

Fig. 10.11 Two rules relevant to program synthesis.

When using backward chaining, the design process begins with the goal state (GS). Note that both (R1) and (R2) in fig. 10.11 contain only goals in their respective condition parts. The rule interpreter matches GS against the rule memory and recognizes (R1) as a match by instantiating Reg to GR1, p and q to a and b respectively, and OP to +. The action part of (R1) establishes the precondition that must prevail in order for the goal stated in the condition part to be achieved. As a result, the single instruction

(I1) ADD GR1, GR2

is generated along with the subgoal

(GS1) GR1 = a ∧ GR2 = b

(GS1) is a conjunction of two goals

(GS11) GR1 = a
(GS12) GR2 = b

Using the linear assumption heuristic (PR1) mentioned in section 10.4, the order

(GS11) ; (GS12)

is established. In order to achieve (GS11) a match to, and the execution of, rule (R2) produces the instruction

(I2) LOAD GR1, X

and the subgoal

(GS111) $X = a$

This, in fact, is contained in the initial state (IS). Similarly (GS12) matches against (R2) resulting in the generation of the instruction

(I3) LOAD GR2, Y

and the subgoal

(GS121) $Y = b$

which is also known to be true according to (IS). The resulting code fragment must, of course, be ordered in the reverse sequence to which they were generated:

(I3) LOAD GR2, Y
(I2) LOAD GR1, X
(I1) ADD GR1, GR2

The search tree produced by this exercise is depicted in fig. 10.12.
End Example

The use of backward chaining in the manner just shown was one of the heuristic methods employed by Mueller and Varghese (1985) in their system for automatic microcode synthesis. Gero and Coyne (1987) have also illustrated the use of backward (as well as forward) chaining in designing room configurations.

One of the most celebrated of the weak methods is *means-ends analysis*. This was proposed by Newell, Simon and their associates in the late 1950s and first used in the General Problem Solver (GPS) one of the earliest and most influential systems developed within the problem space/heuristic search paradigm (Newell, Shaw and Simon 1960, Ernst and Newell 1969, Newell and Simon 1972).

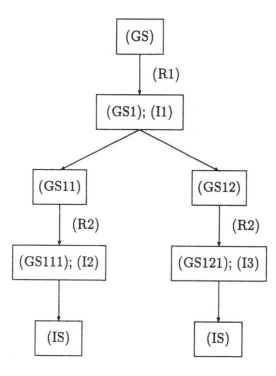

Fig. 10.12 Search tree for example 10.10.

Means-ends analysis relies on the idea that in a particular task domain, *differences* between possible 'current' and goal states can be identified and classified such that for each type of difference, *operators* can be defined that can *reduce* the difference.

The differences and their corresponding operators are encoded in an *operator-differ-ence table*. Associated with each operator is also a *precondition* that the current state must satisfy in order for the operator to be actually applied.

Given an initial or current state and a goal state, means-ends analysis determines the difference between the two. It then attempts to reduce this difference by applying the relevant operator. If, however, the precondition for the operator is not satisfied, means-ends analysis is applied recursively to reduce the difference between the current state and the precondition.

Example 10.11
Consider the automatic synthesis of microcode mentioned earlier (Mueller and Vargh-ese 1985). Simplifying matters somewhat, we may say that the objective is, given a precondition PRE and a postcondition POST, to generate a sequence of micro-

operations M such that the Hoare formula

$$\{PRE\} \ M \ \{POST\}$$

is valid. That is, if the state of memory and registers in the micro-architectural machine level is such that PRE is true to begin with, then the execution of M will leave the memory and registers in such a state that POST will be true.[12]

One of the tasks of microcode is to fetch instructions from memory (at addresses specified by the program counter, PC) into an instruction register, IR, and to update PC in preparation for fetching the next instruction in sequence. The pre- and postconditions for this may be stated as

$$PRE \quad : \ PC \ = \ pc_0$$
$$POST : \ IR \ = \ Mem[pc_0] \ \wedge \ pc \ = \ pc_0 \ + \ 1$$

where pc_0 is a symbolic value. PRE and POST, thus, constitute the initial or current state CS_0 and the goal state GS respectively.

DIFFERENCE	PRECONDITION	OPERATOR
$D1$: PC = X **NOT** PC = $X + 1$	$C1$: **true**	$O1$: PC $\leftarrow$ PC + 1
$D2$: IR = ? **NOT** IR = Mem[X]	$C2$: MBR = Mem[X]	$O2$: IR $\leftarrow$ MBR
$D3$: MBR = ? **NOT** MBR = Mem[X]	$C3$: MAR = X	$O3$: MBR $\leftarrow$ Mem[MAR]
$D4$: MAR = ? **NOT** MAR = X	$C4$: PC = X	$O4$: MAR $\leftarrow$ PC

Fig. 10.13 A partial operator-difference table.

For this particular task domain, fig. 10.13 shows a part of the operator-difference table. Each difference is of the form

$$A \ \textbf{NOT} \ B$$

meaning that the state of affairs is such that A is true whereas what is desired to be true is B. The corresponding operator is a micro-operation the execution of which would reduce or eliminate the difference provided that the associated precondition is true prior to the operator being applied.

---

[12] See chapter 8 for a discussion of Hoare formulas.

The elements PC, IR, MBR, and MAR denote register while Mem signifies main memory. The symbol '?' denotes an unknown or indeterminate value.

Fig. 10.14 depicts the tree of operations that would be performed by a designer/design system using means-ends analysis. The initial objective is to transform CS_0 to GS. This requires two subgoals to be achieved: reduce the difference between CS_0 and GS by producing a new current state CS_1 (step 1); and transform CS_1 to GS (step 2).

To achieve the first of these, the differences between CS_0 and GS are identified, viz., $D1$ and $D2$. This is a *choice point* in that one of these differences must be selected. We suppose that $D2$ is the difference chosen to reduce. Operator O_2 must be applied (step 3).

The operator-difference table (fig. 10.13) reveals that the (instantiated) precondition

$$MBR \ = \ Mem[pc_0]$$

must be satisfied by the current state in order for O_2 to apply (step 4). The difference between CS_0 and this precondition is given by $D3$ and so O_3 must be applied (step 5).

The precondition for O_3 to apply is, according to the operator-difference table:

$$MAR \ = \ pc_0$$

This is determined in step 6. The difference between CS_0 and this precondition is $D4$, hence O_4 should be applied (step 7). The precondition for O_4 is

$$PC \ = \ pc_0$$

and is indeed satisfied by CS_0 (step 8). The process then returns up the tree. O_4 can be applied thus generating the micro-operation

$$MAR \ = \ PC$$

in step 9. Operator O_3 can now apply. This generates the micro-operation

$$MBR \ = \ Mem[MAR]$$

in step 10. Similarly, step 11 applies O_2 producing the micro-operation

$$IR \ \leftarrow \ MBR$$

The difference between CS_0 and GS has now been reduced. The new current state is

$$CS1: \ \ PC \ = \ pc_0 \ \wedge \ IR \ = \ Mem[pc_0]$$

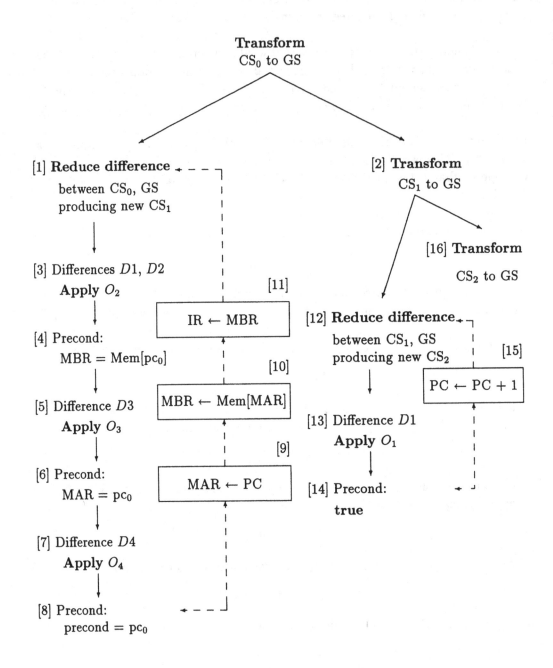

Fig. 10.14 Tree of operations using means–ends analysis for example 10.11.

CS_1 must now be transformed to GS (step 2). This, in turn, involves reducing the difference between CS_1 and GS, producing a new current state CS_2 (step 12) and transforming CS_2 to GS (step 16).

The difference between CS_1 and GS is identified as $D1$ and so O_1 must apply (step 13). The precondition for O_1 is the predicate **true** (step 14), hence O_1 is applied generating the micro-operation (in step 15):

$$PC \leftarrow PC + 1$$

and a new current state

$$CS_2 : \quad PC = pc_0 + 1 \wedge IR = Mem[pc_0]$$

Since $CS_2 = GS$, the transformation of CS_2 to GS is done and the search terminates.

It will be recalled that step 2 represented a choice point in that either $D1$ or $D2$ could be selected for reduction. In the search shown in fig. 10.14 $D2$ happens to have been selected. It can be verified that had $D1$ been chosen at this stage a difference would have eventually been determined for which none of the operators in the operator-difference table would apply. The search process would then have backtracked to the choice point of step 2 and $D2$ would then have been selected.
End Example

10.6 MULTIPLE GOAL RESOLUTION
In discussing example 10.9 (section 10.4) we saw that the presence of multiple goals required the use of additional metarules. Instances of these were the planning heuristics (PR1) and (PR2). In general, many different strategies may have to be identified and explicated in order to handle multiple goals. Mostow (1985) presents a most illuminating discussion of the thorny problem of multiple goals. He first pointed out that two goals $G1$ and $G2$ may relate to one another in a number of ways:

(i) $G1$, $G2$ may be *mutually independent*.
(ii) $G1$, $G2$ *cooperate* with one another in that the achievement of one goal facilitates the attainment of the other.
(iii) $G1$, $G2$ *compete* or are *mutually exclusive* in that the achievement of $G1$ precludes the achievement of $G2$ and vice versa.
(iv) $G1$, $G2$ *interfere* with one another or are *mutually interdependent* in that the satisfaction of one goal is constrained by the need to satisfy the other.

Assuming that which of these relationships holds between a particular pair of goals can be appropriately recognized the question arises as to what strategies should be used in response. Mostow proposed several heuristics all of which are domain-independent:

(A) In the case of cooperating goals achieving the *prerequisite* goal should be attempted first; or if one goal implies the other then the *more general* goal should be attempted first.

(B) In the case of mutual exclusion the less important goal (if so identifiable) can be *sacrificed*. In the event that both goals are equally important one of the goals may be *weakened* so as to eliminate the condition of mutual exclusion. Finally, the goals may be viewed as constituting a *trade-off*; in this event a design may be attempted to satisfy both the goals to an extent as to meet some other (satisficing or optimizing) constraint.

(C) When goals are mutually interdependent several strategies are relevant. They may be *serialized* so that first one goal is satisfied and then the design is transformed so as to satisfy the other. A second strategy is to order the goals so that the *most critical decisions* are made first and then other decisions are 'built around' the latter. A third heuristic is the *least commitment* strategy according to which goals are ordered so that the earlier decisions impose the fewest restrictions on later decisions and, therefore, on the form of the design. Fourthly, one goal $G1$ may serve as a *selection criterion* for obtaining a solution to the other goal $G2$ in the sense that $G1$ may serve to prune the search space of solutions to $G2$ that do not also satisfy $G1$. Finally, one may attempt to use goals to what Mostow (1985) termed *budget* a solution – that is, perform a parallel decomposition of the goals into subgoals.

Example 10.12
Consider (once again) the design of the exo-architecture of a computer. Recall from previous discussions that the main components of exo-architecture are the following:

(i) The types and organization of *programmable storage*.

(ii) The definition and characterization of the *data types* to be supported by the computer.

(iii) *Addressing modes*: the different methods of specifying the addresses of stored objects.

(iv) *Instruction set*: specification of the composition and semantics of the instructions supported by the computer.

(v) *Instruction formats*: the distinct modes of representing instructions in memory.

(vi) *Word length*: the unit (measured as number of bits) of information transfer between memory and processor.

In designing an exo-architecture the objective is to establish precise forms for each of these components so as to satisfy certain conditions. An example of such a condition is that the architecture is *efficient* in the sense that this property was defined in example 9.10 (chapter 9, section 9.10):

SIZE: For all programs $p \in$ BENCHMARKS:
        Size(obj_code(p, inst_set)) $\leq$ LOWSIZE(p)
TIME: For all programs $p \in$ BENCHMARKS:
        Exec_time(obj_code(p, inst_set)) $\leq$ LOWTIME(p)

That is, given a particular set of benchmark programs BENCHMARKS, the exo-architecture design will be deemed efficient if it satisfies both the SIZE and TIME constraints. The former stipulates that the object code produced for each program p in BENCHMARKS using the designed (or about to be designed) instruction set must be less than a constant value LOWSIZE(p); the latter states that the time to execute the object code for each program p must be less than a constant LOWTIME(p).

At the very early stages of the design process the relationship between SIZE and TIME may not be very clear. Assuming that there is likely to be *some* interaction between them the appropriate initial strategy may be Mostow's budgeting heuristic: that is, to refine in parallel the goals SIZE and TIME to more primitive subgoals.

At a later stage of design it may be realized or evidence may be found that SIZE and TIME are mutually exclusive in that one cannot simultaneously satisfy both goals as they are defined. This conflict may be resolved in a number of ways. First, it may be decided that TIME is the more significant constraint for this particular design problem in which case TIME is retained as *the* goal and SIZE is *sacrificed*. Or, even admitting the primacy of TIME the designer may realize that by *weakening* the SIZE constraint – by increasing the values LOWSIZE(p) for one or more programs p – the conflict may in fact be eliminated. Yet another possibility is to weaken both goals.

At some stage of the design, decisions have to be made as to the precise value of the word length, the specific composition of the instruction set, and the nature of the data types and instruction formats. These are mutually interdependent goals. In this situation the designer may decide that, given the TIME constraint, instructions must be fetched from memory into the processor in a single memory cycle. The composition of the instruction set is thus identified as the *most critical component* and decisions concerning this have primacy over other decisions.

Consider as another scenario, the situation involving the determination of the data types and the instruction set. In fact here, the goals *cooperate* in Mostow's sense in

that the nature of the instructions to be made available on the computer is determined by the types of data that are supported. Once the data types are determined the instruction set will almost 'naturally' emerge. Data type definition is, then, a prerequisite for instruction set identification.
End Example

As this example illustrates, different combinations of the various multiple goal resolution strategies will generally be used in the course of a given design.

10.7 THE NOTION OF STYLE AS A KNOWLEDGE TYPE

To recapitulate its main features, the AI design paradigm is founded on the problem space/heuristic search model of intelligent problem solving. Design, according to this paradigm, is a process of search through a problem space for a form that satisfies some requirements.

We have seen by way of the various examples in this chapter that search entails knowledge of various kinds. There is, firstly, rather low level domain-specific knowledge which is used to effect the transitions from one state to the next in the problem space. These are referred to as operators in the problem space/heuristic search model and are represented by the domain-specific rules in the rule memory of a production system. Fig. 10.5 exemplifies such items of knowledge relevant to the design of micro-architectures.

Level of abstraction	Knowledge type: examples
1. Task/domain-specific	State transition operators: Rules (R1)–(R16) of Fig. 10.5; Rules (R1), (R2) of Fig. 10.11
2. Task/domain-specific	Control strategies/planning heuristics: (MR1) in example 10.8
3. Domain-independent	Control strategies/planning heuristics: (PR1), (PR2) in example 10.9; Multiple-goal-resolution strategies (e.g., goal weakening, goal sacrificing, least commitment, etc.)
4. Domain-independent	Grand search strategies: Forward chaining; Backward chaining; Means–ends analysis

Fig. 10.15 Types of knowledge relevant to design.

Then there is a more abstract kind of domain-specific knowledge that serves to establish overall, domain-specific plans of action to guide the design process. An example of this type of knowledge is the metarule (MR1) from example 10.8.

At a still higher abstraction level is knowledge that is essentially domain-independent and which serves to establish plans of action applicable across a range of design domains. Instances are the planning heuristics (PR1) and (PR2) encountered in example 10.9 and the various multiple-goal-resolution strategies appearing in (A), (B) and (C) in section 10.6.

Finally, at the most abstract or general level are the 'weakest' of the weak methods such as forward and backward chaining, and means-ends analysis.[13]

Fig. 10.15 summarizes these various types and levels of knowledge.

There is, however, an important aspect of the general process of design that is not reflected, at least explicitly, in the knowledge types listed in fig. 10.15. To understand this, let us consider the following design scenarios.

Example 10.13
Consider a *loopfree program flowgraph* G defined as follows: $G = \langle V, E \rangle$ is an acyclic directed graph in which (i) each vertex $V_i \in V$ denotes a basic block of code;[14] (ii) there is an edge $e_{ij} \in E$ from V_i to V_j, V_i, $V_j \in V$, if upon execution of V_i the flow of control may transfer to V_j; (iii) there is a distinguished vertex $V_b \in V$ – called the 'begin' vertex – such that V_b has no incoming edge; and (iv) there is a distinguished vertex $V_e \in V$ – called the 'end' vertex – such that there is no outgoing edge from V_e.[15]

Define a *maximal path* (MP) tree $T(G)$ corresponding to G as a tree such that

(a) $T(G)$ is rooted at a vertex that corresponds to V_b in G.
(b) For each vertex $V_i(T)$ in $T(G)$ there exists an offspring $V_j(T)$ in $T(G)$ if and only if there is an edge e_{ij} from V_i to V_j in G.

---

[13] In passing, it should be noted that the AI literature contains many other weak methods than those discussed here. For a recent discussion and enumeration of the many weak methods see Laird, Newell and Rosenbloom (1987, section 3.2).

[14] A *basic block* $B = \langle I_1, I_2, \ldots, I_n \rangle$ is a linearly ordered set of statements or instructions such that there is a single entry point to B, viz., I_1 and a single exit point from B, viz., I_n.

[15] In more formal graph theoretic terms, indegree(V_b) = 0 and outdegree(V_e) = 0.

In other words, a MP tree $T(G)$ is a tree that shows all paths in G from the begin vertex to the end vertex. Fig. 10.17 shows the MP tree for the program flowgraph of fig. 10.16.

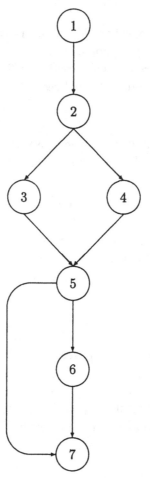

Fig. 10.16 A program flowgraph $G1$.

A person P is required to develop, find, or design an algorithm to generate MP trees from flowgraphs. P consults the textbooks on algorithm design and finds that in the domain of graph theoretic algorithms, there is an efficient *algorithmic form* called 'depth first search' (Aho, Hopcroft and Ullman 1974) which can be suitably modified to yield the desired algorithm.
End Example

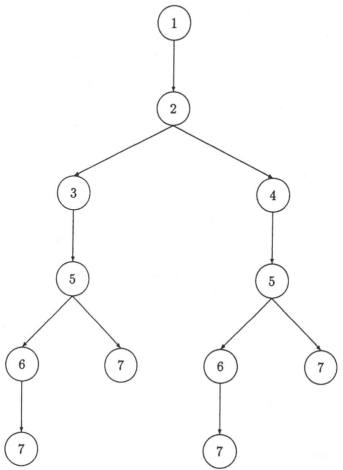

Fig. 10.17 Maximal path tree $T(G1)$ corresponding to $G1$.

Example 10.14

A programming language L is in the process of being developed. It is required to define the syntax of L in terms of a formal grammar G such that G will serve to specify the language for the purpose of constructing the front ends (scanners and parsers) of compilers for L. The person entrusted with the task of designing G takes as the starting point, a type of context-free grammar called *simple precedence grammar* which has the merit of being easy to construct and is known to be unambiguous (Gries 1971, Aho and Ullman 1972).

End Example

Example 10.15

The development of a new 32-bit microprocessor is under way. This microprocessor is intended to be a successor to, and 'upwardly' compatible with, the manufacturer's previous 16-bit microprocessor and an early design decision has been made to implement the control unit in microcode (as had been the case with the predecessor). However, the constraints on the design have been changed because of the wider data paths in the new processor.

In order to 'minimize' the chip area devoted to the control unit, the processor architects decide to explore the viability of using a two-level, microstore–nanostore control unit scheme that had been successfully used in a well known 'competitive' microprocessor.[16]

End Example

Example 10.16

A multiple user time-shared mainframe computer system is in the process of being designed. One of the major requirement for this system is that it must support a powerful, flexible protection mechanism for all programs and data residing in main memory. The design group makes two early decisions regarding the protection mechanism and the basic units or entities to be protected: the system will be based on the *capability-based* protection model; and the entities that will be the smallest units of protection would be *objects*. Thus, the initial conceptual model of the system to be designed combined the principles of *object orientation* and capability-based protection.[17,18]

End Example

Example 10.17

A parallel processing system is being designed to support object oriented programming. At the most abstract level the system is to consist of a collection of objects which, internally, are control-flow-based, imperatively executed, sequential entities that can be dynamically created upon request from other objects. Furthermore, each object maintains its own data objects and cannot directly access the data space of any other object. Objects can be running in parallel.

A decision has to be made as to how objects are to communicate or be synchronized

---

[16] For a discussion of two-level control stores the interested reader may refer to Dasgupta (1989a, chapter 5) or Hayes (1988, chapter 4).

[17] Briefly stated, a *capability* is an entity that contains the name (identifier) of a program or data segment in main memory and the access rights to that segment. Any process that requires access to a given segment must own a capability for that segment. For more on capability based protection, see Dasgupta (1989a, chapter 8), Myers (1982), Wilkes and Needham (1979) or Levy (1984).

[18] An *object* is, roughly speaking, synonymous with 'data abstraction'; it consists of one or more related items of data and a set of operations (procedures) that are the only means of accessing the data. For more on object oriented systems see Myers (1982) and Shriver and Wegner (1987).

with one another. Based on the general abstract nature of the system it is decided that inter-object communication and synchronization would be based on a *synchronized message-passing* scheme.

End Example

The point of these examples is the following: when posed a design problem the designer is likely to use some special features of the problem – that is, of the requirements defining the problem – to identify one or a small number of *styles* that are known for the target artifact. In the terminology of AI such *style recognition and selection* constitute yet another type of planning or control strategy which may be used to sharply limit the size of the problem space to be searched for a solution.

The concept of style has already appeared earlier in this book (see chapter 5, section 5.1; chapter 7, section 7.4). The role of style in the design process was first examined in a very general way by Simon (1975). Starting with Simon's ideas, Dasgupta (1984) analyzed the place of style in the domain of computer architecture and its influence on the architecture design process.

Consider a particular class of artifacts or systems that are intended to serve some common purpose (e.g., the classes of formal grammars, user-interfaces, imperative programming languages, uniprocessors, etc.).

Given such a class of artifacts, *a style is any complex of characteristics or features that sets apart one group of artifacts from another in that same class.*

Such characteristics may range from the formal (as in the case of specific types of grammars; see example 10.14) to the vague and/or ambiguous (as, e.g., in delineating the RISC style of architecture). Styles may be associated with the artifact as a whole (example 10.13) or with a component or an aspect of the artifact. That is, an artifact may result from the mingling of multiple styles. For instance, the parallel processing system of example 10.17 is a composite of (at least) the object oriented programming and message-based multiprocessor styles.

A style represents choice. For one thing, a style comes into existence whenever there are more ways than one of doing something. As Simon (1975) pointed out, where there is only one way of designing a product – where form inexorably follows function – the question of style does not arise. Styles come into existence when there are no unique and optimal solutions to problems but there are many satisficing solutions to the same problem. Conversely, the designer when faced with a particular set of requirements may choose, as a basis for search and exploration, one of several different styles that relate to the requirements set.

The sources of an artifact's style (or that of an artifact's component) appear essentially to be threefold (Simon 1975, Dasgupta 1984). Accordingly, I shall distinguish between

(a) Morphological styles
(b) Manufacturing styles
(c) Design styles

In the most usual situation a style is associated with specific structural features manifest in the artifact's *form* –that is, in the nature of the components and the relationship between the components. Such distinctive structural features of an artifact constitute its *morphological style*.

Example 10.18
In the domain of *building* architecture structural features are so strongly articulated that even the common viewer can identify building styles (Gothic, Romanesque, Baroque, etc.).[19]
End Example

Example 10.19
In the domain of *computer* architecture morphological styles are many: at the exo-architecture level the distinction is made between register, stack, and object oriented styles; along a different dimension the reduced instruction set computer (RISC) has come to be established as a distinct style. In the context of parallel processing systems, pipelining, shared memory von Neumann multiprocessing, message-based von Neumann multiprocessing, vector processing and data flow are all instances of morphological styles.[20]
End Example

A style may also be associated with an artifact in terms of the process or method used to manufacture the artifact. We may then refer to these as *manufacturing styles*. Manufacturing and morphological styles may influence one another; quite often the manufacturing process may impose constraints on the form of the artifact resulting in distinctive structural features and, in turn, a distinctive morphological

---

[19] In architecture, of course, styles have also come to be associated with specific historical periods so that by recognizing a style one can also predict the building's period. See Pevsner (1963) for a detailed discussion of architectural styles.

[20] For characteristics of such styles, the interested reader may consult Hwang and Briggs (1984), Stone (1987), Hayes (1988) or Dasgupta (1989a, 1989b).

style. Conversely, the desire to establish a particular morphological style may suggest a particular style of manufacture.

Example 10.20

If we interpret the word 'manufacturing' to mean physical realization then manufacturing styles are immediately recognizable in the domain of computer hardware (or digital systems in general). In fact computers have been categorized into 'generations' (first, second, third, fourth and currently fifth) primarily on the basis of the technology used to physically realize them.[21] As is well known, each of these 'generations' is dominated by a particular circuit technology – these being respectively: the vacuum tube; the discrete transistor; the small- and medium-scale integrated circuits (with up to about 100 gates/chip); large-scale integrated circuits (with up to 10,000 gates/chip); and very large-scale integration (of the order of 100,000 gates/chip). As manufacturing styles, these circuit technologies have had considerable influence on the structural and other characteristics of computers.[22]
End Example

Example 10.21

To take an example from an entirely different domain, scholars of ancient metallurgy and technology frequently distinguish between metallic artifacts according to the techniques used for their manufacture – e.g., the 'lost wax' casting process or the technique called 'repousse' (Doeringer, Mitten and Steinberg 1970).
End Example

Example 10.22

Probably no engineering domain has been so profoundly influenced by manufacturing style as structural engineering. As Billington (1983) has so elegantly (and eloquently) shown, different structural forms of bridges, tall buildings, and towers emerged from the use of new structural materials – from cast iron, through steel and reinforced concrete to prestressed concrete. Each such material defined a distinct mode or style for the manufacture of structures; each such manufacturing style gave rise to distinctive possibilities for structural form.
End Example

---

[21] Roughly speaking, the 'first generation' computers belonged to the period 1946–1958; the 'second generation' spanned the period 1958–1964; the 'third generation' belonged to the time frame 1964–1972; and the 'fourth generation' spanned 1972–1978. 'Fifth generation' computers are currently 'in fashion'.

[22] See e.g., Hayes (1984) for a detailed discussion of these technologies and their influence on the design of digital systems.

Finally, a style may be associated with an artifact in terms of the process used to design the artifact. We may refer to such styles as *design styles*. The various design paradigms discussed in Part II of this book are instances of design styles at a rather abstract level. Many more concrete design styles may be identified as instantiations of the paradigms and these may be both domain-independent and domain-specific. As in the relationship between morphological and manufacturing styles, there may be an interplay between morphological and design styles: one may influence the other.

Example 10.23

An interesting example of how design and morphological styles may be intertwined is seen in the case of *algorithms*. Horowitz and Sahni (1978) have organized their entire survey of algorithms in terms of the strategies that may be used to *design* them. These strategies – algorithm design styles – include the 'greedy method', 'backtracking', 'branch and bound', 'dynamic programming' and so on.

Consider the *greedy method*; this, in fact, turns out to be both a methodological prescription for the designer – that is, a design style – as well as a characterization of the form algorithms will take when designed according to the design style; that is, it also characterizes a morphological style.

As a design style, the greedy method may be described as follows:

> Given a problem with a set of inputs I_1, I_2, ..., I_n such that the algorithm is required to produce a subset of the inputs satisfying a particular set of constraints, consider the inputs one at a time in some order and determine whether that input is part of the solution.

In its role as a morphological style, the greedy method can be characterized by the following algorithmic form:

> **Input** I_1, I_2, ..., I_n;
> Current_solution $\leftarrow \phi$;
> **For** $j \leftarrow 1$ **to** n **do**
>   **if** current_solution $\cup I_j$ is a feasible solution
>   **then** current_solution $\leftarrow$ current_solution $\cup I_j$
> **return** current_solution

Similarly, Green and Barstow (1978) in their discussion of the sorting problem refer to the *divide-and-conquer* or *partitioning* strategy as a method for synthesizing sorting programs. It is also possible, however, to view divide-and-conquer as a morphological style insofar as it describes the form that algorithms may take. Specifically, the divide-and-conquer may be described as follows:

Input : Set S of elements;
SPLIT S into sets S_1 and S_2;
SORT S_1, S_2
JOIN sorted S_1, S_2

Note that this description prescribes how one may go about creating a sorting algorithm – a design style – as also the structure or form the algorithm will take – a morphological style.
End Example

It is quite obvious that (using the vocabulary of the AI paradigm), human designers use the concept of, and knowledge about, styles to reduce the size of the problem space and, therefore, the amount of search. In the context of automated or computer-aided design it would seem that the system's 'awareness' about styles could serve a similar purpose. One can imagine an interactive design environment such as the VEXED system (Mitchell, Steinberg and Shulman 1985)[23] in which, given the set of requirements for a particular artifact (or component thereof), key features of the requirements would be identified by the user and the system would respond by identifying the relevant styles as candidates for further exploration. The design process would then proceed by searching a reduced or specialized problem space related to that particular style.

The use of stylistic knowledge seems especially appropriate for those types of design problems which are very well understood or mature in the sense that the form of the artifact, its method of design, and the mode of its manufacture (or some subset of these) are known before the design process actually begins. In other words, the *overall* design of the artifact is known quite precisely beforehand. It follows that the general nature of the requirements that are satisfied by this design is also known *a priori*. The task of the designer is essentially to *instantiate* the artifact's style so as to meet the *particular* requirements posed by the design problem.

---

[23] VEXED is an interactive knowledge-based 'consultant' for the design of VLSI circuits. Typically, given a circuit design problem, the system uses its knowledge to advise the user about possible choices or paths of exploration at each step of the design process. Upon the user selecting a particular choice or course of action, the system executes the command – that is, extends or refines the design – and computes or infers consequences of the extension for other parts of the design form (Mitchell, Steinberg and Schulman 1985).

Brown and Chandrasekaran (1985, 1986) refer to such design situations as *routine* or *Class 3* designs.[24] They make the interesting point that routine design is likely to be the type of design situation that is most susceptible to automation using the AI paradigm. We may claim, then, that routine design constitutes an activity that is quite securely grounded in knowledge on the part of the designer or design system of the relevant morphological/manufacture/design style (or styles) of the artifact in question.

Given the ubiquity of styles, an unstructured or undifferentiated set of rather primitive domain-specific rules of the type encoded in the rule memory of a rule-based design system is likely to reflect poorly the nature of such knowledge. It would seem, referring to fig. 10.15, that explicit stylistic knowledge related to artifact forms, design methods, and manufacturing processes, should be an integral part of the design system's knowledge base.

Example 10.24

Brown and Chandrasekaran (1985, 1986) have explored the organization and control of stylistic knowledge in the context of a particular routine mechanical design problem.

The task is to design air cylinders – a piston and rod arrangement which by moving backward and forward against a spring within a tube controls the to-and-fro movement of some component. The morphological style of the artifact is precisely defined to the extent that it can be characterized as a hierarchical conceptual structure (fig. 10.18). The design task is, in effect, to 'redesign' the form according to the specific data of the space in which the air cylinder is to be enclosed or the intended operating temperatures and pressures.

The relevant design paradigm is, of course, the AI paradigm as I have discussed in

---

[24] Their Class 1 represents the most difficult or previously unencountered design situations that are likely to lead to entirely new classes of designs or even artifacts. In terms of our discussion of design problems (chapter 3), Class 1 designs correspond to what I called conceptual design problems. Class 2 designs, in Brown and Chandrasekaran's terms, also involve creative or innovative problem solving; but these are likely to be encountered either as originating in Class 3 design or as subgoals thereof. An example of how this may happen is illustrated by Stritter and Tredennick's (1978) design of the control unit of the Motorola MC 68000 microprocessor. The task – of designing a microprogrammed control unit as part of the processor chip – was basically routine in that a very well defined morphological style for such control units exists. However, the specific constraints of *their* design problem (in particular, chip area limitations) led Stritter and Tredennick to explore alternative solutions and, eventually to an almost forgotten approach that had been proposed several years before, viz., the use of dual level control store. This, then, became a new morphological style for control unit design.

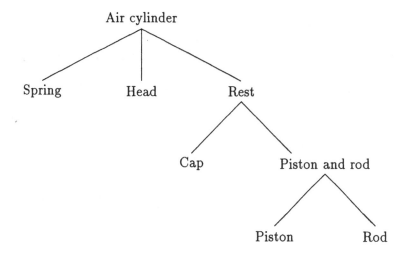

Fig. 10.18 Hierarchical structure of air cylinders (based on Brown and Chandrasekaran (1986)).

```
PLAN
    NAME Air Cylinder Design Plan
    USED BY Air Cylinder SPECIALISTS
    USES Spring, Head, Rest SPECIALISTS

    . . .

    TO DO
        Validate and Process Requirements
        ROUGH DESIGN Air Cylinder
        PARALLEL DESIGN Spring AND Head
        TEST Head AND Spring Compatible?
        DESIGN Rest
```

Fig. 10.19 Top level plan for air cylinder design (based on Brown and Chandrasekaran (1986)).

this chapter. Within the framework of this paradigm, a method or design style called *plan selection and refinement* is used and the morphological style of air cylinders is integrated into the design style itself. [25] Thus, for example, fig. 10.19 shows the salient aspects of the 'top level' plan for air cylinder design.

---

[25] Plan selection and refinement is one of a number of what Chandrasekaran (1986) calls 'generic tasks' that serve as high level building blocks for knowledge based problem solving.

Note that the plan reflects the most distinct structural features of the artifact as well as defining a partially ordered set of actions to be performed. The actions in turn invoke tasks (e.g., 'Validate and Process Requirements') and *specialists* responsible for enacting other plans. The structure of the design process itself reflects the structure – and thus, the precise morphological style – of the artifact.
End Example

10.8 THE TPD PARADIGM REVISITED

As remarked earlier in this chapter (section 10.3) the TPD paradigm is quite explicitly knowledge-based; yet the organization of this knowledge has not been addressed (as yet) within the paradigm itself. In contrast, the AI paradigm, because of the imperative of automation, is intimately involved with knowledge representation and organization issues.

The AI paradigm does provide further insight into TPD. Consider once more the key aspect of TPD: a design is developed in terms of an organized set of plausibility statements each of which is concerned with a specific constraint; and a TPD-based design is the organized set of constraints themselves. The task of a plausibility statement is to establish the grounds for believing that the constraint is in such and such plausibility state.

In particular, given a constraint C, one constructs a plausibility statement

$$S = \langle C, A, R, V, P \rangle$$

where (i) R is a logical formula involving other constraints $C_1, \ldots, C_n$ (for convenience denote this as $R(C_1, \ldots, C_n)$) such that

> if $R(C_1, \ldots, C_n)$ is in plausibility state P
>   then C is in plausibility state P

and (ii) the verification of R being in plausibility state P relies on some means V and some knowledge specified in A.

Knowledge, thus, participates in two ways in this exercise: (a) to justify that $R(C_1, \ldots, C_n)$ does indeed imply C; that is, there are grounds for supposing that the constraints $C_1, \ldots, C_n$ formed into a relationship R is a valid *interpretation* or *refinement* of C; and (b) to serve as evidence for or against the claim that $R(C_1, \ldots, C_n)$ is, in fact, in plausibility state P.

The latter issue (b) is resolved in TPD by decomposing $R(C_1, \ldots, C_n)$ into smaller components by using the laws of plausibility statements (see section 9.7, chapter 9) and ultimately reducing the task to one of establishing that $C_1, \ldots, C_n$ are in specific plausibility states. This is achieved either directly by using proof techniques, simulation or whatever, or by generating new plausibility statements for the individual constraints.

With regard to (a) it seems that one way of justifying that $R(C_1, \ldots, C_n)$ does indeed imply, or is a valid interpretation of, or is a valid refinement of, C, is by invoking and instantiating domain-specific production rules from TPD's knowledge base. The rules would be of the form

> IF the goal is to establish a plausibility state P
>   for a constraint of type C
> THEN attempt to establish that a relationship of
>   type R is in plausibility state P.

As a specific instance, taking computer architecture as the domain of interest,

> IF the goal is to establish the efficiency of an
>   instruction set I
> THEN try to establish that for a given set B of
>   benchmark programs, the object code compiled
>   from B onto I meets predefined execution
>   time and space constraints.

Such a rule was, in fact, implicit in constructing the plausibility statement $(S1)$ in example 9.10 (chapter 9, section 9.10).

Chapter 11

Algorithms for Design

11.1 INTRODUCTION

'Classical' design automation, of course, relied on the use of algorithms. That is, the earliest applications of computing techniques to design problem solving were all based on algorithms for producing designs. We may, therefore, refer to this approach as the *algorithmic design paradigm*.

A necessary (though not sufficient) condition for the algorithmic paradigm to be applicable is that the design problem be *well-structured*. Such problems are characterized by the fact that the requirements are *all* empirical in nature in the sense that one knows exactly how to determine whether or not a given design meets such requirements (see chapter 3, section 3.3). And although most interesting design problems are ill-structured many of their subproblems or components may turn out to be well-structured – in which case, the algorithmic paradigm may apply. Strictly speaking, then, one should think of the algorithmic paradigm as, so to speak, a *tool* that can be invoked by other more general paradigms such as TPD or even ASE to solve well-structured components of a given design problem.

11.2 COMPILING AS AN ALGORITHMIC STYLE

In the domain of computing systems design the algorithmic paradigm is perhaps most well represented by an important family of methods which may be collectively termed *compiling*. This is a technique or style which is 'classical' in that it was invented at a relatively early stage in the history of computer science; and it has been enormously successful as an instance of the algorithmic paradigm in the automation of software, firmware and hardware design.

The central task of compiling may be described as follows.

A system design or description language L is said to support an *operational* mode of description when its user can define the behavior of a system in terms of a program or algorithm. [1] Assume that the system S to be designed is specified in terms of an operational description (of its behavior) in some design language L_0. In other words, it is possible, by inspecting this description of S in L_0, to determine how the system will behave in the particular state space implicit in L_0. Call this specification $D(S, L_0)$.

The task of compiling is to *translate* this operational specification into a specification of structure and/or behavior appropriate for implementation; that is, to translate $D(S, L_0)$ into a description $D(S, L_1)$ of S in an implementable design language L_1.

In very general terms, the compilation process is characterized by an internal structure of the form shown in fig. 11.1. Compiling is decomposed into four logically sequential and functionally distinct subtasks.

In the first task, *parsing*, $D(S, L_0)$ is analyzed for syntactic correctness and, if found correct, is *translated* into an abstract and possibly inefficient ('naive') design expressed in a language L' which serves to bridge the 'semantic gap' between the specification language L_0 and the implementable design language L_1. Thus the parser accepts $D(S, L_0)$ and translates it to $D'(S, L')$.

The second task is to produce a more efficient version of the abstract and naive design $D'(S, L')$. This may be performed by an agent termed (in fig. 11.1) the *abstract system optimizer*. Note that the output of this agent is in the same language L' as its input. Thus the objective here is to *transform* $D'(S, L')$ into a more efficient form $D(S, L')$.

The third subtask *translates* $D(S, L')$ into a relatively inefficient ('naive') concrete design expressed in the target, implementable design language L_1. That is, the task agent called *concrete system synthesizer* translates $D(S, L')$ into $D'(S, L_1)$.

---

[1] The word 'operational' in this context originated in the concept of the *operational semantics* of programming languages (Wegner 1972a, 1972b) in which the meaning of the language construct is defined in terms of an observable sequence of state transitions resulting from the execution of some abstract 'computer' interpreting the instruction. Such an operational viewpoint of meaning has a still earlier root in the philosophy of physics called *operationalism* expounded by the physicist P.W. Bridgeman (1927) according to which a scientific concept is defined solely in terms of some experimental procedures or operations. For example, the concept of 'length' is to be defined in terms of operations by which length is measured. One can also trace a connection between the operational concept and the so-called *verification theory of meaning* propounded by the school of philosophers known as the logical positivists according to whom the meaning of a proposition lies in the availability of a method of verifying the proposition (Ayer 1946).

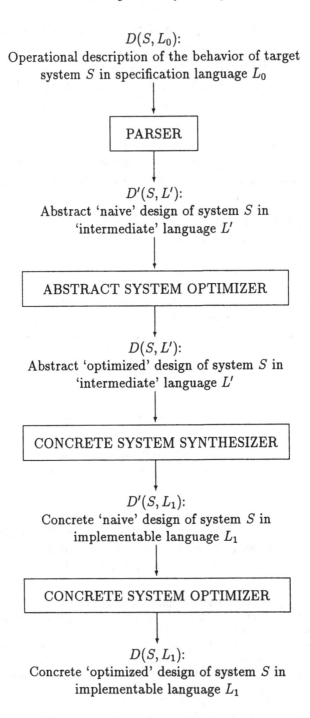

$D(S, L_0)$:
Operational description of the behavior of target
system S in specification language L_0

PARSER

$D'(S, L')$:
Abstract 'naive' design of system S in
'intermediate' language L'

ABSTRACT SYSTEM OPTIMIZER

$D(S, L')$:
Abstract 'optimized' design of system S in
'intermediate' language L'

CONCRETE SYSTEM SYNTHESIZER

$D'(S, L_1)$:
Concrete 'naive' design of system S in
implementable language L_1

CONCRETE SYSTEM OPTIMIZER

$D(S, L_1)$:
Concrete 'optimized' design of system S in
implementable language L_1

Fig. 11.1 Internal structure of a compiler.

Finally, the *concrete system optimizer* produces an efficient ('optimized') version of the concrete design. This is achieved by *transforming* $D'(S, L_1)$ to $D(S, L_1)$.

Compiling, as an instance of the algorithmic paradigm, thus involves (in general) two more specific types of activities, viz., *translation* (from one language to another) and *transformation* (from one form to another in the same language).

Example 11.1
Figs. 11.2, 11.3 and 11.4 show three different instantiations of the compilation schema of fig. 11.1 relevant to the software, firmware, and hardware domains, respectively. In the familiar case of a programming language compiler (fig. 11.2), the intermediate code generator translates the parse tree – the output of the lexical and syntax analyzers (or parser, in terms of fig. 11.1) – into a target-machine-independent language L'. The program represented in L' may be a sequence of abstract instructions of the form

OP source1, source2, destination

where OP is an operation and source1, source2, destination, designate the variables that serve as input sources and destination of OP.

The intermediate code optimizer performs target-machine-independent optimizations on the intermediate code and thereby transforms it into a more efficient form. Code optimization generally involves considerable *analysis* of the input program and is performed both *locally* (that is, within basic blocks) and *globally* (extending to loops and sequences of basic blocks).

The code generator translates the intermediate language code into object code for the target machine in either assembly or machine language form. The main tasks here are allocating target machine registers and memory words to the intermediate code variables and synthesizing instruction sequences corresponding to the instructions in the intermediate code. Finally, further optimization – this time on the target-machine-dependent code – may be performed thereby transforming the object code into a more efficient form.[2]

The compilation scheme for microprograms (fig. 11.3) is almost identical to that for programs in the early steps in that a high level language representation of the microprogram M is translated into a target-machine-independent form.[3]

---

[2] The standard reference on programming language compilers is Aho and Ullman (1977).

[3] Note, however, that the target machine in this case is the computer at the *micro-architectural* level whereas in the case of the programming language compiler, it is the computer at the exo-architectural level.

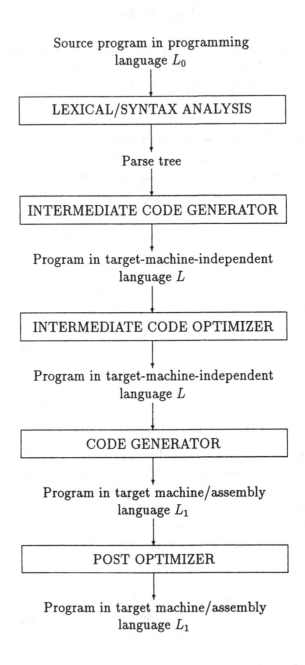

Fig. 11.2 Structure of a programming language compiler.

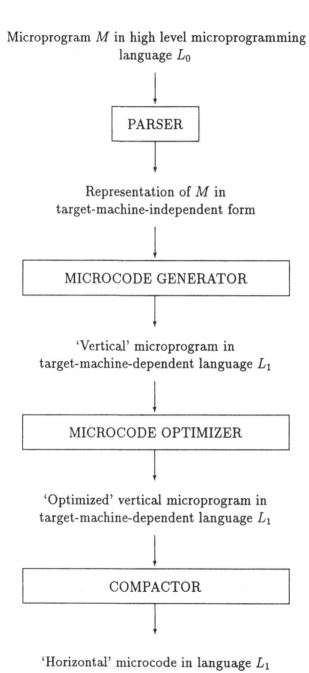

Fig. 11.3 Structure of a microcode compiler.

Behavioral description of processor hardware in
computer hardware description language L_0

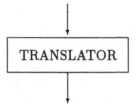

TRANSLATOR

Abstract representation of hardware structure
and behavior in intermediate language L'

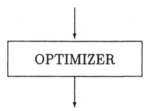

OPTIMIZER

Abstract representation of hardware structure
and behavior in L'

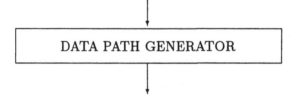

DATA PATH GENERATOR

Specification of data path in implementable
language L_1

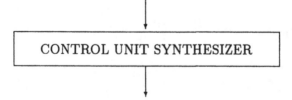

CONTROL UNIT SYNTHESIZER

Specification of the structure and behavior of
processor in L_1

Fig. 11.4 Structure of one type of 'silicon' compiler.

The microcode generator translates the intermediate representation of M into target machine-dependent 'vertical' microcode, that is, a sequence of micro-operations. This microcode form is then transformed by the optimizer into a more efficient vertical form.

Finally, a further step of the transformation is effected in which (for those target machines characterized by 'horizontal' microinstruction forms) the vertical microcode is compacted into a sequence of horizontal microinstructions each of which encodes one or more of the micro-operations appearing in the vertical microcode.[4]

Finally, fig. 11.4 shows the structure of one type of 'silicon compiler'. Here, the earlier translation phase takes as input a description (usually of behavior) of a hardware device in some computer hardware description language L_0 and produces an abstract representation of the hardware. The optimizer transforms this representation into a more efficient form.

The silicon compiler-equivalent to code or microcode generators (in the case of this particular type of silicon compiler[5]) consists of a data path generator and a control unit synthesizer. The first uses the abstract representation to generate a design for the data path part of the processor.[6]

The second component completes the processor design by producing the structure and behavior of a control unit that controls information flow through the data path. *End Example*

11.3 KNOWLEDGE REPRESENTATION IN THE ALGORITHMIC PARADIGM

In chapter 10, we saw that in the case of the AI paradigm, knowledge is largely contained explicitly in a knowledge base. In the examples discussed there, such

---

[4] For more on microcode compilers, see Vegdahl (1986), Mueller *et al.* (1988), Linn (1988), Dasgupta (1989b, chapter 5) and a series of seminal papers assembled by Milutinovic (1989, sections 3–5).

[5] The term *silicon compiler* as originally used by Johannsen (1979) refers to the automatic assembly of VLSI chip layout data. In current parlance the term has come to represent an entire family of schemes for compiling from a relatively high level specification of a hardware processor into a structural form at a relatively lower level of abstraction. Thus, silicon compilation applies as much to the synthesis of micro-architectures (as depicted in fig. 11.4) and logic circuits, as it does to the layout of 'modules' of the complexity of MSI and LSI circuits and of the 'cells' that are the building blocks for modules. For more on silicon compilers, see Gajski (1988) and, in particular, Gajski and Thomas (1988). See also Parker (1984) and Gajski and Kuhn (1983).

[6] Recall chapter 10, section 10.4, in which a similar task was discussed within the framework of the AI design paradigm.

knowledge was mostly formulated as rules and metarules. The design problem solver
– as represented by the interpreter or inference engine – also had some knowledge
built into it; the interpreter is basically a state machine that moves through the states
'match', 'select' and 'execute' in sequential fashion (section 10.3).

One is tempted to say that the interpreter knows what to do but does not have explicit
knowledge *of* this knowledge. This is precisely the characteristic of an algorithm; the
interpreter itself is, thus, an algorithm-driven organ.

In general then, algorithms are problem solving systems that do not have *explicit*
access to *external* knowledge; rather, the knowledge is contained in the algorithm
itself. More precisely, control strategy and knowledge about the task domain are
intertwined and together *define* the algorithm.[7]

This is the *basic* difference between the algorithmic and AI design paradigms; but
there is more. We have seen that in the case of the AI paradigm knowledge can
be in part domain-specific and in part domain-independent. The more the problem
solving system relies on domain-specific knowledge the *stronger* is the problem solving
method itself. The so-called expert systems are instances of such strong methods.
However, a typical AI-based design system relies on at least some domain-independent
heuristics to guide the selection of rules and establish strategies for searching through
the problem space.

In the case of the algorithmic paradigm, what I have earlier termed *algorithmic design
styles* (chapter 10, section 10.7, example 10.23) correspond to the domain-independent
heuristics of AI. The greedy method, divide-and-conquer, branch-and-bound, and
other algorithmic design styles (Horowitz and Sahni 1978) are precisely of this category. However, the domain-specific items of knowledge contained in algorithms are
generally *fewer* in number but of *greater scope, granularity* and *power* than the rule-
based type of knowledge seen in AI systems. In such situations the algorithm design
system can converge to a solution with virtually no search of the problem space.

Example 11.2

As a simple example of this difference consider the problem of solving pairs of simul-

---

[7] This may seem a rather obvious point; yet there still remains confusion on the part of some
of those involved in computer-aided design as to the distinction between 'knowledge-based' CAD
systems (i.e., CAD systems based on the AI paradigm) and algorithmic CAD systems. See, e.g.,
the 'panel' discussion on 'Knowledge based CAD' in the *IEEE Design and Test*, August 1989.

taneous linear equations of the form[8]

$$Ax + By = U$$
$$Cx + Dy = V$$

the solution of which is of the form

$$x = P, \quad y = Q$$

This is an extremely well-structured problem. But viewed first as an exercise in AI problem solving suppose that we use means–ends analysis as a basis for its solution (see chapter 10, section 10.5; in particular, example 10.11). An operator-difference table for this problem is shown in fig. 11.5.

Let the initial state of a particular instance of the problem be

$$\text{CS}_0 : \quad 3x + 4y = 36 \tag{1}$$
$$5x + 8y = 68 \tag{2}$$

The goal state will be

$$\text{GS} : \quad x = P, \quad y = Q \qquad \text{for some integers } P, Q.$$

Fig. 11.6 shows a particular tree of operations that may be generated by means-ends analysis in searching for a solution to this problem. It is assumed that any state that succeeds CS_0 will not continue to contain both (1) and (2) of CS_0; rather, one of these equations will be discarded in the new state. Tracing through fig. 11.6 the successive states generated are[9]

$$\text{CS}_1 : \quad 3x + 4y = 36, \quad 4x = 16$$
$$\text{CS}_2 : \quad 3x + 4y = 36, \quad x = 4$$
$$\text{CS}_3 : \quad 4y = 24, \quad x = 4$$
$$\text{CS}_4 : \quad y = 6, \quad x = 4$$

Of course, this search process is not necessary for this problem. Fig. 11.7 shows the algorithmic solution to the problem. The point to note is that the knowledge that in the means–ends analysis situation is embedded in the operator-difference table is contained directly and more succinctly in the algorithm itself.
End Example

---

[8] This example was largely inspired by a discussion by Newell and Simon (1976) of a similar algebraic problem (see also Langley *et al.* 1987, chapter 1)

[9] Here it is assumed that equation (2) rather than (1) is discarded.

	Difference	Precondition	Operator
(D1)	$Ax + By = U$ (1) $Cx + Dy = V$ (2) **NOT** $ADx + BDy = UD$ $BCx + BDy = VB$	true	(O1) Multiply (1) by D Multiply (2) by B
(D2)	$Ax + By = U$ (1) $Cx + Dy = V$ (2) **NOT** $ACx + BCy = UC$ $ACx + ADy = VA$	true	(O2) Multiply (1) by C Multiply (2) by A
(D3)	$Ex = W$ (1) **NOT** $x = W'$	true	(O3) Divide (1) by E
(D4)	$Fy = Z$ (1) **NOT** $y = Z'$	true	(O4) Divide (1) by F
(D5)	$Ax + By = U$ (1) $Cx + Dy = V$ (2) **NOT** $x = P$ $y = Q$	$ADx + BDy = UD$ (3) $BCx + BDy = VB$ (4)	(3)–(4)
(D6)	$Ax + By = U$ (1) $Cx + Dy = V$ (2) **NOT** $x = P$ $y = Q$	$ACx + BCy = UC$ (3) $ACx + ADy = VA$ (4)	(3)–(4)
(D7)	$Ax + By = U$ (1) $x = P$ (2) **NOT** $By = Q$	true	Substitute (2) in (1) and subtract AP from both sides of (1)
(D8)	$Ax + By = U$ (1) $y = Q$ (2) **NOT** $Ax = P$	true	Substitute (2) in (1) and subtract BQ from both sides of (1)

Fig. 11.5 Operator-difference table for example 11.2.

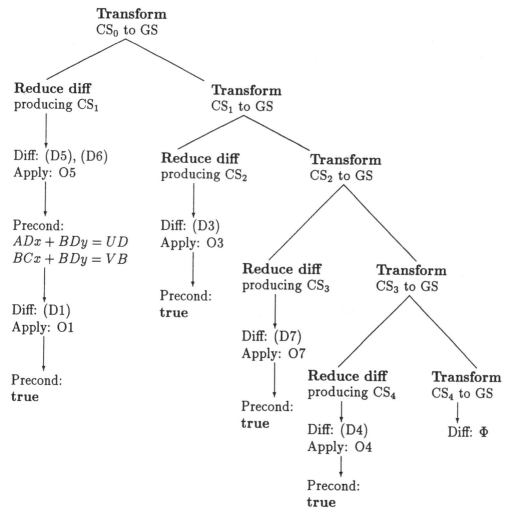

Fig. 11.6 Tree operations using means–ends analysis for example 11.2.

11.4 ALGORITHMIC TRANSLATION

We have noted that compiling is a rather important instance of the algorithmic design paradigm; and that compiling involves in turn two types of activities, viz.: translation from one language to another; and transformation of one form to another in the same language.

In general, the *translation* task takes as input, a design description $D(S, L_i)$ of a system S in language L_i and produces as output, a design description $D(S, L_{i+1})$ in a language L_{i+1} such that $D(S, L_{i+1})$ is a realization of $D(S, L_i)$; i.e., $D(S, L_{i+1})$ is a design that satisfies the requirements or goals implicit in $D(S, L_i)$.

Input Eqn1 : $Ax + By = U$
       Eqn2 : $Cx + Dy = V$
Output $x = P, y = Q$ for some integer P, Q
Local   Eqn3, Eqn4

[1] Eqn3 $\leftarrow$ Eqn1 * D; Eqn4 $\leftarrow$ Eqn2 * B;
[2] Eqn3 $\leftarrow$ Eqn3 – Eqn4;
[3] Eqn3 $\leftarrow$ Eqn3 ÷ coefficient of x in Eqn3
[4] Eqn4 $\leftarrow$ Substitute Eqn3 for x in Eqn1
[5] Eqn4 $\leftarrow$ Subtract constant on left hand side of Eqn4 from both sides of
          Eqn4
[6] Eqn4 $\leftarrow$ Eqn4 ÷ coefficient of y in Eqn4
[7] **Return** Eqn3, Eqn4

Fig. 11.7 Algorithmic solution for the simultaneous equation problem.

What is entailed here is a process wherein for each significant element or component e of $D(S, L_i)$ the translator must *select* or *synthesize* one or more components E in $D(S, L_{i+1})$ such that E is a realization of e.

Example 11.3
Recall from section 10.4, chapter 10, the design of the data path using the AI paradigm. An example of an algorithmic approach to a similar problem is provided by the EMUCS program developed by Thomas *et al.* (1983) as part of the CMU-DA design automation system developed at Carnegie-Mellon University.

The input to EMUCS is an entity called a *value trace* (VT); this is a directed acyclic graph representation of an ISPS description of hardware behavior. Since ISPS (Barbacci *et al.* 1978, Barbacci 1981) is an operational hardware description language the ISPS description is operational in form and so is the VT representation of this description. Both the ISPS descriptions and the VT representation can be viewed as different types of *abstract microprograms* defining the operational behavior of the hardware.[10]

A VT is similar to data flowgraphs used as internal (or intermediate) representations by programming language compilers with certain idiosyncrasies:

---

[10] Note that the ISPS-to-VT conversion is also a translation performed by an agent that corresponds to the parser in fig. 11.4. It is also the case that the VT obtained from this 'front end' of the ISPS compiler is further subject to certain optimizations as depicted in fig. 11.4 (Thomas *et al.* 1983).

(i) The nodes of a VT, called activities or operators, represent operations to be performed.

(ii) The edges of a VT represent dataflow from one operator to another.

(iii) In addition, VTs contain control constructs to denote conditionals and sub-routines.

The VT representation that serves as input to EMUCS also includes an allocation of VT operators to specific time slots called *control steps*. Such an allocation establishes the sequencing constraints or the potential parallelism between operations.

The output from EMUCS is a specification of a data path that (a) is capable of *realizing* the VT behavior and (b) consists of a 'minimal cost' realization for each local segment of the VT, called a VT *body*.[11]

---

while there remains an element of the VT body to bind
do
    COMPUTE_COST: For each unbound VT element compute the
    cost of binding that element to a hardware component
    SELECT_ELEMENT: Select the VT element to bind according
    to the 'min-max' criterion
    BIND: Bind the selected element and modify the data path
end

Fig. 11.8 The EMUCS algorithm.

The EMUCS algorithm (due to McFarland (1983)) is described in fig. 11.8 and operates on one VT body at a time. The elementary step of translation performed by the algorithm is that of *binding* an element of the VT body – that is, to allocate an operator in the VT to a hardware functional unit and to assign values generated by operators to registers.

As fig. 11.8 indicates, EMUCS iterates through a fixed sequence of steps until all elements in a VT body have been bound. The critical aspect of the binding process is to determine in each iteration which element of the VT body to select next for translation. This is done as follows.

In the COMPUTE_COST step, a *cost table* is generated showing the cost of binding each VT element to a relevant hardware component. Costs are computed based on

---

[11] More specifically, the VT corresponding to an ISPS description is partitioned into subgraphs called VT bodies. The partitioning is determined by the organization of the original ISPS description and occurs at the boundaries of ISPS procedures and/or labeled blocks.

parameters that reflect the cost of adding a new component to which the VT element is bound, the cost of binding the element to an existing component, and the cost of modifying the existing data path to accommodate either of these actions.

The SELECT_ELEMENT step chooses the next VT element for binding on the basis of the following heuristic:

min_max:
> For each unbound element e_i in the VT body identify the two lowest binding costs C_{i1}, C_{i2} ($C_{i1} \leq C_{i2}$) from the cost table; select from amongst these, the element e_j such that $C_{j2} - C_{j1}$ is the maximum and use the binding corresponding to cost C_{j1}.

The idea behind this heuristic is the following: if C_{i1}, C_{i2} are the two lowest costs of binding for element e_i ($C_{i1} \leq C_{i2}$) and if e_i is not bound according to its minimal cost C_{i1} in a given iteration, then in the next iteration the minimal cost binding may not be available; the best option available then, may be the next least cost C_{i2}. In that case the difference $C_{i2} - C_{i1}$ is a measure of the price that may have to be paid if e_i cannot be bound in the present iteration according to the least binding cost C_i. The *min_max* heuristic identifies the largest of the prices that may have to be paid and selects the corresponding element e_j for binding.

Finally, the BIND step performs the actual binding of the selected element and modifies the data path.

Note that since the *min_max* value is computed from the cost table and the latter is recomputed in each iteration, the *min_max* heuristic constitutes an optimization criterion that is based solely on the information available in each iteration. It is thus an extreme case of a *local optimization criterion*. The algorithm actually *imposes* severe bounds on the rationality of the decision making process.

To illuminate the workings of this algorithm we may consider the following example due to Thomas *et al.* (1983). Suppose that for a given VT body, allocation of registers is done before binding operators to functional units.[12] Fig. 11.9 shows the state of a partially bound VT body consisting of two control steps. The values Val1, Val4 and

---

[12] Note that register allocation and operator assignment to functional units are interdependent activities in that decisions concerning one influence the efficacy of the decisions concerning the other. Allocating the registers first and then assigning the operators is an instance of *serializing* goals – one of the strategies described by Mostow (1985) and discussed earlier in chapter 10, section 10.6. In the compiling literature this is also referred to as *phase decoupling* (Vegdahl 1982, Mueller *et al.* 1988).

Val5 have been bound to register Reg1, and Val2, Val3 and Val6 have been assigned to register Reg2. The operator OP3 has been assigned to functional unit Fu1. Let us suppose that an iteration of the EMUCS algorithm will now be executed.

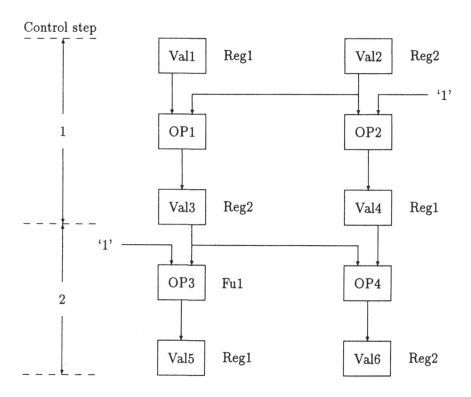

Fig. 11.9 A partially bound two-control-step VT body (Thomas *et al.* (1983) ©IEEE 1983).

| Operator | FUNCTIONAL UNIT | | | min-max |
	Fu1	Fu2	Fu3	cost
OP1	40	30	30	0
OP2	0	35	35	35
OP3	–	–	–	–
OP4	–	30	30	0

Fig. 11.10 Cost table for the unbound operators of Fig. 11.9 (Thomas *et al.* (1983), ©IEEE 1983)

Fig. 11.10 shows the cost table computed by COMPUTE_COST. As the values have already been bound to registers only the costs of binding the operators to three possible types of functional units are shown here. Note that OP4 cannot be bound to Fu1 since (i) OP3 has already been bound to Fu1 and (ii) OP3, OP4 are specified as potentially parallel operators in the same control step in fig. 11.9.

The cost computation can be understood by considering, as an example, the cost of binding OP2 to Fu3. Note first that OP2 is to be activated in control step 1 and Fu3 is not (as yet) in use in this control step. To simplify matters for the purpose of this example it is assumed that functional units can be added 'for free' and that all costs are related to establishing the interconnections necessitated by the addition of Fu3 to the data path. Thus, the cost of binding OP2 to Fu3 may consist of the following elements:

Let

$C1$: Cost of connecting Reg2 to one input of Fu3 = 10 units
$C2$: Cost of connecting the constant '1' to the other input of Fu3 = 10 units
$C3$: Cost of connecting output of Fu3 to input of Reg1 = 15 units

Then the cost of binding OP2 to Fu3 is $C_1 + C_2 + C_3 = 35$ units. The cost of other bindings are computed similarly by COMPUTE_COST.

The SELECT_ELEMENT step then computes the difference between the two smallest costs for each operator; these values are shown on the rightmost column of fig. 11.10. This step then applies the *min_max* heuristic and selects OP2 to bind. The BIND step will then allocate OP2 to Fu1 as this has the smallest cost.[13] Fig. 11.11 shows the state of affairs on completing this iteration of the algorithm.
End Example

From the perspective of algorithmic design styles EMUCS follows the greedy method (see chapter 10, section 10.7, example 10.23). In each iteration the algorithm selects an element to bind using as a selection criterion a limited amount of information available at that point of time, adds it to the partial design available at the start of the iteration, and creates a new partial design.

---

[13] Notice that the binding cost of OP2 to Fu1 is 0. This is to be expected as this binding entails no new component or connections. Fu1 already has Reg2 and the constant '1' as inputs and its output is connected to Reg1 by previous bindings (fig. 11.9). The binding of OP2 to Fu1 requires precisely these same connections.

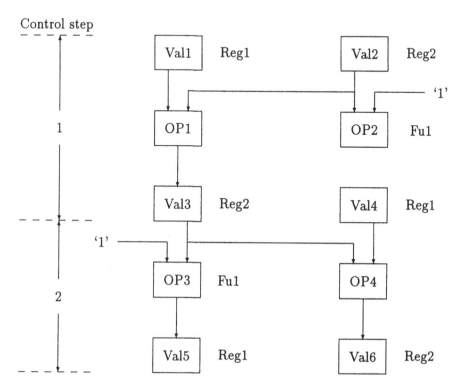

Fig. 11.11 Partially bound VT body resulting from an iteration of the EMUCS algorithm based on cost table Fig. 11.10.

From the perspective of the evolutionary model of design (see chapter 5, section 5.3, fig. 5.5) each iteration of the algorithm corresponds to a cycle of evolution; in this sense the *granularity* of the evolutionary process is very fine indeed. Misfit identification in each cycle consists of the detection of the remaining unbound elements from the original VT body (implicitly performed by COMPUTE_COST). Misfit elimination does not attempt to eliminate all the detected misfits in one swoop but just one. This completes the iteration of the algorithm and, consequently, one cycle of the evolutionary process.

It seems appropriate at this point to note the following: the fine-grained, one-element-at-a-time nature of the conversion performed by EMUCS here exemplifies what is called the *transformational paradigm* by some authors (see, e.g., Mostow and Balzer

1983, Mostow 1985).[14] This may lead to terminological confusion since earlier in this chapter I have used the word 'transformation' to mean the conversion of one form to another *in the same language*. The 'transformational paradigm' of Mostow and others applies both to mapping from one language to another *and* to transformations of one form to another in the same language!

To resolve this terminological confusion, I shall refer to the one-element-at-a-time conversion as *fine-grained evolution* and reserve the word 'transformation' for the sense I have previously defined.

Finally, the question once more arises as to how EMUCS uses knowledge to eliminate having to search through the problem space. Generally speaking the data path synthesis problem is ill-structured. Whether one starts with a VT-like data-flow graph (as above) or with a set of micro-operations (as in section 10.4, chapter 10), it is difficult to determine firm criteria for establishing whether the design is efficient or not. And, even if optimizing or satisficing criteria (such as 'minimal cost' or 'a cost less than such and such') are predefined, the problem space to be searched may be enormous. For example the designer may need to consider different orderings of register allocation and operator assignment, different ways of doing register allocation, alternative data path architectural styles (see chapter 10, section 10.7), different technologies, and so on before the efficiency criterion is met.

The algorithmic approach dramatically curtails the search (to the point of, usually, eliminating it) by limiting sharply the amount of admissible knowledge and by establishing criteria of satisfaction (or optimization) that are myopic but computable. By such expediencies an ill-structured problem is reduced to a well-structured form for which an algorithmic solution can be devised.

11.5 ALGORITHMIC TRANSFORMATION
The other side of the compiling coin is the activity called transformation which, as previously discussed, takes a design form $D(S, L_i)$ of a system described in language L_i and alters it to a form $D'(S, L_i)$ expressed in the same language.

The separation of transformation from translation is another example of the serialization strategies used to cope with multiple, interacting goals (see chapter 10, section 10.6; also Mostow 1985). The idea is that the general problem of compiling a form $D(S, L_i)$ in one language L_i to an *efficient, functionally equivalent* form $D(S, L_j)$ in another language L_j is decomposed into the task of addressing first the functional

---

[14] The synthesis of a data path using the rule-based AI approach in chapter 10, section 10.4 also exhibits this characteristic.

equivalence subproblem and *then* the efficiency subproblem.[15] Thus, translation produces a relatively 'naive' but functionally correct realization $D'(S, L_i)$. In a very obvious sense, then, the broader aim of the transformation task is to *improve* the design.[16]

Example 11.4

The so-called optimizing compilers (Wulf *et al.* 1975, Aho and Ullman 1977, chapters 12–14) perform a variety of transformations on either the intermediate or the object/assembly language code in order to improve the executable program's size and speed of execution (fig. 11.2). The usual strategy is to detect and recognize certain types of code segments and replace them with more efficient equivalents. These optimization strategies apply as much to code for execution on *vector computers* as they do to code intended for *uniprocessor* computers.[17] A specific instance of the latter is provided by Wulf *et al.* (1975) who describe the kinds of optimizing transformations used in the BLISS-11 compiler. This is a compiler for the systems programming language BLISS to generate code for the PDP-11. Transformations are applied both during and after the code generation phase.

An example of an optimizing compiler for vector computers is the PARAFRASE system due to Kuck *et al.* (1980, 1981). This is actually a compiler *preprocessor* that performs a series of transformations on FORTRAN programs and includes both target-machine-independent transformations as well as target-machine-specific optimizations.

An important type of transformation performed by such compilers is *loop optimization*. A widely observed empirical feature of programs is that most of the program's execution time is spent in a relatively small segment of the program and this is usually in inner loops.[18] Thus such loops are obvious candidates for optimizing transformations. In the following examples the code fragments are all stated in a high level language form for the sake of readability.

---

[15] In the context of program development, Dijkstra in his various writings has referred to this as a principle of the *separation of concerns* (see, e.g., Dijkstra 1976, chapter 27).

[16] As depicted in figs. 11.1–11.4, the term 'optimization' is the euphemism used to denote such improvements. The place of 'real' optimization in algorithmic design is discussed in section 11.6.

[17] The aim of code optimization for vector computers is also called *vectorization*. The objective is to transform code so as to enhance its suitability for parallel execution on vector computers (Hwang and Briggs 1984, Dasgupta 1989b, chapter 7).

[18] This phenomenon is often pithily referred to as the '90–10 rule': that 90% of a program's execution time is spent in 10% of the code. One of the earliest empirical documentations of this phenomenon is due to Knuth (1971).

(a) Induction variable substitution

A variable I which only appears within a loop in the form

$$I := I \pm \text{constant}$$

is called an *induction variable* (Aho and Ullman 1977). Induction variable substitution (or elimination) replaces the right hand side of such an assignment by a linear function of the loop index variable. For instance, in the following code segment B is an induction variable:

```
B := 0;
  for I := 1 until 20 do
    B := B + 1
    . . .
```

This can be transformed to

```
B := 0;
  for I := 1 until 20 do
    B := I
    . . .
```

Such a transformation may be useful in different ways. Most obviously, by replacing $B := B + 1$ by $B := I$, an ADD instruction at the target machine code level can be avoided. That is, instead of the code

```
LOAD B, Reg1
ADD 1, Reg1
STORE B, Reg1
```

the code generator would produce

```
LOAD I, Reg1
STORE I, Reg1
```

In the context of vector computers, induction variable substitution eliminates a recurrence relation within a loop and thereby increases the vectorizability of the program.[19]

---

[19] See Kuck (1978) or Kuck *et al.* (1980) for more on the implications of recurrence relations for vectorizability.

(b) Loop unrolling
Consider the following loop:

```
I := 1;
while I ≤ 100 do
    S1 :  A[I]  :=  B[I] + C[I];
    S2 :  I := I + 1
end
```

Notice that each of $S1$ and $S2$ will execute 100 times and that the test of $I \leq 100$ will also be executed 100 times. However, the number of such test executions can be halved by *unrolling* the loop:

```
I := 1;
while I ≤ 100 do
    [I] := B[I] + C[I];
    I := I + 1
    A[I] := B[I] + C[I];
    I := I + 1
end
```

(c) Scalar forward substitution
Consider the following code:

```
R := 8 − A;
Q := 10 − A;
for I := 1 until 20 do
    S1 : B(I, Q) := B(I, R) * D(I)
```

In the context of vectorization without knowing the values of R and Q the compiler would not be able to determine whether $S1$ is a recurrence or not. However, by substituting for the scalar variables R, Q in $S1$ so as to obtain

```
R := 8 − A;
Q := 10 − A;
for I := 1 until 20 do
    S1 : B(I, 10 − A) := B(I, 8 − A) * D(I)
```

the problem can be resolved.

(d) Dead code elimination

Any statement that assigns a value to a variable such that the value is never used again is an instance of *dead code*. Dead code usually arises as a result of other transformations and can be consequently eliminated. For example, an outcome of the scalar forward substitution performed above is that the first two assignments may become dead code.

(e) Reduction in operator strength

Consider a code fragment of the form

$$I := 1;$$
while $I \leq 100$ **do**
    $B := 2 * I;$
    $I := I + 1$
end

Here, B takes on successive values of $2, 4, 6, \ldots, 200$ through 100 execution of the '$*$' operation. However '$*$' is one of the more 'expensive' (i.e., time consuming) of the arithmetic and logical operations. The above code can be transformed to

$$B := 0;$$
$$I := 1;$$
while $I \leq 100$ **do**
    $B := B + 2;$

in which the 'cheaper' operation '$+$' replaces the '$*$'. This type of transformation is called *reduction in strength*.

All the above (as well as other types of) transformations can be performed algorithmically. Examples of some of these algorithms are described in Aho and Ullman (1977), Kuck (1978) and Allen, Cocke and Kennedy (1981).
End Example

Example 11.5

Another class of transformations involves, not replacing one fragment of a design by another, but *rearranging* their components so as to enhance performance. An important example of this type of transformation is *microprogram compaction* (fig. 11.3) in which a vertical microprogram (i.e., a linearly ordered set of micro-operations) is transformed into a horizontal form – i.e., a sequence of horizontal microinstructions each of which consists of one or more of the original micro-operations such that the execution of a microinstruction entails the parallel execution of its constituent micro-operations (Landskov *et al.* 1980, Davidson *et al.* 1981, Fisher 1981, Dasgupta and Shriver 1985, Dasgupta 1989b, chapter 5).

Microcode compaction principles are used not only to produce microprograms for conventional horizontal micro-architectures but also to compile programs written in FORTRAN and other high level programming languages into object code for special classes of horizontal exo-architectures, viz., the so-called attached array processors (Touzeau 1984) and the class of Very Large Instruction Word (VLIW) computers (Fisher 1983, Fisher *et al.* 1984).

Microcode compaction techniques fall into two classes: *local compaction*, the domain of which is a single basic block (i.e., a straight line micro-operation sequence); and *global compaction* in which the domain of compaction extends across several basic blocks.

As a specific example, we consider here a local compaction technique called, variously, the First Come First Served (FCFS) or the Linear algorithm. This is a greedy algorithm originally developed by Dasgupta and Tartar (1976) and later enhanced by Landskov *et al.* (1980) (see also Davidson *et al.* 1981).

Given a basic block

$$S = \langle M_1; M_2; \ldots; M_n \rangle$$

and an initially empty list of microinstructions, for each successive micro-operation M_i in S, the FCFS algorithm tries to place M_i in the earliest possible existing microinstruction provided that this placement neither violates the data precedence relationship nor generates resource conflicts.[20] If this is not possible – either because of a resource conflict between M_i and at least one micro-operation in each of the existing microinstructions or because data precedence relationships preclude inserting M_i into any of the existing microinstructions – a *new* microinstruction is created to hold M_i. If M_i is such that M_i is data-independent of all the micro-operations in all the existing microinstructions, the new microinstruction is created ahead of the

---

[20] Stated very informally, given a pair of micro-operations M_i, M_j in S such that M_i precedes M_j in S, M_i *data precedes* M_j (M_i **dp** M_j) if (i) M_i writes into a register (or memory) that is read by M_j; or (ii) M_i reads a register (or memory) that is written into by M_j; or (iii) M_i, M_j both write to the same register (or memory). If M_i **dp** M_j, then M_i *must* be executed before M_j as there is a data dependency between M_i and M_j. If for a pair M_i, M_j in S, $m_i \neg$ **dp** M_j then M_i, M_j are said to be *data independent*. Furthermore, if M_i, M_j are such that their simultaneous execution requires the use of the same functional unit then M_i, M_j are said to have a *resource conflict* (M_i **rc** M_j). In that case, either M_i must execute before M_j or vice versa. For a more formal treatment of these relationships see Dasgupta and Tartar (1976), Landskov *et al.* (1980).

current microinstruction sequence. Otherwise – that is, if this is not possible – the new microinstruction is created at the end of the current microinstruction sequence.

$M1$: ail := reg1;
$M2$: mbr := mem[ir.opd];
$M3$: air := mbr;
$M4$: aout := ail + air;
$M5$: reg1 := aout;
$M6$: pc := pc + 1;
$M7$: ir := mem[pc]

Fig. 11.12 A basic block of vertical micro-operations.

Fig. 11.12 shows a basic block of micro-operations. For the sake of simplicity it is assumed that all these micro-operations require a single clock cycle to execute.[21] It is further assumed that both the '+' operations are performed by a single arithmetic logic unit (ALU).

Micro-instruction generated	Basic block						
	$M1$	$M2$	$M3$	$M4$	$M5$	$M6$	$M7$
I1	$(M1)$	$(M1,M2)$	$(M1,M2)$	$(M1,M2)$	$(M1,M2)$	$(M1,M2,M6)$	$(M1,M2,M6)$
I2			$(M3)$	$(M3)$	$(M3)$	$(M3)$	$(M3,M7)$
I3				$(M4)$	$(M4)$	$(M4)$	$(M4)$
I4					$(M5)$	$(M5)$	$(M5)$

Fig. 11.13 Compaction of the basic block of Fig. 11.12 by the FCFS algorithm.

Fig. 11.13 shows the way that the algorithm produces the sequence of horizontal microinstructions. $I1$ will first consist of only $M1$. $M2$ can, then, also be placed in $I1$ as $M1$, $M2$ are data-independent and free of resource conflicts. For $M3$, a new 'later' microinstruction $I2$ has to be created as there is a data precedence between $M2$ and $M3$. Similarly, new microinstructions $I3$, $I4$ are successively created to hold $M4$ and $M5$ because of data precedence relationships.

$M6$ is quite independent of all the microoperations in the 'current' microinstruction list and (in spite of a resource conflict between $M4$ and $M6$) can be placed in the

---

[21] For a discussion of the complications arising from various timing issues see Dasgupta and Tartar (1976), Landskov *et al.* (1980).

earliest existing microinstruction $I1$. As for $M7$, this is independent of the micro-operations in $I3$, $I4$, $I5$; however there are data precedences between $M2$ and $M7$ and between $M6$ and $M7$. Thus $M7$ is placed in $I2$. The resulting sequence of microinstructions is

$I1 : (M1, M2, M6)$
$I2 : (M3, M7)$
$I3 : (M4)$
$I4 : (M5)$
End Example

11.6 THE ISSUE OF 'REAL' OPTIMIZATION

The algorithmic design paradigm is, then, relevant to well-structured design problems or, more commonly, to well-structured components of what are, more generally, ill-structured problems. An obvious question arises as to the possibility of the algorithmic design of *optimal* solutions to such well-structured candidates.

In fact, this issue was considered at length in chapter 5. In section 5.2, several examples were presented of well-structured design problems that could be formulated as *mathematical optimization problems* such that their solutions would constitute optimal designs in a mathematical sense. Included among these examples were

(i) Compiler-generation of a *smallest* or a *fastest* executable program that is functionally equivalent to an operational description in some high level language (example 5.3).
(ii) Compacting a vertical microprogram into a *smallest* sequence of horizontal microinstructions (example 5.4).
(iii) Encoding a set of micro-operations into a horizontal microinstruction format that *minimized* the microinstruction word length (example 5.5).
(iv) Placement of integrated circuit modules or cells on a chip or board so as to *minimize* the cost of interconnecting the modules (example 5.6(a)).
(v) Routing of wires on a chip so as to satisfy certain connectivity requirements such that the total wire length is *minimized* (example 5.6(b)).

As I pointed out in section 5.2 of chapter 5, the crucial point of these and many other similar examples is not that they cannot be algorithmically solved; but that these solutions require algorithms of exponential time (or sometimes, space) complexity. Computationally speaking, such design problems are NP-hard (see footnote 13, chapter 5). In other words, the *cost of computing* optimal solutions for such problems is so high as to make it often practically infeasible to apply optimizing algorithms. Thus, the *general* problems of optimal object code production, microcode compaction, module placement, wire routing, etc., are not guaranteed to be solved in polynomial time (although as noted in section 5.2, *special cases* of these problems may, in fact, be optimally solvable using efficient – that is, polynomial time – algorithms). It is because of the general intractability of optimal design problems that even algorithmic approaches to design problems are satisficing in nature.

11.7 CONCLUSIONS

In summary, where design problems are well-structured, algorithms may be constructed to produce designs that satisfy the requirements for such problems. Given the general fact that most design problems of any reasonable level of complexity or interest are ill-structured, however, the algorithmic paradigm is not likely to be of use for most such design situations. The dilemma can be circumvented either by simplifying a given problem so as to *make* it well-structured, or by decomposing it into a number of components some of which are well-structured.

In other words, if we imagine a general, computer-aided design environment in which design problems are addressed, the algorithmic paradigm may best be regarded as the basis of design support, management, and specialist *tools* at the disposal of the user.

For example, given the problem of designing a program for execution on a particular system, where the requirements are stated as a set of functional, performance, reliability and other characteristics (see chapter 3), the compiler can be invoked as a tool when the program has been synthesized in an appropriate programming language. Other paradigms, such as ASE, FD, TPD, or AI, would have to produce this operational form.

Finally, in spite of the optimization potential of many well-structured design problems inherently large problem spaces attend such problems. This results in exponential time complexities for algorithmic solutions that are optimal in a formal sense. Thus, the algorithmic design paradigm usually produces 'good' (or satisficing) rather than optimal solutions.

Part III

Design and Science

Chapter 12

Design as Scientific Discovery

12.1 INTRODUCTION

Recall (from chapter 5) that according to the evolutionary model a design at any stage of its development is best viewed as a tentative or conjectural solution; in other words, as a *hypothesis* which must be tested in the course of that evolutionary cycle and its successors.

It may also be recalled that in the TPD paradigm (chapter 9) the plausibility state of a constraint is determined by the evidence invoked in support of or against the plausibility of that constraint. Accordingly, it was noted (in section 9.4) that there is an analogy between plausibility states in TPD and the states of hypotheses or conjectures in science (see fig. 9.3).

Finally, in discussing the nature of program correctness proofs in chapter 8 (section 8.9), we noted Fetzer's (1988) suggestion that computer programs be viewed not as mathematical theorems (as is assumed in the FD paradigm) but as empirical, refutable, conjectures.

These various discussions appearing in diverse parts of this book collectively seem to suggest that there is *some* sort of a connection between the method of design and the method of science.

The subject of this penultimate chapter is precisely this issue. More exactly, I wish to examine whether, or under what conditions, the design process may legitimately be viewed as a process of scientific theory construction. I will anticipate later arguments by stating in advance the following thesis. Provided certain conditions are met

design problem solving is a special instance of (and is indistinguishable from) the process of scientific discovery.

I shall refer to this proposition as the *Design-as-Scientific-Discovery* (DSD) hypothesis.[1]

The DSD hypothesis is, in a sense, the culmination of our investigation of the design process as described in this book. And it has one significant implication. If the hypothesis is valid – if there are strong empirical grounds for believing it – it will shed some very useful light on (and perhaps help to dispel) a longstanding myth: that there is a fundamental difference between 'science' (meaning the natural sciences) and 'engineering' (that is, the artificial sciences).

This so-called distinction was discussed earlier in chapter 2 (section 2.1) where various accounts of its nature – some simple-minded, others quite sophisticated – were cited. However, as I pointed out there, while it is mostly true that the *aims* of the natural sciences and the sciences of the artificial differ one should not confuse differences in aims for differences in *methodology* or *process*. Thus, if the DSD hypothesis is accepted as valid it will signify that science and engineering share a common methodological basis: that is, science and design are methodologically indistinguishable.

12.2 A REFERENCE MODEL OF SCIENCE

Crucial to any argument supporting the DSD hypothesis is a stipulation as to what is meant by the term 'process of scientific discovery'. We must, therefore, establish a *reference model of science*.

While philosophers and methodologists of science continue to debate over the detailed ontology of science, considerable progress has been made during the past several decades – partly through philosophical investigations and partly through historical studies – in furthering our understanding of the nature of science and the 'scientific method' (Harre 1985, Losee 1980, Suppe 1977b). In particular, using the ideas of Popper (1965, 1968), Hanson (1972), Kuhn (1962), Lakatos (1978) and Laudan (1977) it is possible to construct what seems (empirically) to be a substantially accurate *broad picture* of the nature of the scientific process. While fully cognisant of its incompleteness in many respects, I shall, therefore, adopt this broad picture as my reference model of science. Its features are depicted schematically in fig. 12.1 and explained as follows.

(I) The problem

Scientific problem solving or discovery begins with an unexplained phenomenon or unsolved problem P. P may be either an *empirical* or a *conceptual* problem. An

---

[1] A preliminary account of the DSD hypothesis was given in Dasgupta (1989c). The present chapter is a greatly expanded, revised and detailed discussion of this earlier account.

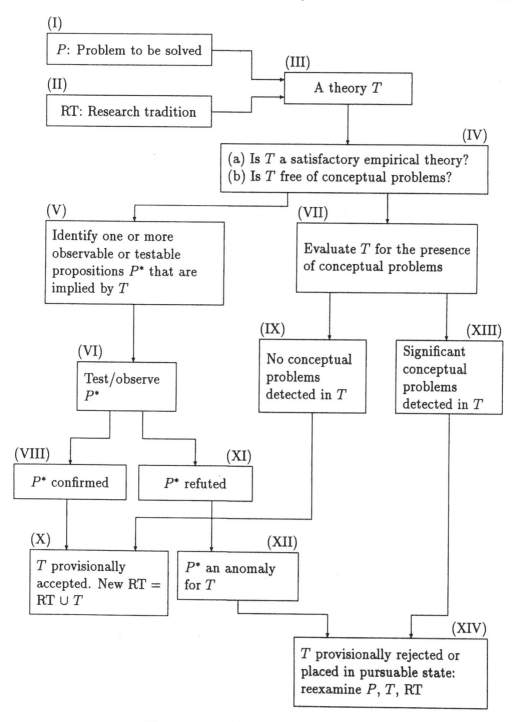

Fig. 12.1 A reference model of science.

empirical problem is posed by the observation or detection of some phenomenon in the natural world that demands an explanation. A conceptual problem arises in the context of a previously established or proposed theory where the theory is perceived to be unsatisfactory on logical, philosophical, or even aesthetic grounds rather than due to some empirical flaw.

Example 12.1

A classic example of a conceptual problem was posed by Ptolemy's geocentric theory of planetary motion. Ptolemy's model – or rather, the *Ptolemaic* model constructed originally by Ptolemy and gradually amended by other astronomers – based on uniform circular motion of the sun and the planets round the earth did indeed explain the then known data concerning the movements of the planets; but this was achieved at the price of a highly complicated geometry involving some *70* simultaneous motions of the sun, the moon and the five planets then known (Mercury, Venus, Mars, Jupiter and Saturn). To Copernicus the presence of such a complex science was, in his own words, 'not sufficiently pleasing to the mind'. It thus posed a *conceptual* problem. His subsequent heliocentric theory not only explained the data as well as the geocentric model; it also solved the conceptual problem attending the Ptolemaic model by its assumption of a far less complex geometry (Holton 1952, chapters 6,7; Kuhn 1957, chapters 2,5).

In contrast, the basic problem posed later to Kepler was that new data available on the orbit of Mars could not be explained by (or 'fitted into') the Copernican system of uniform motion. This was, then, an *empirical* problem which was solved by Kepler with his laws of elliptical motion (Holton 1952, chapter 9; Hanson 1972, chapter 4). *End Example*

(II) The research tradition

The problem solving process occurs in the context of an integrated network of theories, facts, methods, assumptions, and values. The most well known discussion of the nature of such a network or 'global background' is due to Kuhn (1962) through his concept of the *paradigm*.

The composition of Kuhnian paradigms was described at some length in chapter 6, section 6.2 and I shall not elaborate on their nature any further here. However, while the broad concept of the Kuhnian paradigm was accepted, Kuhn's detailed account of how paradigms function in scientific practice has been subject to considerable criticism (Shapere 1964, Lakatos and Musgrave 1970). This first led Lakatos (1970, 1978) to propose his notion of *research programs* as a correction to the paradigm concept and then to Laudan's (1977) articulation of the yet more elaborate idea of a *research tradition*. Since Laudan's research tradition is more comprehensive than, and subsumes the earlier concepts due to both Kuhn and Lakatos, I shall adhere to this term and the concepts that the term entails.

Laudan (1977) characterizes a research tradition (RT) in terms of the following:

(a) A RT contains one or more *specific theories* some of which may be successors to earlier ones while others are 'current' and coexisting at some given time. By a theory, Laudan means assertions, propositions, hypotheses or principles that can lead to specific, empirically testable predictions or can provide detailed explanations of phenomena. A theory is, thus, fundamentally descriptive in nature. Furthermore, the constituent theories within a RT need not all be consistent with respect to one another.

(b) Every RT is characterized by certain *metaphysical models* and *methodological commitments* which collectively distinguish one RT from another.

(c) Because of possible inconsistencies among its constituent theories, a RT may (in order to resolve these inconsistencies) *evolve* through several versions. Generally, then, RTs have long histories.

(d) Unlike theories (in Laudan's sense) RTs are *themselves* neither explanatory nor predictive. Firstly, they are too general for specific explanation or predictions to emanate from them. Secondly, since RTs are grounded on certain philosophical and methodological commitments they have strong prescriptive roles which by their very nature make them unsuitable for detailed explanation or prediction.[2]

Example 12.2

Two significant examples of research traditions in physics are classical mechanics and the quantum theory. The former includes as specific theories, Kepler's laws of planetary motion, Newton's laws of motion, and his law of universal gravitation. Note that classical mechanics *itself* is not a theory; it is a framework within which theories have been constructed. Similarly, the quantum theory, as a newly emerged RT in the early part of this century provided the basis of Einstein's photon theory of light which, in turn, served to explain the photoelectric effect (Holton 1952, chapter 23). Note, in passing, that classical mechanics has not been supplanted by quantum or relativistic mechanics. Classical mechanics remains quite valid as a RT for dealing

---

[2] This, highly abbreviated account cannot obviously do full justice to Laudan's theory of research traditions. The reader, in comparing the features described here with those of the Kuhnian paradigm discussed in chapter 6, may conclude that in broad outline they are very similar. Indeed, in broad outline they are. The critical points of departure for Laudan's theory lie in his detailed account of the relationship between a research tradition and its constituent theories, and between the theories themselves; and in the fact that RTs evolve and may coexist rather than be replaced as is the case with Kuhnian paradigms.

with 'ordinary' bodies and motions of such bodies whereas quantum and relativistic mechanics become the relevant RTs when one considers subatomic particles and motions of bodies near the speed of light.
End Example

(III) Theory proposal

Referring to fig. 12.1, given a problem P and a research tradition RT, the scientist proposes a *theory* T as a solution to (or explanation of) P. There is *no one specific method* by which T may be arrived at. T may have been constructed using some form of *inductive* inference from a given set of data; or by *analogical* reasoning; or by some sort of *gestalt-like* perception; or simply by informative *guesswork*. In other words the process by which a theory T is arrived at given P and RT *may* indeed be rationally explainable but, on the other hand, it may not.[3]

However, I agree with Hanson (1972) that the *general* reasoning leading to the proposal of a theory T follows what the 19th century philosopher C.S. Pierce called *abductive* or *retroductive* reasoning, characterized by the following inference rule schema:

1. Some phenomenon or problem P is observed
2. P would be explained if theory T were true

---

3. There is, thus, reason to believe that T is true[4]

T, then, constitutes a proposition that explains P and, thus, *might* be a correct theory. At this stage, T is a conjecture or hypothesis.

---

[3] I have previously discussed (in chapter 7, section 7.3) the 'myth of inductivism' as a logical basis for scientific discovery. As remarked there, induction – in the sense of inferring a theory from a set of 'observations' or 'facts' – may indeed be *one* method that is used in specific circumstances but it is by no means the only one. Thus, e.g., Langley *et al.* (1987) describe how Kepler's third law of planetary motion *can* be arrived at by their rule-based computer program BACON.1 using a process of induction from given data on the motions of the planets. However, there is no reason to suppose that this kind of induction was actually used by Kepler. In fact, implicit in BACON.1's 'discovery' of the third law is the assumption that there is indeed a law to be discovered. However, as Holton (1952, chapter 9) has pointed out (see also section 12.3 below), the discovery of the third law by Kepler was prompted by a a conceptual problem of a kind that is quite different from the very narrow empirical problem that BACON.1 solves; it would thus be a gross distortion of the documentary evidence (Hanson 1972, chapter 4) to assume that Kepler followed the inductive procedure inherent in BACON.1. Many philosophers of science in fact regard the issue of how a theory is actually arrived at as a problem that does not properly belong to the methodology of science but rather to the psychology of problem solving (see, e.g., Popper 1965, 1968; Medawar 1969).

[4] For a comprehensive discussion of abduction see Thagard (1988).

(IV) Satisfactoriness of the theory

Given its conjectural nature, the question arises as to the satisfactoriness of T as a theory for P. In fact, there are two broad questions that must be asked: (a) Is T a satisfactory *empirical* theory? (b) Is T (as a potential constituent of RT) free of *conceptual* problems?

(V–VII) Testing the theory

With respect to the empirical question (a), it is necessary but not sufficient that T solves (or explains) P; it is also required that any other predicted *consequences* of T must also be empirically true. Thus, some observable or testable proposition P^* that is entailed by T is identified (V) and experiments are performed to confirm or refute P^* (VI). Likewise, with respect to the conceptual question (b), T is assessed for consistency with respect to other relevant contemporaneous theories, assumptions or values in RT (VII).

(VIII–X) Corroboration of the theory

If P^* is indeed confirmed (VIII) *and* T is found not to exhibit any significant conceptual problem (IX), then T may be said to be *corroborated*. The theory is *accepted* and *assimilated* into the research tradition RT as a new constituent thereby enlarging RT (X).

(XI–XIV) Refutation of the theory

On the other hand, if P^* is empirically refuted (XI) then at the very least, P^* constitutes an *anomaly* for T – in the sense that T cannot be accepted until the anomaly has been resolved (XII). Alternatively, there may be found a significant conceptual conflict between T and one or more of the constituents of RT (XIII). In either case, T may be *rejected* outright and the investigation of the original problem P be resumed; or T may be provisionally placed in the 'pursuable' state in the sense that the anomaly and/or the conceptual conflict may be viewed as possible *new* problems that must be pursued (XIV).

In addition to the characteristics just cited, the following important features also attend the reference model.

(A) Nonmonotonicity of science: A theory T that has, at some point, been accepted and assimilated into RT may later be rejected on the basis of new data or solutions to other problems. In other words, scientific reasoning is *nonmonotonic* (Reiter 1987).[5]

---

[5] In this context, recall the nonmonotonic nature of plausibility-driven design (chapter 9, section 9.8).

(B) Emergence of new research traditions: The situation may arise in which a particular (and possibly small) subset of the relevant scientific community may determine that a given problem P is not solvable or satisfactorily explicable in the given research tradition, RT. This may lead to the birth of a *new* or *alternative* research tradition RT' within which P *is* explicable. RT' may, but *need not*, supplant RT; rather they may *coexist* for significant durations of time.[6]

(C) Falsifiability of theories: As Popper (1965, 1968) has articulated, the most effective mode of testing the theory T must involve experiments or predictions P^* that attempt to explicitly *falsify* T. Furthermore, while fig. 12.1 and our discussion appear to be concerned with a single testable proposition P^*, for the more important or significant theories, *many* such propositions must be tested and confirmed before such theories are accepted.

(D) Time span of the scientific 'cycle': Finally, the time frame from theory proposal to its acceptance (conclusively or even tentatively) or rejection may be quite short or very large, possibly spanning decades.

12.3 TWO EXAMPLES OF SCIENTIFIC DISCOVERIES FROM PHYSICS

This, then, is a concise statement of the model of science that will serve as the reference framework for the DSD hypothesis. This model was stated – necessarily – in somewhat abstract terms. In order to drape this model in more concrete clothing I shall recapitulate in this section examples of two fundamental scientific discoveries taken from the domain of physics and map these on to the reference model of science. The sourcebook for these examples is the historical account given by Holton (1952).

Example 12.3
Kepler's *three laws of planetary motion* are as follows:

> *Law 1* (Law of Elliptical Paths): Planets move in elliptical paths with the sun at one focus of the ellipse.

---

[6] This is essentially Laudan's (1977) model of the dynamics of research traditions which differs quite sharply from the dynamics of Kuhnian paradigms (Kuhn 1962). According to Kuhn, a 'scientific revolution' occurs when one paradigm is *replaced* by another and the entire community of relevant scientists accepts the new paradigm. In Laudan's scheme (a) a new research tradition does not necessarily replace another; (b) scientific revolutions are less revolutionary than Kuhn would have us believe since different research traditions may well coexist for considerable periods of time; and (c) insofar as there are scientific revolutions, such a revolution takes place in a particular discipline when a relatively *small* group of scientists choose to break away from one research tradition in order to create another. For more on this see Laudan (1977, chapter 4). For a magisterial discussion of revolutions in science from a historical point of view see Cohen (1985).

Law 2 (Law of Equal Areas): During a given time interval a line from a planet to the sun sweeps out an equal area anywhere along its elliptical path.

Law 3 (The Harmonic Law): If t is the period of any chosen planet and r the mean orbital radius of that planet then

$$t^2 \; = \; kr^3$$

where k is a constant having the same value for *all* planets.

The first and second laws were published together by Kepler in 1609 while the third law appeared in 1619. In terms of the reference model of science, these laws constituted a *theory* (or a set of theories) that solved a specific set of *problems*. Precisely what were these problems?

To begin with, the *research tradition* (RT) within which the problems were identified was constituted by the Copernican heliocentric model according to which planets moved on concentric spheres in uniform circular motion around the sun. However, this was only one part – the 'theory' part – of the RT. Another constituent was the metaphysical belief or assumption in the perfect geometric harmony or order of the universe – a belief that can be traced back to the ancient Greeks. Kepler's main intention was to refine and make more perfect the heliocentric theory within the confines of this metaphysic (Holton 1952, chapter 9).[7]

However, the very basic *problem* ($P1$) posed to Kepler was that new data available on the orbit of Mars could not be explained by the Copernican system of uniform circular motion. This was, then, quite obviously, an *empirical* problem but with such momentous consequences as to also generate a *conceptual* problem as it raised questions about the fundamental Copernican metaphysic.

After years of detailed plotting of the planetary paths Kepler arrived at his first law, the Law of Elliptical Paths as a solution for the problem $P1$. However, it did more than just solve $P1$; it provided a *simpler* model of planetary motion than either the Copernican or the earlier Ptolemaic systems by eliminating the necessity of complicated systems of uniform circular motions involving epicycles and eccentrics.

Kepler's discovery of the Elliptical Law, then, originated in the empirical data. [8] Thus, in some sense, its plausibility lay in its very construction and in its compelling

---

[7] For a detailed discussion of Kepler's metaphysical beliefs see also Holton (1952, chapter 2).

[8] For an account of the kind of (abductive) reasoning used by Kepler in arriving at his Elliptical Law, see Hanson (1972, chapter 4).

simplicity. However, the Elliptical Law in turn produced a *fresh problem* (P2): it does not allow one to *predict* when a particular planet will be in a particular point in its elliptical path. Without such a predictive capability the law, even though it solved problem P1, and in spite of its conceptual attractiveness, would remain rather ineffective from an astronomical perspective – especially as prior theories did possess such predictive capabilities. Thus, as Holton (1952, chapter 9) points out, the confirmation of the Elliptical Law as an acceptable solution to the original problem P1 lay, critically, in a solution to problem P2.

Kepler's second law, the Law of Equal Areas is a solution to P2. Consider now the confirmation of this law. It turns out that if this law is correct then one of its consequences as demonstrated by Holton (1952, chapter 9) is that for a given planet

$$rv = r'v' \tag{12.1}$$

where v is the velocity of the planet at a distance r from the sun and v' is its velocity at distance r'. Therefore given *by observation* the planet's velocity v at distance r from the sun, equation (12.1) allows us to compute the velocity v' at some other distance r'. And, if this predicted value v' can be confirmed by observation, the Equal Area Law is also corroborated thus further corroborating the Elliptical Path Law. Thereafter, equation (12.1) can be routinely used for predictive computations.

In arriving at his third law, the Harmonic Law, Kepler strove to solve what was fundamentally a *conceptual* problem motivated by the research tradition within which he worked. The problem (call it P3) was to establish a connection between – or an overall pattern involving – the motion of the different planets. As Holton (1952, p.156) points out, there is no *empirical* reason why such a connection should exist. The driving force in this case was Kepler's metaphysics – his belief in the simplicity and uniformity of nature.

In what way does the Harmonic Law solve P3? It does so by virtue of the constant k which is a constant *for all planets*. One can confirm the constancy of k by measuring t and r for a set of planets. And, given t_i, r_i (by observation or calculation) for planet i, t_j (or r_j) for any other planet j can be computed given r_j (or t_j).
End Example

Example 12.4
Consider the developments that led to Newton's *Universal Law of Gravitation*. In his celebrated *Principia* (published in 1687) Newton laid out four 'rules of reasoning' intended to serve as methodological guidelines for the construction of scientific hypotheses. In a very strong sense (as we shall see below) these rules are constituents of Newton's research tradition. The rules are (Holton 1952, chapter 11)

(a) Principle of Parsimony: Nature is basically simple; thus one should introduce the smallest number of hypotheses that are necessary and sufficient for explaining a phenomenon.

(b) First Principle of Unity: Similar effects must have similar causes.

(c) Second Principle of Unity: Properties found to hold for all bodies within the scope of observation or experiment are taken to hold (albeit tentatively) for all bodies in general.

(d) Principle of Faith: Hypotheses arrived at inductively are to be viewed as true until they are explicitly shown (experimentally or empirically) to be otherwise.

In the terminology of AI (see chapter 10) one might term these metarules.

Newton's original *problem* (call it $P4$) was to explain the nature of the force that kept planets in their elliptical paths round the sun (see example 12.3). The main gist of the argument leading up to the Law of Universal Gravitation is paraphrased after Holton (1952, section 11.4) as follows:

(i) Newton showed that since planets sweep equal areas per unit time (Kepler's second law) the force acting on each must be a continuous centrally directed (i.e., *centripetal*) force. Conversely if a centripetal force is applied on a body at equal time intervals Δt then in the limit (as $\Delta t \rightarrow 0$) the body describes a continuous curved path satisfying Kepler's second law. This independent derivation of Kepler's second law, the Law of Equal Areas, thus serves as a basis for the confirmation of the hypothesis (theory) that the force is centripetal in nature; the latter, in turn, is a theory that (at least qualitatively) solves $P4$.

(ii) What is the quantitative nature of this centripetal force? Newton showed that for paths following *any* conic section (i.e., parabolas, hyperbolas, ellipses and circles) the centripetal force F on the moving body at any instant is given by

$$F = \frac{k}{r^2} \tag{12.2}$$

where k is a constant for that body and r is the distance of the body from the center (i.e., the focus). This equation (the *Inverse Square Law*) is, therefore, true for a body obeying Kepler's Elliptical Law (see example 12.3).

(iii) If equation (12.2) is assumed true for a body then it can be shown that the body also obeys the relationship

$$t^2 = kr^3 \tag{12.3}$$

Since (12.3) is Kepler's third law – and was derived independently by Kepler – the Inverse Square Law can be said to be confirmed. That is, the Inverse

Square Law – which is a theory that *quantitatively* solves problem $P4$ – is confirmed by the fact that one of its consequences is Kepler's third law, the Harmonic Law which had previously been derived independently and was believed to be true.

(iv) The next problem ($P5$) is the *origin* of the centripetal force acting on the planets. Newton's solution to $P5$ was that the centripetal force on a planet is the *gravitational* pull of the sun and (invoking his second rule of reasoning – the First Principle of Unity) the centripetal force on a planet's satellite is the gravitational pull of the planet.

(v) In order to confirm this hypothesis consider the case of the moon on its path round the earth. For this case it can be shown that if the centripetal force acting on the moon rotating about the earth at distance r with a period t is indeed identical to the gravitational pull of the earth on the moon then

$$t^2 = \left(\frac{4\pi^2}{gR^2}\right) r^3 \tag{12.4}$$

where R is the earth's radius and g is the acceleration due to gravity. By substituting measured values for t, g, R and r, if equation (12.4) holds then the hypothesis is confirmed.

(vi) Having established the preceding theory in the case of the moon's path round the earth, Newton invoked his rules of reasoning (a), (b) and (d) to hypothesize that the same type of gravitational pull is the source of the centripetal force keeping planets in their orbits round the sun.

(vii) A clear confirmation of this theory can be effected if one were able to establish *quantitative* laws for gravitational and centripetal forces and then by showing, either experimentally or through prior results, that these forces are numerically the same.

Consider, first, the derivation of a formula for the gravitational force. Extending the Inverse Square Law (equation 12.2) to the domain of gravitational forces (i.e., by invoking Newton's rules of reasoning (a) and (b)) one may hypothesize that for any two spherical symmetrical bodies with masses m_1, m_2 that are distance r apart, that

$$F_g \propto \frac{1}{r^2} \tag{12.5}$$

where F_g is the gravitational force. And by arguing from Newton's laws of motion one may further postulate that

$$F_g \propto m_1, \quad F_g \propto m_2 \tag{12.6}$$

and thus

$$F_g = \frac{G\,m_1 m_2}{r^2} \tag{12.7}$$

where G is the constant of proportionality.

Furthermore, in the specific case of the earth moving round the sun the centripetal force F_c has been previously established as

$$F_c = \frac{m_e\, 4\pi^2 r_{es}}{t^2} \tag{12.8}$$

where m_e is the earth's mass, t its period, and r_{es} the distance between (the centers of) the earth and the sun. By our hypothesis

$$F_g = F_c$$

or

$$t^2 = \left(\frac{4\pi^2}{Gm_e}\right) r_{es}^3 \tag{12.9}$$

Assuming that G *is* constant for all planets, equation (12.9) is nothing but Kepler's Harmonic Law. Thus if the Law of Universal Gravitation (equation 12.7)) *is* true and if the centripetal force exerted by the sun on the earth *is* identical to the former's gravitational pull on the latter, Kepler's third law is obtained. Since the latter has been independently confirmed, the Universal Law of Gravitation and the identity of centripetal and gravitational forces are confirmed.

(viii) By virtue of Newton's rule of reasoning (c) one may (provisionally at least) accept the above conclusions for all planets orbiting the sun.

 (ix) A crucial assumption in the foregoing argument is that G is indeed a constant. Newton was unable to devise experiments to determine the value of G; he did, however, construct a proof for its constancy. It was left to Henry Cavendish 100 years after the publication of the *Principia* to determine experimentally the value of G and thereby show that G is indeed a constant.[9]

End Example

12.4 THE DSD MODEL

In section 12.1 I had stated the DSD hypothesis with little preamble or explanation. Now that we have established a reference model of science we can proceed to construct a basis for the hypothesis.

In the course of this book various models of the design process have been presented. Part I concluded with the evolutionary model (in chapter 5) which is intended to be

---

[9] The interested reader wishing to pursue further the Newtonian style of reasoning and the historical details of his work may consult *inter alia* Koyre (1968), Cohen (1980) and Cohen (1985, chapter 10).

a *descriptive* model of the design process; that is, a hypothesis about the nature of the design process based on the empirical evidence.

In contrast, the various paradigms discussed in Part II are founded on different *prescriptive* (or normative) models – that is, models of how the design process *should* be conducted according to the proponents of the respective paradigms.

Our concern in this section is to propose another descriptive model which is not quite as general as the evolutionary model of chapter 5; rather it may be taken as a special case of the latter. I shall refer to it as the *DSD model* and it provides the basis for the DSD hypothesis.

Fig. 12.2 depicts the structure of the DSD model of the design process. Its main features are explained immediately below while illustrative examples are presented in section 12.5.

(I) The design problem

Design begins with a set of requirements R that defines a *design problem*. We have previously (in chapter 3) considered at length the nature of such problems and we noted that in general, problems can be *empirical* (and thus, well-structured) or *conceptual* (and, thereby, ill-structured). In the present context not all forms of requirement statements are admissible in the DSD model. In order to count as a *DSD-valid* design problem, R must consist of predicates such that it is possible to devise *a priori* critical tests to confirm or refute the satisfiability of R by any subsequently proposed design.

(II) The knowledge base

The design problem R is given context by a *knowledge base* KB_d relevant to the design domain d associated with R. The form and function of KB_d must be such that

(i) It provides the necessary 'knowledge' that may serve to supply evidence for testing any empirical claim made about a design. The nature of such evidence is described in (V) below.

(ii) It characterizes explicitly, the conceptual assumptions and values underlying the design domain d (and that led to the birth and growth of d). Explicit description of the conceptual background is required (i) to determine whether or not a design D poses fresh conceptual problems with respect to the prevailing assumptions and values; or (ii) to establish the conceptual limits of d, thus leading to the possible emergence of *new* conceptual problems and, consequently, new design domains. Conceptual design problems very often lead

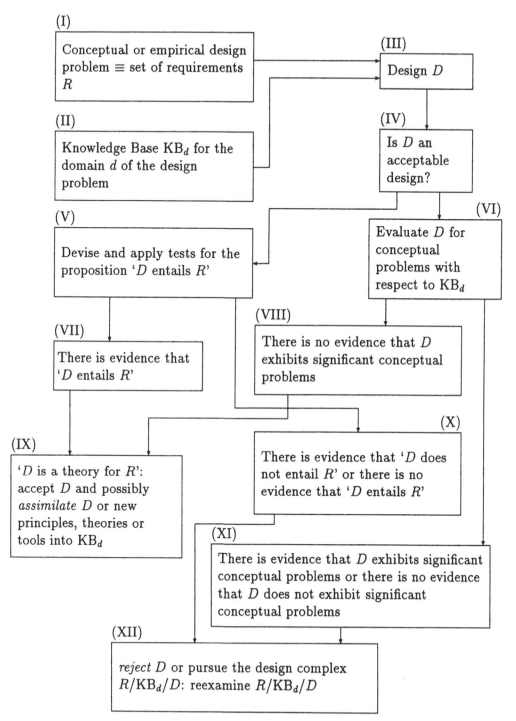

Fig. 12.2 The DSD model.

to important *research programs* in a particular discipline (see example 12.6 below; also, chapter 3, section 3.2).

The contents of KB_d may, then, be expected to consist of the following components.

(a) A data base of *heuristic laws* or *rules* concerning the structure, behavior, performance, cost and other properties of artifacts relevant to d.

(b) A repertoire of mathematical theories (e.g., graph theory, queuing theory, etc.) and formal systems (e.g., first order logic, forms of temporal logic, etc.) relevant to d.

(c) Descriptions of significant *archetypal designs, styles* or *exemplars* belonging to d.

(d) A repertoire of *design paradigms* relevant to d that may be used in design development.

(e) Explicit statements about the conceptual assumptions and values governing d.

Clearly, such a knowledge base, KB_d relevant to a domain d corresponds to the research tradition in our reference model of science. Indeed, when we consider highly innovative or original design (what Brown and Chandrasekaran (1986) called Type I design) KB_d *is* the research tradition.

(III) The design-as-theory
Using KB_d as a source of knowledge, the designer arrives tentatively at a design D – that is, a symbolic description of an artifact such that if the artifact is implemented according to D the designer *expects* it to satisfy R.

Let us consider in more detail exactly what D is. Recall that in science, a theory T is a solution to a problem P if T can *explain* why (or how) P happens to be the case. For example, Kepler's Elliptical Law explains (qualitatively) *why* the new data on Mars's orbit could not be accounted for by the Copernican theory. His second law then explains *why* planets are in particular points in their orbits at particular instances of time. The Harmonic Law explains *in what way* or *how* the orbital motions of the planets are related to one another.[10]

Furthermore, theories can be hierarchically related in that some 'higher level' theories can serve to explain 'lower level' theories. Thus Newton's Law of Gravitation is an

---

[10] For various views of the concept of explanation, see Hempel (1965), Thagard (1988, chapter 3), Hanson (1972, chapter 4).

explanation of, *inter alia*, why Kepler's laws hold – in the sense that one can derive Kepler's laws from the Gravitational Law.[11]

Consider, in the light of this, the role of a design D. D is a proposed solution to the problem defined by R in that it explains how or in what form an artifact may be constructed so as to satisfy the properties stated in R. In other words, insofar as D *explains* how R may obtain in an artifact, D *is a theory for R.*

In the DSD model it is not, however, enough for D to serve *merely* as a theory. The theory must be *testable* – or more accurately *falsifiable* – and for this it is necessary for D to be described in a language such that using valid forms of evidence (see below) and relevant items for KB_d it can be shown that D is indeed (or is not) an acceptable theory for R.

The DSD model itself stipulates nothing concerning how D is arrived at. It may have been derived using one of the design paradigms discussed in Part II or some other paradigm. *In general*, however, we can suggest the following abductive reasoning scheme:

1. Given a design problem R
2. If an artifact is implemented according to D then it will satisfy R

---

3. There is good reason to believe that D is a correct solution for R

It may be objected that while D may indeed be a theory for R it is a very *particular* theory for a *particular* problem and may not possess the generality or universality of theories in the natural sciences. I will address this issue in section 12.6.

(IV–VI) Evaluation of a design

To determine whether D is an acceptable design (or theory) for R two questions need to be asked: (a) Is R entailed by D? and (b) Is D free of any conceptual problems relative to the 'current' knowledge base KB_d?

To answer (a) *tests* are devised to confirm or falsify the proposition 'D entails R'. The exact nature of such tests will depend on the *form of the evidence* sought. In the DSD model the only forms of evidence that are admissible (i.e., are 'DSD valid') are those that demonstrate a *causal structure* between D and R and will include only the following:

---

[11] Although, as example 12.4 shows, it is the fact that Kepler's laws were independently confirmed that served as the confirmational basis for Newton's Gravitational Law!

(a) *Formal proofs*: Where a proposition can be shown to be logically implied by a design according to the axioms and rules of some formal system. An example is the use of Hoare Logic.

(b) *Experimental evidence*: Where it can be shown through *repeatable* experiments that some proposition is, in effect (within margins of experimental error), caused by some component of a design. The means for obtaining such evidence includes simulation and use of prototypes.

(c) *Mathematical (or analytical) modeling:* Where mathematical theories are used to derive, analytically, the evidence. Examples include queuing theory and graph theory.

(d) *Heuristic laws*: As is well known, designers rely a great deal on 'expertise' and 'experience' in order to both design and evaluate designs. Not all such heuristic knowledge however, is admissible in the DSD model. Such knowledge may be more 'rules of thumb' or 'intuitive' having no empirical or known causal basis. An example from the domain of computer architecture is the assertion 'a register-based instruction set is more efficient than a memory-based instruction set' which seems intuitively plausible enough but for which (without further qualification) we have no strong theoretical or empirical justification (see Dasgupta 1984, chapter 13).

On the other hand, certain items of heuristic knowledge are useful *distillations* of formally established principles or empirically observed facts. An example of the former is the logic design rule 'any logic circuit can be designed using NAND gates only' – a rule that is explained by (or has a formal basis in) the laws of boolean algebra. An example from the empirical domain is Moore's law stating that the density of integrated circuit chips doubles every year. We may refer to these sorts of heuristic knowledge as *heuristic laws*. And because they are grounded on formal causal arguments or possess empirical content, they may be legitimately regarded as DSD-valid forms of evidence.

To answer question (b), the design D is evaluated for its consistency with respect to the archetypal designs in KB_d and the conceptual and philosophical assumptions underlying KB_d.

(VII–IX) Acceptance of D

If there is significant evidence that D entails R (and no evidence against this assertion), and there is also no evidence that D poses any significant conceptual problems the proposition 'D is a theory for R' is corroborated. D is accepted as a valid design.

Note, though, that the acceptance of D may only be provisional. For example, the assertion 'D entails R' may have been confirmed on the basis of some evidence at hand at the time of conducting the tests. Later, new knowledge may be introduced into KB$_d$ that results in a falsification of the entailment.

In addition to D being accepted as a valid design, the conditions may merit *assimilating* D (or some aspect of its development or justification) into KB$_d$. This may occur for a variety of reasons or in a variety of ways. *New heuristic laws* may have been discovered in the process of testing D; or R may have signified novel requirements so that D constitutes a wholly *new archetype*; or the testing of D may have necessitated *new mathematical approaches or proof theories* to be applied or even invented; or *new forms of experimental procedures or tools* may have been devised. Assimilating any one of these characteristics into KB$_d$ can result in the modification and enrichment of the latter.

(X–XII) Refutation of D as a theory for R

The tests devised and applied in step (V) may actually falsify the proposition that 'D entails R'. Or it may be the case that in the absence of conclusive falsification there may still be insufficient evidence that D *does* entail R. Alternatively, even if there is significant evidence in favor of the entailment there may be evidence that D is inconsistent with the assumptions or values in KB$_d$ – that is, D poses conceptual problems with respect to KB$_d$.

Due to any one of these reasons (especially if the tests falsify), D may be rejected outright. In that case the original problem must be reconsidered and the cycle begun once more with a new or modified design hypothesized in step (III).

On the other hand – and in particular if a conceptual problem is detected in step (IV) – D may not be immediately rejected. Rather, a new phase of reexamination of the R/KB$_d$/D complex may be pursued to identify or resolve the cause of the falsification or the conceptual problem.

12.5 TWO THOUGHT EXPERIMENTS

As concrete illustrations of design situations that may be interpreted according to the DSD model, let us consider two thought experiments in design taken from the domain of computer architecture.

Example 12.5

Consider the design of a cache memory system. A part of this design involves establishing the following 'key parameters':

(i)   The placement or main memory/cache address mapping policy.

(ii) The size of the blocks to be transferred from main memory to cache.

(iii) The cache size.

The design problem (or *requirement*) R_{cache}, is to establish these parameters so that the cache miss ratio (MR) $\leq M$ for some predefined small fractional constant M.

In order to solve this problem, the architect may examine the *cache knowledge base*, KB_{cache}. In general, this will consist of experimental data involving trade-offs between the various parameters, and the effect of these trade-offs on the miss ratio. Such data may be based, for example, on 'trace simulation' and will be available in the original research literature, in review articles, handbooks, textbooks or in a computer data base.

Based on KB_{cache} the architect may identify a specific set of parameters for the cache. The resulting *cache design*, D_{cache}, can be described in terms of these parameters alone or, perhaps, in a formal architectural description language (ADL). Precisely how D_{cache} was arrived at may differ from one designer to the next (and also on the design paradigm used) but, in general, it would clearly conform to the abductive reasoning schema

(a) Given a design problem R_{cache}

(b) R_{cache} may be satisfied if we assumed a design D_{cache}

(c) Therefore it is reasonable to adopt D_{cache} as a design for the cache memory.

Consider more precisely what D_{cache} actually is: it is a description (in some language) of an artifact (the cache memory) such that if the artifact is implemented according to D_{cache}, the designer *expects* the artifact to satisfy R_{cache}. D_{cache} *explains how* R_{cache} may be realized by an artifact in the sense that if the artifact is implemented according to D_{cache} – so the designer believes – it will exhibit the properties specified as R_{cache}. D_{cache} is thus a theory that solves the design problem. D_{cache} *is a theory for* R_{cache}.

But what grounds do we have in *accepting* D_{cache} as a theory? In the case of the cache problem we do not anticipate any important conceptual issue at stake. Consider rather the empirical issue, the specific form of which is the 'testing condition':

TC_{cache}: D_{cache} exhibits a miss ratio (MR) $\leq M$

We may attempt to answer this question in one of two ways:

Method A: Conduct an experiment and show that D_{cache} exhibits a MR $\leq M$ for a set of benchmarks. The experiment may take the form of a simulation of the cache (as per the design D_{cache}) and observations of its simulated performance on traces generated from the benchmarks; or (more expensively) by constructing a prototype and observing the latter's performance on the benchmarks.

Method B: Show that D_{cache} falls within a class C of cache designs where according to KB_{cache} it is known that every member of C exhibits a MR $\leq M_{\max}$ for some $M_{\max} \leq M$. In other words, KB_{cache} contains data for a class C of cache designs satisfying the required MR such that C includes D_{cache}.

Note that if method A was attempted and was successful then we will have confirmed that D_{cache} is a theory for R_{cache} – but *no more*. If method B was attempted and found successful then we will actually have confirmed a more *general* proposition: that the class C is a theory for R_{cache} and, since D_{cache} is in C, D_{cache} is also a theory for R_{cache}. The confirmation attempt may *fail* however. If method B was first tried and it failed, this implies that the current theory and principles of cache memory design as embodied in KB_{cache} are inadequate for this $R_{\text{cache}}/D_{\text{cache}}$ complex. Method A may then be tried. It may be possible that the experiment actually *refutes* TC_{cache}. In that case, either the problem, R_{cache}, would have to be reconsidered – to decide, for example, whether the MR constraint can be relaxed – or the arguments leading to the design, D_{cache}, would have to be reevaluated. In either case, a (possibly new) requirement R'_{cache} and a new design D'_{cache} would eventually emerge.
End Example

Example 12.6
Consider (once more) the design of a RISC-style architecture. [12] Recall that such machines are characterized as follows (Colwell *et al.* 1985, Katevenis 1985, Patterson 1985, Dasgupta 1989a):

(a) A small set of instructions ($\leq \approx 40$) and a small set of addressing modes ($\leq \approx 4$).
(b) All instructions except LOAD and STORE operate only upon register operands and leave the results in the registers.
(c) All instructions except LOAD and STORE complete execution in a single processor cycle.
(d) Fixed-length and simple fixed-format instructions that do not cross main memory word boundaries.
(e) The use of hardwired rather than microcoded control.

---

[12] See also chapter 9, section 9.10 for a discussion of the design of a RISC-style architecture using the TPD paradigm.

At the time of beginning the design we assume the existence of KB_{RISC}, a knowledge base for the RISC style. KB_{RISC} contains various archetypal designs of RISC architectures and data and results of various studies conducted on RISC-related issues (see, e.g., Colwell *et al.* 1985).

The design begins with a set of requirements, R_{RISC}, comprising of (i) a general requirement R_{gen}, that the design should conform to the RISC style, and (ii) a more specific set of requirements, R_{spec}. Suppose one element of R_{spec} is

R_{eff}: The instruction set must be efficient

For a proposed design D_{RISC}, two conditions of acceptance immediately arise:

$TC1_{RISC}$: D_{RISC} satisfies R_{eff}
$TC2_{RISC}$: D_{RISC} is in the RISC-style

Clearly $TC1_{RISC}$ is an *empirical* proposition since R_{eff} is a desired performance characteristic of the proposed system. Consider its confirmation. Given the 'definition' of R_{eff} one cannot immediately devise a test that could even attempt to falsify $TC1_{RISC}$. One must construct a *testable* (or more accurately, falsifiable) equivalent of R_{eff}. Call this R'_{eff} and, following Aguero (1987), suppose we define it as

$$R'_{eff} : (\forall\ x \in HLL\_benchmark\_set)(Size(Code(x, Inst\_set)) \leq LOWSIZE$$
$$\land\ Exec\_time((Code(x, Inst\_set)) \leq LOWTIME)$$

where

(i) LOWSIZE and LOWTIME are constants denoting object code size (in bytes) and execution time (in processor cycles) respectively.
(ii) HLL_benchmark_set denotes a particular set of benchmark programs written in a particular set of high level languages.
(iii) Code(x, Inst_set) denotes the object code for benchmark program x in terms of the instructions in the Inst_set.
(iv) Inst_set is the instruction set designed as part of D_{RISC}.
(v) Size (Code (..)) denotes the size in bytes of Code(..).
(vi) Exec_time (Code(..)) denotes the execution time in processor cycles of Code(..).

The new condition of acceptance is

$TC1'_{RISC}$: R'_{eff} is a consequence of D_{RISC}.

An experiment can now be designed to confirm or refute $TC1'_{RISC}$. As in the case of the cache example, it may be possible to partially or totally avoid such an experiment. For instance, KB_{RISC} may contain data regarding the performance characteristics of certain classes of RISC machines one item of which is the rule that

> **If** an architecture design is a member of a class K
> **then** $(\forall\, x \in \text{HLL\_benchmark\_set})(\text{Exec\_time}(\text{Code}(x, \text{Inst\_set}_K)) \leq \text{MAX})$

where $\text{MAX} \leq \text{LOWTIME}$ and Inst_set_K is the characteristic instruction set for the class K. In this case TC'_{RISC} may be partially confirmed if it could be shown that $D_{RISC} \in K$.

Consider now the proposition $TC2_{RISC}$. In contrast to $TC1_{RISC}$, this is a *conceptual* condition. To further appreciate this, we consider the following scenario: suppose we find that D_{RISC} satisfies R'_{eff} (and all other empirically important requirements stated in R_{spec}) and *yet violates the RISC style* in the following way: in addition to LOAD and STORE several other instructions require multiple processor cycles. As things stand, D_{RISC} is *not* a theory for $R_{RISC} = \langle R_{gen}, R_{spec}\rangle$ though it *is* a theory for R_{spec}. Would D_{RISC} be accepted as a design for this particular target system? The architect may first attempt to *modify* D_{RISC} such that it satisfies R_{spec} without violating R_{gen}, but finds that he or she is unable to produce such a design. Under such circumstances, D_{RISC} *may* be accepted since it solves the empirical requirements R_{spec}. But in turn, it will have generated a new *conceptual design problem* – viz., the identification of some class of architectural design problems for which the RISC style (previously assumed to be valid) is now found to be partially invalid.
End Example

12.6 ON THE RICHNESS OF DESIGNS-AS-THEORIES

Fig. 12.3 summarizes the relationship between the reference model of science and the DSD model expressed in terms of the correspondences between their respective concepts. In this regard, the reader may also keep in mind fig. 9.3 in chapter 9, which displayed the correspondences between the plausibility states in TPD and the states of hypotheses/conjectures in science.

There remains, however, one important issue: *Is a design D in the DSD model a theory in the same sense that T is a theory in the reference model?* Let us address this question.

(A) In science, in the case that P is an empirical problem, a theory T explains P. For instance as we saw by way of examples 12.2 and 12.3, the original empirical

Reference model of science	DSD model
Unexplained problem/phenomenon (P)	Empirical/Conceptual design problem (R)
Research tradition (RT)	Knowledge Base (KB)
Theory T that explains/solves P	Design D that solves/satisfies R
Confirmation/falsification test for T using predictions P^* entailed by T	Confirmation/falsification test for D by showing that D does/does not entail R
Corroboration of T and acceptance into RT	Acceptance of D and incorporation into KB
Refutation of T as a satisfactory theory; rejection of T or reexamination of the P/T/RT complex	Refutation of D as an acceptable design; rejection of D or reexamination of the R/D/KB complex

Fig. 12.3 Relationship between the reference model of science and the DSD model.

problem for Kepler was that the (then) new data on Mars's orbit could not be explained by the Copernican scheme of uniform circular motion. Kepler's first two laws solved the problem: it explained the data for Mars as well as for the other planets then known.

In the event that P is a conceptual problem one may also interpret T as *explaining how* P may be resolved. For Copernicus, Ptolemy's geocentric model was – geometrically speaking – unduly complicated (see example 12.1); thus it posed a conceptual problem: how is it possible to explain the data that the Ptolemaic model explained but with a simpler geometry? The Copernican model solved this conceptual problem by explaining how the known body of data could be accounted for by a simpler model.

Thus, regardless of the nature of a scientific problem P, a hypothesis or conjecture T is a theory for P when it serves to explain P.

But the *acceptability* of T as a theory will critically depend on the nature of the evidence in its support. If the only evidence in favor of T is the fact that T entails P this would be regarded as dubious support for T. The acceptability of T would, so to speak, be put on hold. For T to be accepted as a theory for P the evidence must not only be P itself, but *other* testable phenomena P^* entailed by T. Thus, in order for T to be accepted there must be *independently testable* consequences of T that are indeed found to be true. The larger the set of such testable predictions of T that are confirmed or the more significant the confirmed consequences of T, the richer, more plausible, and more acceptable will T be.

Consider now, a design D. As described, D is an explanation of how R may obtain in an artifact; it is enough, so the designer claims, for the artifact to be implemented according to D for it to satisfy R. It is because D serves this explanatory function that I am claiming, *via* the DSD model, that D is a theory for R.

However, according to the DSD model the *acceptability* of D as a theory for R is fundamentally determined by whether or not it entails R.[13] For instance, if the empirical requirement for the development of a microprocessor were

> R': A maximum throughput of at least 10 MIPS
> *and*
> The functionality of the Berkeley RISC-I processor

then a design D' is acceptable as a theory for R' if it can be shown that D' entails R'. If R' was the *only* requirement, it is not necessary for *any other* prediction of D' to be generated and tested.

Thus, in terms of what it takes for a design to be acceptable, designs-as-theories are evidently *less rich* than theories in science in that the range of corroborated consequences demanded of designs-as-theories is less than that demanded of scientific theories.

(B) Consider on the other hand, the situation in science where *two rival theories* T_1 and T_2 both explain a phenomenon P in the sense that P is entailed by both T_1 and T_2. In this case the other independently testable consequence of T_1 and T_2, viz., P_1^* and P_2^* respectively would serve as the basis for deciding which of T_1 and T_2 is more acceptable.[14]

Similarly, consider two *alternative designs* D_1 and D_2 each of which entails a set of requirements R. In this case, other properties R_1^*, R_2^* that are also entailed by D_1, D_2 respectively could serve to decide which of D_1 and D_2 is the 'more' acceptable design.

Suppose, for example, that two alternative microprocessor designs D_1', D_2' both satisfy the requirements R' stated earlier. D_1', however, entails a simpler wire routing scheme on the processor chip than D_2'. This may make D_1' more acceptable as a design than D_2'.

Thus, as in the case of choosing between rival theories in science, choosing between alternative or rival designs that equally satisfactorily solve a *given* problem R would be determined by *other predicted consequences* of the respective designs.

---

[13] In addition, one must show the absence of any conceptual problems *vis-à-vis* the knowledge base KB. For our present needs I shall assume the absence of any such conceptual problems.

[14] This is a highly simplified picture of the whole issue of choosing between rival theories in science. For an examination of this problem see Laudan (1977, chapter 4) and, in particular, Laudan (1984, chapters 2 and 3). For an interesting discussion of the issue from a computational perspective, see Thagard (1988, chapter 5).

(C) The aim in science is to construct laws that are 'universal' in some sense. However, in a particular scientific domain all theories may not have the same level of richness or universality. Two theories T_1, T_2 may be such that (i) T_1 is explained by T_2 (i.e., T_2 entails T_1) or (ii) T_2 explains everything T_1 does and more. T_1 and T_2 are then related to one another *hierarchically* with T_1 placed lower in the hierarchy than T_2.

For example, the universal gas law $PV = nRT$ (where P, V, T are, respectively, the pressure, volume and temperature of a volume of n moles of gas, and R is the universal gas constant) summarizes and explains the empirical behavior of gases. However, this law can also be derived from (i.e., is entailed by) the kinetic theory of gases (Holton 1952). The kinetic theory is a richer and more universal theory than the universal gas law; the two theories form (or are part of) a hierarchy.

In the domain of artifacts, designs may also be observed to constitute theories of progressively increasing richness. Consider the following examples from the domain of algorithm design. Denote by

LM: A *local* microcode compaction algorithm that produces horizontal microcode from basic blocks of vertical microcode for the class of *monophase* micromachines.

LP: A *local* microcode compaction algorithm that produces microcode from basic blocks of vertical microcode for the class of *polyphase* micromachines.

GP: A *global* microcode compaction algorithm that produces horizontal microcode from arbitrarily structured vertical microprograms for the class of *polyphase* micromachines.[15]

Furthermore, let

$R_M \equiv$ the requirement that horizontal microcode is to be produced for the class of monophase micromachines.

$R_P \equiv$ the requirement that horizontal microcode is to be produced for the class of polyphase micromachines.

Then LM is a theory for R_M only; LP is a theory for R_P and (as monophase micromachines form a limiting case of polyphase micromachines) by implication,

---

[15] A *monophase* micromachine is a computer viewed at the micro-architectural level of abstraction in which a single phase clock cycle controls the operation of the computer. In a *polyphase* micromachine, a clock cycle with sequentially ordered phases controls the computer (Dasgupta 1989a, chapter 5).

is also a theory for R_M. GP is also a theory for R_P; it may also be a theory for other requirements or properties R', e.g., that 'more' optimal code is to be produced. Thus, we find that

> LP does everything that LM does and more.
> GP does everything that LP does and more.

LM, LP and GP thus form a hierarchy of designs-as-theories of progressively increasing richness and universality.

12.7 CONCLUSIONS

I have suggested in this chapter that provided certain conditions are met, design problem solving is a special case of (and indistinguishable from) the process of scientific discovery. I termed this the DSD hypothesis; in section 12.4, a descriptive model of the design process called the DSD model was outlined that laid out the conditions underpinning the DSD hypothesis.

The most interesting aspect of the DSD hypothesis – if it is accepted – is that it establishes a strong link between the natural and the artificial sciences. Note that this link is very different from the usual perception of how the natural and the artificial sciences are connected. Conventional wisdom has it that the latter are *applications* of the former. Thus, for example, the 'science' in metallurgy is the physics and chemistry of metals and alloys; the 'science' in mechanical engineering is in the underlying thermodynamics and mechanics; and so on. In a sense it was Simon (1981) who, in the first edition (published in 1964) of his seminal book, pointed out that there is indeed a 'science' in the artificial sciences that is not simply the underlying physics or chemistry or whatever.

The DSD hypothesis seeks to go still further: it wishes to assert that, methodologically speaking, the 'science' of the natural sciences and that of the artificial sciences are fundamentally alike. That these activities share a common methodology – what we have come to know broadly as the 'scientific method' or 'process' – is not something that is easily admitted either by the natural scientists or by the engineers or engineering theorists.

Finally, it is important to note that the DSD hypothesis is proposed here as a *testable hypothesis*. I have provided some small examples and 'thought experiments' in support of the hypothesis but clearly it must be subjected to considerably more rigorous and extensive empirical tests before one can reasonably claim to have corroborated it.

The most obvious *modus operandi* for testing the DSD hypothesis seems to be the approach taken by the more historically minded philosophers of science such as Hanson, Kuhn or Laudan; and that is, to examine, using documentary evidence, the historical development of specific design domains and determine whether their respective evolutions can convincingly support or definitely refute the hypothesis.

References

Agerwala, T. (1976) 'Microprogram Optimization: A Survey', *IEEE Trans. on Computers*, **C-25**, 10, Oct., 962–973.

Aguero, U. (1987) 'A Theory of Plausibility for Computer Architecture Designs', Ph.D. Thesis, Center for Advanced Computer Studies, University of Southwestern Louisiana, Lafayette, LA.

Aguero, U. and Dasgupta, S. (1987) 'A Plausibility Driven Approach to Computer Architecture Design', *Comm. ACM*, **30**, 11, Nov., 922–932.

Aho, A.V., Hopcroft, J.E., and Ullman, J.D. (1974) *The Design and Analysis of Computer Algorithms*, Addison-Wesley, Reading, MA.

Aho, A.V. and Ullman, J.D. (1972) *The Theory of Parsing, Translation and Compiling, Vol. 1: Parsing*, Prentice-Hall, Englewood Cliffs, NJ.

Aho, A.V. and Ullman, J.D. (1977) *Principles of Compiler Design*, Addison-Wesley, Reading, MA.

Alagic, S. and Arbib, M.A. (1978) *The Design of Well-Structured and Correct Programs*, Springer-Verlag, Berlin.

Alberti, L.B. (1955 1726) *Ten Books on Architecture*, A. Tiranti, London.

Alexander, C. (1963) 'The Determination of Components for an Indian Village', in *Conference on Design Methods*, J.C. Jones and D. Thornley (Eds.), Pergamon Press, Oxford. Reprinted in Cross (1984) 33–56.

Alexander, C. (1964) *Notes on the Synthesis of Form*, Harvard University Press, Cambridge, MA.

Alexander, C. (1971a) 'Preface to the Paperback Edition', *Notes on the Synthesis of Form*, Harvard University Press, Cambridge, MA.

Alexander, C. (1971b) 'The State of the Art in Design Methods' (Interview with M. Jacobson), *Design Methods Group Newsletter*, **5**, 3, 3–7. Reprinted in Cross (1984), 309–316.

Alford, M.W. (1977), 'A Requirements Engineering Methodology for Real Time Processing Requirements', *IEEE Trans. on Soft. Engg.*, **SE-3**, 1, 60–69.

Alford, M.W. (1985) 'SREM at the Age of Eight: The Distributed Computing Design System', *Computer*, **18**, 4, April, 36–46.

Allen, F.E., Cocke, J. and Kennedy, K. (1981) 'Reduction of Operator Strength', in *Program Flow Analysis*, S.S. Muchnick and N.D. Jones (Eds.), Prentice-Hall, Englewood Cliffs, NJ, 79–101.

Anderson, J.R. (1980) *Cognitive Psychology and its Implications*, W.H. Freeman & Co., San Francisco, CA.

Anderson, J.R. (1983) *The Architecture of Cognition*, Harvard University Press, Cambridge, MA.

Anderson, T. and Lee, P.A. (1981) *Fault Tolerance: Principles and Practice*, Prentice-Hall International, Englewood Cliffs, NJ.

Andrews, G.R. and Schneider, F.B. (1983) 'Concepts and Notations for Parallel Programming', *ACM Comp. Surveys*, **15**, 1, March, 3–44.

Appel, K.I. (1984) 'The Use of the Computer in the Proof of the Four Color Theorem', *Proc. Am. Phil. Soc.*, **128**, 1, 35–39.

Appleman, P. (Ed.) (1970) *Darwin, A Norton Critical Edition*, W.W. Norton & Co., New York.

Arvind and Gostelow, K.P. (1982) 'The U-Interpreter', *Computer*, **15**, 2, Feb. 42–50.

Asimow, M. (1962) *Introduction to Design*, Prentice-Hall. Englewood Cliffs, NJ.

Atkinson, R.C. and Shiffrin, R.M. (1968) 'Human Memory: A Proposed System and its Control Processes', in *The Psychology of Learning and Motivation*, Vol 2, K. Spence and J. Spence (Eds.), Academic Press, New York.

Ayer, A.J. (1946) *Language, Truth and Logic*, (Reprint of 1936 Edition with new introduction), Victor Gollancz, London (Penguin Edition 1971).

Backhouse, R.C. (1986) *Program Construction and Verification*, Prentice-Hall International, Englewood Cliffs, NJ.

Backus, J. (1978) 'Can Programming be Liberated from the von Neumann Style? A Functional Style and its Algebra of Programs' (ACM Turing Award Lecture), *Comm. ACM*, **21**, 8, Aug., 613–41.

Banerji, D.K. and Raymond, J. (1982) *Elements of Microprogramming*, Prentice-Hall, Englewood Cliffs, NJ.

Barbacci, M.R. (1981) 'Instruction Set Processor Specification (ISPS): The Notation and its Application', *IEEE Trans. on Comput.*, **C-30**, 1, Jan., 26–40.

Barbacci, M.R. and Parker, A. (1980) 'Using Emulation to Verify Formal Architecture Descriptions', *Computer*, **13**, 5, May, 51–56.

Barbacci, M.R. and Siewiorek, D.P. (1982), *The Design and Analysis of Instruction Set Processors*, McGraw-Hill, New York.

Barbacci, M.R. *et al.* (1978) 'The ISPS Computer Description Language', Dept. of Comp. Science, Carnegie-Mellon University, Pittsburgh, PA.

Barbe, D.F. (1981) 'VHSIC Systems and Technology', *Computer*, **14**, 2, Feb., 13–22.

Barr, A. and Feigenbaum, E.A. (1981) *The Handbook of Artificial Intelligence*, Vol. 1, HeurisTech Press, Stanford, and William Kaufmann, Inc., Los Altos, CA.

Barstow, D.R. (1985) 'Domain Specific Automatic Programming', *IEEE Trans. on Soft. Engg.*, **SE-11**, 11, Nov., 1321–1336.

Belady, L.A. and Lehman, M.M. (1976) 'A Model of Large Program Development', *IBM Systems J.*, **15**, 3, 225–252. Reprinted in Lehman and Belady (1985), 165–200.

Belady, L.A. and Lehman, M.M. (1979) 'Characteristics of Large Systems', in *Research Directions in Software Technology*, P. Wegner (Ed.), MIT Press, Cambridge, MA, 106–138.

Bell, C.G. (1977), 'What Have We Learned from the PDP-11?', in *Computer Architecture*, G.G. Boulaye and D.W. Lewin (Eds.), D. Riedel, Boston, MA, 1–38.

Bell, C.G. & Mudge, J.C. (1978) 'The Evolution of the PDP-11', in Bell, Mudge and McNamara (1978), 379–408.

Bell, C.G., Mudge, J.C. and McNamara, J.E. (Eds.) (1978) *Computer Engineering: A DEC View of Hardware Systems Design*, Digital Press, Bedford, MA.

Bell, C.G. and Newell, A. (1971) *Computer Structures: Readings and Examples*, McGraw-Hill, New York.

Bell, C.G. and Strecker, W.D. (1976), 'Computer Structures: What Have We Learned from the PDP-11?' *Proc. 3rd Annual Symposium on Computer Architecture*, ACM/IEEE, New York, 1–14.

Bell, C.G. *et al.* (1978) 'The Evolution of the DECsystem-10', in Bell, Mudge and McNamara (1978), 489–518.

Bendall, D.G. (Ed.) (1983) *Evolution from Molecules to Men*, Cambridge University Press, Cambridge, U.K.

Berry, A.J. (1954) *From Classical to Modern Chemistry*, Dover, New York.

Billington, D.P. (1979) *Robert Maillart's Bridges: The Art of Engineering*, Princeton Univ. Press, Princeton, NJ.

Billington, D.P. (1983) *The Tower and the Bridge*, Basic Books, New York.

Blaauw, G.A. and Brooks, F.P. (1964) 'The Structure of System/360 Part I: Outline of Logical Structure, *IBM Systems, J.*, **3**, 2 & 3, 119–135.

Blumrich, J.F. (1970), 'Design', *Science*, **168**, 1551–1554.

Boehm, B. (1981) *Software Engineering Economics*, Prentice-Hall, Englewood Cliffs, NJ.

Boehm, B. (1984) 'Software LifeCycle Factors', in *Handbook of Software Engineering*, C.R. Vick and C.V. Ramamoorthy (Eds.), Van Nostrand-Reinhold, New York, 494–518.

Bohm, C. and Jacopini, G. (1966) 'Flow Diagrams, Turing Machines and Languages with only Two Formation Rules', *Comm. ACM*, **9**, 5, May, 366–371.

Boyd, D.L. and Pizzarello, A. (1978) 'An Introduction to the WELLMADE Design Methodology', *IEEE Trans. on Soft. Engg.*, **SE-4**, 4, July, 276–282.

Brachman, R.J. and Levesque, H.J. (Eds.) (1985) *Readings in Knowledge Representation*, Morgan Kaufmann, San Mateo, CA.

Bridgeman, P.W. (1927) *The Logic of Modern Physics*, Macmillan, New York.

Brinch Hansen, P. (1977) *The Architecture of Concurrent Programs*, Prentice-Hall, Englewood Cliffs, NJ.

Brinch Hansen, P. (1982) *Programming a Personal Computer*, Prentice-Hall, Englewood Cliffs, NJ.

Brown, D.C. and Chandrasekaran, B. (1985) 'Expert Systems for a Class of Mechanical Design Activity', in Gero (1985), 259–282.

Brown, D.C. and Chandrasekaran, B. (1986), 'Knowledge and Control for a Mechanical Design Expert System', *Computer*, **19**, 7, July, 92–100.

Brown, H., Tong, C. and Foyster, G. (1983) 'Palladio: An Exploratory Environment for Circuit Design', *Computer*, **16**, 12, Dec., 41–56.

Burks, A.W., Goldstine, H.H. and von Neumann, J. (1946) 'Preliminary Discussion of the Logical Design of an Electronic Computing Instrument', Institute for Advanced Study, Princeton, NJ. Reprinted in Bell and Newell (1971), 92–119.

Butterfield, H. (1968) *The Origins of Modern Science 1300–1800*, Clarke, Irwin & Co., Toronto.

Camilleri, A., Gordon, M. and Melham, T. (1987) 'Hardware Verification Using Higher Order Logic', in *From HDL Descriptions to Guaranteed Correct Circuit Designs*, D. Borrione (Ed.), North-Holland, Amsterdam, 43–67.

Campbell, D.T. (1974) 'Evolutionary Epistemology', in *The Philosophy of Karl Popper*, P. Schlipp (Ed.), Open Court, LaSalle, IL.

Carnap, R. (1966) *Philosophical Foundations of Physics*, Basic Books, New York.

Carter, W.C., Joyner, W.H. and Brand, D. (1978), 'Microprogram Verification Considered Necessary', *Proc. National Comp. Conf.*, AFIPS Press, Arlington, VA, 657–664.

Chandrasekaran, B. (1986) 'Generic Tasks in Knowledge-Based Reasoning: High Level Building Blocks for Expert System Design', *IEEE Expert*, 1, 3, 23–30.

Chandrasekhar, S. (1987) *Truth and Beauty: Aesthetics and Motivation in Science*, University of Chicago Press, Chicago.

Chandy, K.M. and Misra, J. (1988) *Parallel Program Design: A Foundation*, Addison-Wesley, Reading, MA.

Charniak, E. and McDermott, D. (1985) *Introduction to Artificial Intelligence*, Addison-Wesley, Reading, MA.

Chomsky, N. (1957) *Syntactic Structures*, Mouton, The Hague, (Eighth printing 1969).

Coelho, D. (1989) *The VHDL Handbook*, Kluwer Academic Publishers, Boston, MA.

Coffman, E.G. and Denning, P.J. (1973) *Operating Systems Theory*, Prentice-Hall, Englewood Cliffs, NJ.

Cohen, I.B. (1980) *The Newtonian Revolution: With Illustrations of the Transformation of Scientific Ideas*, Cambridge University Press, Cambridge, U.K.

Cohen, I.B. (1985) *Revolution in Science*, The Belknap Press of the Harvard University Press, Cambridge, MA.

Cohen, P.R. and Feigenbaum, E.A. (Eds.) (1982) *The Handbook of Artificial Intelligence, Vol. 3*, HeuriTech Press, Stanford, and William Kaufmann, Inc., Los Altos, CA.

Colwell, R.P. *et al.* (1985) 'Computers, Complexity and Controversy', *Computer*, **18**, 9, Sept., 8–20.

Courtois, P.J. (1977) *Decomposability*, Academic Press, New York.

Crocker, S.D. Marcus, L. and van Mierop, D. (1980) 'The ISI Microcode Verification System' in *Firmware, Microprogramming and Restructurable Hardware*, North-Holland, Amsterdam, 89–102.

Cross, N. (Ed.) (1984) *Developments in Design Methodology*, John Wiley & Sons, New York.

Damm, W. (1984) 'Automatic Generation of Simulation Tools: A Case Study in the Design of a Retargetable Firmware Development System', in *Advances in Microprocessing and Microprogramming*, B. Myrhaug and D.R. Wilson (Eds.), North-Holland, Amsterdam, 165–176.

Damm, W. (1985) 'Design and Specification of Microprogrammed Computer Architectures', *Proc. 18th Annual Microprogramming Workshop*, IEEE Comp. Soc. Press, Los Alamitos, CA, 3–10.

Damm, W. (1988) 'A Microprogramming Logic', *IEEE Trans. on Soft. Engg.*, **14**, 5, May, 559–574.

Damm, W. and Doehmen, G. (1985) 'Verification of Microprogrammed Computer Architectures in the S*-System: A Case Study', *Proc. 18th Annual Microprogramming Workshop*, IEEE Comp. Soc. Press, Los Alamitos, CA, 61–73.

Damm, W. and Doehmen, G. (1987) 'An Axiomatic Approach to the Specification of Distributed Computer Architectures', *Proc. Conf. Parallel Architectures and Languages Europe* (PARLE), Lecture Notes on Computer Science, Springer-Verlag, Berlin.

Damm, W. *et al.* (1986) 'The AADL/S* Approach to Firmware Design and Verification', *IEEE Software*, **3**, 4, 27–37.

Dantzig, G.B. (1963) *Linear Programming and Extensions*, Princeton University Press, Princeton, NJ.

Das, S.R., Banerji, D.K. and Chattopadhyay, A. (1973) 'On Control Memory Minimization in Microprogrammed Digital Computers', *IEEE Trans. on Comput.*, **C-22**, 9, Sept., 845–848.

Dasgupta, S. (1977) 'The Design of Some Language Constructs for Horizontal Microprogramming', *Proc. 4th Annual Symp. on Comp. Architecture*, ACM/IEEE, New York, 10–16.

Dasgupta, S. (1978) 'Towards a Microprogramming Language Schema', *Proc. 11th Annual Microprogramming Workshop*, (MICRO.11), ACM/IEEE, New York, 144–153.

Dasgupta, S. (1979) 'The Organization of Microprogram Stores', *ACM Computing Surveys*, **12**, 3, March, 295–324.

Dasgupta, S. (1980a) 'Some Implications of Programming Methodology for Microprogramming Language Design', in *Firmware, Microprogramming and Restructurable Hardware*, G. Chroust and J. Mulbacher (Eds.), North-Holland, Amsterdam, 243–252.

Dasgupta, S. (1980b) 'Some Aspects of High Level Microprogramming', *ACM Comp. Surveys*, **12**, 3, Sept., 295–324.

Dasgupta, S. (1982) 'Computer Design and Description Languages', in *Advances in Computers, Vol. 21*, M.C. Yovits (Ed.), Academic Press, New York, 91–155.

Dasgupta, S. (1983) 'On the Verification of Computer Architectures Using an Architecture Description Lnaguage', *Proc. 10th Annual Symposium on Computer Architecture*, IEEE Computer Society Press, New York, 158–167.

Dasgupta, S. (1984) *The Design and Description of Computer Architectures*, John Wiley & Sons, New York.

Dasgupta, S. (1985) 'Hardware Description Languages in Microprogramming Systems', *Computer*, **18**, 2, Feb., 67–76.

Dasgupta, S. (1988) 'Principles of Firmware Verification', in Habib (1988), 433–482.

Dasgupta, S. (1989a) *Computer Architecture: A Modern Synthesis, Vol. 1: Foundations*, John Wiley & Sons, New York.

Dasgupta, S. (1989b) *Computer Architecture: A Modern Synthesis, Vol. 2: Advanced Topics.* John Wiley & Sons, New York.

Dasgupta, S. (1989c) 'The Structure of Design Processes', in *Advances in Computers, Vol. 28*, M.C. Yovits (Ed.), Academic Press, New York, 1–67.

Dasgupta, S. and Aguero, U. (1987) 'On the Plausibility of Architectural Designs', *Proc. 8th Int. Conf. on Computer Hardware Description Languages and Their Applications* (CHDL 87), M.R. Barbacci and C.J. Koomen (Eds.), Elsevier Science Publishers, Amsterdam, 177–194.

Dasgupta, S. and Heinanen, J. (1985) 'On the Axiomatic Specification of Computer Architectures', in *Computer Hardware Description Languages and Their Applications, Proc. of the 7th International Symposium* (CHDL-85), C.J. Koomen & T.Moto-oka (Eds.), North-Holland, Amsterdam, 1–15.

Dasgupta, S. and Shriver, B.D. (1985) 'Developments in Firmware Engineering', in *Advances in Computers, Vol. 24*, M.C. Yovits (Ed.), Academic Press, New York, 101–176.

Dasgupta, S. and Tartar, J. (1976) 'The Identification of Maximal Parallelism in Straight Line Microprograms, *IEEE Trans. on Computers*, **C-25**, 10, Oct., 986–992.

Dasgupta, S. and Wagner, A. (1984) 'The Use of Hoare Logic in the Verification of Horizontal Microprograms', *Int. J. of Comp. & Info. Sciences*, **13**, 6, 461–490.

Dasgupta, S., Wilsey, P.A. and Heinanen, J. (1986) 'Axiomatic Specifications in Firmware Development Systems', *IEEE Software*, 3, 4, July, 49–58.

Davidson, S. (1986), 'Progress in High Level Microprogramming', *IEEE Software*, **3**, 4, July, 18–26.

Davidson, S. *et al.* (1981), 'Some Experiments in Local Microcode Compaction for Horizontal Machines', *IEEE Trans. on Computers*, **C-30**, 7, July, 460–477.

Davidson, S. (1988), 'High Level Microprogramming Languages' in Habib (1988), 145–190.

Dawkins, R. (1986) *The Blind Watchmaker*, W.W. Norton & Company, New York.

de Bakker, J. (1980), *Mathematical Theory of Program Correctness*, Prentice-Hall International, Englewood Cliffs, NJ.

de Kleer, J. (1986a) 'An Assumption-based TMS', *Artificial Intelligence*, **28**, 127–162.

de Kleer, J. (1986b) 'Extending the ATMS', *Artificial Intelligence*, **28**, 163–196.

de Kleer, J. (1986c) 'Problem Solving with the ATMS', *Artificial Intelligence*, **28**, 197–224.

de Kleer, J. (1988) 'A General Labeling Algorithm for Assumption-based Truth Maintenance', *Proc. AAAI-Conf.* (AAAI-88), 199–204.

de Millo, R., Lipton, R.J. and Perlis, A. (1979) 'Social Processes and Proofs of Theorems and Programs', *Comm. ACM*, **22**, 5, May, 271–280.

Dennis, J.B. (1974) 'First Version of A Data Flow Procedural Language', *Proc. Colloque sur la Programmation*, Lecture Notes in Computer Science, Springer-Verlag, Berlin, 362–376.

Dewey, A. (1983) 'VHSIC Hardware Description (VHDL) Development Program', *Proc. 20th Design Automation Conf.*, IEEE Press, New York.

Dieter, G.E. (1983), *Engineering Design: A Materials and Processing Approach*, McGraw-Hill, New York.

Dijkstra, E.W. (1968), 'Go to Statements Considered Harmful' (Letter to the Editor), *Comm. ACM*, **11**, 3, March, 147–148.

Dijkstra, E.W. (1972) 'Notes on Structured Programming' in O.J. Dahl, E.W. Dijkstra, and C.A.R. Hoare, *Structured Programming*, Academic Press, New York.

Dijkstra, E.W. (1976) *A Discipline of Programming*, Prentice-Hall, Englewood Cliffs, NJ.

Dijkstra, E.W. (1980) 'Some Beautiful Arguments Using Mathematical Induction', *Acta Informatica*, **13**, 1, Jan.

Djordjevic, J., Ibbett, R.N. and Barbacci, M.R. (1980) 'Evaluation of Computer Architecture Using ISPS', *Proc. IEE (U.K.)*, **127**, 4, Part E, 126–135.

Doeringer, S., Mitten, D.G. and Steinberg, A. (Eds.) (1970) *Art and Technology: A Symposium on Classical Bronzes*, MIT Press, Cambridge, MA.

Doran, R.W. (1979) *Computer Architecture: A Structured Approach*, Academic Press, New York.

Dworkin, R. (1986) *Law's Empire*, Belknap Press of the Harvard University Press, Cambridge, MA.

Doyle, J. (1979a) 'A Truth Maintenance System', *Artificial Intelligence*, **12**, 231–272.

Doyle, J. (1979b) 'A Glimpse of Truth Maintenance', in *Artificial Intelligence: An MIT Perspective*, P.H. Winston and R.H. Brown (Eds.), MIT Press, Cambridge, MA, 119–136.

Eckhouse, R.H. Jr. (1971) 'A High Level Microprogramming Language (MPL)', Ph.D. Thesis, Dept. of Computer Science, State University of New York, Buffalo, N.Y.

Ernst, G.W. and Newell, A. (1969) *GPS: A Case Study in Generality and Problem Solving*, Academic Press, New York.

Fetzer, J.H. (1988) 'Program Verification: The Very Idea', *Comm. ACM*, **31**, 9, Sept., 1048–1063.

Feyerabend, P. (1978) *Against Method*, Verso, London.

Fisher, J.A. (1981) 'Trace Scheduling: A Technique for Global Microcode Compaction', *IEEE Trans. on Comput.*, **C-30**, 7, July, 478–490.

Fisher, J.A. (1983) 'Very Long Instruction Word Architectures and the ELI-512', in *Proc. 10th Annual Int. Symp. on Comp. Arch.*, IEEE Comp. Soc. Press, New York, 140–150.

Fisher, J.A. *et al.* (1984) 'Parallel Processing: A Smart Compiler and a Dumb Machine', *Proc. SIGPLAN Symp. on Compiler Construction*, ACM, New York, 37–47.

Floyd, R.W. (1961) 'A Descriptive Language for Symbol Manipulation', *J. ACM*, **8**, 4, 579–584.

Floyd, R.W. (1967) 'Assigning Meaning to Programs', *Mathematical Aspects of Computer Science*, Amer. Math. Soc., Providence, R.I.

Flynn, M.J. (1980) 'Directions and Issues in Architecture and Language', *Computer*, **13**, 10, Oct., 5–22.

Flynn, M.J. and Huck, J.C. (1984) 'Emulation' in *Handbook of Software Engineering*, C.R. Vick and C.V. Ramamoorthy (Eds.), van Nostrand-Reinhold, New York, 134–148.

Freeman, P. (1980a) 'The Context of Design' in *Software Design Techniques*, P. Freeman and A.J. Wasserman (Eds.), IEEE, New York, 2–5.

Freeman, P. (1980b) 'The Central Role of Design in Software Engineering: Implications for Research', in *Software Engineering*, H. Freeman and P.M. Lewis II (Eds.), Academic Press, New York.

Freeman, P. (1987) *Software Perspectives*, Addison-Wesley, Reading, MA.

Gajski, D. (Ed.) (1988) *Silicon Compilation*, Addison-Wesley, Reading, MA.

Gajski, D.D. and Kuhn, R.H. (1983) 'New VLSI Tools', *Computer*, **16**, 12, Dec., 11–14.

Gajski, D.D. and Thomas, D.E. (1988) 'Introduction to Silicon Compilation', in Gajski (1988), 1–48.

Garey, M.R. and Johnson, D.S. (1979) *Computers and Intractability: A Guide to the Theory of NP-Completeness*, W.H. Freeman & Co., San Francisco, CA.

Genesereth, M.R. and Nilsson, N.J. (1987) *Logical Foundations of Artificial Intelligence*, Morgan Kauffman, Los Altos, CA.

Gero, J.S. (Ed.) (1985) *Knowledge Engineering in Computer-Aided Design*, North-Holland, Amsterdam.

Gero, J.S. and Coyne, R.D. (1987) 'Knowledge-Based Planning as a Design Paradigm', in *Design Theory for CAD*, H. Yoshikawa and E.A. Warman (Eds.), Elsevier Science Publishers, Amsterdam, 339–373.

Gilman, A.S. (1986) 'VHDL – The Designer Environment', *IEEE Design & Test of Computers*, **3**, 2, April, 42–47.

Gombrich, E.H. (1972) *The Story of Art*, 13th Edition, Phaidon Press, London.

Gopalakrishnan, G.C., Smith, D.R. and Srivas, M.K. (1985), 'An Algebraic Approach to the Specification and Realization of VLSI Designs', in *Proc. 7th Int. Symp. on Computer Hardware Desc. Languages & Their Applications* (CHDL-85), C.J. Koomen and T. Moko-oka (Eds.), North-Holland, Amsterdam, 16–38.

Gopalakrishnan, G.C., Srivas, M.K. and Smith, D.R. (1987), 'From Algebraic Specifications to Correct VLSI Circuits', in *From HDL Descriptions to Guaranteed Correct Circuit Design*, D. Borrione (Ed.), North-Holland, Amsterdam.

Gordon, M.J.C. (1979), *The Denotational Description of Programming Languages*, Springer-Verlag, Berlin.

Gordon, M.J.C. (1986) 'Why Higher-Order Logic is a Good Formalism for Specifying and Verifying Hardware, in *Formal Aspects of VLSI Design*, G.J. Milne and P.A. Subrahmanayam (Eds.), Elsevier Science Publishers, Amsterdam, 153–177.

Gordon, M.J.C. (1988a) *Programming Language Theory and its Implementation*, Prentice-Hall, New York.

Gordon, M.J.C. (1988b) 'HOL – A Proof Generating System for Higher Order Logic', in *VLSI Specification, Verification and Synthesis*, G. Birtwistle and P.A. Subrahmanayam (Eds.), Kluwer Academic Publishers, Boston, MA. 73–128.

Gould, S.J. (1977) *Ontogeny and Phylogeny*, Belknap Press of the Harvard University Press, Cambridge, MA.

Grasselli, A. and Montanari, U. (1970) 'On the Minimization of Read-Only Memories in Microprogrammed Digital Computers', *IEEE Trans. on Comput,* **C-19**, 11, Nov., 1111–1114.

Green, C. and Barstow, D. (1978) 'On Program Synthesis Knowledge', *Artificial Intelligence,* **10**, 241–279.

Gries, D.G. (1971) *Compiler Construction for Digital Computers,* John Wiley, New York.

Gries, D.G. (1981) *The Science of Programming,* Springer-Verlag, New York.

Habib, S. (Ed.) (1988) *Microprogramming and Firmware Engineering Methods,* van Nostrand-Reinhold, New York.

Hadley, G.F. (1962) *Linear Programming,* Addison-Wesley, Reading, MA.

Hadley, G.F. (1967) *Introduction to Probability and Statistical Decision Theory,* Holden-Day, San Francisco, CA.

Haken, W., Appel, K. and Koch, J. (1977) 'Every Planar Map is Four Colorable', *Illinois J. Math.,* **21**, 84, 429–567.

Hanna, F.K. and Daeche, N. (1985) 'Specification and Verification Using Higher Order Logic', in *Proc. 7th Int. Symp. on Computer Hardware Description Languages and Their Applications (CHDL 85),* C.J. Koomen and T. Moto-oka (Eds.), North-Holland, Amsterdam, 418–433.

Hanson, N.R. (1972) *Patterns of Discovery,* Cambridge University Press, Cambridge, U.K.

Harré, R. (1985) *The Philosophies of Science: An Introductory Survey,* Oxford University Press, Oxford.

Hayes, I. (1985), 'Specification Case Studies', Tech. Monograph PRG-46, Programming Research Group, Oxford University Computing Laboratory, Oxford, U.K.

Hayes, J.P. (1984) *Digital Systems and Microprocessors,* McGraw-Hall, New York.

Hayes, J.P. (1988) *Computer Architecture and Organization,* McGraw-Hill, New York.

Heidegger, M. (1962), *Being and Time*, Harper and Row, New York.

Hempel, C.G. (1965) *Aspects of Scientific Explanation*, Free Press, New York.

Henderson, P. (1980) *Functional Programming: Application and Implementation*, Prentice-Hall International, Englewood Cliffs, NJ.

Hennessy, J.L. (1984) 'VLSI Processor Architecture', *IEEE Trans. Computers*, **C-33**, 12, Dec., 1221–1246.

Hennessy, J.L. and Gross, T. (1983) 'Postpass Code Optimization of Pipeline Constraints', *ACM Trans. Prog. Lang. & Syst.*, **5**, 3, 422–448.

Hoare, C.A.R. (1969) 'An Axiomatic Approach to Computer Programming', *Comm. ACM*, **12**, 10, Oct., 576–580, 583.

Hoare, C.A.R. (1985) *Communicating Sequential Processes*, Prentice-Hall International, Englewood Cliffs, NJ.

Hoare, C.A.R. (1986) 'The Mathematics of Programming', Inaugural Lecture, Univ. of Oxford, Clarendon Press, Oxford, U.K.

Hoare, C.A.R. (1987) 'An Overview of Some Formal Methods for Program Design', *Computer*, **20**, 9, Sept., 85–91.

Hoare, C.A.R. and Shepherdson, J.C. (Eds.) (1985) *Mathematical Logic and Programming Languages*, Prentice-Hall, Englewood Cliffs, NJ.

Hoare, C.A.R. and Wirth, N. (1973), 'An Axiomatic Definition of the Programming Language Pascal', *Acta Informatica*, **2**, 335–355.

Hoevel, L.W. (1974) 'Ideal Directly Executed Languages: An Analytical Argument for Emulation', *IEEE Trans. on Comput.*, **C-23**, 8, Aug., 759–767.

Hoevel, L.W. and Flynn, M.J. (1977) 'The Structure of Directly Executed Languages: A New Theory of Interpretive System Design', Tech. Rept. 130, Computer Syst. Lab., Stanford University, Stanford, CA.

Holton, G. (1952) *Introduction to Concepts and Theories in Physical Science*, Addison-Wesley, Reading, MA.

Holton, G. and Elkana, Y. (Eds.) (1982) *Albert Einstein: Historical and Cultural Perspectives*, Princeton University Press, Princeton, NJ.

Hooton, A. (1987) 'The Plausible Design of CASE: A Computer Architecture Simulation Engine', M.S. Thesis, Center for Advanced Computer Studies, University of Southwestern Louisiana, Lafayette, LA.

Hooton, A., Aguero, U. and Dasgupta, S. (1988), 'An Exercise in Plausibility Driven Design', *Computer*, **21**, 7, July, 21–31.

Horowitz, E. and Sahni, S. (1978) *Fundamentals of Computer Algorithms*, Computer Science Press, Rockville, MD.

Hume, D. (1977) *An Enquiry Concerning Human Understanding* (First published 1748), Edited by E. Steinberg, Hackett Publishing Co., Indianapolis, IN.

Hunt, W.A. (1987) 'The Mechanical Verification of a Microprocessor Design', in *From HDL Descriptions to Guaranteed Correct Circuit Designs*, D. Borrione (Ed.), North-Holland, Amsterdam, 89–129.

Hwang, K. and Briggs, F.A. (1984) *Computer Architecture and Parallel Processing*, McGraw-Hill, New York.

IBM (1981) *IBM System/370 Principles of Operation*, GA 22-7000-8, IBM Corporation, White Plains, N.Y.

IEEE (1988) Special Report on Good Design, *IEEE Spectrum*, **24**, 5.

IEEE (1988) 'Standard VHDL Language Reference Manual – Std 1076-1987', IEEE, New York.

Inmos (1984), *Occam Programming Manual*, Inmos Ltd., Prentice-Hall International, Englewood Cliffs, NJ.

Intermetrics (1984a) 'VHDL Language Requirements' Rept. IR-MD-020-1, July 1984, Intermetrics, Inc., Bethesda, MD.

Intermetrics (1984b) 'VHDL Language Reference Manual: Version 5.O.', Rept. IR-MD-025-1, July 1984, Intermetrics, Inc., Bethesda, MD.

Intermetrics (1985) 'VHDL Language Reference Manual, Version 7.2', Rept. IR-MD-045-2, Aug., Intermetrics, Inc., Bethesda, MD.

Jackson, L.W. and Dasgupta, S. (1974), 'The Identification of Parallel Microoperations', *Information Proc. Letters*, **2**, March, 180–184.

Jackson, M.A. (1983) *System Development*, Prentice-Hall International, Englewood Cliffs, NJ.

Jammer, M. (1982) 'Einstein and Quantum Physics' in Holton and Elkana (1982), 59–78.

Jansen, H.W. (1969) *History of Art*, Prentice-Hall, Englewood Cliffs, NJ. and Harry N. Abrams, New York.

Jenkins, G.M. and Watts, D.G. (1968) *Spectral Analysis and its Applications*, Holden-Day, San Francisco, CA.

Johannsen, D. (1979) 'Bristle Blocks: A Silicon Compiler', *Proc. 16th Design Automation Conference*, ACM, New York, 310–313.

Johnson-Laird, P.N. (1988), *The Computer and the Mind*, Harvard University Press, Cambridge, MA.

Jones, C.B. (1980) *Software Development – A Rigorous Approach*, Prentice-Hall International, Englewood Cliffs, NJ.

Jones, C.B. (1986) *Systematic Software Development using VDM*, Prentice-Hall International, Englewood Cliffs, NJ.

Jones, J.C. (1963) 'A Method of Systematic Design', in *Conference on Design Methods*, J.C. Jones and D. Thornley (Eds.), Pergamon Press, Oxford, 10–31. Reprinted in Cross (1984), 9–32.

Jones, J.C. (1980), *Design Methods: Seeds of Human Futures*, 2nd Edition, John Wiley & Sons, New York.

Jones, J.C. (1984) *Essays in Design*, John Wiley & Sons, New York.

Joyce, J.J. (1988) 'Formal Verification and Implementation of a Microprocessor', in *VLSI Specification, Verification and Synthesis,*, G. Birtwistle and P.A. Subrahmanayam (Eds.), Kluwer Academic Publishers, Boston, MA. 129–157.

Kachian, L.G. (1979) 'A Polynomial Algorithm in Linear Programming', *Soviet Math. Dokl.*, **20**, 191–194.

Kalay, Y.E. (1987), 'Preface' in *Computability of Design*, Y.E. Kalay (Ed.), John Wiley and Sons, New York, xi–xiii.

Kant, E. (1985) 'Understanding and Automating Algorithm Design', *IEEE Trans. on Soft. Engg.*, **SE-11**, 11, Nov., 1361–1374.

Kant, E. and Newell, A. (1984) 'Problem Solving Techniques for the Design of Algorithms', *Info.Proc. and Mgmt.*, **20**, 1–2, 97–118.

Katevenis, M.G.H. (1985) *Reduced Instruction Set Computer Architectures for VLSI*, MIT Press, Cambridge, MA.

Katsuki, D. *et al.* (1978) 'Pluribus – An Operational Fault-Tolerant Multiprocessor', *Proc. IEEE*, **66**, 10, Oct., 1146–1159.

Katzman, J.A. (1977) 'The Tandem 16: A Fault Tolerant Computing System', Tandem Computers Inc. Reprinted in Siewiorek, Bell and Newell (1982), 470–480.

Kettlewell, H.B.D. (1959) 'Darwin's Missing Evidence', *Scientific American*, March. Reprinted in *Facets of Genetics*, A.A. Srb, R.D. Owen and R.S. Edgar (Eds.), W.H. Freeman, San Francisco, CA, 1969.

Klassen, A. and Dasgupta, S. (1981) 'S*(QM-1): An Instantiation of the High Level Microprogramming Language Schema S* for the Nanodata QM-1'. *Proc. 14th Annual Microprogramming Workshop* (MICRO-14), IEEE Comp. Soc. Press, New York, 126–130.

Kleir, R.L. and Ramamoorthy, C.V. (1971), 'Optimization Strategies for Microprograms', *IEEE Trans. on Computers*, **C-20**, 7, July, 783–795.

Knuth, D.E. (1971) 'An Empirical Study of FORTRAN Programs', *Software – Practice and Experience*, **1**, 105–133.

Knuth, D.E. (1974), 'Structured Programming with Go To Statements', *ACM Comp. Surveys*, **5**, 4, Dec., 261–301.

Kogge, P.M. (1981) *The Architecture of Pipelined Computers*, McGraw-Hill, New York.

Kohavi, Z. (1970) *Switching and Finite Automata Theory*, McGraw-Hill, New York.

Kowalski, T.J. (1985) *An Artificial Intelligence Approach to VLSI Design*, Kluwer, Boston, MA.

Kowalski, T.J. (1988) 'The VLSI Design Automation Assistance: An Architecture Compiler', in Gajski (1988), 122–152.

Kowalski, T.J. and Thomas, D.E. (1984) 'The VLSI Design Automation Assistant: An IBM System/370 Design', *IEEE Design and Test*, **1**, 1, Feb., 60–69.

Kowalski, T.J. *et al.* (1985) 'The VLSI Design Automation Assistant: From Algorithms to Silicon', *IEEE Design and Test*, **2**, 3, Aug., 33–43.

Koyre, A. (1968) *Newtonian Studies*, University of Chicago Press, Chicago, IL.

Kraft, G.P. and Toy, W.N. (1981) *Microprogrammed Control and Reliable Design of Small Computers*, Prentice-Hall, Englewood Cliffs, NJ.

Kuck, D.J. (1978) *The Structure of Computers and Computation*, Vol. 1, John Wiley, New York.

Kuck, D.J. *et al.* (1980) 'The Structure of an Advanced Retargetable Vectorizer', *Proc. of COMPSAC 80*, IEEE Comp. Soc., New York.

Kuck, D.J. *et al.* (1981) 'Dependence Graphs and Compiler Organization', *Proc. 8th Annual ACM Symp. on Principles of Prog. Lang.*, ACM, New York, 207–218.

Kuhn, T.S. (1957) *The Copernican Revolution*, Harvard University Press, Cambridge, MA.

Kuhn, T.S. (1962) *The Structure of Scientific Revolutions*, University of Chicago Press, Chicago, IL.

Kuhn, T.S. (1970a) 'Postscript – 1969' in *The Structure of Scientific Revolutions*, Enlarged 2nd Edition, University of Chicago Press, Chicago, IL, 174–210.

Kuhn, T.S. (1970b) 'Reflections on my Critics', in Lakatos and Musgrave (1970), 231–278.

Kuhn, T.S. (1977) 'Second Thoughts on Paradigms' in Suppe (1977b), 459–482. Reprinted in T.S. Kuhn, *The Essential Tension*, University of Chicago Press, Chicago, IL, 1977.

Lachman, R., Lachman, J.L. and Butterfield, E.C. (1979), *Cognitive Psychology and Information Processing*, Lawrence Erlbaum Associates, Hillsdale, NJ.

Laird, J.E., Newell, A. and Rosenbloom, P.S. (1987) 'SOAR: An Architecture for General Intelligence', *Artificial Intelligence*, **33**, 1–64.

Lakatos, I. (1970) 'Falsification and the Methodology of Scientific Research Programmes', in Lakatos and Musgrave (1970), 91–196.

Lakatos, I. (1976) *Proofs and Refutations*, Cambridge University Press, Cambridge, U.K.

Lakatos, I. (1978) *The Methodology of Scientific Research Programmes*, Cambridge University Press, Cambridge, U.K.

Lakatos, I. and Musgrave, A. (Eds.) (1970) *Criticism and the Growth of Knowledge*, Cambridge University Press, Cambridge, U.K.

Landry, S. *et al.* (1988) 'PDI: A Plausibility-Driven User Interface for UNIX', Working Documents, Center for Advanced Computer Studies, University of Southwestern Louisiana, Lafayette, LA.

Landskov, D. *et al.* (1980) 'Local Microcode Compaction Techniques', *ACM Comp. Surveys*, **12**, 3, Sept., 261–294.

Langdon, G.G. Jr., (1974), *Logic Design: A Review of Theory and Practice*, Academic Press, New York.

Langley, P. *et al.* (1987) *Scientific Discovery: Computational Explorations of the Creative Processes*, MIT Press, Cambridge, MA.

Laudan, L. (1977) *Progress and Its Problems*, University of California Press, Los Angeles.

Laudan, L. (1984), *Science and Values*, University of California Press, Berkeley, CA.

Lawrence, M.J. (1982) 'An Examination of Evolution Dynamics', *Proc. 6th Int. Conf. on Soft. Engg.*, IEEE Comp. Soc. Press, New York, 188–196.

Lawson, B. (1980), *How Designers Think: The Design Process Demystified*, Architectural Press, London.

Leeman, G.B., Carter, W.C. and Birman, A. (1974), 'Some Techniques for Microprogram Validation', in *Information Processing 74* (Proc. IFIP Congress), North-Holland, Amsterdam, 76–80.

Lehman, M.M. (1974) 'Programs, Cities and Students – Limits to Growth?', Inaug. Lect., Imperial College of Science and Technology. Reprinted in *Programming Methodology*, D. Gries (Ed.), Springer-Verlag, Berlin, 42–69.

Lehman, M.M. (1980a) 'Programs, Life Cycles and Laws of Program Evolution', *Proc. IEEE*, **68**, 9, 1060–1076. Reprinted in Lehman and Belady (1985), 393–450.

Lehman, M.M. (1980b) 'On Understanding Laws, Evolution and Conservation in Large Program Life Cycles', *J. Syst. and Software*, **1**, 3. Reprinted in Lehman and Belady (1985), 375–392.

Lehman, M.M. (1984) 'Program Evolution', *Info. Proc. and Mgmt.*, **20**, 1–2, 19–36.

Lehman, M.M. and Belady, L.A. (1985) *Program Evolution: Processes of Software Change*, Academic Press, New York.

Lenat, D.B. (1982) 'The Nature of Heuristics', *Artificial Intelligence*, **19**, 2, 189–249.

Levy, H.M. (1984) *Capability-Based Computer Systems*, Digital Press, Bedford, MA.

Levy, L.M. and Pollacia, L.F. (1988) 'PDI Constraints', Working Document, Project on PDI: A Plausibility Driven User Interface, Center for Advanced Computer Studies, University of Southwestern Louisiana, Lafayette, LA.

Linn, J.L. (1988) 'Horizontal Microcode Compaction', in Habib (1988), 381–432.

Lipsett, R., Schaefer, C. and Ussery, C. (1989), *VHDL: Hardware Description and Design*, Kluwer Academic Publishers, Boston, MA.

Liskov, B. (1980) 'Modular Program Construction Using Abstractions', in *Abstract Software Specifications*, D. Bjorner (Ed.), Lecture Notes in Computer Science, Springer-Verlag, Berlin.

Liskov, B. and Guttag, J. (1986) *Abstraction and Specification in Program Development*, MIT Press, Cambridge, MA.

Liu, Y.-C and Gibson, G.A. (1986) *Microcomputer Systems: The 8086/8088 Family*, 2nd Edition, Prentice-Hall, Englewood Cliffs, NJ.

Losee, J. (1980) *Historical Introduction to the Philosophy of Science*, Oxford University Press, Oxford.

McCluskey, E.J. (1986) *Logic Design Principles with Emphasis on Testable Semicustom Circuits*, Prentice-Hall, Englewood Cliffs, NJ.

McDermott, J. (1982) 'R1: A Rule-Based Configurer of Computer Systems', *Artificial Intelligence*, **19**, 1, Sept., 39–88.

McFarland, M.C., S.J. (1983) 'Computer-Aided Partitioning of Behavioral Hardware Descriptions', *Proc. 20th Design Automation Conf.*, ACM/IEEE, New York.

Maher, M.L. (1988) 'HI-RISE: An Expert System for Preliminary Structural Design', in Rychener (1988), 37–52.

Makarenko, D.D. (1982) 'Simulating Computer Architectures Using the Architecture Description Language S*A', M.Sc. Thesis, Dept. of Computing Science, University of Alberta, Edmonton, Alberta.

Manna, Z. (1974) *Mathematical Theory of Computation*, McGraw-Hill, New York.

March, L. (Ed.) (1976) *The Architecture of Form*, Cambridge University Press, Cambridge, U.K.

Marcus, L., Crocker, S.D. and Landauer, J.R. (1984) 'SDVS: A System for Verifying Microcode Correctness', *Proc. 17th Annual Microprogramming Workshop*, IEEE Comp. Soc. Press, New York, 246–255.

Marsland, T.A. and Demco, J. (1978) 'A Case Study of Computer Emulation', *INFOR* (Canada), **16**, 2, 112–131.

Masterman, M. (1970) 'The Nature of a Paradigm', in Lakatos and Musgrave (1970), 59–90.

Maynard Smith, J. (1975) *The Theory of Evolution*, 3rd Edition, Penguin Books, Harmondsworth, Middlesex.

Mayr. E. (1982) *The Growth of Biological Thought*, The Belknap Press of Harvard University Press, Cambridge, MA.

Medawar, P.B. (1969) 'Induction and Intuition in Scientific Thought', Jayne Lectures for 1968, Amer. Phil. Soc., Philadelphia, PA. Reprinted in Medawar (1982), 73–114.

Medawar, P.B. (1963), 'Hypothesis and Imagination', *Times Literary Supplement*, Oct. 25. Reprinted in Medawar (1982), 115–135.

Medawar, P.B. (1975) 'Technology and Evolution', in *Technology and the Frontiers of Knowledge* (The Frank Nelson Doubleday Lectures 1972–73), Doubleday, New York. Reprinted in Medawar (1982), 184–190.

Medawar, P.B. (1982) *Pluto's Republic*, Oxford University Press, Oxford.

Middendorf, W.H. (1986) *Design of Devices and Systems*, Marcel Dekker, New York.

Miller, G.A. (1956) 'The Magical Number Seven, Plus or Minus Two: Some Limits on Our Capacity for Information Processing', *Psychological Review*, **63**, 81–97.

Miller, G.A., Galanter, E. and Pribram, K.H. (1960) *Plans and the Structure of Behavior*, Henry Holt & Co., New York.

Mills, H.D. (1975) 'The New Math of Computer Programming', *Comm. ACM*, **18**, 1, 43–48.

Mills, H.D. (1976) 'Software Development', *IEEE Trans. on Soft. Engg.*, **SE-2**, 4, Dec.

Milner, R. (1980) *A Calculus of Communicating Systems*, Lecture Notes in Computer Science, Springer-Verlag, Berlin.

Milutinovic, V. (Ed.) (1989) *Tutorial: Microprogramming and Firmware Engineering*, IEEE Comp. Soc. Press, Washington, D.C.

Minsky, M. (1967) *Computation: Finite and Infinite Machines*, Prentice-Hall, Englewood Cliffs, NJ.

Mitchell, T.M., Steinberg, L.I. and Shulman, J.S. (1985) 'A Knowledge-Based Approach to Design', *IEEE Trans. on Pattern Anal. & Machine Int.*, **PAMI-7**, 5, Sept., 502–510.

Morse, S.P., Isaacson, E.J. and Albert, D.J. (1987) *The 80386/387 Architecture*, John Wiley & Sons, New York.

Mostow, J. (1985) 'Towards Better Models of Design Processes', *AI Magazine*, Spring, 44–57.

Mostow, J. and Balzer, R. (1983) 'A Program-Transformation Approach to VLSI Design', in *Report: VLSI and Software Engineering Workshop*, IEEE Comp. Soc. Press, Silver Spring, MD, 126–133.

Mueller, R.A. and Varghese, J. (1985) 'Knowledge-Based Code Selection in Retargetable Microcode Synthesis', *IEEE Design and Test*, **2**, 3, 44–55.

Mueller, R.A. and Varghese, J. (1988) 'Fundamental Concepts of Microprogramming', in Habib (1988), 33–94.

Mueller, R.A. *et al.* (1988) 'Horizon: A Retargetable Compiler for Horizontal Microarchitectures', *IEEE Trans. on Soft. Engg.*, **14**, 5, May, 515–583.

Muroga, S. (1982), *VLSI System Design*, John Wiley and Sons, New York.

Musa, J.D. (1980), 'Software Reliability Measurement', *J. of Systems and Software*, **1**, 3, 223–241.

Musa, J.D. (1984) 'Software Reliability', in *Software Engineering Handbook*, C.R. Vick and C.V. Ramamoorthy (Eds.), van Nostrand-Reinhold, New York, 392–412.

Myers, G.J. (1982) *Advances in Computer Architecture*, John Wiley, New York.

Nanodata (1979) *The QM-1 Hardware Level User's Manual*, Nanodata Corporation, Williamsburg, N.Y.

Nash, J.D. and Saunders, L.F. (1986) 'VHDL Critique', *IEEE Design and Test*, **3**, 2, April, 54–65.

Naur, P. (Ed.) (1963) 'Revised Report on the Algorithmic Language Algol 60', *Numerische Mathematik*, **4**, 420–453.

Nervi, P.L. (1957), *The Works of Pier Luigi Nervi*, F.A. Praeger, New York.

Nervi, P.L. (1966) *Aesthetics and Technology in Building* (The Charles Eliot Norton Lectures), Harvard University Press, Cambridge, MA.

Neuhauser, C.J. and Flynn, M.J. (1988) 'An Emulation Environment and its Application', in Habib (1988), 275–336.

Newell, A., Shaw, J.C. and Simon, H.A. (1960) 'Report on a General Problem-Solving Program for a Computer', in *Information Processing* (Proc. of the International Conference on Information Processing), UNESCO, Paris, 256–264.

Newell, A. and Simon, H.A. (1972) *Human Problem Solving*, Prentice-Hall, Englewood Cliffs, NJ.

Newell, A. and Simon, H.A. (1976), 'Computer Science as Empirical Inquiry: Symbols and Search' (ACM Turing Award Lecture), *Comm. ACM*, **19**, 3, March, 113–126.

Norman, D.A. (1981) 'The Trouble with Unix', *Datamation*, Nov., 139–150.

Norman, D.A. (1986) 'Cognitive Engineering', *User Centered System Design*, D.A. Norman and S.W. Draper (Eds.), Erlbaum Associates, Hillsdale, NJ.

Olafsson, M. (1981) 'The QM-C: A C-Oriented Instruction Set Architecture for the Nanodata QM-1', Tech. Rept. TR81-11, Dept. of Computing Science, University of Alberta, Edmonton, Alberta.

Owicki, S. and Gries, D.G. (1976) 'An Axiomatic Proof Technique for Parallel Programs', *Acta Informatica*, **6**, 319–340.

Owicki, S. and Lamport, L. (1982) 'Proving Liveness Properties of Concurrent Programs', *ACM. Trans. on Prog. Lang. & Syst.*, **4**, 3, July, 455–495.

Pais, A. (1982) *'Subtle is the Lord. . .': The Science and Life of Albert Einstein*, Oxford University Press, Oxford.

Papert, S. (1988) 'One AI or Many', *Daedalus*, Winter; also *Proc. Amer. Academy of Arts and Sciences*, **117**, 1, 1–14.

Parnas, D.L. (1972) 'On the Criteria to be Used in Decomposing Systems into Modules', *Comm. ACM*, **5**, 12, Dec., 1053–1058.

Parnas, D.L. (1979) 'The Role of Program Specifications', in *Research Directions in Software Technology*, P. Wegner (Ed.), MIT Press, Cambridge, MA, 364–370.

Parker, A.C. (1984) 'Automated Synthesis of Digital Systems', *IEEE Design and Test*, **1**, 4, 75–81.

Partington, J.R. (1960) *A Short History of Chemistry*, 3rd Edition, MacMillan & Co., London.

Patel, S. (1990) 'Computer-Aided Tools for Plausibility-Driven Designs', Ph.D. Thesis, Center for Advanced Computer Studies, University of Southwestern Louisiana, Lafayette, LA.

Patel, S. and Dasgupta, S. (1989) 'Automated Belief Revision in Plausibility-Driven Designs', Tech. Rept. TR-89-2-1, Center for Advanced Computer Studies, University of Southwestern Louisiana, Lafayette, LA.

Patterson, D.A. (1976), 'STRUM: A Structured Microprogram Development System for Correct Firmware', *IEEE Trans. on Computers*, **C-25**, 10, Oct., 974–985.

Patterson, D.A. (1985) 'Reduced Instruction Set Computers', *Comm. ACM*, **28**, 1, Jan., 8–21.

Patterson, D.A. and Dietzel, D. (1980) 'The Case for the Reduced Instruction Set Computer', *Computer Architecture News* (SIGARCH), **8**, 6, 25–33.

Patterson, D.A. and Sequin, C. (1981) 'RISC I: A Reduced Instruction Set Computer', *Proc. 8th Ann. Int. Symp. on Comp. Architecture*, IEEE Comp. Soc. Press, Los Angeles, 443–458.

Patterson, D.A. and Sequin, C. (1982), 'A VLSI RISC', *Computer*, **15**, 9, Sept. 8–21.

Pevsner, N. (1963) *An Outline of European Architlecture*, Penguin Books, Harmondsworth, Middlesex.

Piloty, R. and Borrione, D. (1985) 'The Conlan Project: Concepts, Implementations and Applications', *Computer*, **18**, 2, Feb., 81–93.

Piloty, R. *et al.* (1983) *CONLAN Report*, Lecture Notes in Computer Science, Springer-Verlag, Berlin.

Pitchumani, V. and Stabler, E.P. (1983) 'An Inductive Assertion Method for Register Transfer Level Design Verification', *IEEE Trans. on Comput.*, **C-32**, 12, Dec., 1073–1080.

Pólya, G. (1945) *How to Solve It*, Princeton University Press, Princeton, NJ. (2nd Edition, 1957).

Popper, K.R. (1965) *Conjectures and Refutations: The Growth of Scientific Knowledge*, Harper and Row, New York.

Popper, K.R. (1968) *The Logic of Scientific Discovery*, Harper and Row, New York.

Popper, K.R. (1972) *Objective Knowledge: An Evolutionary Approach*, Clarendon Press, Oxford.

Post, E. (1943) 'Formal Reductions of the General Combinatorial Decision Problem, *Amer. J. of Math.*, **65**, 197–268.

Ramamoorthy, C.V. and Tsuchiya, M. (1974) 'A High-Level Language for Horizontal Microprogramming', *IEEE Trans. on Computers*, **C-23**, 8, Aug., 791–801.

Ramamoorthy, C.V. *et al.* (1987) 'Issues in the Development of Large, Distributed and Reliable Software', in *Advances in Computers*, Vol. 26, M.C. Yovits (Ed.), Academic Press, New York, 393–443.

Rehak, D.R., Howard, H.C. and Sriram, D. (1985) 'Architecture of an Integrated Knowledge Based Environment for Structural Engineering Applications', in Gero (1985), 89–117.

Reiter, R. (1987) 'Nonmonotonic Reasoning' *Annual Review of Computer Science*, **2**, 147–186.

Rittell, H.W. and Webber, M.M. (1973) 'Planning Problems are Wicked Problems', *Policy Sciences*, **4**, 155–169. Reprinted in Cross (1984), 135–144.

Ross, D.T. (1977) 'Structured Analysis (SA): A Language for Communicating Ideas', *IEEE Trans. on Soft. Engg.*, **SE-3**, 1, 15–34.

Ross, D.T. (1985), 'Applications and Extensions of SADT', *Computer*, **18**, 4, April, 25–34.

Ross, D.T. and Schoman, K.E. (1977) 'Structured Analysis for Requirements Definition', *IEEE Trans. on Soft. Engg.*, **SE-3**, 1, Jan., 6–15.

Rubin, S.M. (1987), *Computer Aids for VLSI Design*, Addison-Wesley, Reading, MA.

Ruse, M. (1986) *Taking Darwin Seriously*, Basil Blackwell, Oxford.

Rychener, M.D. (Ed.) (1988) *Expert Systems for Engineering Design*, Academic Press, New York.

Sacerdoti, E.D. (1977) *A Structure for Plans and Behavior*, Elsevier, New York.

Sahni, S. and Bhatt, A. (1980) 'The Complexity of Design Automation Problems', *Proc. 17th Design Automation Conference*, ACM/IEEE, New York, 402–411.

Salisbury, A.B. (1976) *Microprogrammable Computer Architectures*, Elsevier, New York.

Scherlis, W.L. and Scott, D.S. (1983) 'First Steps Towards Inferential Programming', *Information Processing* **83** (Proc. IFIP Congress), North-Holland, Amsterdam, 199–212.

Schön, D.A. (1983) *The Reflective Practitioner*, Basic Books, New York.

Scott, D. (1970) 'Outline of a Mathematical Theory of Computation', *Proc. 4th Annual Princeton Conf. on Info. Sciences & Systems*, Princeton, NJ., 169–176.

Sedgewick, R. (1983) *Algorithms*, Addison-Wesley, Reading, MA.

Shahdad, M. *et al.* (1985) 'VHDL Hardware Description Language', *Computer*, **18**, 2, Feb., 94–103.

Shapere, D. (1964) 'The Structure of Scientific Revolutions', *Philosophical Review*, **73**, 383–394.

Shapere, D. (1966) 'Meaning and Scientific Change' in *Mind & Cosmos: Essays in Contemporary Science and Philosophy*, R.G. Colodny (Ed.), University of Pittsburgh Press, Pittsburgh, PA, 41–85.

Shoenfield, J.R. (1967) *Mathematical Logic*, Addison-Wesley, Reading, MA.

Shostak, R.E. (1983) 'Formal Verification of Circuit Designs', *Proc. 6th Int. Symp. on Computer Hardware Description Languages and Their Applications (CHDL 83)*, T. Uehara and M.R. Barbacci (Eds.), North-Holland, Amsterdam, 13–30.

Siddall, J.N. (1982) *Optimal Engineering Design: Principles and Applications*, M. Dekker, New York.

Siewiorek, D.P., Bell, C.G., and Newell, A. (1982) *Computer Structures: Principles and Examples*, McGraw-Hill, New York.

Siewiorek, D.P. and Swarz, R.S. (1982) *The Theory and Practice of Reliable System Design*, Digital Press, Bedford, MA.

Siewiorek, D.P. *et al.* (1978), 'C.Vmp: A Voted Multiprocessor', *Proc. IEEE*, **66**, 10, Oct., 1190–1198.

Simon, H.A. (1973), 'The Structure of Ill Structured Problems', *Artificial Intelligence*, 4, 181–200. Reprinted in Cross (1984), 145–165.

Simon, H.A. (1975) 'Style in Design' in *Spatial Synthesis in Computer Aided Building Design*, C.M. Eastman (Ed.), John Wiley & Sons, New York.

Simon, H.A. (1976) *Administrative Behavior*, 3rd Edition, The Free Press, New York.

Simon, H.A. (1981), *The Sciences of the Artificial*, 2nd Edition, MIT Press, Cambridge, MA.

Simon, H.A. (1982) *Models of Bounded Rationality, Vol. 2*, MIT Press, Cambridge, MA.

Sint, M. (1980) 'A Survey of High Level Microprogramming Languages', *Proc 13th Annual Workshop on Microprogramming*, ACM/IEEE, New York, 141–153.

Smith, A.J. (1982) 'Cache Memories', *ACM Comp. Surveys*, 14, 3, Sept., 473–529.

Smith, B.C. (1985) 'Prologue to "Reflection and Semantics in a Procedural Language" ', in Brachman and Levesque (1985), 31–40.

Sommerville, I. (1985) *Software Engineering*, 2nd Edition, Addison-Wesley, Reading, MA.

Soundarajan, N. (1984) 'A Proof Technique for Parallel Programs', *Theoretical Computer Science*, **31**, 1 & 2, May, 13–29.

Shriver, B.D. and Wegner, P. (Eds.) (1987) *Research Directions in Object Oriented Programming*, MIT Press, Cambridge, MA.

Sriram, D., Maher, M.L. and Fenves, S.J. (1984) 'Knowledge-Based Expert Systems in Structural Design', Tech. Rept. DRC-12-24-84, Engineering Design Research Center, Carnegie-Mellon University, Pittsburgh, PA.

Steadman, P. (1979) *The Evolution of Designs*, Cambridge University Press, Cambridge, U.K.

Stone, H.S. (1987) *High Performance Computer Architecture*, Addison-Wesley, Reading, MA.

Stoy, J.E. (1977) *Denotational Semantics: The Scott–Strachey Approach to Programming Language Theory*, MIT Press, Cambridge, MA.

Strecker, W.D. and Clark, D.W. (1980) 'Comments on "The Case for the Reduced Instruction Set Computer" by Patterson and Ditzel', *Computer Architecture News* (SIGARCH), **8**, 6, 34–38.

Stritter, S. and Tredennick, N. (1978) 'Microprogrammed Implementation of a Single Chip Microprocessor', in *Proc. 11th Annual Microprogramming Workshop*, ACM/IEEE, New York, 8–16.

Sturt, G. (1923) *The Wheelwright's Shop*, Cambridge University Press, Cambridge, U.K.

Suppe, F. (1977a), 'The Search for Philosophic Understanding of Scientific Theories', in Suppe (1977b), 3–24.

Suppe, F. (Ed.) (1977b) *The Structure of Scientific Theories*, University of Illinois Press, Urbana, IL.

Sussman, G.J. (1975) *A Computational Model of Skill Acquisition*, American Elsevier, New York.

Swartout, W. and Balzer, R. (1982) 'On the Inevitable Intertwining of Specification and Implementation', *Comm. ACM*, **25**, 7, July, 438–440.

Thagard, P. (1988) *Computational Philosophy of Science*, MIT Press, Cambridge, MA.

Thomas, D.E. *et al.* (1983) 'Automatic Data Path Synthesis', *Computer*, **16**, 12, Dec., 59–70.

Thompson, D.W.T. (1917) *On Growth and Form*, Abridged Edition 1961, J.T. Bonner (Ed.), Cambridge University Press, Cambridge, U.K.

Toulmin, S. (1972) *Human Understanding*, Princeton University Press, Princeton, NJ.

Touzeau, R.F. (1984) 'A Fortran Compiler for the FPS-164 Scientific Computer', in *Proc. SIGPLAN Symp. on Compiler Construction*, ACM, New York, 48–57.

Tsuchiya, M. and Gonzales, M.J. (1976), 'Towards Optimization of Horizontal Microprograms', IEEE Trans. on Computers, **C-25**, 10, Oct., 992–999.

Turing, A. (1949), 'Checking a Large Routine', *Report on the Conference on High Speed Automatic Calculating Machines*, University Mathematical Laboratory, Cambridge, U.K., 67–68.

U.S. Department of Defense (1981) *ADA Language Reference Manual*, Springer-Verlag, Berlin.

U.S. Department of Defense (1983) 'Requirements for Hardware Description Languages', Institute for Defense Analysis, Alexandria, VA, Jan.

Varian (1975) *Varian Microprogramming Guide*, Varian Data Machines, Irvine, CA.

Vegdahl, S.R. (1982) 'Phase Coupling and Constant Generation in an Optimizing Microcode Compiler', *Proc. 15th Annual Microprogramming Workshop*, IEEE Comp. Soc. Press, Los Angeles, 125–133.

Vegdahl, S.R. (1986) 'Microcode Optimization: Examples and Approaches', *IEEE Software*, **3**, 4, July, 59–68.

Wagner, A. and Dasgupta, S. (1982) 'Axiomatic Proof Rules for a Machine Specific Microprogramming Language', *Proc. 16th Annual Microprogramming Workshop*, (MICRO-16), IEEE Comp. Soc. Press, Los Angeles, 151–158.

Wakerly, J.F. (1989), *Microcomputer Architecture and Programming: The 68000 Family*, John Wiley & Sons, New York.

Wegner, P. (1972a) 'The Vienna Definition Language', *ACM Comp. Surveys*, 4, 1, March, 5–63.

Wegner, P. (1972b) 'Programming Language Semantics', in *Formal Semantics of Programming Languages*, R. Rustin (Ed.), Prentice-Hall, Englewood Cliffs, NJ., 149–248.

Wensley, J.H. *et al.* (1978), 'SIFT: Design and Analysis of a Fault-Tolerant Computer for Aircraft Control', *Proc. IEEE*, **66**, Oct., 1240–1255.

Whewell, W. (1967) *The Philosophy of the Inductive Sciences*, 2nd Edition, John W. Parker, London (originally published 1847); 1967 Impression, Frank Cass, London.

Wiener, R. and Sincovec, R. (1984) *Software Engineering with Modula-2 and Ada*, John Wiley, New York.

Wilkes, M.V. (1951) 'The Best Way to Design an Automatic Calculating Machine, *Report of the Manchester University Computer Inaugural Conference*, University of Manchester, Manchester, U.K. 266–270. Reprinted in *Annals of the History of Computing*, **8**, 2, April 1986, 118–121.

Wilkes, M.V. and Needham, R.M. (1979) *The Cambridge CAP Computer and its Operating System*, North-Holland, New York.

Wilsey, P.A. (1985) 'S*M: An Axiomatic Nonprocedural Hardware Description Language for Clocked Architectures', M.S. Thesis, Center for Advanced Computer Studies, University of Southwestern Louisiana, Lafayette, LA.

Wilsey, P.A. (1987) 'A Hardware description Language for Multilevel Design Automation Systems', Ph.D. Thesis, Center for Advanced Computer Studies, University of Southwestern Louisiana, Lafayette, LA.

Wilsey, P.A. and Dasgupta, S. (1988) 'A Formal Model of Computer Architectures for Computer System Design Environments', in *Design Methodologies for VLSI and Computer Architecture*, D.A. Edwards (Ed.), North-Holland, Amsterdam.

Wilsey, P.A. and Dasgupta, S. (1989) 'Functional and Operational Specifications of Computer Architectures', *Proc. 9th Int. Symp. on Computer Hardware Description Languages and their Applications* (CHDL-89), J.A. Darringer and F.J. Rammig (Eds.), Elsevier, Amsterdam, 209–224.

Wilsey, P.A. and Dasgupta, S. (1990) 'A Formal Model of Computer Architectures for Digital System Design Environments,' *IEEE Trans. on Computer Aided Design for Integrated Circuits and Systems*, 9, 5, May, 473–86.

Wilsey, P.A. *et al.* (1987) 'An S*M Execution Environment' Tech. Rept. TR87-3-1, Center for Advanced Computer Studies, University of Southwestern Louisiana, Lafayette, LA, Feb.

Winograd, T. and Flores, F. (1987), *Understanding Computers and Cognition*, Addison-Wesley, Reading, MA.

Winston, P.H. (1977) *Artificial Intelligence*, Addison-Wesley, Reading, MA.

Wirth, N. (1971) 'Program Development by Stepwise Refinement', *Comm. ACM*, **14**, 4, April, 221–227.

Wirth, N. (1973) *Systematic Programming: An Introduction*, Prentice-Hall, Englewood Cliffs, NJ.

Wirth, N. (1977), 'Modula: A Language for Modular Multiprogramming', *Software Practice and Experience*, **7**, 3–35.

Wirth, N. (1985a) *Programming in Modula-2*, Springer-Verlag, New York.

Wirth, N. (1985b) 'From Programming Language Design to Computer Construction', (ACM Turing Award Lecture), *Comm. ACM*, **28**, 2, Feb., 159–164.

Wulf, W.A., Russell, D.B. and Habermann, A.N. (1971) 'BLISS: A Language for Systems Programming', *Comm. ACM*, **1**, 12, Dec., 780–790.

Wulf, W.A. *et al.* (1975) *The Design of an Optimizing Compiler*, American Elsevier, New York.

Yau, S.S., Schowe, A.C. and Tsuchiya, M. (1974) 'On Storage Optimization for Horizontal Microprograms' *Proc. 7th Annual Workshop on Microprogramming*, ACM/IEEE, New York, 98–106.

Yeh, R.T. *et al.* (1984) 'Software Requirements: New Directions and Perspectives', in *Handbook of Software Engineering*, C.R. Vick and C.V. Ramamoorthy (Eds.), van Nostrand-Reinhold, New York, 519–543.

Zelkowitz, M.V., Shaw, A.C. and Gannon, J.D. (1979), *Principles of Software Engineering and Design*, Prentice-Hall, Englewood Cliffs, NJ.

Zemanek, H. (1980) 'Abstract Architecture', in *Abstract Software Specification*, D. Bjorner (Ed.), Lecture Notes in Computer Science, Springer-Verlag, New York.

Zurcher, W. and Randell, B. (1968) 'Iterative Multilevel Modeling: A Methodology for Computer System Design', *Information Processing 68* (Proc. IFIP Congress), North-Holland, Amsterdam, D138–D142.

INDEX

Printed in the United States
By Bookmasters